France
TravelBook

Ninth Edition

Written by Laurence Phillips
Ninth edition verified by Big World Productions Ltd
Project Editor: Sheila Hawkins Ltd

Published by AAA Publishing, 1000 AAA Drive, Heathrow, Florida 32746.
The *AAA France TravelBook* was created and produced for AAA Publishing by AA
Media Limited, Fanum House, Basing View, Basingstoke, Hampshire, RG21 4EA, UK.

Text © AAA Publishing 2013, 9th edition.

Maps © AA Media Limited 2013
Traffic signs © Crown copyright. Reproduced under the terms of the Open
Government Licence.

© Tele-Atlas N.V. 2013 Tele Atlas

ISBN: 978-1-59508-521-4

Cover photos
Main cover photo and spine: Moulin Rouge, Paris, France
© Steve Vidler / eStock Photo
Back cover: Lavender fields, Provence, France
© SIME / eStock Photo

Cataloging-in-Publication Data is on file with the Library of Congress.

Color separations by Digital Department AA Publishing.
Printed in China by C & C Offset Printing Co. Ltd.

A04764

Beautiful Cap Ferrat on the Côte d'Azur

Foreword

You're ready to plan a vacation to France. As you consider your itinerary, this book will guide you through the fascinating areas this country offers. Explore the places you always hear about: Paris, with its renowned museums and elegant parks and gardens; thriving and cultured Bordeaux; Strasbourg, laced with canals and looking up at its majestic cathedral; the ski resorts in the Alps; and the glittering Côte d'Azur.

But let some of France's quieter corners tempt you. The small town of Sarlat-la-Canéda is an exquisitely beautiful medieval mélange of cobbled passageways and stone houses. Rocamadour, a tiny village with steep staircases and streets, clings improbably to the side of a cliff. Inland from the frantic Riviera and high above the coastline, the more low-key "perched villages," such as Vence, afford stunning views of the sea around every corner. And the northwest region of Brittany, protruding far into the Atlantic, features bustling towns, rugged coastlines and fresh seafood.

The AAA France TravelBook will stir your imagination with evocative descriptions and photographs of these places and many more. Its practical information will help you decide where you want to go, and its maps will show you how to get there. Useful suggestions for eating, drinking and shopping appear throughout the book. Included walking and driving tours will lead you through selected areas with a more in-depth focus. Everything to help you get the most from your French vacation is here.

4

Contents

Key to symbols
🞤 map page number and coordinates
✉ address
☎ telephone number
🕐 opening times
Ⓜ nearest subway station
🚌 nearest bus/trolley bus/tram/funicular route
⛴ ferry
🍴 restaurant
💷 admission charge
🛈 information
For conversion charts, see the inside back cover

Introduction to France

"How is it possible to govern a country that produces more than 370 different cheeses?" So demanded Charles de Gaulle, war hero and the nation's most famous 20th-century leader. It's no easier to define the land that also boasts in excess of 500 registered wines. The very essence of France can be identified in its diversity.

Administrative boundaries may change on the whim of politicians, but tradition is made of sterner stuff. Local pride and a healthy mistrust of other regions stem from the different cultures that created each part of the land, which first united against outside invasion in the sixth century. Such pride means towns and villages still nurse their centuries-old prejudices, lick their wounds and respect their heritage, offering the visitor a selection of more than 4,000 museums and over 42,000 historic monuments, with 1,500 private châteaux open to the public.

Culture

The arts are part of everyday life. The Académie Française may rail against Americanization of French culture, complaining of words such as *le weekend* falling into their dictionaries and insisting on the spelling *mél* to replace the blatantly Anglo-Saxon "e-mail." However, France has always loved its American dream. Its youth icons remain Marilyn Monroe and 1950s Hollywood. France gave America its denim, and the U.S. returned it wrapping up James Dean, just as literature and philosophy share French prime-time television with imported soaps and game shows. Culture is not reserved for the elite: Many museums are open free once a month, and some stay open late at night

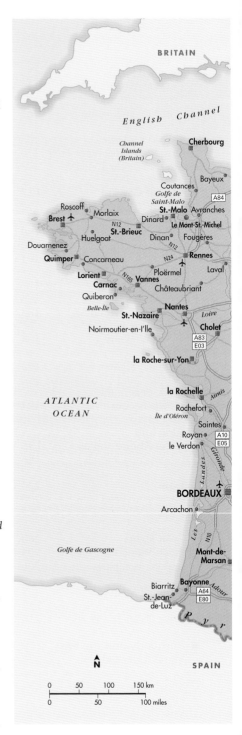

Pas de Calais

Dunkerque
Calais
St.-Omer Lille
Boulogne-sur-Mer
le Touqet Béthune
BELGIUM
Lens
Valenciennes
Abbeville Douai Maubeuge
Dieppe Arras Cambrai
Fécamp Amiens la Capelle Charleville- LUXEMBOURG
Etretat Ardennes Mézières
Le Havre Roye St.-Quentin Montmédy
Honfleur Beauvais Laon Rethel Thionville Forbach Sarreguemines
Jumièges Rouen Compiègne Soissons Reims Verdun Metz Haguenau
Caen les Andelys Pontoise Chantilly Épernay STRASBOURG
Falaise Lisieux Giverny Meaux Châlons-en-Champagne Nancy
Argentan Evreux Mantes Versailles PARIS Disneyland Bar-le-Duc
Bagnoles-de- Verneuil- Resort Paris St.-Dizier Domrémy- St.-Dié
l'Orne sur-Avre Etampes Melun la-Pucelle
Alençon Chartres Barbizon Fontainebleau Troyes Vittel Colmar
le Mans Châteaudun Sens Châtillon- Chaumont Epinal Gérardmer
la Flèche Vendôme Orléans Montargis sur-Seine Langres Ronchamp Thann
Angers Blois Gien Auxerre Chablis Montbard Vesoul Mulhouse
Tours Chaumont-sur-Loire Vézelay Avallon Dijon Besançon Belfort
Saumur Amboise Sancerre Cosne Montbéliard
Chinon Vierzon Bourges Beaune Dole
Loches Nevers Chalon- Lons-le-Saunier
Parthenay Châtellerault Châteauroux Autun sur-Saône
Poitiers Argenton- Moulins Cluny
Niort sur-Creuse Mâcon Bourg- Annemasse
Montluçon Vichy Roanne en-Bresse Chamonix
Ruffec Bellac Gueret Villefranche- Annecy Megève
Cognac Aubusson Clermont- sur-Saône Aix-les-Bains
Angoulême Limoges Ferrand LYON Chambéry Val d'Isère
le Mont-Doré Vienne Voiron Courchevel
Brive-la- 1885m St.-Étienne Grenoble
Périgueux Gaillarde Tulle Puy de Sancy Le Puy en Vizille Briançon
Grotte de St.-Flour Velay Valence Gap
Bergerac Lascaux Central Privas
Rocamadour Aurillac
Langon Conques Mende Montélimar
Figeac Gorges du Gorges de Serres
Cahors Tarn l'Ardèche Digne-
Agen Rodez Millau Alès Orange les-Bains NICE Menton
Houeillès Moissac Montauban Pont Avignon Manosque MONACO
Auch Albi Cirque de du Gard Nîmes les Baux Aix-en- Grasse Antibes
Toulouse Navacelles Castres Montpellier Arles Provence Cannes
Pau Muret Béziers Sète Aigues- St.-Tropez Fréjus
Tarbes Carcassonne Mortes Martigues Marseille Cassis Toulon
Lourdes St.-Bertrand- Narbonne Golfe du Lion
de-Comminges St.-Girons Quillan
Cirque de Foix Bourg- Perpignan MEDITERRANEAN
Gavarnie ANDORRA Madame SEA

GERMANY

SWITZERLAND

ITALY

Bastia
Calvi
Corte
Corse
Ajaccio
Porto-
Vecchio
Bonifacio

since art appreciation is regarded as a social activity. When the country feels good about itself, art flourishes. The wealth that built châteaux lured Renaissance artists from Italy. The 19th-century reinvention of France as a republic saw the beginnings of the Impressionist movement.

Take-out Tradition

Although large supermarkets on the edge of towns have tolled the death knell of many small businesses, the French still support specialty food stores. France has 35,000 *boulangeries* (bakeries), where *baguettes* and *flûtes* (loafs) are freshly baked throughout the day. After a hard day's work, people choose quality prepared foods from the local *traiteur* – a cross between a caterer and a deli – rather than a mass-produced TV dinner.

The art of the pastry chef is widely respected (even restaurants have specialty chefs to prepare desserts), so there is no shame in buying a fruit tart or rich *gâteau* for dessert. All towns and most villages have at least one *pâtisserie* selling wonderful homemade cakes and irresistible pastries.

The Nobility

France may be a republic, but it still has its aristocracy. Although international banks own most vineyard châteaux in Bordeaux, many châteaux of the Loire still belong to dukes, counts and princes.

Laws have been relaxed to allow heirs and pretenders to the French throne, who were once forced into exile, to live in France. Since 1998, the once-ruling classes annually return to Versailles to host a sumptuous New Year's Eve charity ball as in the days of Louis XIV.

Bienvenue au Château (the association of château owners offering bed and breakfast) ✉ Centre d'Affaires Les Alizés, la Rigourdière, 35510 Cesson Sevigne; www.bienvenueauchateau.com.

Religion and Race

Although church and state are formally separate entities and marriages are sanctioned at the local town hall, 63 percent of French people still consider themselves Catholic. Thirty percent declare themselves without religion. Minority religions are most active. Less than 2 percent of the population are Protestant, persecuted throughout the nation's history, and immigrant Jewish and Muslim communities thrive in major cities.

The well-documented rise of the National Front, under Jean-Marie Le Pen, led to the extreme right-wing party gaining political control in some areas of the south. However, a strong anti-racist movement – S.O.S. Racisme, founded by the improbably named Harlem Désir with the slogan *Touche pas à mon pote* (hands off my pal) – did much to unite the country in support of minority groups in the 1980s. When Dior's lead designer John Galliano was discovered to have made anti-Semitic comments in a bar in Paris in early 2011, he was dismissed by the fashion house and fined by the French authorities.

The mainstream has adopted the distinctive youth culture and music of second-generation north Africans (*les Beurs*) and black communities, and success for multiracial national sports teams has built many bridges. Visitors are unlikely to encounter any tension outside the poorer suburbs of Paris and other large cities.

National Pride

With the revival of its sporting fortunes in the late 1990s came proof that despite regional affiliations, *la patrie* (the homeland) is alive and well. For most of the past 150 years, France has been a republic, with the French Revolution giving the world a model for liberty, equality and brotherhood.

Opposite: Interior of Cathédrale Ste.-Réparate in the old quarter of Nice, Côte d'Azur

Boules players in the course of a game in the alpine town of Gap in Provence

The blue, white and red *tricolore* flag flies above most public buildings. The symbol of France is the face of Marianne, displayed in city halls and on stamps and coins. Models for the figure have included actresses Brigitte Bardot and Catherine Deneuve. There was a cause célèbre in April 2000 when the then Marianne, L'Oréal and Victoria's Secret model Laetitia Casta, decided to live in London; politicians regarded her action as treason.

Pastimes

Winter sports, particularly skiing and boarding in the mountains of the Pyrénées and the Alps, thrive in France, which has the largest skiing area in Europe. Rugby is the game of the southwest, especially around Toulouse, and soccer is a national obsession. The wide beaches of the north and west attract sailboarders, and surfers congregate at Biarritz. Pétanque, the great game of boules from the south, is played in public squares all over France.

Geography

Known as the "hexagon," France has mountain or sea borders on all six sides. The coastline – 3,418 miles – faces the English Channel (la Manche), the Atlantic Ocean and the Mediterranean Sea. Europe's largest beach is attributed to France at la Baule-Escoublac.

Within the hexagon are almost 65 million people, clustered in cities or spread over the vast and varied countryside, which, at 212,000 square miles in area, is roughly the size of Texas. The country's 36,000 towns and villages are linked by 670,000 miles of roads and 19,847 miles of railroad.

France is divided into a series of 96 administrative departments, numbered in their alphabetical order and often

Reaching speeds of up to 200 mph, the TGV (Train à Grande Vitesse) slashed travel times between major cities and allowed depressed agricultural and mining regions to reinvent themselves as European business centers.

The northern city of Lille (see pages 242–247), with a population of less than 150,000, went from a run-down industrial zone with extremely high unemployment in 1970s to a major financial hub when the trains brought Brussels, Paris, Britain and Germany within 90 minutes. As former Prime Minister Pierre Mauroy explained, "Distance in France is now measured in time not kilometers."

Private Pleasures

On the bridge that spans the fast-flowing Vézère river in the hamlet of le Saillant, local lads gather to fish, smoke and watch the traffic that passes through from Brive to the Limousin countryside. Ask the boys if there is anything special to see in le Saillant, and they shrug, inhale and laughingly suggest the chapel. There is no chapel in sight. "Yes, the chapel – in that house over there," they say, pointing over to a workman's terraced cottage. "A man came from Provence to do the windows."

Naturally, the house is locked, but perhaps a neighbor lends a key. Inside, the tiny parlor-sized chapel is lit by six stained-glass windows by Marc Chagall: luminous sketches of the harvest, the forest and the fishing, in blues and reds, gold and black.

This is the magic of traveling through France. Every corner presents a treasure. Chagall's art attracts countless thousands to the museum in Nice, the Paris Opéra and Reims Cathedral, but for the villagers of le Saillant, his glasswork remains a mirror of their working lives. The modest village is featured on no tourist map, and France delights in many such private pleasures. Hikers' paths and vacation highways can be pathways to serendipity.

named after the rivers or mountain ranges that cross them. Each one is run by a prefect and general council. Postal codes contain the department number; for example, Paris is 75.

Six mountain ranges and 37 million acres of forests run through a land at the heart of both northern and southern Europe. France's temperate climate covers several climatic zones: cold winters and hot summers in much of the country's mountainous regions, a moist western seaboard that has cool summers, and the Mediterranean zone in the south that experiences mild winters and soaring temperatures during the sweltering summers.

The regional traditions of daily life permitted each corner of the country to exist in isolation for centuries. However, the 1970s witnessed a railroad revolution that united the country and allowed it to become a leading player in the European community.

Public Joys

Food and drink are naturally part of any celebration. Turkeys trot through the streets of Licques as their brethren are sacrificed at Christmas. Cherries in the east and olive oil in the south inspire music and dancing. And wine flows throughout the year.

Jazz is another favorite for a festival: twilight jam sessions under springtime Normandy apple blossoms in Coutances, or living legends playing by starlight in the pine groves of Antibes, in the small town of Marciac or among Roman ruins in Nice and Vienne.

Classical music, too, is not always restrained within the plush velvet of the concert hall. Strasbourg's summer festival has the great orchestras. In Reims, the *Flâneries d'été* are a glorious game of hide-and-seek with free recitals tucked away on street corners and spilling into parks. Winter is the season of gala concerts at Évian-les-Bains, with the backdrop of snowcapped peaks.

Local people add that special touch. After a *fest-noz* (after-dark party) of sea shanties and feasting in a Brittany port, take a moonlight boat trip and listen to fishermen's tales as a sound-and-light enactment of *Jonathan Livingston Seagull* teases the horizon from a distant cliff top. Or at Charleville's puppet festival, stumble across a full-scale curbside production of *Dracula* at 11 p.m., the Transylvanian spell broken only by the sound of a motorcycle and the furious yapping of a nervous terrier.

Enviable collections of Impressionist canvases vie for gallery space with local sources of pride. Grasse has its perfume, Lorraine its glassware, Limoges that famous porcelain. Some collections bordering on the eccentric can be found in the most unlikely places – a beret museum in the Pyrenees, or the Musée Imaginaire de la Sardine in Hérault. The private, and unusual, Melon in Art collection, accumulated by restaurateur

Jean-Jacques Prévôt in Cavaillon, features watercolors with paint made from local melon seeds and skins.

France *en Fête*

But no one better exemplifies French *joie de vivre* than ordinary people at their local town fairs and festivals. Year round, there is always some excuse to dress up and take to the streets. February is carnival time on the Riviera. Summer sees sound-and-light shows at Loire châteaux. Sometimes you find a pageant where you least expect it, as a village commemorates a long-forgotten poet or local hero. In the most unassuming of farmsteads, 10, 20, 40, 50, then 60 masked figures might creep into the

The ancient Roman theater in Orange, Provence, hosts plays on summer nights

courtyard softly singing sacred music, the flames from their torches licking the night sky. Later, audience and players will adjourn to the farmhouse cellar for food, wine and general conviviality. Someone may start to sing a country song; one by one, other voices will join in the chorus.

Later, as you wander through the trees to the parking lot and turn toward the unblinking stars of a summer night, reflect that once again France has opened one of her private doors to you – as she may to other lucky souls in a Brittany fishing boat, to jazz lovers in Roman theaters of the south, or to anyone lucky enough to cross the bridge over the Vézère at le Saillant.

Dining

Fatty foods, creamy sauces and strong red wine are daily treats – yet this nation has one of the lowest incidences of heart disease in the world. Rich French cuisine appears to break all the medical establishment rules without clogging the arteries.

Food is an essential part of French life. Even in the age of business and fitness – when lunchtime wine may be replaced by mineral water, and heavy casseroles by fish – the midday meal will usually still last two hours.

Fortunately, *cuisine nouvelle*, once described as "a little bit of nothing on a big white plate," has faded from fashion, although the food presentation itself remains an art form. Regional cuisine has its own robust identity, in which local ingredients always have pride of place; look for it on the *menu du terroir* of any good local restaurant.

Supermarket convenience foods may be found in the freezers of Parisian department stores, and fast-food emporia sprout on many a city street corner. However, in provincial France and family homes throughout the land, evening and weekend meals remain social occasions. At Christmas and family celebrations, six-, seven- or eight-course meals are not uncommon, with wine and spirits served to nudge the digestion.

Dining out is always a joy, whether in stylish formal restaurants or local bistros. Choose your restaurant with the same care you would select a show or other entertainment. Menus must be displayed outside, so browse. Often the humble café, complete with locals, will be more rewarding than the starchy establishment farther down the road.

Three to four courses are the norm. You can eat à la carte from the wider menu or choose from recommended set menus at a fixed price. A range is usually available, from modest two- to three-course options to the *menu gastronomique* (gourmet selection) in high-class venues, perhaps featuring an *amuse-gueule* or *amuse-bouche* appetizer, soup, salad, fish, main course (usually meat), cheese and dessert, followed by coffee with *gourmandises* (candies). Often a sorbet or calvados (apple brandy) is served before the main course as a *trou Normand* (see page 61).

All restaurants offer the fixed-price option. Budget diners should opt for the *plat du jour* (daily special), usually an excellent-value local specialty. Top-of-the-range restaurants often have lunch menus at less than half the price of the dinner ones. In restaurants where working people go to eat, it can be harder to get a table at midday than in the evening. The better restaurants often close in August and January.

Diners at a sidewalk restaurant on cours Saleya in the old quarter of Nice, on the Côte d'Azur

Wine

The French have a word for it: *terroir*, or native soil. It's what makes every French wine different from its neighbor bottled across the valley. It's that magic something a wine gets from its own soil, its hometown and the people who love and raise it. To meet a wine on its home soil is a bit like being introduced to the family. That is how a wine lover goes from a one-glass stand to a serious affair.

Each wine region proclaims that its *terroir* makes its wines special, and a willingness to try something local will bring its own rewards. Of course, the *grand crus* of Bordeaux (those classified wines within the individual château areas) and the celebrated Burgundy vintages will take top billing on restaurant wine lists in Paris. However, if you take advice from your local waiter in the provinces, you will be pleasantly surprised for far fewer euros.

Invariably, local cuisine evolves around the characteristics of local wines, so sometimes a modest table wine will better serve your meal than the town's most expensive bottle.

Wines labeled *appellation d'origine contrôlée* (A.O.C.) meet strict standards before they are permitted to be sold under the regional or vineyard name. *Vin du pays* (country wine) will name the region, and *vin de table* is an unpretentious everyday wine sometimes blended from various sources.

The principal wine-producing regions of France are:

Alsace, which is known for its refreshing white wines. Unlike most French varieties, bottles boldly state the grape type rather than town of origin, such as Riesling (dry), Gerwürztraminer (more complex) and Pinot Gris (nutty dry).

Beaujolais produces respected wines as well as the famous nouveau wines.

Bordeaux Bergerac is renowned for its premier cru red wines. **Sauternes** dessert wines include the legendary Château d'Yquem.

Enjoying a selection of wines at a restaurant by the Canal St.-Martin in Paris

Burgundy, where classic wines are celebrated heartily with a calendar of traditional festivals.

Champagne The world's finest fizz founded the region's fortunes.

Jura in Franche-Comté; try the excellent *vin jaune* (yellow wine).

Languedoc-Roussillon, which is beginning to gain a reputation for extremely palatable everyday wines at reasonable prices.

Loire, which now boasts a choice of more than 100 wines – mainly whites, but also a popular rosé d'Anjou and a fine red Gamay – grown along the longest river in France. Saumur produces the best sparkling wines outside Champagne.

Provence, which includes such surprises as the local Bellet rosé and white wines served by both café owners and award-winning restaurateurs alike. Provence wines are unlikely to be offered outside the region.

Rhône From world-famous Châteauneuf du Pape to favorite table wines, vineyards line the river.

The Summer Break
The French tend to take their vacations within France and at the same time.

For six weeks or so from the July 14 Bastille Day celebrations to the first week in September, Parisians leave their city for the coasts and countryside. Many Parisian families have second homes and decamp to them for the duration of the summer.

Meanwhile, the wealthier quarters of Paris are strangely deserted. Major restaurants and many stores and

Events		September	Braderie street market in Lille, Paris fashion shows, National Heritage Days (third weekend)
January	Monte Carlo Rally, Paris fashion shows		
February	Nice and Menton carnivals	October	Grand Prix de l'Arc de Triomphe horse race in Paris
March	Paris Book Show		
April	Paris Marathon	November	Beaujolais Nouveau released on third Thursday
May	Cannes Film Festival, Monaco Grand Prix, Paris French Open Tennis Championship		
		December	St. Nicolas' Day celebrations in Alsace, Lorraine and Franche-Comté (5th), St. Sylvestre's Day – New Year's Eve (31st)
June	Paris French Open Tennis Championship le Mans 24-Hour Car Race, National Music Day		
July	Bastille Day celebrations (14th), Tour de France, Avignon Festival		

Competitors in the Tour de France reach the summit of Col de la Colombière, in the Alps

theaters close their doors. Even the best ice-cream parlor shuts down for July and August.

The last weekend of the summer holiday, the *Rentrée*, is the busiest time of the year on French roads. Highways to the sunshine can be a nightmare in July and August as millions of travelers clog the network and contribute to record numbers of accidents. To combat this, the state organizes summer festivals at rest areas to persuade motorists to pull over for a break every two hours.

The *relais bébé* sign designates staffed baby changing and feeding units. Local history and wildlife excursions are offered in some areas, as are free eye and reflex tests for drivers.

Autoroute-Infos, Europe's largest highway information system, continuously broadcasts information about more than 8,000 miles of highway and on a single frequency (tune into 107.7 MHz). For information visit the website www.autoroutes.fr, which has excellent information in English.

Some facilities are offered only on peak travel days, but leaflets detailing busy periods and programs of events are available from service areas. Ports and national tourist offices offer a free road map called *Le Bison Futé*, which features alternative routes to the main freeways in an attempt to relieve congestion.

Tour de France

One way to see the infinite variety of France is to follow the progress of the Tour de France. For three weeks in July, the world's greatest bicycle race covers 2,260 miles of the country – from the harshest mountain passes to the coast roads, from Disneyland's Sleeping Beauty Castle to the châteaux of the Loire. Each grueling daily stage and time trial brings thousands of well-wishers to cheer on the leading media caravan and the riders following in its wake who vie to win the coveted yellow jersey. Despite drug-taking scandals in recent years, teamwork is the key to the Tour's success and nationalism comes second place to hero worship. When Texan Lance Armstrong, who holds the record for most wins (seven, 1999–2005), cycled up the Champs-Élysées, even Parisian taxi drivers tooted their horns in congratulation.

Timeline

15,000 BC	Prehistoric groups occupy caves in southwest France.
4,000 BC	Tribes in Brittany erect megalithic tombs.
600 BC	Greek traders found Marseille as a trading post.
58–51 BC	Julius Caesar conquers Gaul and begins cultural Romanization.
AD 500	King Clovis unites tribes to form Francia.
AD 800	Charlemagne, king of the Franks, is crowned Holy Roman Emperor.
1309–77	The popes reside at Avignon during their exile from Rome.
1333	Edward III of England claims the throne of France, leading to the Hundred Years War (1337–1453).
1431	Patriotism movement begins after Joan of Arc is burned at the stake as a heretic in Rouen.
1547–59	Henri II persecutes the Huguenots. After his death, his widow Catherine de Médicis becomes politically influential.
1603	A French colony is established in Canada.
1624–42	Cardinal Richelieu becomes Louis XIII's chief minister.
1635	The Académie Française is established to promote art and learning.
1643–1715	Louis XIV, the Sun King, rules with autocratic extravagance.
1715–74	During the reign of Louis XV, France loses its American colonies to Britain after the Seven Years War.
1789–99	The French Revolution begins with a challenge to the authority of Louis XVI and ends with a coup installing Napoléon Bonaparte in power.
1804–15	Napoléon, emperor of France, seizes power across Europe. He is defeated by a British-led army at Waterloo in 1815.
1814–24	The Bourbon monarchy is restored. King Louis XVIII creates a new constitution.
1824–30	Charles X tries to restore old-style monarchy. Paris revolts against him in 1830 and Charles abdicates. Louis-Philippe, Duke of Orléans, becomes the *roi citoyen* (citizen king).

U.S. reinforcement troops arrive on the Normandy coast in June 1944

1848	The February Revolution leads to abdication, the establishment of the Second Republic and democratic elections to the National Assembly.
1870	The Republic is restored.
1874	The first exhibition of Impressionist art is held.
1889	The Eiffel Tower is built for the Paris Exhibition. The belle époque begins.
1894	The Lumière brothers develop the cinematograph.
1896–1906	Jewish officer Alfred Dreyfus is falsely imprisoned for spying. The issue is resolved after Émile Zola publishes *J'Accuse*.
1914–18	France joins Britain and Russia against Germany and Austria-Hungary in World War I.
1919	Victory for the Allies is finalized in the Treaty of Versailles.
1939–45	World War II is declared in September 1939. Charles de Gaulle forms a government in exile in Britain.
1944–45	June D-Day landings take place in Normandy. Paris is liberated. Charles de Gaulle becomes president.
1946	The Fourth Republic is declared.
1958	France is a founding member of the European Economic Community (called the European Union/E.U. since 1993).
1968	Student and trade union unrest almost bring down the government of President Charles de Gaulle.
1981–95	François Mitterrand's two-term socialist presidency launches the *grands projets*, through which major monuments are constructed around the country.
1994	The tunnel under the Channel links France and Britain.
1995	Conservative Jacques Chirac is elected as the French President.
1999	France is among the first E.U. nations to debut the euro currency. Christmas storms damage forests and parkland.
2007	Nicolas Sarkozy is elected as the French President.
2011	France is chosen to host the 2018 Ryder Cup golf tournament.
2012	Socialist François Hollande is elected as the French President.

The French Revolution

Political factions at court, and later revisionism, liked to paint Queen Marie Antoinette as the Austrian bimbo who shrugged, "Let them eat cake," when told that the poor were starving because they had no bread. Yet it was economic mismanagement under the *ancien régime* and grievances about the inequality of society that led to civil unrest, beginning with the storming of the Bastille prison on July 14, 1789. This led to the deposing of the monarchy and the "Reign of Terror", during which Robespierre and the Committee of Public Safety dispatched aristocrats and other enemies of the Revolution to Madame la Guillotine. Louis XVI and Marie Antoinette were executed in 1793. When Robespierre himself lost his head in 1794, the Reign of Terror abated.

Survival Guide

■ Although in Paris, the Riviera and most cities English is spoken in the more obvious tourist areas, people generally prefer you to at least begin a conversation in French. The phrase "*Parlez-vous anglais?*" is the polite opener to use.

■ Remember that in southern and eastern border areas, English will not be the principal foreign language. Expect fewer English brochures and guidebooks. Spanish, German or Italian may be spoken more widely.

■ Good manners are highly regarded. It's customary to shake hands on meeting, to address shopkeepers as *monsieur* or *madame*, always to say *bonjour* or *bonsoir* and *merci*, and to bid a general *au revoir* when leaving a café or bar.

■ Appearance is important. Even in bars, the well-dressed will receive better service.

■ At concerts and in cinemas and theaters, tip the attendant up to €1. They receive no other payment.

■ Bars and cafés always display a list of drink charges with two prices for every drink. Usually the first column shows the lower rate for drinks consumed standing or sitting at the bar. The second price – 30 to 50 percent higher – is that charged for drinks served at a table or on the terrace. In some trendy Parisian bars, the second column is the cost of drinks served after 10 p.m.

■ Unless a bar is crowded or an obvious tourist trap, it isn't customary to pay for drinks in advance. Each drink comes with a price ticket that the bartender or waiter will tear when you pay. Settle the bill for all drinks before leaving.

■ Coffee is usually served black unless you request *café au lait*, *un crème* or *un grand crème*. French coffee is strong espresso. For weaker, filtered coffee ask for *café américain*, or order a glass of water (*un verre d'eau*) on the side.

■ Sodas and soft drinks can occasionally be more expensive than buying wine and beer.

■ Tap water is safe for drinking. Restaurants are legally obligated to provide a glass or carafe on request, so don't be forced to buy mineral water against your wishes.

■ Smoking is a national institution but the French government introduced a smoking ban in all restaurants, cafés and bars at the start of 2008, which has been well received and adhered to by the French people. Smoking is still allowed on restaurant terraces and other outside spaces.

■ Vegetarianism isn't widely understood. A "meatless" meal might include bacon, a cheese sandwich could include ham unless you specify otherwise, and vegetable dishes are often prepared in a meat stock. Remember always to be specific about your dietary requirements.

■ When invited to a French home, bring a gift of pastry or chocolates for your hostess. If you wish to take flowers, seek advice from the florist since some blooms are at the heart of local superstitions or have religious significance, and might cause some people offense.

■ Many offices and small stores close for a long lunch break. Most stores close Sundays although bakers and florists open Sunday mornings, and all but the big supermarkets are closed Monday in many places.

■ Numbered seats on the subway and buses are reserved for the war wounded, pregnant women, the elderly or the infirm.

■ When telephoning for a taxi you will be charged for the driver's journey to get to where you are, in addition to your own trip.

- Keep small bags with you in taxis; there's a charge for each case carried in the trunk.
- French motorists are often aggressive, and city driving can be intimidating. Since local insurance companies refuse to pay when accidents occur on place Charles-de-Gaulle in Paris, you will often find cars being pushed into side streets after collisions, so that the crash can be recorded as occurring elsewhere. Highways and tunnels charge tolls (*péage*).
- All prices are displayed very clearly at toll booths in euros.
- Restrooms in museums and the more modern restaurants have flushing toilets. However, in a few small cafés and rural areas the old-fashioned hole in the ground with porcelain footrests for squatting may, very occasionally, still be in use. Use facilities in hotels and restaurants whenever possible.
- Many restroom facilities have an attendant – slang nickname "Madame Pipi" (pronounced "Peepee"), but never to her face – who will expect a tip of about 50¢. The price is usually displayed.

- Bidets: These low-level fixtures resembling toilets with faucets are for purposes of intimate hygiene.
- Telephones: Since hotels usually mark up call charges 100 to 200 percent, phone from public pay phones. Most use phone cards (*une télécarte*), which are available from post offices and tobacco shops (*tabac*) in 50- and 120-unit versions. The cheapest time to call the United States and Canada, with 50 percent extra time, is from 7:30 p.m. to 1:30 a.m. daily and all weekend. Some phone cards include a list of discount rates. Details can also be obtained from any post office. Phone booths displaying a blue bell sign may receive incoming calls.
- If your credit card is refused, don't panic. Most French credit cards are now equipped with a microchip (*puce*) to avoid fraud. International cards often contain the same information on a magnetic strip, which may not always be easily read. If a clerk or waiter is suspicious of your card, simply explain: "*Les cartes internationales ne sont pas des cartes à puce, mais à bande magnétique.*"

Admiring colorful blooms at the flower market on the Île de la Cité, in Paris

France

Opposite: The town of Villefranche-sur-Mer, on the Côte d'Azur, has a deep natural harbor

Paris and the Île-de-France

Opposite: The iconic Eiffel Tower – the best-known symbol of Paris

Paris and the Île-de-France

Arrogant and romantic, flirtatious and self-indulgent, the city of lights with more than a million secret shadows, Paris belongs to the world. Its enduring image is of romantic interludes, cultural treasures and a constant cosmopolitan bustle on its fashionable boulevards. So it's always a shock to find the city of Paris nestled in the heart of a sleepy, gentle and oh-so-French region, the Île-de-France.

Long, unbending, tree-lined country roads. Extravagant, wide-open spaces. Rural farms and medieval churches. These are the timeless treats of the region for which Francophiles will cheerfully trek to some of the most inaccessible corners of the land.

An Island City

Yet, so close to the city much of the region is served by the RER underground and overground express rail service that runs parallel with the urban subway network (*métro*). These connections, and the fact that all roads in France seem to lead to and from Paris, offer the opportunity to escape from the bustle of the city for a few hours or a weekend.

Perhaps spend an afternoon browsing around the 13th-century marketplace of Luzarches or discovering the medieval underground world of the town of Pontoise. Or enjoy a couple of days of total self-indulgence at the region's only lakeside thermal spa resort, Enghien-les-Bains. Stroll along the promenade, wrap, steam and spray yourself fit, or dress to the nines for a night at the casino.

A ring of illustrious châteaux and beautiful royal palaces, standing in vast

The magnificent Latona Fountain, in the grounds of the palace of Versailles

The *métro* subway serves the city and suburbs

The Impressionists were drawn to the Île-de-France, seeing similarities to the moody skies and ambiguous landscapes of Normandy nearby.

The countryside and rivers of the Oise valley attracted Pierre-Auguste Renoir, Paul Cézanne, Paul Gauguin and Vincent van Gogh, and many of the views we see today are familiar from their gallery versions. Lovers of Claude Monet will instantly recognize the Seine at Vétheuil. You can explore Impressionist country by boat on the Oise or by hot-air balloon.

parks and estates, is a reminder that the woods and waterways were once the playground of kings and princes. Even today, aristocrats who would once have been successors to the royal throne of France choose to live in the region. The Count of Paris, direct descendant of the last king, set up his Fondation Condé at Chantilly, where the beautiful château appears to float on a lake.

Tickets

A standard single central Paris subway ticket won't take you out to the Île-de-France. To travel extensively within this region, buy a tourist pass that includes the wider region, or buy a one-way (*aller simple*) or round-trip (*aller-retour*) ticket to the châteaux or market town you wish to visit, from one of the automatic ticket machines.

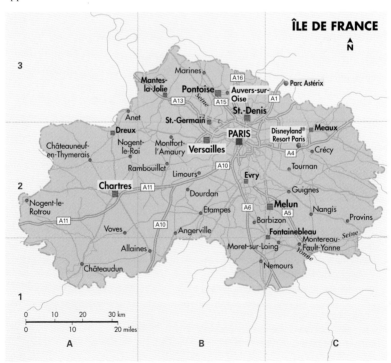

Paris

The 2.2 million genuine Parisians live within the 21-mile ring road (le Périphérique). Even if you've never visited Paris, you are likely to know the city is divided into the southern, left bank and the right bank.

Once you arrive, you discover life is never that simple. The city is divided into a shell-like spiral of 20 *arrondissements* (districts), each an individual village in its own right. Literary romantics need never leave the Latin Quarter (see page 47). Lovers of glamor stay firmly in the area between the Champs-Élysées and the Opéra.

True bohemia departed the left bank and Montmartre many years ago, but young cosmopolitan artistic communities thrive in the northeast of the city at Belleville. For four days each May, potters and painters throw open the doors and skylights of their studios and garrets and welcome visitors to a Paris most of us dream about.

Sightseeing

Even though this is a city of high fashion, don't be afraid to wear comfortable shoes. Attractions are so close together that you may find yourself on your feet for hours.

Riverboats (see page 33) will offer you spectacular views of Paris from the Seine. Best are the dinner cruises at night on the Bateaux Mouches (www.bateaux-mouches.fr).

L'Open Tour (www.parislopentour. com), an open-top double-decker bus with English commentary, travels from the Arc de Triomphe to Notre-Dame, with branches up to Montmartre and across to Bercy. One ticket allows one, two or three consecutive days of unlimited use. Buses depart at 15- to 30-minute intervals for the full two-hour, 15-minute circuit all day,

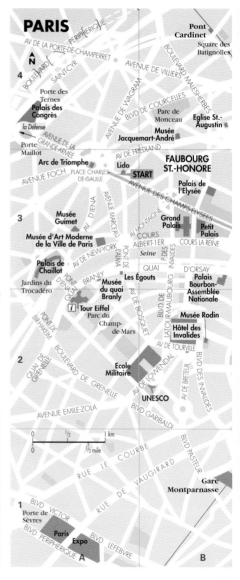

Pick up a Pass

The Paris Museum Pass offers direct admission and unlimited access to more than 60 museums and monuments in the city and surrounding area. You can buy passes for two, four or six consecutive days from participating attractions, main subway stations, tourist offices and from FNAC ticket counters. For more information look online at www.parismuseumpass.com.

every day. Tickets may be purchased on board, at principal subway stations and tourist offices. More traditional guided tours with an ongoing audio commentary are offered on some distinctive buses marked Cityrama (www.pariscityrama.fr) and Paris Vision (www.parisvision.com). If you decide to purchase a travel pass, everyday public buses provide an

excellent Parisian's eye view of the city. Route No. 47 crosses the river, passes Notre-Dame cathedral on the Île de la Cité and provides a glimpse of the Pompidou Center. The No. 24 bus travels along the banks of the romantic Seine, taking in the Madeleine church, the place de la Concorde and the Louvre on the right bank, the Musée d'Orsay on the left bank and the Île de la Cité.

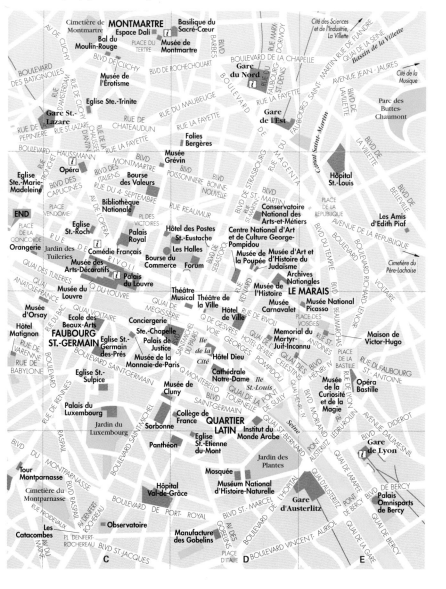

Paris Music

Cole Porter and the Gershwins hinted at it. But there is a headiness about the combination of Paris and music that suggests it should be kept out of the reach of children and the easily led. In most cities, music is played. In Paris, music happens. Walk through a subway station and hear tribal sounds. Travelers happily miss their trains and lean against poster-shellacked walls to listen. Past midnight on rue St.-André-des-Arts on the left bank, a lone sax player might play the blues as a window opens across the narrow street and a piano jams along. This is what the French refer to as a *boeuf* – and Anglo-Saxons call improbable.

Midsummer's Eve is Fête de la Musique and a party spirit descends (www.fetedelamusique.culture.fr). Every year, on June 21, song takes over street corners and train stations.

When opera houses close for summer, 20 parks provide free jazz. Another seasonal idyll may not be free, but it's certainly priceless: a season of Frédéric Chopin recitals in the Parc de Bagatelle's Orangerie in June and July and at the Musée de la Vie Romantique (George Sand Museum), 16 rue Chaptal. Most major museums stage concerts for a modest door charge.

Parisians regard music as a basic human right. Just as the city provides clean drinking water and a constant supply of haute- and cold-running couture and Impressionist painting, year-round music is available practically on demand. Churches offer free performances of Johann Sebastian Bach and Antonio Vivaldi. The Sunday concert at Notre-Dame (see page 46), at 4:30 p.m., is always packed and is superb if you can ignore the video-whirring and camera-clicking. The American Church on quai d'Orsay has piano and guitar recitals. In the heart of the Marais (see pages 39–40), the Église des Billettes hosts great choral concerts. Other churches with regular music performances include Église Saint-Germain-des-Prés and Ste. Chapelle on Île de la Cité.

That's Entertainment

The box office of the Comédie Française doesn't recommend its cheaper seats. Apparently, all one can see from these is the play. At the Comédie Française, one still goes to the theater to be seen and to notice who is sitting with whom. Accordingly, the more expensive seats are at right angles to the stage, facing the audience. In nearly all other Paris theaters, keen enthusiasm for the plays and shows suppresses that snobbery.

Paris loves American and English theater. Larger playhouses offer Arthur Miller, William Shakespeare and Neil Simon in French. Smaller bilingual companies stage English-language productions. Broadway musicals are treated like opera, with English performances subtitled in French. But new French musicals are worth catching. (Remember, this is where *Les Misérables* started out.)

Most theaters close on Monday but offer Sunday matinées. Prices are much cheaper than New York, and half-price, same-day tickets are sold from noon at a booth in place de la Madeleine.

Paris has more cinema screens than any other city and a vast choice of movies every week. On advertisements "vf" means dubbed versions are shown and "vo" usually means the original English version is screened with subtitles. The Opéra de Paris-Bastille (see page 34) stages operas, and the Opéra Garnier is home to the ballet.

The traditional Parisian cabaret exists for the city's visitors, as locals tend to prefer jazz and comedy clubs. Regardless, the slick productions provide enjoyable, undemanding entertainment with no language barriers. Since the image of the leggy showgirl is about six inches taller than the average Parisienne, today's belle of Belleville is

The impressive Opéra Garnier, with its golden statues, is illuminated at night

most likely to hail from Portland, Oregon, or Baltimore, Maryland. The Moulin Rouge cancan pays homage to the days of Maurice Chevalier and Joséphine Baker, and the Lido's Vegas-style floor show flourishes with special effects. The Folies Bergère now stages French musicals and concerts.

Information about the theater, movies and operas is the focus of the Wednesday magazine *Pariscope*, which has an English-language supplement. If you have access to the internet, you can also check out www.timeout.com/paris.

Shopping
In a city of the arts, one of the most popular pastimes is shopping. Big department stores on boulevard Haussmann spread over several buildings. Here also are the covered arcades of the Grands Boulevards (see page 38). Bargains at the lower end of the market may be found between Gare du Nord and Montmartre (see page 41). For fine foods as gifts, try Fauchon and its neighbors on place de la Madeleine.

Buried Treasure
There are several flea markets in Paris, but the best – arguably the best in Europe – is the Marché aux Puces at Porte de St.-Ouen/Clignancourt (Sat. 9–6, Sun. 10–6 and Mon. 11–5). Antiques, rugs, clothes, bric-a-brac and furniture are among the varied offerings. To snap up a real bargain, arrive before dawn and try the small dealers on the outskirts of this enormous market. These smaller markets are well marked: Marché Malik for old clothes and knicknacks, records, canes and tin boxes; Marché Jules Vallès for dolls, toys and theatrical trunks; Marché Paul Bert

A statue for sale at the Marché aux Puces at Porte de St.-Ouen

for crystal, mirrors and furniture; Marché Michelet for new clothes and shoes; and Marché Vernaison for antique furniture as well as silverware. Pickpockets frequent the markets, so keep a close eye on your personal belongings.

Antiques shops abound in the backstreets of poorer districts. Shops with an eye for the tourist trade are located around place des Vosges. Dealers around avenue Matignon and the St.-Honoré district advertise in the trade press and have showings in their own houses. The classiest – and most expensive – area is the Carré Rive Gauche, where numerous shops and galleries are lined along rues Allent, du Bac, de Beaune, de Lille, Jacob, des St.-Pères, de l'Université, de Verneuil and quai Voltaire. Details are on the website: www.carrerivegauche.com. The right bank version, the Louvre des Antiquaires on the place du Palais-Royal, in the shadow of the Louvre, is a collectors' corner for the very wealthy. Like many dealers, the antiques shops are closed during the Parisian summer holiday in August and also on Sundays.

Parks and Gardens

Most visitors to Paris tend to stroll in the Jardin des Tuileries, in front of the Louvre, but Paris is a city that is blessed with a lot of green spaces. The two main expanses of city-center countryside are the Bois de Boulogne and Bois de Vincennes, which each spring hosts the famous Foire du Trône fair (www.foiredutrone.com). Bois de Boulogne has 2,000 acres of woodland with open-air restaurants, a Shakespearean garden, seven lakes, an amusement park and a racetrack. It also has a notorious red-light district, so take local advice before embarking on any nighttime strolls. Victor Hugo set up *Les Misérables* lovers in the Jardin du Luxembourg, now a city haven for retired men playing boules, students laden with books and friends engaged in genteel games of croquet.

The rugged Parc des Buttes Chaumont features ravines, hills and even a temple of love nestling in a quiet dormitory quarter; while on the left bank, the Arènes de Lutèce Roman arena is a legacy of the city that ancient Rome named Lutetia.

Subterranean Paris

Under Paris there is another city with a beauty and interest of its own. You can visit the catacombs and sewers, but there is plenty of interest to see without even leaving the subway. Several *métro* stations have been decorated in strikingly original styles. Arts et Métiers evokes Jules Verne's *20,000 Leagues Under the Sea*, the staircase in Abbesses has a patchwork fresco by Montmartre artists and Concorde is plastered with the text of the Declaration of the Rights of Man and of the Citizen.

Essential Information

Tourist Information

☎ 0892 68 30 00 (toll call); www.parisinfo. com. The Paris Tourist Office has five offices open daily throughout the year. The main office is at 25 rue des Pyramides. Other branches are Anvers, Gare du Nord, Gare de l'Est, Gare du Lyon. The office at Paris Expo, Porte de Versailles is open daily during trade shows. There are also five information kiosks open daily from mid-May to mid-Sep. These are found at place du Tertre, Montmartre, Champs-Élysées at Clemenceau, Hôtel de Ville, parvis du Notre-Dame and place de la Bastille.

Urban Transportation

You are never more than 200 yards from a *métro* (subway) station. Trains run from 5:20 a.m. to 1:20 a.m. When you leave a subway train, follow either the blue-and-white signs marked *Sortie* for the exit or the orange-and-white signs marked *Correspondances* for interchanges. The subway links with an underground-overground express service called the RER, which stretches into the Île-de-France, Disneyland Paris, the airports and Versailles. Buses run Mon.–Sat. 5:30 a.m. to 8:30 p.m.; some have a reduced service until 12:30 a.m. and on Sunday. Night buses (Noctilien) cover the city from place du Châtelet. Tickets are available individually or in books of 10 from subway stations, and are interchangeable. Free maps are also available. Tourist tickets – ParisVisite – are valid for one, two, three or five days. Validate and keep your ticket with you, as you can be fined for traveling without a valid ticket. For information ☎ 32 46; www.ratp.fr.

Almost year-round, Batobus operates a hop-on, hop-off river bus at sights between the Eiffel Tower and Jardin des Plantes ☎ 08 25 05 01 01; www.batobus.com ⏰ Daily 10–9:30 every 20 minutes, early Apr.–Sep.; 10–7 every 25 minutes, rest of year.

Taxi stands can be found near subway and main train stations, although there is often an extra charge for pick-ups from the stands. Hail a taxi in the street if the white light on the roof is switched on. The maximum number of passengers most taxis will carry is four. Call taxis on ☎ 36 07; www.taxisg7.fr.

The Eurostar Channel Tunnel train (journey time two hours, 15 minutes from London) and other high-speed TGV services from northern Europe arrive at Gare du Nord. Trains for the east depart from Gare de l'Est, the south from Gare de Lyon, the southwest from Gare d'Austerlitz, Normandy from Gare St.-Lazare, and the west, including Brittany, the Loire and Aquitaine, from Gare Montparnasse.

Airport Information

Paris has two international airports, Orly and Roissy-Charles-de-Gaulle (for both: ☎ 39 50 from within France, ☎ 011 33 1 70 36 39 50 from the U.S.; www.aeroportsdeparis.fr). Most U.S. flights arrive at Roissy, 14 miles north of Paris. Shuttle buses run every 20 minutes to and from both airports, but the quickest route is the RER connection to the subway, which runs every 15 minutes around 5 a.m. to midnight. From Roissy, services on RER line B depart directly from the airport complex. From Orly, shuttle bus "Orlybus" takes you to RER line C, or shuttle bus "Orlyval" takes you to RER line B for onward connection.

Climate – average highs and lows for the month

Jan.	Feb.	Mar.	Apr.	May	Jun.	Jul.	Aug.	Sep.	Oct.	Nov.	Dec.
6°C	7°C	10°C	13°C	18°C	21°C	24°C	24°C	20°C	14°C	9°C	8°C
43°F	45°F	50°F	55°F	64°F	70°F	75°F	75°F	68°F	57°F	48°F	46°F
2°C	2°C	4°C	5°C	9°C	12°C	14°C	14°C	12°C	8°C	4°C	2°C
36°F	36°F	39°F	41°F	48°F	54°F	57°F	57°F	54°F	46°F	39°F	36°F

Paris and the Île-de-France

Paris Sights

Bastille

The famous Bastille prison, where the French Revolution started, was completely destroyed on July 14, 1789, although the outline of the fortress is marked on the paving stones of the square. Place de la Bastille has at its center the July Column topped by the winged *Spirit of Liberty*, sculpted in memory of the victims of the 1830 and 1848 uprisings immortalized in *Les Misérables*. The opera house, designed by Canadian Carlos Ott, is a confection of gray, silver and sunlight and seats 2,700 music lovers. Rue de Lappe is the gateway to trendy jazzland and old-style dance halls, once the haunt of Edith Piaf. Some platforms of the busy subway interchange rise above ground to overlook the Arsenal Basin, pleasure port of the Seine. After years of decline, this area has been reborn as eatery country, with fashionable restaurants on the edge of the new bohemia of the Marais.

⊞ E2 ✉ place de la Bastille, 75012 🍴 Chez Paul, see page 259 Ⓜ Bastille

Les Catacombes and Les Égouts

The Catacombs – a labyrinth of man-made tunnels beneath Paris – aren't for the claustrophobic. Dating back to Roman times, one corner of the vast network was given over to a ghoulish rehousing program for the dead. When Paris was being redesigned after the Revolution, it was decided to rebuild the cemeteries. Remains of 6 million occupants of the former graveyards were taken to the old catacombs and reburied in 1810. In the true spirit of post-Revolutionary bureaucratic efficiency, the remains weren't classified by name but stacked neatly as femurs and skulls for the

The Centre Pompidou holds an acclaimed collection of modern art

The Opéra Bastille was inaugurated on July 13, 1989, 200 years after the prison was destroyed

discerning visitor who braves the winding tunnels. The gallery of Port-Mahon reveals a detailed sculpture of the fortress of Mahon on Menorca, one of the Balearic Islands of the Mediterranean, carved by a veteran soldier of the army of Louis XV who had been imprisoned there during wars against the British. It reopened in 2008 after a long renovation program.

Elsewhere, the remarkable sewer system, Les Égouts, is well worth a visit. Ventilated with fresh air, a small section of the elaborate network of tunnels and squares, which mirror the street grid of the city above, is open for guided tours. Although an illegal youth subculture may have colonized some of the huge main drains elsewhere in town, this well-maintained showcase features an exhibition about the history of sanitation that is actually almost entertaining and affords glimpses of Paris' most-hidden architecture.

Catacombes de Paris ✚ C1 ✉ 1 avenue Colonel Henri Rol-Tanguy, 75014 ☎ 01 43 22 47 63; www.catacombes-de-paris.fr 🕐 Tue.–Sun. 10–5 (last admission 4 p.m.) Ⓜ Denfert-Rochereau 🎟 $$
Musée des Égouts de Paris ✚ A3 ✉ Opposite 93 quai d'Orsay, 75007 ☎ 01 53 68 27 81; www.paris.fr 🕐 Sat.–Wed. 11–5, May–Sep.;

11–4, rest of year. Closed two weeks in Jan. Ⓜ Alma-Marceau 🎟 $

Centre Pompidou

Known internationally as the Pompidou Center, this is probably more famous for its architecture than its collections. The controversial inside-out design by Richard Rogers and Renzo Piano makes it as much a landmark meeting place as an exhibition center. The Musée National d'Art Moderne housed in the center now has two distinct themes: 1905–60 modern art, and works from the 1960s to the present day. Henri Matisse, Salvador Dalí, Amedeo Modigliani, Marc Chagall and Andy Warhol are among 20th-century giants whose creations span movements from Cubism and Surrealism to pop art. Outside, a sunken piazza is a popular sprawling ground for backpackers and a showplace for street entertainers.

✚ D3 ✉ place Georges-Pompidou, 75004 ☎ 01 44 78 12 33; www.centrepompidou.fr 🕐 Wed.–Mon. 11–9; occasionally Thu. 11–11 depending on the exhibition. Ticket counters close at 8 p.m. 🍴 Café Beaubourg, see page 259 Ⓜ Hôtel de Ville, Rambuteau, Châtelet 🎟 Center free; museum $$$ (free first Sun. of the month)

Conciergerie

Poor Marie Antoinette, wife of Louis XVI, has had bad press over the years. The "let them eat cake" remark was taken out of context, and accounts of her eccentric lifestyle at Versailles (see page 52) denied her public sympathy.

A visit to her prison cell at the elegant fortress of the Conciergerie on the Île de la Cité should soften even the hardest hearts.

It was here that Marie Antoinette and other victims of the Reign of Terror were held before being taken across the river to their public execution at the guillotine on place de la Révolution, today's place de la Concorde. Here, the final turbulent nights of Danton and Madame du Barry, Robespierre and the poet André Chénier were also spent.

Although the events of the French Revolution in the late 1800s dominate the public image of the Conciergerie, the building has a much longer history. The site of the palace of the Merovingian kings since the 10th century, much of the fabric of the building was already more than 500 years old when Marie Antoinette was imprisoned here. The Guardroom and Grand Hall of the Men at Arms were built during the 13th century, while the vast kitchens were built in the 14th century. In addition to the cells, all of these fine examples of Gothic architecture are open for the public to visit.

Paris' first public clock is mounted on the building's great square tower.

✚ C2 ✉ 2 boulevard du Palais, 75001 ☎ 01 53 40 60 80; www.monuments-nationaux.fr ⏰ Daily 9:30–6. Last admission 30 minutes before closing 🚇 Cité 💰 $$ (free first Sun. of the month)

La Défense

The Grande Arche de la Défense is the newest of the triumphant gateways to the city. Less a traditional arch, it is more a gigantic hollow cube of glass and white Carrara marble, symbolizing a window open to the world. Inaugurated in 1989 for the bicentennial of the French Revolution, the arch dominates the Parvis, a modern square studded with contemporary statuary and home to an IMAX cinema (the Dome) and a superb shopping complex known as Les Quatre Temps.

At first, in the 1960s, La Défense district seemed harsh and alien, but it has softened over time into a modern community, and this dream of president and war hero Charles de Gaulle is now matched by the other grand monuments conceived across town by his 1980s successor, François Mitterrand.

Good restaurants serve the business community of La Défense, and fast public transportation links this most western quarter of Paris with the city center in just minutes.

Grande Arche de la Défense ✚ Off map A4 ✉ Paris la Défense, 92040 ☎ 01 49 07 27 27; www.grandearche.com 🚇 La-Défense-Grande-Arche

The Grande Arche de la Défense is made of glass and Carrara marble

The Champs-Élysées sweeps up to the Arc de Triomphe from place de la Concorde

Walk
Along the Champs-Élysées

Refer to route marked on city map on pages 28–29

Here Parisians gather to see in the New Year, to welcome the Tour de France and to toot horns on election night. Bustling and brilliant, France's most famous avenue has never looked lovelier.

After decades of erosion by traffic, building work and fast-food emporia, the Champs-Élysées has been reborn as the most civilized downhill stroll in town. At its crest – and at the center of the Étoile, a star-shaped intersection of 12 avenues – is the Arc de Triomphe, a 164-foot Napoleonic monument, home to the tomb of the unknown soldier. This 1.5-mile walk begins here.

Cross to the top of the avenue des Champs-Élysées.

The sidewalks have been widened, parking moved underground and broad paths planted with trees reflecting the original design of landscape gardener André Le Nôtre. The top section is lined with cafés, car showrooms, cinemas, restaurants and shops. Most famous are the Lido floor show and Fouquet's restaurant (you pronounce the "t") on the corner of avenue George-V, which still forbids women on their own to drink at the bar.

Midway down the avenue, cross the intersection of Rond-Point (traffic circle), marking the start of the *champs* or fields. Gardens border the art and exhibition galleries Grand Palais and Petit Palais (from 1900); opposite is a memorial to Jean Moulin, French Resistance hero. The avenue opens out to the magnificent 18th-century place de la Concorde, with its pink granite obelisk from the Palace of Luxor in Egypt. To the right is the Seine, with the Assemblée Nationale parliament building across the bridge. To the left is the start of the colonnades of rue de Rivoli. Straight ahead is the majestic Jardin des Tuileries and the Louvre beyond.

Arc de Triomphe ✉ place Charles-de-Gaulle, 75008 ☎ 01 55 37 73 77; www.monuments-nationaux.fr 🕐 Daily 10 a.m.–11 p.m., Apr.–Sep.; 10 a.m.–10:30 p.m., rest of year 🚇 Charles de Gaulle-Étoile ✋ $$ (free first Sun. of the month)

Grand Palais ✉ Public entrances on avenue Winston-Churchill and avenue Franklin D. Roosevelt ☎ 01 44 13 17 17; www.grandpalais.fr 🕐 Tue.–Sat. 9:30–6, Sun. 10–7 (times of exhibitions may vary) 🚇 Champs-Élysées-Clémenceau ✋ Exhibitions $$

Petit Palais ✉ avenue Winston-Churchill, 75008 ☎ 01 53 43 40 00; www.petitpalais.paris.fr 🕐 Tue.–Sun. 10–6 🚇 Champs-Élysées-Clémenceau ✋ Free (charge for temporary exhibitions)

Assemblée Nationale ✉ 126 rue de l'Université, 75007 ☎ 01 40 63 60 00 🕐 Closed to the public. Visits only by invitation from a member of the National Assembly 🚇 Assemblée Nationale

Grands Boulevards

Choked by traffic snarling from République to the Opéra and beyond, Haussmann's wide streets might be dismissed as mere rat runs. Don't miss out on the real Paris. On wide sidewalks shaded from the sun by tall trees and taller buildings, bankers on skates avoid the rush-hour crowds on the subway, and honeymooners stroll in no particular hurry to find a spot for coffee.

A fair smattering of 19th-century theaters, which put on light entertainment and farces, offer performances late enough that patrons can grab an early supper at a neighboring restaurant. Famous Parisian galleries and passages and glass-roofed shopping arcades have discreet entrances on the boulevards themselves. Within are art and toy shops, the occasional small theater or such tucked-away sights as the Musée Grévin, Paris' waxworks museum.

The eastern section of the boulevards, nearer République, was once home to indoor circuses but now is a bit run-down. However, the two gateways to Paris, the Porte St.-Denis and Porte St.-Martin, have been beautifully restored. The sophisticated west serves the Opéra and Opéra-Comique audiences. As a rule of thumb, side streets in the southern financial district, home to great restaurants, are quieter, and streets in the north, which serve the more working-class districts between the boulevards and the fleshpots of Pigalle, are livelier. A well-chosen café table can afford a superb glimpse of Montmartre.

Musée Grévin ➕ C3 ✉ 10 boulevard Montmartre, 75009 ☎ 01 47 70 85 05; www.grevin.com 🕐 Daily 9:30–7, early Jul.–early Sep. (school vacations); Mon.–Fri. 10–6:30, Sat.–Sun. 10–7, rest of year 🍴 Chez Georges, see page 259 🚇 Grands-Boulevards 💲 $$$

Les Halles

Despite the less-than-flattering local nickname "le Trou" (the hole), this is one hole in the ground that is well worth a visit. When the old wrought-iron framed halls of the market – the city's principal food market for 800 years – were demolished in 1969, an ambitious glass cascade was constructed to bathe the underground shopping mall in natural light. The streets above have become a pedestrian-friendly zone of restaurants, bars, cafés and nightlife, from the seedy and bright neon promises of the rue St.-Denis red-light district to the restaurants serving seafood and onion soup to theatergoers at midnight and party revelers at dawn. In 2011

Offbeat Museums

Experienced shoppers start at the Musée de la Contrefaçon, where you can test your abilities in discriminating between quality items and plain old junk. This is one of Paris' most unusual museums (this in a city that boasts a gallery devoted to 4,500 years of bread!), where the discerning can show shrewd skills in detecting forgery. Here, you can see counterfeit Cartiers and Louis Vuittons that never saw the inside of a designer's workroom. A shrine to the greatest French singer of the 20th century makes a touching detour: The Musée Edith Piaf is a private museum dedicated to her memory and life. Enjoy a dash of whimsy at the Musée de la Magie (Magic Museum) in the Marais, something of an interactive wonderland with 19th-century curios, magic tricks and futuristic robots.

Musée de la Contrefaçon ➕ Off map A3 ✉ 16 rue de la Faisanderie, 75116 ☎ 01 56 26 14 03; www.unifab.com 🕐 Tue.–Sun. 2–5:30. Closed weekends in Aug. 🚇 Porte Dauphine 💲 $

Musée Edith Piaf ➕ E3 ✉ 5 rue Crespin-du-Gast, 75011 ☎ 01 43 55 52 72 🕐 Mon.–Thu. 1–6, but phone to make an appointment 🚇 Ménilmontant 💲 Free (donation appreciated)

Musée de la Magie ➕ E2 ✉ Academie de Magie, 11 rue St.-Paul, 75004 ☎ 01 42 72 13 26; www.museedelamagie.com 🕐 Wed. and Sat.–Sun. 2–7 🚇 St.-Paul, Bastille, Sully-Morland 💲 $$

Les Halles began a long process of renovation which will continue until 2016. During this time, various sections and elements of the complex will sport a futuristic translucent canopy, by French architects Patrick Berger and Jacques Anziutti, but Les Halles will remain open to visitors.

➕ D3 ✉ rue Pierre-Lescot, rue Rambuteau, rue Berger ☎ 01 44 76 96 56; www.forumdeshalles.com 🕐 Shops: Mon.–Sat. 10–8 (restaurants open Sun.); cinemas 9:30 a.m.–10:30 p.m. 🍴 Le Grand Vefour, see page 260 🚇 Les Halles

Hôtel des Invalides

The elegance of Louis XIV military architecture is never more striking than around the grand arcaded courtyard of Les Invalides. Some visitors just make a whistlestop halt here to see Napoléon's tomb, but it's worth your while to view the other treasures in this 17th-century retreat from modern Paris. Originally constructed as a home for military pensioners, it's still the residence of 100 veterans. The soldiers' Église St.-Louis-des-Invalides is decked with flags and pennants from 300 years of military campaigns. The imposing Église du Dôme, designed by Jules Hardouin-Mansart, houses the six-layer coffin of Emperor Napoléon.

The Musée de l'Armée is among the world's finest museums of warfare, and the fourth-floor Musée des Plans-Reliefs (www.museedesplansreliefs.culture.fr) contains a unique national treasure, hidden from the public for some 200 years. Louis XIV commissioned the military architect Sébastien le Prestre de Vauban to create miniature models of all the fortified towns in the kingdom. The bulk of the collection is on display here; the remaining section, covering northern France and Flanders, is held at the Palais des Beaux-Arts in Lille.

➕ B2 ✉ 129 rue de Grenelle, 75009 (entrance on esplanade des Invalides) ☎ 0810 11 33 99 (in France only); www.invalides.org 🕐 Tue. 10–9, Sun. 10–6:30, Wed.–Sat. 10–6, Apr.–Sep. (Dome open to 7 p.m. Jul.–Aug.); Sun. 10–5:30, Mon.–Sat. 10–5, rest of year

Napoléon Bonaparte is buried in Église du Dôme

🍴 Restaurant 🚇 Latour-Maubourg and Invalides 🎟 Combined ticket $$

Le Marais

Mozart and matzos, majesty and marshland: The treasures of the Marais are hidden behind high walls in the quaint 17th-century streets and alleys of the right bank, just north of Notre-Dame, and east of the Pompidou Center. Past narrow byways and creaking houses where the young Wolfgang Amadeus Mozart once played, come upon place des Vosges – once place Royale – the last great pre-Revolution square, where ladies lunch under shady arcades. Victor Hugo's house at No. 6 is now a museum dedicated to the author.

The area was once a slushy bog to the north of the island that was Paris, uninhabitable until the 13th century when monks managed to reclaim the swamps around rue St.-Antoine for farmland. Gradually the Marais became a fashionable alternative to the city center. In the late 14th century, it even became a royal retreat for Charles VI.

The joy of the Marais lies in its many secret courtyards. *Hôtels particuliers* are grand private residences whose tall street gates hide some stunning entrances. Worth a visit are the Hôtels

The neo-Byzantine marble basilica of Sacré-Coeur, atop Montmartre hill

Carnavalet, now a museum of Paris history, Salé (Picasso Museum, see page 44), Rohan-Guéménée (Maison de Victor-Hugo) and Soubise. The buildings are floodlit at certain times of the year.

For generations, the Marais was known for its Jewish quarter, with its bakers and restaurants along rue des Rosiers.

Since the 1980s, when the gay community adopted rue Ste.-Croix-de-la-Bretonnerie and its tributaries, unlikely neighbors have become the best of friends and the area has become very fashionable once again. Town planners readily issue preservation orders, and every season ushers in new museums, such as the little-known Musée de la Poupée, home to hundreds of dolls in impasse Berthaud. Café theater flourishes at Point-Virgule and Les Blancs Manteaux, and you might find a thing of beauty, if not quite a bargain, from the antiques dealers around Église St.-Paul-St.-Louis. Today's Marais attracts a fashionable element whose penthouse apartments overlook old streets where new shopfronts are more likely to display designer cuff links than groceries. Nonetheless, a true sense of people and place remains.

Musée Carnavalet – Histoire de Paris ✚ D2 ✉ 23 rue de Sévigné, 75003 ☎ 01 44 59 58 58 🕐 Tue.–Sun. 10–6 🚇 St.-Paul 🎟 Free (temporary exhibitions $–$$)

Musée de la Poupée ✚ D3 ✉ impasse Berthaud, off rue Beaubourg, near No. 22, 75003 ☎ 01 42 72 73 11; www.museedelapoupeeparis.com 🕐 Tue.–Sun. 10–6 🍴 Café Beaubourg, see page 259 🚇 Rambuteau 🎟 $$

Maison de Victor-Hugo ✚ E2 ✉ Hôtel de Rohan-Guéménée, 6 place des Vosges ☎ 01 42 72 10 16 🕐 Tue.–Sun. 10–6 🚇 Chemin-Vert, St.-Paul, Bastille 🎟 Free (temporary exhibitions $–$$)

Montmartre

Montmartre was always a village. Originally outside the city limits, when the cancan was banned from theaters, the public balls of Montmartre welcomed revelers to enjoy the gavotte performed by the prostitutes of the hill. Today, a sanitized dance is the finale of the floor show at the Moulin Rouge, named for the windmills that once dotted the hill. Pierre-Auguste Renoir's quaint "Moulin de la Galette" can still be seen here.

Take the funicular (you need the exact fare – they don't give change) up the final slopes to the Sacré-Coeur basilica, completed in 1910 as penance for the Franco-Prussian War. Hardy types climb the extra 295 feet to the dome. Around the corner at place du Tertre, a permanent rush hour of waiters serving sidewalk tables and portrait-hustlers continues as accordion tunes mingle with the constant honking of buses passing the white marble domes. If the garish daubs of the street artists don't appeal, the nearby Espace Dalí, a museum devoted to the great Surrealist, may prove more interesting.

Montmartre remains true to its past. Private mansions lie behind locked gates and rickety steps climb sidewalks so steep that they have banisters in the middle of the street. Snack on *frites* (fries) and mustard under a 19th-century lamp with the city spread at your feet, or savor a midnight crêpe and modern jazz in a cramped basement bar.

The area is home to a tiny vineyard, an exclusive cemetery, and more than one alley or facade that might have been painted by Toulouse-Lautrec or the bohemians of yore.

The lower slopes lead to the bustling cliché of Clichy, home to a Museum of Erotica (Musée de l'Érotisme), fairground shows and Tati, the famous bazaar where store security guards keep at bay hordes of local shoppers determined to secure a pair of pants for €10, a €15 skirt or an entire wardrobe for less than €75. The carnival spirit bustles all year round, and it isn't only locals who come here. The well-to-do put on dark glasses and Hermès scarves to join the crush. A world leader once arrived late for a summit conference because the lure of the Tati racks proved too strong for his wife.

Basilique du Sacré-Coeur ✚ D4 ✉ place du Parvis-du-Sacré-Coeur, 75018 ☎ 01 53 41 89 00; www.sacre-coeur-montmartre.com Ⓖ Basilica: daily 6:30 a.m.– 10:30 p.m. Dome and crypt: daily 9–7, in summer; 9–6, rest of year Ⓜ Anvers Ⓦ Basilica and crypt free; dome $$

Espace Dalí ✚ C4 ✉ 11 rue Poulbot, 75018 ☎ 01 42 64 40 10; www.daliparis.com Ⓖ Daily 10–6 (until 8 p.m. Jul.–Aug.) Ⓜ Anvers, Abbesses, Lamarck-Caulaincourt Ⓦ $$$

Musée de l'Érotisme ✚ C4 ✉ 72 boulevard de Clichy, 75018 ☎ 01 42 58 28 73; www.musee-erotisme.com Ⓖ Daily 10 a.m.–2 a.m. Ⓜ Blanche Ⓦ $$$

Musée d'Art et d'Histoire du Judaïsme

The Hôtel de St.-Aignan in the Marais is the elegant setting for the Jewish Art and History Museum, containing relics of French Jewish communities dating back hundreds of years before the Spanish Inquisition. Artifacts and icons from the Diaspora across Europe and north Africa are at the heart of a fascinating, informative and moving collection depicting Jewish life. Paintings of religious festivities in Venice, menorahs and Chanukah candleholders from Poland to the Ottoman Empire and models of *shtetl* villages and synagogues from eastern Europe are among highlights of the historical wings.

The works of Marc Chagall and fellow Jewish artists form the second collection. An interactive audio guide provides a fascinating insight into Jewish history and the Sephardi and Ashkenazi cultures. Original papers and pamphlets from the Dreyfus Affair and firsthand accounts of anti-Semitism bring the collection into the 20th century.

The Holocaust is referred to only by an exhibit charting the fate of the wartime inhabitants of the Marais mansion itself. For a sobering reflection of life in occupied France, the Memorial to the Unknown Jewish Martyr is dedicated to the memory of 6 million Jews who died during World War II. The memorial is now part of a larger complex, called the Memorial de la Shoah, which was opened on January 27, 2005 to mark the 60th anniversary of the discovery by Allied forces of Auschwitz.

➕ D3 ✉ Hôtel de St.-Aignan, 71 rue du Temple, 75003 ☎ 01 53 01 86 53; www.mahj.org ⏰ Mon.–Fri. 11–6, Sun. 10–6. Closed some Jewish holidays 🍴 Café 🚇 Rambuteau, Hôtel de Ville 💲 $$ (audio-guided tours available)

Memorial de la Shoah ✉ 17 rue Geoffroy-l'Asnier, 75004 ☎ 01 42 77 44 72; www.memorialdelashoah. org ⏰ Sun.–Fri. 10–6 (Thu. until 10 p.m.) 🚇 Pont-Marie, St.-Paul, Hôtel de Ville 💲 Free

Musée d'Art Moderne de la Ville de Paris

In a city that positively groans under the weight of the greatest artworks from the Renaissance to the Impressionists, it would be all too easy to forget that

A wooden sculpture at the Musée d'Art Moderne de la Ville de Paris

the 20th century has left its own treasure chest.

Not to be confused with the national collection at Centre Pompidou (see page 35), light, airy rooms in the Museum of Modern Art at the Palais de Tokyo – itself a fabulous example of 1937 modern architecture – are the fitting home to a collection of works by Henri Matisse, Pablo Picasso, Maurice Utrillo, Georges Braque and many others, encompassing Fauvim, Cubism, Surrealism, Abstract art and Nouveau Réalisme. Though these canvases are the main attraction, the museum offers more than this – the permanent collection includes installation and video art and a range of art deco furniture and modern tapestries.

➕ A3 ✉ 11 avenue du Président-Wilson, 75116 ☎ 01 53 67 40 00; www.mam.paris.fr ⏰ Tue.–Sun. 10–6 🚇 Alma-Marceau, Iéna 💲 Permanent collections free; temporary exhibitions $$

Musée Jacquemart-André

This perfect contrast to the sprawling Louvre is an elegant private art collection in a 19th-century home on boulevard Haussmann. Wealthy banker Edouard André and his wife Nélie Jacquemart accumulated a fabulous collection of art and furniture, bequeathed to the Institut de France just before World War II. Mostly 18th-century French art, from François Boucher to Antoine Watteau and 17th-century Flemish masters, is housed in the library. A Renaissance collection includes works by Donatello and Sandro Botticelli.

Visitors may also enjoy a glimpse of life as it was lived behind the high walls of this city mansion, with some of the family rooms restored to their original splendor. An audio guide is available in eight languages.

➕ B4 ✉ 158 boulevard Haussmann, 75008 ☎ 01 45 62 11 59; www.musee-jacquemart-andre.com ⏰ Daily 10–6 (also Mon. and Sat. 6–9 p.m. for temporary exhibitions) 🍴 Tearoom 🚇 Miromesnil, St.-Philippe-du-Roule 💲 $$$ (includes audio guide)

Musée du Louvre

The only way to arrive at I. M. Pei's Pyramide is from below. Leaving the subway, enter the Carrousel du Louvre, a high-class shopping mall and underground temple to today's highest culture. Inside the glass pyramid, a balletic spiral staircase whisks you into daylight, and the most glamorous wheelchair elevator spins to street level. The great glass structure reflects the grandeur of its setting in a kaleidoscope of constant architecture and ever-changing skies. This was the first sign of the Grand Louvre, President François Mitterrand's imperial plan to revive a building that was museum, royal palace, government offices and city landmark three subway stations long.

Because the Louvre is really seven museums in one sprawling three-winged palace, the Pyramide offers three entrances. It's impossible to walk the reputed 5 miles of galleries in one day, so first-timers should take the Sully entrance to see the 12th-century fortress, hidden underneath the Royal Palace until 1989. Above on two levels are the Egyptian collections. Discover daily life from bread-making to mummification, then walk through to explore the reigns of the pharaohs. In room seven of the Sully Wing, you will

> ### The Louvre in a Hurry
> If you simply want to see the three most famous attractions in record time, then beat the crowds in the Denon wing. Take the elevator to the second floor, turn into room six for *Mona Lisa*, back past the elevator for *Winged Victory*, then head downstairs to room seven of the Sully Wing for *Venus de Milo*. When you are done, follow the exit sign to the subway.

find the *Venus de Milo*, dating from the late second century BC.

The Apollo Gallery in the Denon wing houses the Crown Jewels, removed from regal necks before Madame Guillotine descended. See the dynamic *Winged Victory of Samothrace* atop the staircase, then wander among 13th-through 15th-century Italian paintings, including Leonardo da Vinci's *Mona Lisa* behind bullet-proof glass in room six. The renowned piece is smaller and more like a postcard than you might expect.

Back on the first floor, pass through the first sculpture gallery, taking in Michelangelo's *Dying Slave*, and stroll through treasures of ancient Greece and Rome.

The Richelieu wing has two covered courtyards studded with marble statues

One of the works by celebrated 17th-century sculptor, architect and painter Pierre Puget in the Louvre

Art has replaced locomotives in the former train station that is now the Musée d'Orsay

of the gods – all of which are woefully overlooked by the beautiful people noshing at Café Marly. Upstairs are the Renaissance galleries, Emperor Napoléon III's state apartments and the works of French, Flemish and Dutch old masters, including Jean Baptiste Camille Corot, Antoine Watteau and Jan Vermeer.

➕ C3 ✉ La Pyramide, cour Napoléon, 75001 ☎ 01 40 20 53 17; www.louvre.fr 🕐 Wed.–Mon. 9–6 (Wed. and Fri. until 9:45 p.m.) 🍴 Restaurants and cafés 🚇 Palais-Royal-Musée du Louvre 💰 $$ (less expensive Wed. and Fri. 6 p.m.–9:45 p.m.; additional charge for temporary exhibitions; free first Sun. of the month and Jul. 14)

Musée National Picasso

Some 200 of Pablo Picasso's paintings, dozens of sculptures and hundreds of drawings and sketches are housed in the elegant Hôtel Salé, an imposing Marais mansion rescued from years of neglect by a major cultural project. The visit takes the form of a chronological walk through the various ages, periods and styles of the artist from the early blue to the pink to the final Cubist phases in this comprehensive collection of the most prominent and prolific painter of the 20th century. The sensitivity and detail of the young painter's canvases

often strike visitors, who are mostly familiar with his later work.

The collection, donated to the state by the family in lieu of death duties, also features works acquired by Picasso during his lifetime, in particular paintings by Pierre-Auguste Renoir, Paul Cézanne and his contemporary Georges Braque.

➕ E2 ✉ Hôtel Salé, 5 rue de Thorigny, 75003 ☎ 01 42 71 25 21; www.musee-picasso.fr 🕐 Closed for renovation until summer 2013 🍴 Restaurant 🚇 St.-Paul 🎫 Guided tour in English 💰 $$ (free first Sun. of the month)

Musée d'Orsay

Every pane in the glass roof, the big clock and the vast light and airy space itself conjures the tingle of anticipation that only a train station built in 1900 could inspire. In 1986, the building was reincarnated as the home of 1848–1914 art, the missing link between the Louvre (see pages 43–44) and the Modern Art Museum (see page 42). The museum has fine examples of masters of art nouveau and realism, but the most popular exhibits are from the prestigious collection of Impressionist and post-Impressionist art. Claude Monet's *Houses of Parliament* and *Rouen Cathedral*, Vincent van Gogh's

Church at Auvers-sur-Oise, Pierre-Auguste Renoir's *Bathers* and Edgar Degas' *Blue Dancers*, to name but a few, highlight a lineup that features the best of Henri de Toulouse-Lautrec, Paul Cézanne, Paul Gauguin, Edouard Manet and Alfred Sisley. The belle-époque station decor reflects an age of inspiration and encourages visitors to linger. Sit in the tearoom at sunset, and watch the hands of the clock orchestrate shadows across the Seine.

B2 ✉ 1 rue de la Légion-d'Honneur, 75007 ☎ 01 40 49 48 14; www.musee-orsay.fr ⏰ Tue.–Sun. 9:30–6 (also Thu. 6–9:45 p.m.) 🍴 Restaurant and café 🚇 Solférino 💶 $$ (less expensive after 4:15 p.m. or 6 p.m. on Thu.; free first Sun. of the month)

Musée du quai Branly

Opened in 2006 and housed in a striking edifice designed by Jean Nouvel, and with a huge garden, the museum is a center of excellence for non-Western arts. There are collections from cultures throughout Africa, the Americas, Asia and Oceania, comprising over 5,000 artifacts from textiles to wood carvings.

A3 ✉ 37 quai Branly, 75007 ☎ 01 56 61 70 00; www.quaibranly.fr ⏰ Thu.–Sat. 11–9, Tue.–Wed. and Sun. 11–7 🍴 Restaurant and café 🚇 École Militaire or Alma-Marceau 🚌 42, 63, 69, 72, 80, 82, 90 💶 $$

Musée Rodin

The most celebrated work of the great sculptor Auguste Rodin (1840–1917) cannot be found in any room of the museum that bears his name. *The Thinker*, along with the *Burghers of Calais*, is discovered in the tranquil gardens that make this left-bank gallery so special. The roses, trees and pathways in the grounds of the 18th-century Hôtel Biron form a stunning backdrop to set off the larger works perfectly.

The mansion was home to Rodin in his later years and also numbered Jean Cocteau, Henri Matisse and Isadora Duncan among its illustrious residents. After the artist's death, the state opened the house as a permanent memorial to a national hero. His much-copied work, *The Kiss*, is among exhibits displayed within the indoor galleries.

B2 ✉ Hôtel Biron, 79 rue de Varenne, 75007 ☎ 01 44 18 61 10; www.musee-rodin.fr ⏰ Tue.–Sun. 10–5:45 (park closes at 6 p.m. Apr.–Sep.; 5 p.m. rest of year) 🍴 Restaurant 🚇 Varenne 💶 $$ (free first Sun. of the month)

Père-Lachaise, Cimetière du

A vast sprawling town in its own right, this cemetery is the last home of some of the world's greatest talents. The most famous resident is Oscar Wilde, whose once-magnificent Sphinx-guarded tomb has been hacked by souvenir hunters. His most private trinkets are said to serve as paperweights in some curator's office.

Père-Lachaise Cemetery is a full day out. Pay your respects to Marcel Proust, Honoré de Balzac, Sarah Bernhardt, Gertrude Stein, Abelard and Héloïse and, of course, Edith Piaf and Yves Montand. The Doors' lead singer Jim Morrison's graffiti-spattered monument is a gathering point for most visitors to this vast park of past glories. But there are also some peaceful corners for quiet reflection. The Mur des Fédérés, for example, is where more than 100 of the last members of the Commune (the alliance of revolutionaries that briefly ruled the city in 1871) were lined up against the cemetery wall and shot dead.

Père-Lachaise is only one of Paris' many last resting places. At Montmartre Cemetery, the guest list includes Jacques Offenbach, Léo Delibes, Hector Berlioz, Alexandre Dumas, François Truffaut, Vaslav Nijinsky, Jean-Paul Sartre and Charles Baudelaire.

Off map E3 ✉ 8 boulevard de Ménilmontant ☎ 01 55 25 82 10 ⏰ Mon.–Fri. 8–6, Sat. 8:30–6, Sun. 9–6, mid-Mar. to early Nov.; closes 5:30 rest of year 🍴 Pavillon Puebla 🚇 Père Lachaise or Philipe Auguste 💶 Free (guided tours $$; ☎ 06 20 46 23 87) **Cimetière de Montmartre** C4 ✉ 20 avenue Rachel, 75018 ☎ 01 53 42 36 30 ⏰ Mon.–Fri. 8–6, Sat. 8.30–6, Sun. 9–6, mid-Mar. to early Nov.; closes

5:30 p.m. rest of year 🚇 Blanche or Place de Clichy 💳 Free (guided tours $$; ☎ 06 20 46 23 87)

Cimitière du Montparnasse ✚ B1–C1 ✉ 3 boulevard Edgar-Quinet, 75014 ☎ 01 44 10 86 50 🕐 Mon.–Fri. 8–6, Sat. 8:30–6, Sun. 9–6, mid-Mar. to early Nov.; closes 5:30 rest of year 🚇 Raspail 💳 Free (guided tours $$ ☎ 06 20 46 23 87)

The Seine and the Islands

When Paris was born, the Seine ran around it – the Île de la Cité. This island and its more subdued twin, the Île St.-Louis, are the heart of Paris to this day, between the bustle and commerce of the modern right bank and the more romantic reflections of the left bank (see page 47). The Île de la Cité is home to the Conciergerie (see page 36), the Palais de Justice, the bird and flower market at place Louis-Lépine and the peaceful, old-style place Dauphine.

The main attraction is the Gothic Cathédrale Notre-Dame. Built from 1163 to 1345, the edifice is 426 feet

Notre-Dame cathedral's soaring interior

long, with towers creating a skyline at 226 feet. It's a magnet for tourists, who tend to crowd the place with too many camcorders. Arrive early in the day to appreciate the exquisite rose window and the view from the top of the towers of Eugène Viollet-le-Duc's celebrated 19th-century gargoyles. Two areas of contemplation sit beside the cathedral: the Hôtel Dieu's cloister across the parvis, and at the eastern tip of the island, the tiny cell that serves as a memorial to deported concentration-camp prisoners. A little bridge leads to the much quieter Île St.-Louis, with its many discreet restaurants and hotels.

On both banks are *bouquinistes*, dealers of second-hand books and prints who trade from lock-up cabinets at street level. Below, by the waterside, are dusty, shaded footpaths where lovers stroll into the evening and where, on summer Sunday mornings, fire-service cadets practice their water drill below quai Voltaire.

The metal Pont des Arts footbridge offers the best view of the city's sunset. Other bridges to cross include the famous Pont Neuf (literally "new bridge," but actually the oldest surviving crossing in town) by Île de la Cité, with its statue of Henri IV on horseback – he galloped across on its opening in 1607 – and the flamboyant Pont Alexandre III, a gift from the czar in 1900, with gilded cupids atop columns. Cross the Pont de Grenelle for its miniature Statue of Liberty facing westward to her big sister across the Atlantic.

Bateaux Mouche floating restaurants depart from Pont de l'Alma and smaller sightseeing craft from Pont Neuf. The Batobus (see page 33) plies the central stretch of the Seine almost year-round as a hop-on, hop-off alternative to the subway.

Notre-Dame ✚ D2 ✉ place du Parvis-de-Notre-Dame, 75004 ☎ 01 42 34 56 10; www.notredamedeparis.fr 🕐 Mon.–Fri. 8–6:45, Sat.–Sun. 8–7:15. Visits are limited during religious services 🚇 Cité 💳 Free

Rive Gauche

The *rive gauche*, or left bank, is more than simply the southern half of Paris. Marked by boulevards St.-Germain and St.-Michel, the left bank is a time and place apart.

The Romans developed the Quartier Latin (Latin Quarter) at the time the Île de la Cité was being colonized, but it was the establishment of the universities in the Middle Ages that gave the area its name and character. The 13th-century Sorbonne is the heart of the scholastic district. Largely escaping the grand designs that shaped the boulevards of the rest of Paris, the left bank remains a place where students hold discussions in cafés and cheap bookstores and where midnight is no excuse to retire. History happens at the table. Around place St.-Germain-des-Près, people flock to the Deux Magots and Café de Flore seeking Jean-Paul Sartre and Ernest Hemingway. At restaurants such as Le Procope, the American Constitution was drafted and debated.

The quarter's true spirit is its love of the arts: Théâtre de la Huchette (www.theatre-huchette.com), with Paris' longest-running play (more than 40 years), Eugène Ionesco's *La Cantatrice Chauve* (The Bald Prima Donna); scores of tiny cinemas, especially the essential Action chain, screening late-night Cary Grant and Katharine Hepburn classics; and, most of all, Shakespeare & Co. on rue de la Bûcherie, an American bookstore, previously owned by George Whitman (12.12.1913–12.14.2011), that acts as a magnet for budding writers and where there are readings and workshops. The sign over the door reads, "Be not inhospitable to strangers, lest they be angels in disguise."

The left bank is the Paris of legend for sitting and sipping rather than rushing and ticking a checklist of sights. Should you need a soundtrack, the Roman ruins of the Musée de Cluny and the nearby small 13th-century Église St.-Julien-le-Pauvre, where student councils were held until tempers flew too high in the 16th century, both host classical concerts on midweek afternoons. As the boulevards reach the area around the Musée d'Orsay and rue du Bac, the streets become less bohemian and art galleries more and more exclusive.

Le Procope, on the left bank, is a well-known Paris institution and dates back to 1686

The Eiffel Tower – a temporary exhibit that became Paris' most enduring landmark

Tour Eiffel

More than a triumph of 19th-century engineering, this 1,040-foot hunk of ironwork is one of the great personalities of Paris. Built by Gustave Eiffel for the 1889 World Exhibition, the temporary exhibit is still going strong. The world's tallest structure until New York's Chrysler Building was constructed in 1930, the Eiffel Tower took just two years to build and was saved from demolition in 1909 thanks to its radio mast, later boosted another 65 feet to serve as a weather station and TV antenna. Radio signals intercepted during World War I led to the capture of spy Mata Hari. Every fact – it weighs 7,000 tons and is repainted every seven years – is matched by a better anecdote: During the Nazi occupation, resistance fighters hid vital elevator parts so Hitler couldn't be photographed atop the symbol of France. Elevators and 1,710 steps serve the three levels and, in 2007, a summer terrace was opened on the first level. Information, a gift shop and a post office for specially postmarked mail are available on the second floor. The Jules Verne Restaurant occupies the third level. A panoramic viewing platform is perched 906 feet up on the highest level. Here, until his death in 1923, Eiffel maintained an office with the unique address, "Mr. Gustave Eiffel, Tour Eiffel, Paris."

Although on a clear day you can see for miles, the best view in town is of the tower by night when it is illuminated and seen from the Trocadéro. Among the millions of visitors in its first 100 years was an 85-year-old circus elephant that made it to the first level.

➕ A2 ✉ Champs de Mars, 75007 ☎ 01 44 11 23 23; www.tour-eiffel.fr 🕐 Daily 9 a.m.–0:45 a.m., mid-Jun. to end Aug. (final elevator for top floor at 11 p.m., steps close at midnight); 9:30 a.m.–11:45 p.m. (final lift for top floor at 10:30 p.m., steps close at 6:30 p.m.), rest of year 🍴 Restaurants. Jules Verne Restaurant: www.lejulesverne-paris.com 🚇 Bir-Hakeim ♿ First and second platforms $$; top platform $$$

La Villette

The canals and slaughterhouses of northeast Paris had long been dismissed as an area beyond the pale when the Cité des Sciences et de l'Industrie opened its daringly futuristic complex at La Villette. The spherical Géode movie theater is the landmark seen by traffic roaring by on the Périphérique highway circling Paris, but within the museums' halls and auditoriums are plenty of worlds to be uncovered, explored and tested, using up-to-the-minute cinematic and computer graphics technology.

Across the gardens is a piazza containing the Cité de la Musique and its Grande Halle, home to regular classical music and jazz festivals, open-air movies in summer and other major exhibitions. Concert halls and displays of musical instruments dating back to the Renaissance and examples of works of art inspired by music are part of the interesting Musée de la Musique (Museum of Music) housed within the complex.

Just a few steps from La Villette are the Canal de l'Oureq and the Canal St.-Martin, which provide quiet walks from the outskirts of Paris to the Gare de l'Est train station. The arrival of the museums has led to several cafés and restaurants opening by the canal locks and riverbanks.

➕ Off map E4

Cité des Sciences et de l'Industrie

✉ Parc de la Villette, 30 avenue Corentin-Cariou, 75019 ☎ 01 40 05 70 00; www.cite-sciences.fr 🕐 Tue.–Sat. 10–6, Sun. 10–7 🍴 Restaurant 🚇 Porte de la Villette ♿ $$; combined attractions packages $$$

Musée de la Musique ✉ 221 avenue Jean-Jaurès, 75019 ☎ 01 44 84 44 84; www.cite-musique.fr 🕐 Tue.–Sat. noon–6, Sun. 10–6 🍴 Restaurant 🚇 Porte de Pantin ♿ $$; concerts $$$

Cité de la Musique is one of the many and varied attractions at the large, modern park, La Villette

Regional Sights

> **Key to symbols**
> ✚ map coordinates refer to the Île-de-France map on page 27 💷 admission charge:
> $$$ more than €10, $$ €5–€10, $ less than €5
> See page 5 for complete key to symbols

Auvers-sur-Oise

Immortalized by the Impressionists – van Gogh's painting of the church surrounded by slanting rooftops, Cézanne's *House of Dr. Gachet* and countless local views by Corot and Pissarro – the little town on the banks of the Oise river is still an artists' colony. Van Gogh spent the last 70 days of his life here in 1890, creating 70 canvases in a painting frenzy before committing suicide. His room at the Auberge Ravoux has been preserved as he left it and can be visited. Van Gogh is buried in Auvers cemetery beside his brother Théo, and a statue by Ossip Zadkine (1961) stands in Van Gogh Park between the restaurant and the train station. A walk along the "old road" at the foot of the cliffs reveals many of the vistas and 19th-century houses that inspired so many famous works of art.

The last resting place of artist van Gogh, Auvers

The tourist office in the 17th-century Manoir des Colombières has walking and driving routes around the town. The first floor of the manor is a museum devoted to Charles François Daubigny, whose own descendents show visitors around his studio in the family home nearby. Another Auvers attraction is the Musée de l'Absinthe, dedicated to the favorite tipple of some 19th-century painters. Château d'Auvers offers a multimedia tour and audio guide of more than 500 Impressionist works.

✚ B3

Tourist information ✉ Manoir des Colombières, rue de la Sansonne ☎ 01 30 36 10 06; www.auvers-sur-oise.com

Maison de van Gogh ✉ Auberge Ravoux, place de la Marie ☎ 01 30 36 60 60; www.maisondevangogh.fr 🕐 Wed.–Sun. 10–6, Mar.–Oct. 💷 $$

Musée Daubigny ✉ Manoir des Colombières, rue de la Sansonne ☎ 01 30 36 80 20; www.musee-daubigny.com 🕐 Sat.–Sun. 10:30–12:30 and 2–6, Wed.–Fri. 2–5:30, Apr.–Oct.; Sat.–Sun. 10.30–12.30 and 2–5.30, Wed.–Fri. 2–5, rest of year. Closed mid-Dec. to mid-Jan. 💷 $

Maison-Atelier de Daubigny ✉ 61 rue Daubigny ☎ 01 30 36 60 60; www.atelier-daubigny.com 🕐 Thu.–Sun. 2–6:30, Easter to mid-Jul. and mid-Aug. to end Sep. 💷 $$

Musée de l'Absinthe ✉ 44 rue Alphonse-Callé ☎ 01 30 36 83 26; www.musee-absinthe.com 🕐 Wed.–Fri. 1:30–6, Sat.–Sun. 11–6, mid-Jun. to mid-Sep.; Sat.–Sun. 11–6, rest of year. Closed Nov.– early Mar. 💷 $

Château d'Auvers ✉ rue de Léry ☎ 01 34 48 48 48; www.chateau-auvers.fr 🕐 Tue.–Sun. 10:30–6, Apr.–Sep.; Tue.–Sun. 10:30–4:30, rest of year. Closed Christmas to mid-Jan. 🍴 Restaurant 💷 $$$

Chartres

The great Gothic Cathédrale Notre-Dame is worth the 50-mile drive from Paris. Unlike its magnificent sisters throughout Europe, this 13th-century masterpiece has remained untouched by the ravages of war and revolution. The original ninth-century church, built to house the tunic of the Virgin Mary, was burned to the ground in 1194, leaving the holy relic untouched by the flames.

Particularly spectacular are the 25,000 square feet of original stained-glass windows, most dating from the 13th century. Chartres blue glass gives the cathedral a particular light, notably from the Blue Madonna near the steps to the crypt. In 1971, the American Society of Architects donated a window to the south transept. Chartres has been a place of pilgrimage since the days of the first church here. The labyrinth in the nave is traditionally followed by pilgrims shuffling on their knees.

In town, the 17th-century streets have been well restored, a 12th-century grain store has been turned into a stained-glass center, and old mills survive along the Eure River.

✚ A2

Tourist information ✉ place de la Cathédrale
☎ 02 37 18 26 26; www.chartres-tourisme.com
Cathédrale Notre-Dame ✉ place Cathédrale
☎ 02 37 21 75 02; www.cathedrale-chartres.org
🕒 Daily 8:30–7:30 (Tue., Fri. and Sun. to 10 p.m. Jun. to early Sep.) 🚹 Guided visits Tue.–Sat. at noon and 2:45, Easter to Oct. 🎟 Free; towers $$

Statues of Old Testament kings and queens at Chartres' cathedral

Disneyland® Resort Paris

Opened as Euro Disney, Disneyland® Resort Paris has a distinctly French twist on the American dream. It is spread over the usual Fantasyland, Adventureland and Frontierland, as well as a suitably Gallic Discoveryland, with a nicely European 360-degree film adventure featuring Jules Verne and H. G. Wells. White-knuckle rides, flights of fancy and street parades are textbook Disney. Neighboring Walt Disney Studios® Park has four themed studio areas: Front Lot, Backlot, Toon Studio and Production Courtyard®.

Christmas is perhaps the best season to visit, as the domestic charm creates the cozy feel of Charles Dickens meets the Nutcracker Suite. Festival Disney, outside the gates, and cheap summer-evening rates for the park attract locals to Disney by night. The train station links to the Paris subway and airports and a direct international service to London.

✚ C2 ✉ Marne-la-Vallée, 77777 ☎ 0825 30 02 22, from U.S. call 011 33 1 60 30 60 53; www.disneylandparis.com 🕒 Daily. Hours vary each seasonal; call for details 🍴 Choice on site 🚇 RER: Marne-la-Vallée-Chessy 🎟 $$$

Parc Astérix

Based on the European cartoon characters Astérix and Obelix, the Parc Astérix is themed around the Roman occupation of Gaul (France). With the usual rides and splashes, themed foods and souvenirs, Astérix has an educational subtext for the young and unaware, with Latin puns for the mature and overeducated. There is a selection of nonscary family rides for younger children. Smaller than Uncle Walt's place at Marne-la-Vallée and just 21 miles north of Paris, the park boasts five zones, a hotel and enough to keep a family amused for a day or two.

✚ C3 ✉ Plailly, 60128 ☎ 08 26 30 10 40; www.parcasterix.fr 🕒 Daily 10–6, early Apr.–Aug.; Sat.–Sun. 10–6, Sep.–Oct. Also open some days in low season 🍴 Choice on site 🚇 RER: Aéroport-Charles-de-Gaulle 1 then shuttle bus 🚌 Shuttle from Paris (Louvre Museum) daily from 8:45 a.m. 🎟 $$$

Versailles palace is surrounded by wonderful gardens with statues and spectacular water features

Versailles

Versailles is unique. For 100 years it served as the center of French government, and for posterity it's the legacy of a magnificent ego. Louis XIV inherited a modest hunting lodge from his father and throughout his reign hired the greatest architects and landscape artists to embellish the site, transforming it from château to palace to a veritable kingdom in its own right. The result is a palace in 2,350 acres of nature tamed to a royal will.

It is impossible to see everything in a day, so content yourself with the essential visit to the great apartments and the grounds. The best of the château is on the ground floor, with the state apartments and the king's rooms along one wing and the queen's suite on the other.

The wings are linked by the splendid Hall of Mirrors, designed by Jules Hardouin-Mansart in 1687. The hall, with its unrivaled view over the great perspective of fountains and waterways, hosted royal banquets and, later, the historic signing of the Treaty of Versailles in 1919.

Despite the grandeur of decor and furnishings, human aspects still echo through the centuries. Discreet passageways link the bedrooms, where much of court life took place in private. The mantelpiece in Marie Antoinette's bedroom still bears scars of a scramble among courtiers for a good view of the queen giving birth. Visit the private opera house – used in the film *Dangerous Liaisons* (1988) – and the royal chapel before going on to discover the grounds.

The spectacular fountains and statues, particularly the Apollo Basin, are among the set pieces viewed from the flower beds. The Hameau was Marie Antoinette's own pastoral idyll, a model farm where the Austrian outsider might escape from the machinations of the court.

The least known of the gardens is the Potager du Roi, the royal kitchen garden adjoining the estate. Now the national agricultural college, it boasts trellised fruit trees and fascinating vegetable varieties.

✚ B2 ✉ Versailles, 78000 ☎ 01 30 83 78 00; www.chateauversailles.fr 🕐 Château open Tue.–Sun. 9–6:30, Apr.–Oct.; 9–5:30, rest of year. Various times for other attractions 🍽 Restaurant 🚊 RER: Versailles–Rive Gauche 🎟 Château $$$; other attractions $$$; comprehensive pass $$$

Drive
Palaces of
the Île-de-France

Distance: 150 miles
Time: 3 to 4 days

Much of France claims royal status. Reims in Champagne and Rouen in Normandy have staged coronations, but the Île-de-France has more than its fair share of castles, palaces and hunting estates. Some, like Vincennes, are within the Paris subway network. However, the great châteaux and royal towns that encircle the capital make for a country drive in itself.

From Paris, take the A1 to St.-Denis.
Better known today for its national sports stadium, St.-Denis has a rich 2,000-year history. The Basilique St.-Denis is the last resting place of 70 kings and other royals who reigned before Louis XVIII. No mere mausoleum, the early Gothic church has a spectacular collection of medieval and Renaissance sculpture. The city's Museum of Art and History is housed in a Carmelite convent that once was home to Louise de France, sister of Louis XVI. In June and July, St.-Denis hosts a major music festival.

Take the A86 west to Pont de Chatou then the D186 to St.-Germain-en-Laye.
St.-Germain-en-Laye was Louis XIV's birthplace and, before his move to Versailles in 1682, his country estate, famous for its hunting parties in the

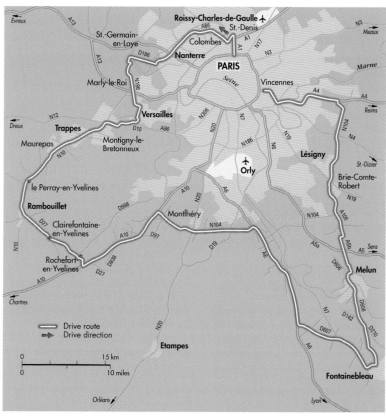

Rich wall coverings in the Tapestry Salon of the château at Fontainebleau

nearby state forest. A strategic fortress since the 14th century, the site was restored and embellished by successive kings in its 17th-century heyday. Royal favorite garden designer Le Nôtre designed the Grande Terrasse, which stretches for nearly 1.5 miles and offers magnificent views of the Seine valley. The garden is best enjoyed in summer, when concerts are held on the terrace bandstand. The château was restored under Napoléon III, who inaugurated the Museum of National Antiquities, with France's archeological treasures displayed in 17 rooms. In town, the birthplace of composer Claude Debussy is open to the public.

Leave St.-Germain south on the D284, following signs to le Pecq for 1 mile, then follow the N13 east for 130 yards to join the D7 for almost 1 mile.

You have to hand it to Louis XIV. Settled into his new and improved home of Versailles, he then decided the main palace was a little too large for himself and his friends. So he commissioned a second country estate at Marly-le-Roi. Less formal than the court, a modest royal pavilion with separate buildings for guests was conceived and constructed by the architect Jules Hardouin-Mansart, who spent the rest of his life perfecting it. It's said that the king himself enjoyed gardening on the grounds. Today, the buildings have gone, but visitors may drive and stroll through the royal park. A must-see is the wonderful Marly Machine, designed to pump water from the Seine to the fountains of Marly and Versailles. Madame du Barry's music pavilion remains from the Golden Age. Worth a visit is the Château of Monte Cristo, a fine Moorish-Renaissance folly built by Alexandre Dumas from the proceeds of his successful novels *The Count of Monte Cristo* and *The Three Musketeers*. The author worked in his Gothic Château d'If, nearby. Marly Forest consists of 5,000 acres of woodland. Some roads may be closed to traffic.

Leave Marly on the D386, drive 1 mile to the N186, leading south to Versailles.

Visit Palace of Versailles (see page 52).

Take the D91 south and turn right onto the N286 to the N12. At the Rambouillet exit, turn left to the A12, continuing on the N10 for 14 miles to Rambouillet.

Something of a storybook castle, Rambouillet is the official summer residence of the French president. Another of Louis XIV's collected châteaux, it was given to the Count of Toulouse and repurchased by Louis XVI, who enjoyed the hunting grounds. Queen Marie Antoinette was less enchanted, so the king commissioned a modest dairy pavilion for her pleasures. Another pretty outbuilding is the seashell-encrusted cottage in the park. The grounds are filled with flower beds and water gardens fit for regal and presidential strolls. Other attractions are the National Sheep Farm, founded by Louis XVI, and the Musée Rambolitrain, with 1,300 feet of miniature railroad track and some 4,000 models.

Leave Rambouillet on the D906, then drive southeast on the D27 for 8 miles, the D149 toward Paris for 1 mile, then join the A10 for 10 miles, leaving at the Lyon-Évry-Orléans exit for the N104. Continue for 11 miles, then take the A6 toward Lyon for 11 miles. Take the Fontainebleau-Montargis exit, turn left onto the N37, then the N7, following signs for the Château de Fontainebleau.

The spring of Bleau gave its name to Fontainebleau. François I tore down much of the medieval palace, and the great Renaissance estate was planned during the 16th century. Each reign saw improvements to the building, and after the revolution, Napoléon and his successors maintained the estate, which is now a World Heritage Site. Around the forest sits the village of Barbizon, home to Jean-François Millet, Pierre-Auguste Renoir and Claude Monet.

Take the N6 north to Melun. Two miles north of the town turn onto the N105 for half a mile to the A5B for 6 miles. Then go north on the N104 for 13 miles. At the Paris exit, turn left and take the N4 for 7 miles. At Joinville, go right onto the A4 and follow signs for the Château de Vincennes.

On the boundary of Paris, the Château de Vincennes is the last habitable, medieval royal fortress in France. The main reception area is housed in the old harnessing rooms, from which a shuttle bus operates to the nearest subway station. Two royal pavilions, the donjon and a chapel are open to the public. The old cartridge factory (*cartoucherie*) is now a theater complex with a varied program throughout the year. Also located here are Paris' zoo (closed until 2014) and the Bois de Vincennes park, a favorite for Sunday outings for Parisians.

Musée d'Art et d'Histoire ✉ 22 bis, rue Gabriel-Péri, St.-Denis, 93200 ☎ 01 42 43 05 10; www.musee-saint-denis.fr 🕔 Mon. and Wed.–Fri. 10–5:30 (to 8 p.m. Thu.), Sat.–Sun. 2–6:30 🚇 St.-Denis-Porte de Paris, RER: Gare de St.-Denis 💵 $$

Château St.-Germain-en-Laye ☎ 01 39 10 13 00; www.musee-archeologienationale.fr 🕔 Wed.–Mon. 10–5:15 🚇 RER: Gare de St.Germain-en-Laye 💵 $$

Maison Claude Debussy ✉ 38 rue au Pain, St.-Germain-en-Laye ☎ Tourist office and museum 01 30 87 20 63 🕔 Tue. and Thu.–Sat. 10–1 and 2–6, Mon. and Wed. 2–6, Sun. 10–1, Mar.–Oct.; Tue. and Thu.–Sat. 10:30–12:30 and 2:30–5:30, Mon. and Wed. 2:30–5:30, rest of year 💵 Free

Musée-promenade de Marly-le-Roi ✉ La Grille Royale, Parc de Marly, Louveciennes, 78430 ☎ 01 39 69 06 26; www.musee-promenade.fr 🕔 Wed.–Sun. 2–5:30; park 8–5:30 🚇 Louveciennes or Marly-le-Roi; RER: St.-Germain-en-Laye, then bus No. 1 to Louveciennes 💵 $

Château de Rambouillet and Laiterie de la Reine ✉ place de la Libération, 78120 Rambouillet ☎ 01 34 83 00 25; Laiterie de la Reine 01 34 83 29 09; www.chateau-rambouillet.monuments-nationaux.fr 🕔 Wed.–Mon. 10–11 and 2–5, Apr.–Sep.; Wed.–Mon. 10–11 and 2–4, rest of year. Closed during presidential stays 💵 $$ (includes Laiterie de la Reine)

Château de Rambouillet, La Bergerie Nationale (National Sheep Farm) ✉ Parc du Château ☎ 01 61 08 68 00; www.bergerie-nationale.educagri.fr 🕔 Wed., Sat.–Sun. 2–5:30, May–Sep.; 2–5, rest of year. Closed Christmas–end Jan. 💵 $$

Château de Rambouillet, Le Musée Rambolitrain ✉ 4 place Jeanne-d'Arc ☎ 01 34 83 15 93; www.rambolitrain.com 🕔 Wed.–Sun. 10–noon and 2–5:30 💵 $

Château de Fontainebleau ✉ place du Général-de-Gaulle, 77300 Fontainebleau ☎ 01 60 71 50 70; www.musee-chateau-fontainebleau.fr 🕔 Wed.–Mon. 9:30–6, Apr.–Sep.; 9:30–5, rest of year 💵 $$

Barbizon tourist information ✉ place Marc-Jacquet, 77630 ☎ 01 60 66 41 87; www.barbizon-tourisme.com

Château de Vincennes ✉ avenue de Paris, 94300 Vincennes ☎ 01 48 08 31 20; http://en.chateau-vincennes.fr 🚇 Château de Vincennes; RER: Vincennes 🕔 Daily 10–6, May–Aug.; 10–5, rest of year 💵 $$

Normandy and Brittany

Opposite: Mont St.-Michel and its abbey silhouetted in front of the setting sun

Normandy and Brittany

Even though Normandy and Brittany share the northwest coast of France, these two regions have fiercely independent histories and identities. The Normans, named Norsemen after fierce Vikings who descended from Scandinavia to take the land and tame a lush fertile region of farms and abundant seas, settled the area now called Normandy in the ninth century. Within 200 years, their regime of churches and ducal government had extended from here to England, and the two nations' histories were bound together for centuries to come.

Normandy's Heritage

The year 1944 saw the Allied D-Day landings and the Battle of Normandy that eventually liberated France. Postwar recuperation and tourism led to the discovery of Normandy's traditional cuisine of cream, cheeses, apples and seafood and it has influenced the world's menus ever since.

Fishing boats in the harbor of Dieppe

The distinctive landscape may be familiar to first-time visitors from its interpretation by the great Impressionists: Claude Monet on land and Pierre Bonnard and Eugène Boudin on the coasts. Sea ports such as Honfleur and Dieppe are popular with fishermen and tourists alike, Deauville is an unashamed holiday resort, and Caen and Cherbourg are principal cities, with their ferry and container ports and thriving commercial centers.

The Normandy capital is Rouen (see pages 62–65), on the Seine, which periodically welcomes international armadas, festivals of ships great and small from all over the world. The upper-eastern section of the region,

Haute-Normandie, is more industrial and certainly wealthier. The economy of the lower half, Basse-Normandie, relies on farming and fishing. This area has plenty in common with the neighboring region of Brittany.

The Land of the Sea

Any resemblance to Normandy is superficial, for Brittany is France's kingdom of the Celts. The past is only ever a few yards away in a land that still guards its identity and joined France only in 1547. Its Breton name is Armorica, the land of the sea. Once a harsh, barren land, today Brittany has a strong farming community, celebrated for its arable produce, including onions and artichokes. The landscape is no less dramatic: From the cliffs ablaze with gorse on the emerald coast, to the treacherous rocks around little coves, to the salt marshes on the Guérande peninsula, where egrets and purple herons stand sentinel over lagoons and pools as salt flakes crystallize while the sea trickles away.

Inland, Brittany is less interesting for visitors, with few cities worth a detour. The new capital is Rennes, though the historic capital was Nantes, where Gilles de Rais, better known as Bluebeard the pirate, was burned at the stake in the 15th century by the Duke of Brittany. Nantes has since been reassigned to the neighboring Loire region.

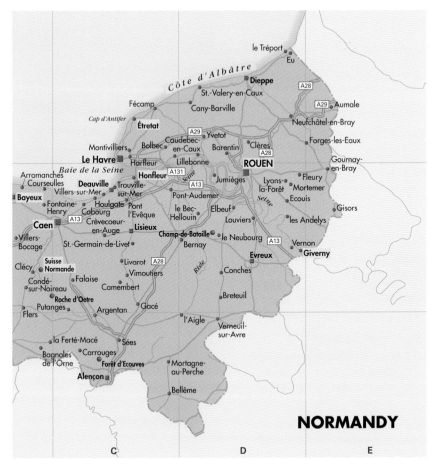

NORMANDY

Try the richly flavored local cider *(cidre)* made in Brittany and Normandy

Celtic Heritage

Celtic festivals, uniting Brittany with Wales, Scotland and Ireland, take place in Quimper (see page 74) and Lorient every summer. Myths of witches and strange creatures abound, especially in the towns and villages to the west of the region. Plenty of folk festivals enable visitors to see colorful traditional costumes and charming lacework, especially in the *coiffes* (lace headdresses) that elderly women still wear to folkloric events. The country crafts of Brittany's heritage are well promoted, but generations of piracy on the high seas tend to be played down. Evidence of pagan times can be seen in the strange stone remains of long lost cultures.

Food

Oysters in Brittany and Normandy, or Brittany's *bélons* from the Bélon river, are rare treasures on any menu, and the region produces many of the finest varieties in France. In Normandy, choose the oysters from St.-Vaast-la-Hougue (see page 77). Brittany's celebrated *crêpes*, flat pancakes folded into wedges, are fabulous, savory or sweet. Every village has its *crêperie*, where fast food is an art. Chefs prize the local sea salt, farmed on salt marshes and sold in stores and by the roadside. Normandy's lush pastures produce great cheeses – Camembert is the best known – and wonderful butter from Isigny-sur-Mer. *Tripes à la mode de Caen* (a savory tripe dish) is a delicacy, as is a starter of *rillettes* (coarse pâté) or

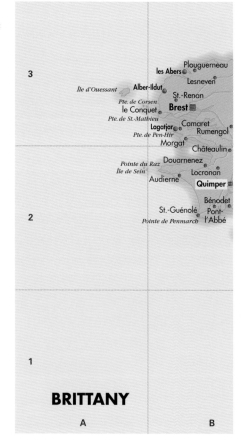

boudin noir (black pudding). The main seafood dish is a fish and shellfish stew, *marmite Dieppoise*. *Tarte Normande* is a delicious dessert pastry made with apples or pears. Those apples provide the staple drink, cider. In Normandy and Brittany, order cider rather than wine with your meal and maybe try a glass of calvados, a potent apple brandy. Calvados is often served as a *trou Normand* (Norman hole), to be downed in one gulp midway through a meal to increase the appetite and make way for yet another few courses.

Les Pardons

The traditional Brittany *pardon* is a colorful local pilgrimage and procession celebrating patron saints, with costumes, parades, dancing and feasting. *Pardons* occur during the summer months and details are available from the local tourist offices.

Language

There has been a keen revival of Celtic, the ancient Breton language, in recent years. It's said that at one time a fisherman from St.-Malo (see page 76) would have been able to converse freely with a Celtic trawlerman from Cornwall in England. Signage is bilingual throughout Brittany, and, in Finistère, a growing number of hotels are moving away from the standard international or typical French styles, to more traditional folk color and design schemes and are using the local language on menus.

Historic timber-framed houses, decorated with flowering plants, front the old marketplace in Rouen

Rouen

Rouen is the city of Joan of Arc. The Norman capital may be an important modern port, but it can never escape its association with one of the great folk martyrs of France. It's centrally placed in rich and rural Normandy, with easy access along the Seine river to the east or through the tunnel from Abbeville. Visitors are greeted by the splendor of the city's Gothic cathedral. Arrival at sunset, when the spire and towers glow with sparkling rich sculptures twinkling like a fairy-tale castle, is an unforgettable experience.

But there is much more to Rouen than St. Joan. Its old quarters haven't been allowed to stagnate. Modern buildings are not self-conscious, and all periods of the port's historic wealth and influence may be seen in the style of buildings and the busy stores and streets.

The city is compact and easy to walk around or you can rent a bicycle from one of the 20 stations dotted around the city. Begin any visit by stopping at the tourist office in the main courtyard of the cathedral where guided tours can be organized. If you plan to stay a while, buy a map – the free version handed out here is plastered with advertisements for stores, obscuring details of historic sites.

Shopping in Rouen is excellent, and is mainly focused on the pedestrian-friendly zone, a maze of cobbled side streets and half-timbered houses. The best area is around the huge one-handed clock on a carved Renaissance arch that straddles rue du Gros-Horloge.

The City of St. Joan

The warrior saint, who heard the voice of St. Catherine and scandalized society by wearing male clothing, was burned at the stake on May 30, 1431, in the old marketplace (place du Vieux-Marché) after Bishop Pierre Cauchon tried her for heresy. A modern commemorative cross stands on the spot where she died. Visit the striking Église Ste.-Jeanne-d'Arc, created in 1979 by a local architect to mark the 550th anniversary of her martyrdom. The boat-shaped church dominates the square, where markets still take place under a canopy matching the new building. The interior is impressive, with notable stained glass, including Renaissance panels removed from Église St.-Vincent before bombings destroyed the original church. Excavations revealed the foundation of another church, St.-Sauveur, destroyed in 1833. The complex is surrounded by gardens and a museum dedicated to St. Joan.

Église Ste.-Jeanne-d'Arc 🛉 A2 ✉ place du Vieux-Marché ☎ 02 35 71 85 65 🕐 Mon.–Thu. and Sat. 10–12 and 2–6, Fri. and Sun. 2–6 🚇 Théâtre des Arts 🎫 Free

Musée de Cire Jeanne d'Arc 🛉 A2 ✉ 33 place du Vieux-Marché ☎ 02 35 88 02 70; www.jeanne-darc.com 🕐 Daily 9:30–1, 1:30–9, mid-Apr. to mid-Sep.; 10–noon and 2–6:30, rest of year 🚇 Théâtre des Arts 🎫 $

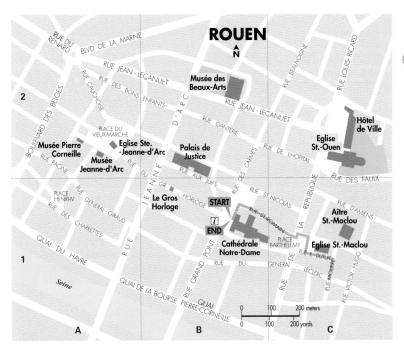

Essential Information

Tourist Information

25 place de la Cathédrale ☎ 02 32 08 32 40;
www.rouentourisme.com

Urban Transportation

A bus and subway system known as
Métrobus serves Rouen and its outlying
districts. However, the central historic part
of town is best explored on foot, and all
sights are within a short walk of the Théâtre
des Arts subway station. Tickets are
inexpensive and should be validated in
machines at stations and on boarding buses.
The Découverte card offers unlimited travel

within a 24-hour period. Transportation
information is available at the bus station,
Espace Métrobus, rue Jeanne-d'Arc ☎ 02 35
52 52 52; www.tcar.fr. Taxis can be hailed in
the street or at stands. Trains to Paris and
other towns in Normandy depart from the
SNCF Gare-rue Verte ✉ place Bernard-Tissot
☎ 36 35 (premium-rate call); www.sncf.fr.

Airport Information

Aéroport Rouen-Vallée-de-Seine is at Boos,
10 miles east of Rouen. Taxis serve the city
center ☎ 02 35 79 41 00;
www.rouen.aeroport.fr.

Climate – average highs and lows for the month

Jan.	Feb.	Mar.	Apr.	May	Jun.	Jul.	Aug.	Sep.	Oct.	Nov.	Dec.
8°C	8°C	10°C	12°C	15°C	18°C	19°C	20°C	19°C	15°C	12°C	10°C
46°F	46°F	50°F	54°F	59°F	64°F	66°F	68°F	66°F	59°F	54°F	50°F
4°C	4°C	5°C	7°C	9°C	12°C	14°C	14°C	13°C	10°C	8°C	5°C
39°F	39°F	41°F	45°F	48°F	54°F	57°F	57°F	55°F	50°F	46°F	41°F

Rouen Sights

> **Key to symbols**
> ✚ map coordinates refer to the Rouen map on
> page 63 ⚜ admission charge: $$$ more than €10,
> $$ €5–€10, $ less than €5
> See page 5 for complete key to symbols

Cathédrale Notre-Dame

A favorite subject for the Impressionist
painter Claude Monet, the white stone
of the beautifully restored Gothic facade
continues to impress and dazzle visitors.
Inside the dusky interior, with its
vaulting arches and airy nave, Gothic
and Renaissance styles are combined.
Among the surviving medieval legacies
are several stained-glass windows – still
in place despite centuries of assault –
with vivid, deep-blue panes.

The tombs of dukes and princes outdo
each other with their opulence and
dignity and, in the crypt, there is a tomb
that, allegedly, contains the heart of
Richard the Lionheart.

The cathedral has been rebuilt and
added to many times over the centuries,
including suffering damage during
World War II, but the 499-foot cast-iron
spire, constructed in the 19th-century,
continues to dominate the city and is
floodlit every night until 1 a.m.

✚ B1 ✉ place de la Cathédrale ☎ 02 35 71 86 65;
www.cathedrale-rouen.net ⏰ Mon. 2–6, Tue.–Sat.
9–7, Sun. 8–6, Apr.–Sep.; Mon. 2–6, Tue.–Sat. 9–12
and 2–6, Sun. 8–6, rest of year 🚇 Théâtre des Arts
⚜ Free

Église St.-Ouen

It's best to visit here during one of the
many fabulous concerts held in this
massive light and airy Gothic arched
church. Only an unattractive modern
altar mars the splendor of the windows
and the sanctuary, with 18th-century
choir gates. The 15th-century abbey
church by the town hall is famous for
the excellent quality of its organs, which
may be heard being played in rehearsal
during the days leading up to a concert.

The church has its own tower and spires
to augment Rouen's skyline. The
building is seen to best effect from the
peaceful gardens at the rear.

✚ C2 ✉ place du Général-de-Gaulle ☎ 02 32 08 31
01 ⏰ Tue.–Thu. and Sat.–Sun. 10–noon and 2–6,
Apr.–Oct.; closes at 5 p.m. rest of year 🚇 Théâtre des
Arts ⚜ Free

Le Gros Horloge

One glance at the huge clock face
straddling an archway across the
bustling rue du Gros-Horloge and you
are tempted to laugh at the original
criticism that locals had trouble seeing
it. But keep in mind that originally it
was placed out of sight high on the clock
tower next door. Moved by public
demand to its present location, the
"Great Clock," with its complicated,
gilded double face showing both time
and date, is now part of a potpourri of
architectural styles. The building is
framed with other unusual details, from
its medieval tower to 17th-century
carved fripperies and an ancient stone
sculpture set in the arch under the
clock. Enjoy a pleasant walk underneath
through this old part of the town.

✚ B1 ✉ rue du Gros-Horloge ☎ 02 32 08 01 90
⏰ Tue.–Sun. 10–1 and 2–7, Apr.–Oct.; Tue.–Sun. 2–6,
rest of year 🚇 Palais de Justice ⚜ $$

Musée des Beaux-Arts

The elegant Square Verdrel has
waterfalls and exotic trees to distract the
visitor for a while before entering the
Classical fine arts museum on one side
of the square. Within is a fine collection
of paintings, from François Clouet's
fleshy nudes to Claude Monet's hazy *The
Seine at Port-Villez*, and his *Vue générale
de Rouen*, plus several works by Alfred
Sisley. Michelangelo da Caravaggio's
Flagellation of Christ shouldn't be
missed. Temporary exhibitions are held
here and guided tours are available.

✚ B2 ✉ esplanade Marcel-Duchamp ☎ 02 35 71 28
40; www.rouen-musees.com ⏰ Wed.–Mon. 10–6.
Closed holidays 🍴 Restaurant 🚇 Palais de Justice
⚜ $$

Walk
Rouen's
Antiques Shops

Refer to route marked on city
map on page 63

You will probably take some of
Rouen's past home with you if you
spend an hour or so foraging through
the backstreets around the cathedral
quarter. This area is rich with good
small antiques shops. Dealers in this
quarter are generally helpful and
knowledgeable, and since most shops
are in the city's famous old buildings,
consider it art, not consumerism!

**Start this mile-long walk facing the
cathedral's facade. Walk left and stroll
along the rue St.-Romain, taking time to
check out the stores on the left side.**
Max Tetelin, specializing in old glass,
porcelain, silver and furniture, is at
Nos. 10–14. Newer, but no less stylish,
is Augy-Carpentier (No. 26), which
sells tableware.
**As you arrive at the busy shopping street
of rue de la République, turn left to find
Boisnard, at No. 54, which was founded in
1910 and is stocked with fine furniture and
art. Cross the road to walk through one of**
the narrow side streets into the intimate
place St.-Barthélémy.
Take time to appreciate the Gothic
Église St.-Maclou, with its five porches
and carved wooden doors dating from
1552. Charming galleries cluster
opposite the bow-fronted church. Signs
direct you to the church's unusual Aître,
a cloistered cemetery with fascinating
wall designs created from bones.
**Walk behind the church to reach
place Barthélémy.**
At No. 2, the Métais family are experts
in antiques and are used by many
insurance companies to assess value
for replacement or damage repair.
Leave the square on rue Eugène-Dutuit,
leading to rue Molière.
**Bertran, at Nos. 108–110, has a remarkably
fine selection of books, porcelain, jewelry
and small paintings.**
Turn back along rue Eugène-Dutuit and
cross the square to return to rue
St.-Romain and the cathedral shops,
which are open Monday through
Saturday until 7 p.m.

Église St.-Maclou ✚ C1 ✉ place Barthélémy
☎ 02 32 08 32 40 🕐 Fri.–Mon. 10–noon and 2–6,
Apr.–Oct.; closes at 5:30 p.m. rest of year 🚊 Théâtre
des Arts ℹ Audio-guided visits available 🎫 Free
Aître St.-Maclou ✚ C1 ✉ 184 rue Martainville
☎ 02 32 08 32 40 🕐 Fri.–Mon. 10–12 and 2–6,
Apr.–Oct.; Fri.–Mon. 10–12 and 2–5:30, rest of year
🚊 Théâtre des Arts 🎫 Free

Cathédrale Notre-Dame marks the start of a walk around the city

Regional Sights

> **Key to symbols**
> ✚ map coordinates refer to the maps on pages
> 58–59 and 60–61 ✋ admission charge:
> $$$ more than €10, $$ €5–€10, $ less than €5
> See page 5 for complete key to symbols

Bayeux

Timbered buildings, clean streets and the splashing of watermills: This city would be worth a visit even without its rich history. However, there is never any escaping the past in Bayeux. The Musée Mémorial de la Bataille de Normandie tells of the 1944 battle.

The 11th-century cathedral, with its frescoes depicting the murder of St. Thomas, was the original home to the Bayeux Tapestry, now displayed nearby. This remarkable 230-foot embroidered epic, commissioned by Odo, bishop of Bayeux and half-brother of William the Conqueror, relates the frame-by-frame drama of William's triumph at the Battle of Hastings and how the duke of Normandy won the crown of England in 1066. More than just propaganda, the detailed craftwork is an 11th-century soap opera, with scenes showing religious intrigue, shipwreck and panic when Halley's Comet warns Saxon king Harold of impending disaster. An excellent exhibition highlights the storytelling and stitching techniques, and an audio guide explains the drama contained within the tapestry.

✚ B2–Normandy
Tourist information ✉ Pont St.-Jean, 14400
☎ 02 31 51 28 28; www.bessin-normandie.fr
Musée Mémorial de la Bataille de Normandie
✉ boulevard Fabian-Ware ☎ 02 31 51 46 90;
www.normandiememoire.com ⏰ Daily 9:30–6:30,
May–Sep.; 10–12:30 and 2–6, rest of year. Closed Jan.
to mid-Feb. ✋ $$
Tapisserie de Bayeux ✉ Centre Guillaume-le-
Conquerant, rue de Nesmond ☎ 02 31 51 25 50;
www.tapisserie-bayeux.fr ⏰ Daily 9–6:15, May–Aug.;
9–5:45, mid-Mar. to Apr. and Oct. to mid-Nov.;
9:30–1:45 and 2–5:50, rest of year. Closed two weeks
in Jan. ✋ $$

Caen

With a castle and two abbeys founded by William the Conqueror as a penance for marrying his cousin Matilda of Flanders, enough of old Caen survived

Colorful borders and shrubs fill the courtyard of the Abbaye aux Dames, in Caen

the bombing in 1944 to make a visit worthwhile. And don't miss the Peace Memorial just outside town. From the 1919 peace pledges, the gallery charts past politicians, press and daily life into the inferno of World War II. Linked cinemas take you from D-Day to the present; you will see a split-screen perception of the landings through home movies of both sides, then a multimedia diary of events. *Esperance* (Hope), the third film, which ends this strange history, is a painful barrage of clips of the state of the world since the end of World War II. Churchill, Eisenhower, de Gaulle, Hitler, J.F.K., King, Stalin, Nixon, Mao. Nazis at Nuremberg declare their innocence to the children of Auschwitz. Nelson Mandela walks free. Rwanda denies food to its own people. The screen provides an unforgiving mirror to the face of world "peace."

✚ C2–Normandy

Tourist information ✉ place St.-Pierre, 14000 ☎ 02 31 27 14 14; www.tourisme.caen.fr

Le Mémorial de Caen ✉ esplanade Général-Eisenhower ☎ 02 31 06 06 45; www.memorial-caen.fr ⏱ Daily 9–7, mid-Feb. to mid-Nov.; 9:30–6, rest of year. Closed early Jan. to late Jan. Closed Mon., mid-Nov. to late Dec. ⑪ Restaurants and café 🍴 $$$

Carnac

Come to wonder at the riddle of the stones, strange alignments erected up to 6,000 years ago and still standing to the north of the town. The megaliths are said to have been arranged for some long-forgotten religious or ritual purpose, and the more distinctive lines can be seen from viewing platforms. Most are now roped off from the public to avoid erosion and vandalism. The tourist offices have pamphlets proposing local myths and legends about the stones, and details of guided tours and seasonal opening hours.

For a more recent historical era, visit Église St.-Cornély, dedicated to the patron saint of horned beasts.

To pay homage to the sun, pass the lagoons to Carnac-Plage, a delightful and modern seaside resort.

✚ C2–Brittany

Tourist information ✉ 74 avenue des Druides, 56342 (Carnac-Plage) ☎ 02 97 52 13 52; www.ot-carnac.fr

Cotentin

The unspoiled Cotentin peninsula is the finger of France pointing toward the Channel Islands (which are part of Great Britain), culminating in the granite cliffs of Cap de la Hague. The rugged coastline from Cherbourg to Caen is better known for the D-Day landings, but William the Conqueror and Richard the Lionheart both sailed from Barfleur, which boasts a lifeboat museum and Normandy's tallest lighthouse (233 feet) at Gateville. St.-Vaast-la-Hougue and the little island of Tatihou (see page 77) are across the atmospheric Val de Saire, an area with France's tiniest town hall at la Pernelle.

At Isigny-sur-Mer, discover France's best butter and cream. Valognes, another city ravaged by bombings, has the regional cider and calvados museums.

On the west side of the peninsula, where there are beautiful dunes, visit the splendid Gothic Cathédrale Notre-Dame at Coutances and Christian Dior's childhood home in the busy fishing port of Granville. From Granville and nearby Barneville-Carteret, ferries run to the Channel Islands of Guernsey (Carteret only) and Jersey.

✚ B2–Normandy

Barfleur tourist information ✉ 2 Rond-Point Guillaume-le-Conquérant, 50760 ☎ 02 33 54 02 48; www.ville-barfleur.fr

Coutances tourist information ✉ place Georges-Leclerc, 50200 ☎ 02 33 19 08 10; www.tourisme-coutances.fr

Granville tourist information ✉ 4 cours Jonville, 50406 ☎ 02 33 91 30 03; www.ville-granville.fr

Musée Christian-Dior ✉ rue d'Estouteville, Granville ☎ 02 33 61 48 21; www.musee-dior-granville.com ⏱ Daily 10–6:30, mid-May to late Sep.; Sat.–Sun. 2–5:30, Oct.–Feb. ⑪ Café 🍴 $$

Côte d'Albâtre

The northeastern strip of coastline from Le Tréport to Le Havre is named for its fast-retreating cliff faces. The white chalk is eroded by several yards each year, and the sea is dotted with lonely shards of rock, showing where a previous generation once stood. Beaches of smooth, blue-gray pebbles and stones are a particular attraction of the many coves and harbors nestling under the cliffs. Most charming is Étretat (see page 70), and most interesting is Fécamp, where the 12th-century Église de la Trinité contains a relic said to be the blood of Christ and a palace still makes the monastic liqueur Bénédictine. Tours and tastings are offered daily.

Le Havre is uncompromisingly modern, with an industrial approach road and little remaining of the prewar port. By contrast, Dieppe has lovely old streets linking the port and the town center, many good seafood restaurants and its 15th-century château containing a museum with a fabulous ivory collection and paintings by Pierre-Auguste Renoir, Eugène Boudin and Camille Pissarro. The pretty harbor is full of boats and the town has a new complex of heated seawater swimming pools, a fitness center and a spa.

➕ C3–D3–Normandy
Fécamp tourist information ✉ quai Sadi-Carnot, 76400 ☎ 02 35 28 51 01; www.fecamptourisme.com
Palais Bénédictine ✉ 110 rue Alexandre-le-Grand, Fécamp, 76400 ☎ 02 35 10 26 10; www.benedictine.fr
🕐 Daily 10–7, early Jul. to end Aug.; 10–1 and 2–6:30, Apr.–early Jul. and Sep. to mid-Oct.; 10:30–12:45 and 2–6, early Feb. to late Mar. and mid-Oct. to end Dec. Closed Jan.–early Feb. 💲 $$
Dieppe tourist information ✉ Pont Ango, quai du Carénage, 76200 ☎ 02 32 14 40 60; www.dieppetourisme.com
Château Musée ✉ rue de Chastes, Dieppe, 76200 ☎ 02 35 06 61 99 🕐 Daily 10–12 and 2–6, May–Sep.; Mon. and Wed.–Sat. 10–12 and 2–5, Sun. 10–12 and 2–6, rest of year 💲 $

Deauville

A summer pleasure ground designed for Parisian and American weekenders, Deauville built its boardwalk (promenade des Planches), casino and racetrack in 1910. Here, Gabrielle "Coco" Chanel invented herself as a couturier, making women's fashions out of fishermen's jerseys; Hollywood stars come for the annual American Film Festival in September or the races, and casino gamblers take time out to enjoy the glitz of the floor show. During July and August, the city's vacation residences are full to bursting.

The beach huts at the glamorous seaside resort of Deauville are named after movie stars of the past

C2–Normandy
Tourist information ✉ 112 rue Victor-Hugo, 14800
☎ 02 31 14 40 00; www.deauville.org

Dinan

If possible, try to arrive at this charming
medieval town by boat. As you sail from
St.-Malo along the Rance river, you will
stock up on lifelong memories. This
most perfectly preserved of walled towns
has been built on such a human scale
that you will hardly believe its charm –
from the little pleasure port, past the
black-roofed gray-stone buildings, to the
fertile green fields and trees on the
sloping hillside.

Start your walk from the town
museum in the castle, and stroll on the
almost complete ramparts dating from
the 13th century. The best views are
from the promenade de la Duchesse-
Anne. Streets are storybook narrow,
steep and arcaded. Many of the old
shops, especially along the medieval
rue du Jerzual, one of the most
photographed streets in all Brittany,
are now tasteful boutiques selling
handicrafts and antiques.

In good weather, take a turn around
the neat Jardin Anglais; on duller days,
visit Église St.-Sauveur, which is the
repository of the heart of Bertrand du
Guesclin, who famously fought a duel
with one Thomas of Canterbury in
Dinan's main square in 1357. Today, a
statue of Bertrand du Guesclin stands in
the square.

D3–Brittany
Tourist information ✉ 9 rue du Château, 22105
☎ 02 96 87 69 76; www.dinan-tourisme.com
Château-Musée ✉ place du Guesclin, 22100
☎ 02 96 39 45 20; www.mairie-dinan.com
Ⓖ Daily 10–6:30, Jun.–Sep.; 1:30–5:30, rest of year.
Closed Jan. 🖊 $

Dinard

Probably the prettiest of the popular
resorts of Brittany is Dinard, with its
lovely Grande Plage and surprisingly
warm summer climate that comes
courtesy of the Gulf Stream.

Historic buildings cling to the hillside at Dinan

Just across the estuary from St.-Malo
(see page 76), this popular resort was
discovered by wealthy Americans in the
mid-19th century and, since then, every
year sees new striped bathing tents and
familiar faces returning to the favorite
beach. The season brings regattas by
day, sound-and-light shows by night,
and thalassotherapy by way of
alternative pampering.

The romantically named Promenade
du Clair de Lune (Moonlight
Promenade) offers wonderful sea views
and fresh sea air, and is a popular
after-lunch stroll in winter or after
dinner during the summer months.

Dinard is an excellent base for
exploring the beautiful Côte d'Emeraude
(Emerald Coast) – ideally by renting a
boat, but it is just as rewarding by car.
Cross the bridge to visit St.-Malo and the
tidal dam that provides Brittany with its
electricity, or enjoy the sandy beaches of
les Sables-d'Or and explore the
magnificent 230-foot-high cliffs of Cap
Fréhel, one of Brittany's most dramatic
promontories, and its lighthouse.

D3–Brittany
Tourist information ✉ 2 boulevard Féart, 35800
☎ 02 99 46 94 12; www.ot-dinard.fr

Étretat

Normandy's most stunning beach resort is best enjoyed out of season, when the bay is deserted and the magnificent chalk headlands may be admired in peace. A cathedral-size cave is accessible from the pebbled beach. Atop the Falaise d'Amont cliff is a sailor's chapel, Notre-Dame de la Garde, and a memorial to aviators Charles Nungesser and François Coli, whose plane *l'Oiseau Blanc* was last seen from these cliffs on its ill-fated bid to fly from Paris to New York in 1927. In the sea just beyond the other cliff, the Falaise d'Aval, stands a 230-foot rock stack known as the Aiguille d'Étretat (the needle). These rocks inspired the great landscape and Impressionist artists Claude Monet, Jean-Baptiste-Camille Corot and Eugène Boudin, who returned here year after year. Writer Maurice Leblanc visited Étretat too, and bought a house here. It is now a museum dedicated to his most famous character, Arsène Lupin. In place du Maréchal-Foch, the town built its wooden covered market in 1926, surrounded by charming 16th-century town houses. A plaque recalls a World War I American hospital on the square.

➕ C3–Normandy

Tourist information ✉ place M.-Guillard, 76790 ☎ 02 35 27 05 21; www.etretat.net

Le Clos Arsène Lupin ✉ 15 rue Guy-de-Maupassant, 76790 ☎ 02 35 10 59 53; www.arsene-lupin.com 🕐 Daily 10–5:45, Apr.–Sep.; Sat.–Sun. 11–4:45 and holidays, rest of year ✋ $$

Giverny

You won't find a single famous canvas by Claude Monet in the charming pink-and-green house where the artist lived until his death in 1926, but reproductions of his classic paintings

are displayed here, along with his personal collection of Japanese prints. The beautiful gardens, with the water-lily pond and bridge, are well known the whole world over.

Maintained with old-style planting, exactly as they've been immortalized in the world's art galleries, these gardens were the artist's constant subject beginning in 1895, when he bought the house he had rented and lived in since 1883. Monet painted a great deal in the countryside and on the coasts of Normandy. His family home was at Le Havre, and he studied in Honfleur. However, it was his later study, *Nymphéas (Water Lilies)*, that many critics consider his masterwork.

The house and gardens, the lily pond and the Clos Normand, now managed by the Fondation Claude Monet, are best seen in early summer and early in the day (before crowds arrive). The favorite spot for photographs is the little green bridge, where delays can occur while everyone takes the same snapshot.

The Musée des Impressionnismes Giverny displays works by disciples of Monet and international artists. It has a restaurant on its grounds and is convenient for art pilgrims doing the full tour, since Giverny is also close to the Impressionist site of Auvers-sur-Oise (see page 50).

(see page 50).

✚ D2–Normandy

Fondation Claude Monet ✉ 84 rue Claude-Monet, 27620 ☎ 02 32 51 28 21; www.fondation-monet.com ⏰ Daily 9:30–6, Apr.–Nov. 🍴 Restaurant 💲 $$

Musée des Impressionnismes Giverny ✉ 99 rue Claude-Monet, 27620 ☎ 02 32 51 94 65; www.mdig.fr ⏰ Daily 10–6 (last admission 5:30), Apr.–Oct. 🍴 Restaurant and café 💲 $$ (free first Sun. in month)

The famous water-lily pond and bridge at Giverny

The charming harbor at Honfleur

Honfleur

The prettiest working port in northern France positively hums with visitors seeking the best table for a seafood dinner, yet it still retains its charm. The quayside view of the Vieux Bassin is always seen through a haze of bobbing masts from little fishing boats and pleasure craft in the harbor. Tall slate-and-oak fronted timber-framed buildings jostle for position and their first floors are now yacht chandlers, art galleries and, of course, restaurants.

Many an adventurer departed from here. A plaque on the wall of the 16th-century Lieutenance building records Samuel de Champlain setting sail for Québec. Local fishermen worked the Newfoundland banks, using Honfleur's great salt store to preserve their catch. René-Robert Cavelier de La Salle embarked for the Mississippi to found Louisiana. The marketplace Église Ste.-Catherine was built of wood in the 15th century by shipbuilders. From here, photograph the 18th-century bell tower across the square.

Honfleur attracted artists: The Musée Eugène-Boudin – named for the town's most-celebrated resident, Eugène Boudin, son of a ferryman – has the artist's works along with views by Jean-Baptiste-Camille Corot, Raoul Dufy and Boudin's student, Claude Monet.

✚ C2–Normandy

Tourist information ✉ quai Lepaulmier, 14600 ☎ 02 31 89 23 30; www.ot-honfleur.fr

Musée Eugène-Boudin ✉ place Erik-Satie, 14600 ☎ 02 31 89 54 00 🕒 Wed.–Mon. 10–noon and 2–6, mid-Mar.to Sep.; Mon. and Wed.–Fri. 2:30–5:30, Sat.–Sun. 10–noon and 2:30–5:30, mid-Feb. to mid-Mar. and Oct.–Dec. Closed Jan. to mid-Feb. 🎫 $$

Le Mont-St.-Michel

An awe-inspiring sight, this centuries-old monastery appears to rise from the sea in the early mist. Mont-St.-Michel, a UNESCO World Heritage Site, has been a symbol of French ingenuity since long before the Eiffel Tower.

Mont St.-Michel towers above the salt marshes of the Couesnon estuary

A 260-foot granite island in the mudflats and salt marshes of the Couesnon estuary stands on the Normandy side of the border with Brittany. Quicksand and sudden tides separate the rock from the mainland. In 2012 a new bridge linking the mount with the mainland was inaugurated. There is no private vehicular access to the island. Access is on foot or by horse-drawn or motorized bus.

Believed originally to be a pagan burial ground, Mont-St.-Michel had the early name Mont Tombe. In the eighth century, the Bishop of Avranches had a vision of the Archangel Michael, said to have ordered the building of a chapel on the site. Successive Carolingian, Romanesque and Gothic buildings crowded on the precarious rock to create the abbey known since the Middle Ages as *la Merveille* (the wonder). It was finally topped out with the placing of a statue of St. Michael on the 515-foot spire in the late 19th century.

The trek through the narrow, winding streets to the ramparts is well worth the effort. Tourists squeeze into the inaccurately named Grande Rue, which would have once been just as crowded, but with pilgrims and penitents.

🚩 A1–Normandy

Tourist information ✉ Corps de Garde de Bourgois ☎ 02 33 60 14 30; www.ot-montsaintmichel.com

Le Mont-St.-Michel 🕐 24 hours

Abbey of le Mont-St.-Michel ☎ 02 33 89 80 00; www.mont-saint-michel.monuments-nationaux.fr 🕐 Daily 9–7 (last admission 6), early May to end Aug.; 9:30–6 (last admission 5), rest of year 💶 $$ (for horse-drawn and motorized bus)

Nantes

Nantes, the former capital of Brittany, now reigns over the neighboring region of Pays de la Loire, and is a gateway to the Loire vineyards and châteaux. Befitting the birthplace of Jules Verne, Nantes is home to Les Machines de l'Île Nantes, a fascinating workshop-exhibition creating amazing mechanical fantasy figures.

Also worth a visit is the Cathédrale St.-Pierre-et-St.-Paul, built of local gleaming-white tufa stone. Built in the 15th through 17th centuries, the airy cathedral holds the Renaissance tomb of François II, last duke of Brittany, who died in 1488.

A few steps away is the renovated 15th- to 16th-century ducal château housing various small museums of local history and traditions. Boat trips along the Erdre river are a pleasant way to see some charming smaller private châteaux.

🚩 D1–Brittany

Tourist information ✉ 3 cours Olivier-de-Clisson, 44000 (open Mon.–Sat.); 2 place Saint-Pierre (open Tue.–Sun.) ☎ 08 92 46 40 44 (toll call); www.nantes-tourisme.com

Les Machines de l'Île Nantes ✉ Les Chantiers, boulevard Léon-Bureau, 44000 ☎ 08 10 12 12 25; www.lesmachines-nantes.fr 🕐 Daily 10–7, mid-Jul. to Aug.; Mon.–Fri. 10–5, Sat.–Sun. 10–6, Sep.–Oct. and mid-Apr. to mid-Jul.; Tue.–Fri. 2–5, Sat.–Sun. 2–6, Nov. to late Dec. and late Feb. to mid-Apr.; Wed.–Sun. 2–6, late Dec.; Tue.–Sun. 2–6 mid- to late Feb. Closed early Jan. to mid-Feb. 🎫 $$

Château ✉ 4 place Marc-Elder, 44000 ☎ 08 11 46 46 44 (toll call) or 02 51 17 49 48; www.chateau-nantes.fr 🕐 Castle: daily 9–8 (Sat. also 8–11 p.m.), Jul.–Aug.; daily 10–7, rest of year. Museum: daily 10–7, Jul.–Aug.; Tue.–Sun. 10–6, rest of year 🍴 Café 🎫 Museums $$; courtyard free

Quimper

The ancient Celtic kingdom of Cornouaille chose Quimper as its capital after the original city of Ys sank in Douarnenez bay in the sixth century. A statue of King Gradlon, founder of the city, stands between the twin spires of the 13th-century Gothic cathedral.

Quimper is the focus of several Breton-Celtic festivals during the year. The other local tradition is lace making, and picturesque roadside stands appear in summer. With its attractive timber-framed houses, cobbled streets and an air of gentility, this large town presents an air of discreet intimacy.

🚩 B2–Brittany

Tourist information ✉ place de la Résistance, 29000 ☎ 02 98 53 04 05; www.quimper-tourisme.com

Picturesque timber-framed houses line many of the streets in the center of Quimper

Capital of Brittany

The city of Rennes stands at the confluence of the Ille and Vilaine rivers. In 1720, a great fire destroyed much of the medieval town. It was replaced with regal squares and wide streets. Rennes is often compared unfavorably with Nantes (see opposite), but traces of unmistakable Breton charm can be found in the oldest corners of the town, with its bulging beamed Renaissance buildings tottering over narrow streets. Just north of the canal, the remaining byways of old Rennes make for a revealing walk. The tourist office is housed in the Chapelle St.-Yves, just off quai Duguay-Trouin, and has a free exhibition of Rennes history in a medieval setting.

Explore the ancient, narrow streets around Église St.-Sauveur. The nearby cathedral is an unremarkable baroque building, but the area around it is intriguing. Follow rue des Dames to the Portes Mordelaises, a medieval corner with entry gate and fortifications. Close by is place des Lices, with its colorful Saturday market. The restored Breton Parliament is on place du Palais, and place de la Mairie has the Hôtel de Ville and an impressive opera house. The Jardin du Thabor gardens are entered from rue de Paris or place St.-Mélaine. The 40-acre green space was once the grounds of a Benedictine abbey.

The spectacular Champs Libres is a cultural center incorporating the library, Science Center and Brittany Museum. The Science Center is a state-of-the-art facility with a planetarium, while the Brittany Museum has diverse collections, from prehistoric relics to domestic items and art.

The Musée des Beaux-Arts (Fine Arts Museum) has Egyptian artifacts and an art gallery with a collection of Impressionist pieces, augmented by works by Breton artists. The museum's jewel is the 17th-century Georges de la Tour's *The Newborn*, a masterpiece of rich color.

Top restaurants and hotels are found on this side of town. Budget places are strung around the station, with its fast train service to and from Paris.

When entering the city, follow signs for Rennes-Sud in order to park near your hotel. The canal and northern section are a good 15-minute walk away, but a taxi to the town center costs around €12.

✚ D2–Brittany

Tourist information ✉ 11 rue St.-Yves, 35064 ☎ 02 99 67 11 11; www.tourisme-rennes.com

Champs Libres ✉ 10 cours des Alliés, 35000 ☎ 02 23 40 66 00; www.leschampslibres.com ◷ Tue. noon–9, Wed.–Fri. noon–7, Sat.–Sun. 2–7 ✋ Free; $ for all museums and temporary exhibitions

Musée des Beaux-Arts ✉ 20 quai Émile-Zola, 35000 ☎ 02 23 62 17 45; www.mbar.org ◷ Tue. 10–6, Wed.–Sun. 10–noon and 2–6 ✋ $$

A traditional *crêperie* open for business in Rennes

The old city area of St.-Malo was faithfully restored after severe damage in August 1944

St.-Malo

The seafaring town of St.-Malo was the homeport for the notorious Corsairs, state-licensed pirates who would board foreign vessels and claim their cargo for France. Officially operating in French waters, these adventurers managed to ride and raid the high seas as far away as the south Atlantic.

At the mouth of the Rance estuary is a walled town – St.-Malo-Intra-Muros – all faithfully restored after wartime bombing. A tour of the sympathetically renovated ramparts is an essential part of any visit. Many imposing 18th-century family homes were built on the proceeds of piracy. Fort National, designed by Vauban, guards the seaward approach to the town. If the weather is pleasant and the tide is out, walk across the sands to the two islands in the bay. Back on the mainland, there are many fine seafood restaurants both in St.-Malo itself and the neighboring resort of St.-Servan, which has a landscaped path, the Aleth Corniche.

✠ D3–Brittany
Tourist information ✉ Esplanade St.-Vincent, 35400
☎ 08 25 13 52 00 (toll call);
www.saint-malo-tourisme.com

Suisse Normande

It may not have any Alps and winter sports are a world away, but the "Norman Switzerland" area around the Orne valley, south of Caen, offers some

Suisse Normande. A none-too-strenuous walk features views from the Pain de Sucre (sugar-loaf) hill.

✚ B2–Normandy

Clécy tourist information ✉ place du Tripot, 14220 ☎ 02 31 69 79 95; www.ot-suisse-normande.com

Thury-Harcourt tourist information
✉ place St.-Sauveur ☎ 02 31 79 70 45

Tatihou, Île de

One of Normandy's least known attractions lies just off the coast of the celebrated oyster-fishing port of St.-Vaast-la-Hougue. Just 69 acres, Tatihou is known for its Vauban fort. The island may be reached on foot across the oyster beds at low tide or by amphibious boat May through September, which is included in admission charges to the fort and maritime and marine heritage museum. Ecology rules limit the maximum number of visitors to 500 per day. Free supervised birding excursions take place during summer months. Also offshore are the Îles St.-Marcouf – Île de Terre and Île du Large – once home to pirates. Each winter, 30,000 gulls come here to nest and rest among cormorants and herons. In summer, fishermen and lifeboat crews take groups for a closer view of these seabird sanctuaries, with their abandoned 19th-century military buildings. In August, Tatihou hosts an international open-air music festival, with free fringe events on the St.-Vaast wharf and music in local bars until late. The port of St.-Vaast has excellent restaurants and superb food shops.

✚ B3–Normandy

Tatihou tourist information ✉ quai Vauban, St.-Vaast-la-Hougue, 50500 ☎ 02 33 23 19 92; tatihou.manche.fr 🚤 Boat departs daily every hour (flood tide) 10–4, Apr.–Sep.; Sat.–Sun. 1–4:30, Oct.; Wed.–Sun. 2–5, Feb.; daily 2–5 during French school holidays and rest of year. Last boat back at 6 p.m. 🛈 Ornithological and historical tours (free), daily, Jul.–Aug., in French only 🚤 Boat (includes fort and museum) $$

St.-Vaast-la-Hougue tourist information ✉ 1 place du Général-de-Gaulle, 50500 ☎ 02 33 23 19 32; www.saint-vaast-reville.com

charming half-timbered buildings, the opportunity for modest rock climbing and plenty of outdoor sports in summer. The river weaves through its attractive valleys and both rafting and canoeing are popular. Horseback riding and hang-gliding are other alternatives. The "Route de la Suisse Normande," a marked circular driving route, is an easier option. Picturesque drives offer ample opportunity to sample local food and drink. Calvados (apple brandy) and farmhouse cider are available everywhere. Thury-Harcourt, with its bombed-out château, has attractive parks and gardens. During summer a scenic train takes excursions to the coast near Caen or inland to Clécy, a stone village that is the unofficial capital of the

Normandy and Brittany

Drive
The D-Day Coast

Distance: 130 miles
Time: 2 to 3 days

D-Day: June 6, 1944. Allied forces stormed the beaches of Normandy to mark the beginning of the end of the war in Europe and the liberation of France. The coast is marked with memorials and museums telling the tale of these remarkable events (www.normandie1944.fr).

At Caen, visit Le Mémorial de Caen (page 67), then take the D515 to Bénouville.
The first target captured by Allies on D-Day, the Pegasus Bridge on the Caen–Ouistreham canal, was a vital strategic link that had to be preserved. Three gliders crash-landed just after midnight, and Pegasus Bridge was in Allied hands by the time reinforcements arrived. The original bridge was removed in 1999. It now abuts the canal, preserved as "Mémorial Pegasus."
Take the D35C then the D514 to the port of Ouistreham.
Visit the Musée du Mur de l'Atlantique (Atlantic Wall Museum). Follow the D514 beside Sword, Juno and Gold beaches. At Bernières-sur-Mer turn left

on D79A for the Canadian Cemetery at Bény-sur-Mer. Turn back to the coast road, stop at Ver-sur-Mer's museum of the Gold Beach landings and the 1927 airmail race between Paris and New York, then head for Arromanches-les-Bains. The remains of the Mulberry Harbor landing pontoons can be seen. Arromanches 360 is an 18-minute, 360-degree movie re-enactment.
Take the D516 to Bayeux (see page 66). Follow the D6 to Port-en-Bessin.
At Omaha Beach, visit the Musée des Épaves-Sous-Marines du Débarquement for the artifacts of ships lost at D-Day. The Cimetière Américain (American Cemetery) at Colleville-sur-Mer overlooking Omaha Beach has a visitor center. At St.-Laurent-sur-Mer, the Musée Omaha 6 Juin 1944 has vehicles and weapons found on the beaches. Pass the cliffs of Pointe du Hoc, where German positions were taken by Colonel Rudder's Rangers; Grandcamp-Maisy has an exhibition devoted to them.
At the intersection of the D514 and the N13, follow signs for Cherbourg to Ste.-Mère-Église.
The Musée Airborne tells the story of the American 82nd and 101st Airborne Divisions.
From the D423, turn right onto D115 then D14 to Ste.-Marie-du-Mont. Turn left toward the beach on the D913 to the Musée du Débarquement d'Utah-Beach.

Part of the Mulberry Harbor used in the D-Day landings, off Arromanches

Along the coast are milestones of liberty, including the Mémorial de Montormel. The Mémorial de la Liberté retrouvée at Quinéville recalls life under the Nazis. **Follow the D42 for 5 miles to join the N13 to Cherbourg.**

As Cherbourg was badly damaged by bombing, many buildings are postwar. Follow the dramatic story of the liberation at the Musée de la Libération.

✛ C2, B2, B3, A3–Normandy

Mémorial Pegasus ✉ avenue du Major-Howard, Ranville, 14600 ☎ 02 31 78 19 44; www.memorial-pegasus.org ◷ Daily Apr.–Oct. 🎟 $$

Musée du Mur de l'Atlantique ✉ 6 avenue du 6-Juin, Ouistreham, 14150 ☎ 02 31 97 28 69; www.musee-grand-bunker.com ◷ Daily 9–7, Apr.–Sep.; 10–6, Feb.–Mar. and Oct.–Dec. Closed Jan. 🎟 $$

Musée America Gold Beach ✉ 2 place Amiral-Byrd, Ver-sur-Mer, 14114 ☎ 02 31 22 58 58; www.goldbeachmusee.org.uk ◷ Daily 10:30–5:30, Jul.–Aug.; Wed–Mon 10:30–5:30, Apr.–Jun. and Sep.–Oct. 🎟 $

Musée du Débarquement ✉ place du 6-Juin, Arromanches-les-Bains, 14117 ☎ 02 31 22 34 31; www.musee-arromanches.fr ◷ Daily 9:30–12:30 and 1:30–5:30 🎟 $$

Arromanches 360 ✉ Chemin du Calvaire, Arromanches-les-Bains, 14050 ☎ 02 31 06 06 44; www.arromanches360.com ◷ Half-hour screening daily from 9:40, Jul.–Aug. and from 10:10, Feb.–Jun. and Sep.–Dec. 🎟 $

Musée des Épaves Sous-Marines du Débarquement ✉ Route de Bayeux, Port-en-Bessin, 14520 ☎ 02 31 21 17 06 ◷ Daily 10–1 and 2–7, Jun.–Sep.; Sat.–Sun. and holidays 10–1 and 2–7, May 🎟 $$

Cimetière Américain Visitor Center ✉ Colleville-sur-Mer ☎ 02 31 51 62 00 ◷ Daily 9–6, Apr.–Sep.; 9–5, rest of year 🎟 Free

Musée Omaha 6 Juin 1944 ✉ avenue de la Liberation, St.-Laurent-sur-Mer, 14710 ☎ 02 31 21 97 44; www.musee-memorial-omaha.com ◷ Daily 9:30–7.30, Jul.–Aug.; 9:30–7, mid-May to Jun. and early Sep.; 9:30–6:30, mid-Mar. to mid-May and mid-Sep. to mid-Nov.; 10–12:30 and 2:30–6 mid-Feb. to mid-Mar. 🎟 $$

Musée des Rangers ✉ 30 quai Crampon, Grandcamp-Maisy, 14450 ☎ 02 31 92 33 51 ◷ Tue. 1:30–6:30, Wed.–Sun. 10–1 and 2:30–6:30, May–Oct.; Tue.–Sun. 1–6, mid-Feb. to Apr. 🎟 $

Musée Airborne ✉ 14 rue Eisenhower, Ste.-Mère-Église, 50480 ☎ 02 33 41 41 35; www.musee-airborne.com ◷ Daily 9–6:45, Apr.–Sep.; 10–5, Feb.–Mar. and Oct.–Dec. 🎟 $$

Musée du Débarquement d'Utah-Beach ✉ Opposite Utah-Beach, Ste.-Marie-du-Mont, 15480 ☎ 02 33 71 53 35; www.utah-beach.com ◷ Daily 9:30–7, Apr.–Oct.; 10–5:30, Feb.–Mar. and Nov. 🎟 $$

Mémorial de la Liberté retrouvée ✉ 18 avenue de la Plage, Quinéville ☎ 02 33 95 95 95; www.memorial-quineville.com ◷ Daily 10–7, late Mar.–Nov. 🎟 $$

Musée de la Libération ✉ Fort du Roule, Cherbourg, 50100 ☎ 02 33 20 14 12 ◷ Tue.–Sat. 10–12 and 2–6, Sun. 2–6, May–Sep.; Tue.–Sun. 2–6, rest of year 🎟 $ (free every Sun.)

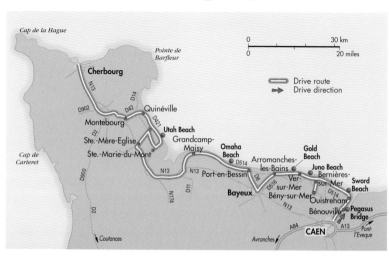

Loire Valley and the Atlantic Coast

Opposite: Formal gardens at the Château de Villandry

Loire Valley and the Atlantic Coast

The Loire is the picture book of France. Every mile offers some spectacular Renaissance indulgences perched on hilltops and on islands, and medieval fortresses guarding bridgeheads and towns. The Loire river, with its many tributaries, serves countless creamy-white châteaux whose turrets and gardens literally inspired the authors and illustrators of the great European fairy tales.

Like in every fairy tale, there are fabulous matriarchs and wicked queens populating the history of the Loire. Eleanor of Aquitaine, Catherine de Médicis and many a king's mistress helped to shape the French past. The region also has strong associations with two women who defied convention and took on the world of men: Joan of Arc (see page 62) and Chopin's lover, George Sand (see page 97).

Sound and Light

Celebration in summer often takes the form of sound-and-light presentations at the grand palaces. Lights, lasers and even fireworks tell the stories of great houses and the kings and princes who lived there.

Best is the *Puy du Fou*: Its name means madman's well, but the spectacle is anything but crazy. Conceived by a local politician, the show – which brings to life 1,000 years of history in an hour and 40 minutes – has entertained more than 5 million people. France's greatest actors and musicians provide the soundtrack for the largest show of its kind in the country. Many performances are given each summer, and their

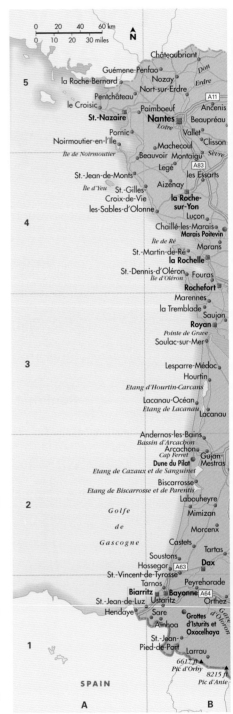

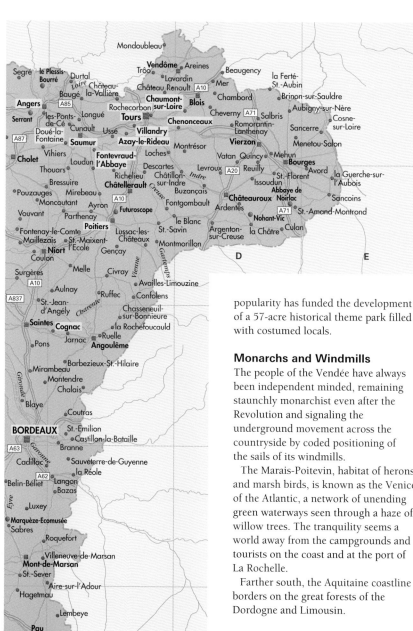

popularity has funded the development of a 57-acre historical theme park filled with costumed locals.

Monarchs and Windmills

The people of the Vendée have always been independent minded, remaining staunchly monarchist even after the Revolution and signaling the underground movement across the countryside by coded positioning of the sails of its windmills.

The Marais-Poitevin, habitat of herons and marsh birds, is known as the Venice of the Atlantic, a network of unending green waterways seen through a haze of willow trees. The tranquility seems a world away from the campgrounds and tourists on the coast and at the port of La Rochelle.

Farther south, the Aquitaine coastline borders on the great forests of the Dordogne and Limousin.

Wining and Dining

This area includes two great wine regions: the Loire and Bordeaux. The whites of the Loire – Hollywood star Gérard Depardieu is counted among the region's winemakers – are crisp and refreshing. The great wines of Bordeaux, of course, are the stuff of legend. Various crus are as carefully considered as gilt-edged stocks and bonds, and large château estates are owned and managed mostly by banks and businesses.

Cognac is the famous brandy of Poitou-Charentes and Cointreau the *digestif* of Anjou, while another splendid brandy, Armagnac, is made in the Gers *département* of the Midi-Pyrénées. Where no wines are made, western France is always inventive. What apples are to Normandy, pears are to the Mayenne. Here, drink *poiré*, an alcoholic fermentation of pears alone, or *pommeau*, calvados mixed with apple or fruit juice.

Generally, restaurants of the Loire serve a lighter, but no less satisfying, cuisine. Freshwater *sandre* (pike perch) and Chalon duck are among delights to discover. This is the region of frog's legs, button mushrooms and *mogettes* (white beans). When dining in Les Landes, don't be surprised to find prunes served with meats and poultry. Bordelais food is richer and more classical, while *foie gras*, walnuts and truffles define the tables of neighboring Dordogne.

A variety of conditions can be treated at one of the many thalassotherapy centers on the coast, from Nantes to Biarritz. Seawater treatment is considered essential for such things as asthma and a general sense of well-being. These spa resorts usually boast highly prized chefs, and the "cure" is taken by the French as a luxury vacation rather than a medical requirement.

Grape Expectations

Au revoir lettuce leaves, *adieu* pills and potions, and *bonjour* and *bienvenue* to the bottle and its bounty. Fitness through claret and its byproducts is the latest treat for the clinically wealthy. Vinotherapy, a range of anti-aging and slimming treatments, is based on extracts from vines and wine, in particular grapeseed polyphenols that

Pomerol is one of the excellent wines produced in the Bordeaux region

protect against ultraviolet rays. The technique was developed in the heart of the Graves vineyards, a stone's throw from Bordeaux. Whether you go for a day's quick fix or a week of indulgence, you will be pampered. After wine and a honey wrap or a barrel-bath in which fresh grapeseed extracts are added to the whirlpool bath, you may set off to discover all the *appellations* of Bordeaux wine with a tour of some of the world's most valuable grapes.

Bordeaux

Naturally enough, in a city of so many classic wines, Bordeaux is rich, dignified and discreet, with many fine flavors. A classic city by any standards, Bordeaux enables visitors to enjoy fine architecture from the 18th century and earlier, as well as grandiose public sculpture added over several periods.

The abiding impression is of unostentatious wealth and well-tended good taste. Mansions have wrought-iron balconies and sculpted facades, both in the central streets and along the wide Garonne river. Sightseeing boats provide an excellent introduction to the city and its region.

Like any thriving French city of its size, Bordeaux is divided into distinct quarters. The northern Chartrons area lines the quayside of the old wine trade.

If you are on a short visit, concentrate on the more central St.-Pierre, Ste.-Croix and St.-Michel districts, where all the principal sights can be found.

There is little overtly modern building to detract from the classic layout of the city, designed in the Paris mold. However, the tourist office will provide information about a walking tour for those eager to discover 20th-century buildings such as the Richard Rogers designed Law Courts completed in 1998. The joy of the center is that it remains surprisingly intimate and convenient for *flâneurs* (strollers). If you arrive with a car, your best bet is to park up near the Pont de Pierre bridge that arches across the Garonne river.

In 2007, about half of the city was designated a World Heritage Site by UNESCO for its beauty and unity of architectural style.

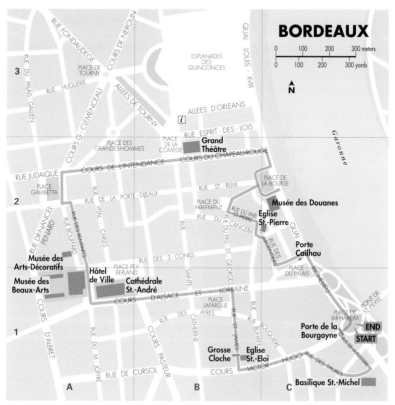

Wines

Since Bordeaux, which is the capital of the region, stands on the navigable Gironde estuary and is surrounded by the great château vineyards, it has developed as much by commerce as by actually producing fine wines. During their various occupations of the region, the English developed the wine known as claret. The original clairette is still on sale here. The classification of the wines was carried out by Thomas Jefferson before he became president of the United States, and it was then that the thriving export business began.

The grand Maison du Vin, opposite the theater, is as much a financial and commercial institution as an information point. The public inquiry desk in the spacious lobby can arrange tours and day or half-day visits to the surrounding wine country. Red wines are produced to the north: Médoc on the west bank of the Gironde, Bourg on the east and St.-Emilion and Pomerol north of the Dordogne. The rest of the area mostly produces white wines: Graves, Sauternes and Entre-deux-Mers. Staff at the

Maison du Vin can point you in the right direction for free wine tastings in the city, suburbs and surrounding countryside, and let you know of any wine festivals.

Culture

In town, people are elegant and have a real sense of civic pride. The compact yet well-laid-out center is always busy, with smartly dressed ladies at lunch and suited business types meeting over a glass of wine and easily outnumbering the more-obvious tourists. There is a friendly hum on commercial streets, such as cours de l'Intendance.

Early in the evening, people loiter on café terraces or meet with friends at the botanic gardens or around place Gambetta. Chic and unmistakably French, this handsome square with an English garden is the best place in town for people-watching. Originally known as place Dauphine, the square boasts 18th-century arcades and mansard roofs from which revolutionary executions were witnessed in 1790. To one side is the 1748 Porte Dijeaux. Off to the rear, the elegant tree-lined cours Clemenceau stretches up to the public garden and Église St.-Louis.

The area fosters a vibrant cultural scene. Check at the tourist office for details of temporary exhibitions and performances. Permanent pleasures and treasures include the famous Grosse Cloche, a well-preserved gate from the 14th through 18th centuries. Set beside a section of the 13th-century town wall, this former chunk of the town hall features a fine profile of stonework and pointed slate roofs, a bell suspended in the arch, and carved water spouts and clock faces on both sides.

The Hôtel de Ville – once the 1784 Hôtel de Rohan – on the wide cathedral square is an early example of French neoclassicism. Pass through a courtyard and enter to discover a memorable staircase and fine paneled salons. Outside the two wings of the Musée

Liberty atop the monument to the Girondins

des Beaux-Arts (see pages 88–89), gilded gateways and a grille of railings surround a formal French garden with a classic carpet of bedding plants, fountains and statues. The garden remains open until early evening.

At the south of the city near Église Ste.-Eulalie, see the monument to the Girondin victims of Robespierre's "reign of terror:" a 164-foot column with a figure of Liberty throwing off her shackles.

Detail of an ornate fountain on esplanade des Quinconces, a large 19th-century square

Essential Information

Tourist Information
✉ 12 cours du 30-Juillet, just behind the theater, 33000 ☎ 05 56 00 66 00; www.bordeaux-tourisme.com 🚌 7, 8; tram B, C ✉ St.-Jean train station, rue Charles-Domercq, 33800 ☎ 05 56 91 64 70 🚌 1, 7, 8, 10, 11, 16, 26, 29, 45, 47, 58, 83; tram C

Public Transportation
There is a frequent bus and tram service all over the city from 5 a.m. to 10 p.m. CGFTE special tickets offer one hour of travel (cheaper on Sundays). Tickets are also sold at newsstands and bookstores. Day tickets and 10-ticket packages offer savings on the single-trip price. The city's many limited-access streets are welcoming to pedestrians. For bus and tram information ☎ 05 57 57 88

88; www.infotbc.com. Taxis can be hailed at Gare St.-Jean ☎ 05 56 91 48 11, and in the city center (Grand Théâtre ☎ 05 56 81 99 15 and cours Georges Clemenceau ☎ 05 56 81 99 05). Les Taxis Touristique offer 90-minute tours of the city ☎ 06 24 88 22 09. Frequent fast trains leave for Paris from Gare St.-Jean 🚆 36 35; www.sncf.fr.

Airport Information
Bordeaux-Mérignac Airport services national and international flights ☎ 05 56 34 50 50; www.bordeaux.aeroport.fr. A shuttle to town-center stops, including Gare St.-Jean (45 minutes) and place Gambetta (30 minutes), operates every 30–45 minutes (Jet'bus runs every 45 minutes throughout the week 🚌 05 56 34 50 50).

Climate – average highs and lows for the month

Jan.	Feb.	Mar.	Apr.	May	Jun.	Jul.	Aug.	Sep.	Oct.	Nov.	Dec.
9°C	11°C	14°C	16°C	19°C	23°C	26°C	26°C	23°C	18°C	13°C	10°C
48°F	52°F	57°F	61°F	66°F	73°F	79°F	79°F	73°F	64°F	55°F	50°F
2°C	3°C	5°C	6°C	10°C	13°C	15°C	15°C	12°C	9°C	5°C	3°C
36°F	37°F	41°F	43°F	50°F	55°F	59°F	59°F	54°F	48°F	41°F	37°F

Bordeaux Sights

> **Key to symbols**
> 🚩 map coordinates refer to the Bordeaux map on
> page 85 💰 admission charge: $$$ more than €10,
> $$ €5–€10, $ less than €5
> See page 5 for complete key to symbols

Basilique St.-Michel

Colorful glass casts blue, red and gray
light in the handsome 14th-century
Gothic basilica. Inside is an extravagant
wooden pulpit and a vast organ set on
stone. To one side of the main building
is a separate bell tower, La Flèche. The
original tower, finished in 1492, was
struck by lightning in 1574 and 1608
and lashed by a hurricane in 1768.
Despite the ravages of the elements and
a period of service as a telegraph station,
the tower was only reconstructed in
1865. It's the highest tower in the south
of France, at 370 feet. The nation's
tallest is at Rouen cathedral (see page
64). The market square around the
church offers a mixture of trash and
treasures spread on the cobblestones.
🚩 C1 ✉ place Canteloup, 33800 🕐 Daily 9–noon
and 2–6 🚋 24, 25; tram C at St.-Michel

Cathédrale St.-André

Listed as a World Heritage Site in 1998,
the Cathedral of St. André is mostly
Gothic but has gathered touches from
most successive periods. A devastating
fire in 1787 destroyed many early
features: The nave survives from the
original church in which Eleanor of
Aquitaine was first married in 1137 to
the future king of France. Today, the
large sanctuary and extensive chapels
impress visitors. A timeless, gentle light
from stained glass gives the effect of an
endless elegant nave. The church faces
the Hôtel de Ville across a wide square.
Twin spires on the cathedral itself are
complemented by a separate bell tower
(the Tour Pey-Berland, 1440–46) with a
statue perched atop like a cork in a
bottle. All around the building is a
cluster of supporting arches and flying
buttresses. Neat gardens alongside offer
seclusion for private reflection.
🚩 A1 ✉ place Pey-Berland, 33000 🕐 Daily. Check
website for details: www.cathedrale-bordeaux.fr
🚋 4, 5, 15, 16; tram A and B

Grand Théâtre

Considered the finest theater in the
country, this handsome Classical
building opened its doors to the wealthy
citizens of Bordeaux in 1780. With 12
Corinthian pillars supporting carved
figures of the muses and gods, the
facility is the masterwork of architect
Louis Victor. Dominating the town
center, it spreads across a vast city block
almost 300 feet long. The focus of the
stone lobby is its sweeping double
stairway, said to have inspired the Paris
opera house. Here you will find the box
office for a varied program of opera and
ballet classics, as well as popular
productions of William Shakespeare.
The spacious interior is exceptional.
If you aren't planning to take in a
performance, then consider arranging a
guided visit of the building (reserve at
the tourist offices, see page 87) to see
the luxurious gilding and blue and
red velvet. Splendid cantilevered boxes
and elegant pillars complete the
majestic effect.
🚩 B2 ✉ place de la Comédie, 33000 ☎ 05 56 00 85
95; www.opera-bordeaux.com 🚋 47; tram B to Grand
Théâtre 💰 Guided tours Wed. at 2:30, 4 and 5:30 ($)

Musée des Beaux-Arts

Set in a pair of Classical two-story
pavilions flanking the gardens of the
Hôtel de Ville (see page 86), the Musée
des Beaux-Arts (Fine Arts Museum)
houses works dating to the 19th century
in one section and a second wing with
modern and contemporary art. A varied
collection ranges from Dutch and
Flemish classics to 19th-century
bourgeois erotica, such as Henri
Gervex's *Rolla*. Eugène Delacroix's
Greece Surveying the Ruins of Missolonghi
is among the city's prized artworks.

Sculpture is arranged around the entry desk. Regular art shows are held at nearby Galerie des Beaux-Arts, place du Colonel-Raynal.

➕ A1 ✉ Jardin de la Mairie, 20 cours d'Albret, 33000
☎ 05 56 10 20 56 🕐 Wed.–Mon. 11–6 🚌 4, 5, 6, 15, 16, 56; tram A and B at Palais de Justice or Meriadeck
💶 Free; exhibitions $

Gothic splendor – the twin spires of Cathédrale St.-André pierce the summer sky

Walk
Stroll Through Bordeaux

Refer to route marked on
city map on page 85

This three-hour stroll through the
city is about 2 miles long and begins
at the oldest bridge in town, the Pont
de Pierre.

**Turn left on rue de la Fusterie into narrow,
cobbled rue des Faures up past Basilique
St.-Michel (see page 88). Continue to turn
left along cours Victor-Hugo shopping street
and cross right into rue St.-James.**
Pause at Grosse Cloche (see page 86).
Still on rue St.-James, peek (right) into
rue St.-Eloi to see the church. Cross
place Lafargue and continue along rue
St.-James to turn left onto cours
d'Alsace-et-Lorraine to place Pey-
Berland, where you will find Cathédrale
St.-André (see page 88) and the Hôtel
de Ville (see page 86). Visit the sights
and the gardens (see page 87).
**From the northwest corner of the square,
follow rue des Remparts past the back of
the Musée des Arts-Décoratifs (Museum of**
Decorative Arts) **and continue up to
charming place Gambetta (see page 86).
Turn right along busy and wide cours
de l'Intendance.**
Handsome buildings go up to the big
block of the theater, with the wine
center nearby (see page 86).
**Continue on cours de l'Intendance to cours
du Chapeau-Rouge, down to the river. Turn
right onto place de la Bourse, with its
Musée Nationale des Douanes (Customs
House Museum) on the corner.**
This wide riverside space on quai de la
Douane has a statue of the Three Graces
replacing the original figure of Louis XV.
In the early 18th century, the square was
known as place Royale.
**Retrace your steps behind the Bourse along
rue Fernand Philippant.**
Note the pretty Second Empire-style
place du Parlement with its fountain.
**Turn left down rue St.-Pierre, crossing the
site of the old port of Bordeaux past Église
St.-Pierre. At the end of rue des Argentiers,
turn left at the bottom to see the 15th-
century arch of the Porte Cailhau, then right,
along quai Richelieu.**
Take time to enjoy the riverside from
Porte Cailhau all the way down to place
de Bir-Hakeim, passing some fine
restaurants. The splendid crescent and
arch of Porte de la Bourgogne faces the
Pont de Pierre, where the walk began.

The Pont de Pierre, or "Stone Bridge," stretches across the Garonne river

Regional Sights

Key to symbols
➕ map coordinates refer to the map on pages
82–83 🖐 admission charge: $$$ more than €10,
$$ €5–€10, $ less than €5
See page 5 for complete key to symbols

Angers

Angers is a city famous for its château.
Looming above the town and built to
protect a flourishing river trade, 17
mossy gray-and-white towers of the
medieval château proclaim this was
originally constructed as a fortress rather
than a palace. The first duke of Anjou,
Louis I, commissioned artworks and
remodeling to adapt the château to a
family home in the 14th century. By the
time of the last duke, poet and patron of
the arts Good King René (1409–80),
Angers had acquired royal status, formal
gardens and a private menagerie of lions
and monkeys. The greatest of Louis'
acquisitions was the remarkable series of
tapestries, *The Apocalypse of St. John the
Evangelist.* Woven by Nicolas Bataille,
the finest artist in his field, these
spectacular, sometimes shocking, works
stand 16 feet high and wrap 328 feet
around a specially customized gallery.
Having been lost in the Revolution, each
fragment was sought and found by the
city's bishop, who commissioned a
major restoration work in 1843. Take
time to enjoy the gardens in the former
moat. Compare the tapestries with
contemporary Jean Lurçat tapestries at
the Musée Jean Lurçat in the Ancien
Hôpital St.-Jean, across the river.
➕ B5
Tourist information ✉ 7 place Kennedy, 49050
☎ 02 41 23 50 00; www.angersloiretourisme.com
Château ✉ 2 promenade du Bout-de-Monde, 49050
☎ 02 41 86 48 77; www.monuments-nationaux.fr
🕐 Daily 9:30–6:30, May–early Sep.; 10–5:30, early
Sep.–end Apr. 🖐 $$
Musée Jean Lurçat ✉ Ancien Hôpital St.-Jean,
4 boulevard Arago, 49050 ☎ 02 41 24 18 45 🕐 Daily
10–6:30, Jun.–Sep.; Tue.–Sun. 10–noon and 2–6,
rest of year 🖐 $

Formal gardens occupy the former moat beneath the round towers of the Chateau d'Angers

Azay-le-Rideau

A rich, dappled, tree-framed vision of an enchanted château floating on the water lures summer wanderers to the ordinary village of Azay-le-Rideau. The blue-black slate turrets and conical spires top Rapunzel towers like icing on a cake. The pretty château is unusual in that it was built in just 11 years, beginning in 1518, and remained faithful to the original plans of the architect Bastien François. Perched on the river foundations of a previous building, the château, remarkably, has been left alone by generations of owners who, in a rare instance of restraint, managed not to rebuild or add to the finished gem in almost 500 years. The towers are delicate adornments, as this was never a fortress, merely a grand country retreat. Note the carved salamander, a symbol of François I, over the main entrance, and the lavish grand staircase among Renaissance tapestries.

🔒 C5

Tourist information ✉ 4 rue du Château, 37190 ☎ 02 47 45 44 40; www.paysazaylerideau.com

Château d'Azay-le-Rideau ✉ Off rue de Pineau, 37190 ☎ 02 47 45 42 04; www.monuments-nationaux. fr 🕐 Daily 9:30–7, Jul.–Aug.; 9:30–6, Apr.–Jun., Sep.; 10–5:15, rest of year 🎟 $$

Château de Chaumont-sur-Loire

Don't be misled by first impressions. The stern drawbridge, cylindrical keep and pathways atop its high ramparts suggest a military fortification. The approach is impressive, as white walls rise behind a veil of cedar trees. From the austerity of the western facade you might expect to find weaponry and bare stone walls. But once inside, you can savor the pleasant

A drawbridge marks the entrance to the Renaissance Château de Chaumont-sur-Loire

Château de Chenonceau, spanning the Cher river, has lovely Renaissance gardens

indulgences of a modest Renaissance home with a selection of tapestries from the 15th through 19th centuries and period furnishings, but no vast display of ostentation. Surprising when you consider that this was the residence of the ambitious and manipulative Catherine de Médicis, wife of King Henri II and mother of three kings – François II, Charles IX and Henri III. Venture out on the 18th-century terrace for superb views across the Loire.

✚ D5

✉ Chaumont-sur-Loire, 41150 ☎ 02 54 20 99 22; www.domaine-chaumont.fr 🕐 Daily 10–6:15, Jul.–Aug.; 10–5:45, early Apr.–Jun. and Sep.; 10–5:15, Oct.–early Nov.; 10–4:50, rest of year. Last admission 45 minutes before closing 🎟 Château $$; château and gardens $$$

Château de Chenonceau

The most popular of the Loire châteaux is famous for its extravagant gallery, which spans the Cher river. Originally a graceful 200-foot bridge in the style of the main château, the gallery was commissioned by Diane de Poitiers, mistress of Henri II. On the king's death, his vengeful wife, Catherine de Médicis, ousted Diane from her home,

embellished the bridge with a two-tier gallery and ordered a landscaped park over Diane's gardens. Diane was sent to live at Chaumont. The grace of the château reflects the styles of the many powerful women who shaped its history, including the Scottish Mary Stuart. The main flight of steps is a straight staircase designed for making an entrance.

Well-presented pamphlets (in English) explain art, furnishings and hangings. For an additional fee, the Galerie des Dames has a wax exhibition featuring 15 tableaux from the glory days, with figures of the famous queens and duchesses. The château also offers a sumptuous *son et lumière* (sound and light) show every evening in July and August. The château's own wines, labeled *Des Dômes de Chenonceau*, are sold in the Bâtiment des Dômes in the Jardin Vert.

✚ D5

✉ Chenonceaux, 37150 ☎ 02 47 23 90 07; www. chenonceau.com 🕐 Daily 9–8, Jul.–Aug.; 9–7:30, Jun. and Sep.; 9–7, Apr.–May; 9–6:30, Oct. 1–late Oct.; 9:30–7, mid- to end Mar.; 9–6, late Oct.–early Nov.; 9:30–6, early Feb. to mid-Mar.; 9:30–5, early Nov.–early Feb. 🍴 Restaurant 🎟 $$$ (including audio guide and/or Galerie des Dames)

Biarritz: The Imperial Resort

Unquestionably one of the most elegant towns in France, Biarritz was little more than a whaling port until an empress discovered and adopted it. Just along the coast from the Basque port of St.-Jean-de-Luz (see page 132) and within easy reach of Spain and the Pyrénées, the resort is the southern showcase of France's Atlantic coast.

In 1854, when the Spanish-born empress Eugénie was the darling of society, she brought her husband Napoléon III to stay in the town. Almost overnight, Biarritz became regarded as the Atlantic's answer to the Riviera, the playground of the rich and famous. A popular saying declared: "If you have to choose between two beaches – one of them is always Biarritz." Life still revolves around the villa Napoléon commissioned for his empress. The town's fortunes continued to rise even after the imperial couple left town, and the ostentatious brick and stone villa became Hôtel du Palais, keeping its imposing gates and pretty formal gardens and adding new wings and even a swimming pool with a sea view. The lobby is over the top, packed with grandiose furnishings and ponderous sculpted chandeliers and light fittings. No visit is complete without enjoying a cup of coffee or tea while taking in the great sea views from the *salle rotonde*, a belle-époque addition to the building. A decided whiff of money lingers in the air even today, from the classy staff to the assured demeanor of the regular guests.

Even if today's Biarritz lacks the Parisian chic of Deauville (see pages 68–69), reminders abound as to the great guests of the past. At the beginning of the 20th century, all European and Russian royals came to this stylish French coastal town to relax, including Queen Victoria, the Shah of Persia and Eugénie's natural successors as a draw for much gossip

Atlantic waves lap the golden sands of Grande Plage, backed by stately hotels

and fascination: Britain's Edward, Duke of Windsor and his American wife, Wallis Simpson.

Touring visitors will arrive through a well-marked knot of narrow streets although the town is served by good rail and air links. The area is ideal for exploring on foot, particularly since place Bellevue and place Clémenceau were made traffic-free, and inevitably is busy from mid-June to mid-September. Hotels are usually open year-round although some close during February. Regardless, there is plenty of life even out of season on a cold, wet March day. Visit Eugénie's imperial chapel for a sense of the flamboyant early days of the resort. From the tourist office in the main square d'Ixelles, you can easily stroll the entire town in half a day. Narrow streets introduce you to stone arcades, nice art deco hotels and casinos, a handful of original 19th-century villas and plenty of views of the Atlantic ocean.

The bulk of the town is spread along the rocky sea front, a welcome route for driving or strolling along the promenades and gardens. On fine days, genteel vacationers take in the air. At the cry "surf's up," a young, fit and tanned generation materializes to make the most of France's best breakers. When strong winds agitate the Bay of Biscay, there is something impressive about green and white spray hurling itself at the lighthouse and headlands. The sea also washes the town's symbol, a modest statue of the Virgin Mary designed by Gustave Eiffel (of Eiffel Tower fame) perched on a rock in the sea just opposite the old port. Seals and sharks await rainy-day visitors to the sea museum, and buses leave place de l'Hôtel-de-Ville during the day for the lighthouse and suburbs.

✚ B1

Tourist information ✉ Javalquinto, 1 square d'Ixelles, 64200 ☎ 05 59 22 37 00; www.biarritz.fr

Cognac

Don't ask for brandy here. The quality tipple is called cognac, after the town. The Dutch developed the drink as "burnt wine" (*brande-wijn* – gently corrupted to brandy), distilling white wine as a means of storing it and avoiding tax, since Cognac was a major wine port on the Charente river. Tour the countryside to see the exclusive area of just 250,000 acres of vines – which have to be specific varieties – matured in barrels of Limousin oak.

The area is divided into Grande Champagne, Petite Champagne, Borderies, Fins Bois, Bons Bois and Bois Ordinaires. A tasting visit to a cellar enables you to learn how the wines are blended. Big names, such as Hennessy, Martel and Rémy Martin, have visitor centers and offer tours. Some lesser-known houses can prove more interesting. Otard, for example, is made in the 13th-century Château de Cognac, birthplace of François I.

✚ C3

Tourist information ✉ 16 rue du 14-Juillet, 16100 ☎ 05 45 82 10 71; www.tourism-cognac.com
Otard, Château de Cognac ✉ 127 boulevard Denfert-Rochereau ☎ 05 45 36 88 86; www.otard.com ⏰ Daily 10–noon and 2–4, Apr.–Oct. Closed 1 May. Call ahead for a reservation 💰 $$

Fontevraud-l'Abbaye

To atone for the death of St. Thomas of Canterbury (Thomas Becket), England's Henry II built the Abbaye Royale de Fontevraud near Saumur. The abbey was home to nuns, monks and lepers, and 14 abbesses were royal princesses, each retiring from the world with dozens of personal servants. Unsurprisingly, entering this cloistered community was something of a social event. Henry's dysfunctional family, the house of Angers, which governed England as the Plantagenets, included his wife Eleanor of Aquitaine (see page 106), who decreed that her favorite son, Richard the Lionheart, should be king of England. Richard kept the job 10 years, never learned English and spent less than 10 months in England, preferring to join the Crusades. Many abbey buildings are gone, but you may visit kitchens, cloisters and a herb garden and see the tombs of Richard, Eleanor and Henry in the church.

✚ C5

✉ Fontevraud-l'Abbaye, 49590 ☎ 02 41 51 73 52; www.abbaye-fontevraud.com ⏰ Daily 9:30–7:30, Jul.–Aug.; 9:30–6:30, early Apr.–end Jun. and Sep.–early Nov; Tue.–Sun. 10–5:30, early Nov.–early Apr. Last admission 30 minutes before closing 💰 $$ (free first Sun. of month, Nov.–Mar.)

Effigies of Eleanor and Henry repose in the abbey church at Fontevraud-l'Abbaye

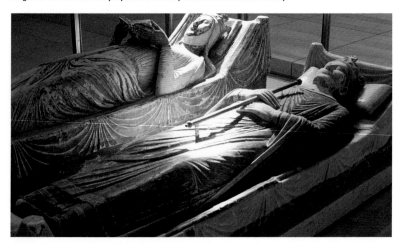

When George Met Frédéric

Nohant-Vic – a discreet hamlet with its tree-lined square and countryside of hedgerows – is set in a sleepy corner of the Berry region. It slipped onto the map thanks to a dynamic woman who lived here from 1804 to 1876.

Although Amandine-Aurore-Lucile Dudevant (née Dupin) lived at the château of Nohant, the baroness was no ordinary chatelaine. "My profession is to be free," she wrote. So, at night, she would disguise herself as a man and sneak out of the château to experience the heartier peasant life of

The statue of Aurore Dupin, better known as George Sand, in La Châtre

nearby La Châtre. Dudevant had another, professional life: She achieved immortality and success as novelist and playwright George Sand.

Separated from her husband in 1831 at the age of 27, she wrote novels set in the countryside she called the Vallée Noire. She scandalized Paris society by smoking and wearing men's clothes. The great love of her life was the Polish-born composer Frédéric Chopin, and the château, now a museum, holds mementoes of their life together. Visit in July for the Chopin Music Festival, when pianists revive the passion of the romantic composer in the house where he created so many masterpieces.

Even if you miss out on the concert season, Sand's home is always worth a visit. Delights include the novelist's additions to the 18th-century château, including the little theater Chopin designed for her. Here, she staged private performances of her own plays. The varied marionettes, made by the novelist's son Maurice, are attired in costumes she made.

Details in her boudoir and study intrigue and delight, but it's the salon that captures the spirit of her secret artistic life. The table is laid ready for a dinner party, and you can almost anticipate the arrival of eminent guests and Chopin himself.

Château de la Vallée Bleue, a nearby manor house once home to the couple's doctor, is now a family-run hotel offering musical candlelit dinners beside the fire and tours of Sand's favorite places.

Tourist information ✉ 134 rue Nationale, La Châtre, 36400 ☎ 02 54 48 22 64; www.pays-george-sand.com

Maison de George Sand ✉ Domaine de George Sand, Nohant-Vic, 36400 ☎ 02 54 31 06 04; www.monuments-nationaux.fr 🕐 Daily 9:30–6:30, Jul.–Aug.; 9:30–12 and 2–6:30, May–Jun.; 10–12:30 and 2–6, Apr. and Sep.; 10–12:30 and 2–5, rest of year. Last admission one hour before closing 🎫 $$

Château de la Vallée Bleue ✉ route de Verneuil, St.-Chartier, 36400 ☎ 02 54 31 01 91; www.chateauvalleebleue.com

Poitiers

Famous for Romanesque churches and a history of key battles against the English and Arabs, Poitiers is the nearest large town to Futuroscope (see panel) and a diversion on the way to the port of La Rochelle. The city's main architectural trophy is Église Notre-Dame la Grande, which is surrounded by a local market. Elsewhere, the fourth-century Baptistère St.-Jean is the oldest Christian building in France and has some medieval frescoes.

In the 12th- to 13th-century Great Hall of the mainly 18th-century Palais de Justice, Joan of Arc successfully faced an ecclesiastical committee.

✚ C4

Tourist information ✉ 45 place Charles-de-Gaulle, 86000 ☎ 05 49 41 21 24; www.ot-poitiers.fr

Saumur

Horses, mushrooms and sparkling white wine carry Saumur's fame from its gleaming white 13th-century château on the banks of the Loire to the outside world. The École Nationale d'Équitation (National Riding School) – with its museums, cavalry horses and legendary Cadre Noir display team – puts on displays in July and sometimes allows visitors to watch equestrian training taking place and show rehearsals.

Half of France's mushrooms are cultivated here in underground cellars and tunnels that aren't used for storing the fabulous red and white still and sparkling wines.

The bridge was a crossing point for pilgrims on the Santiago de Compostela route. The château, built of tufa stone, won immortality when it found its way into the illustrations of the beautiful illuminated medieval book of hours, *Les Très Riches Heures du Duc de Berry*. From the towers and renovated castle walls, the summer brings unforgettable views of the old town at its feet and the Loire dried up to a mere stream, its bed a green park of trees and bushes.

✚ C5

Tourist information ✉ place de la Bilange, 49148 ☎ 02 41 40 20 60; www.ot-saumur.fr

Château de Saumur ☎ 02 41 40 24 40 🕐 Tue.–Sun. 10–6:30, Jul.–Aug.; 10–1 and 2–5:30, Apr.–Jun. and Sep.–early Nov. 🔒 Jul.–Aug. $$; rest of year $

L'École Nationale d'Équitation ✉ St.-Hilaire–St. Florent, 49411 ☎ 02 41 53 50 60; www.cadrenoir.fr

---

Fun at Futuroscope

Futuroscope is the theme park that predated Disney crossing the Atlantic and anticipates wonderful tomorrows. But, unlike Disney, it is a theme park that deals not in making fantasies seem real, but in making reality seem an improbable adventure.

Rides involve more IMAX perspectives than anywhere else on the Continent and use the latest technology to overload visitors' senses through filmmaking. The architecture around the verdant landscape is as challenging as the movies featured: A gigantic domed screen envelops its audience with a stomach-churning ride down the rapids of the upper Nile. Another massive screen rises into the air as the auditorium finds itself by a man-made lake with amazing glass mountains. The past features in one ride through the world of dinosaurs, and the deep sea is explored and exploited in 3D – you can almost touch the jellyfish.

But there's more to Futuroscope than just IMAX. You'll find a whole range of rides, performances and experiences for all ages: Adrenalin-pumping rides to suit teenagers and adults, while there are gentler rides and exploration attractions for younger visitors. These include musical fountains where children can dance around the jets – especially fun on a hot summer day.

Futuroscope, Parc Européen de l'Image ✉ Jaunay-Clan, 86130 ☎ 05 49 49 11 12 (Infoline); www.futuroscope.com 🕐 Daily 9 or 10 a.m. to between 6 and 11 p.m., depending on season. Weekends only off-season. Closed early Jan.–early Feb. 🍴 Choice on site 🔒 $$$

The ornate central porch of Cathédrale St.-Gatien, Tours, features beautiful stained glass

Guided tours only, half-hourly 9:30–11:30 and 2–4, early Apr. to mid-Oct., tours at 9:30 and 11, 2 and 4, mid-Feb. to early Apr. and mid-Oct. to early Nov. $$

Tours

After the destructive heavy bombing of World War II, the university city of Tours was all but left for dead. Then, in the 1960s, plans were made to transform the slums and derelict shells of houses into a conservation area and build today's charming city center. Today, the city is a lively cultural center with several excellent museums, and interesting street markets.

Old Tours is a skillfully blended mixture of the few buildings that survived the bombs and contemporary creations constructed from traditional materials. Now fashionable cafés, artists' quarters, galleries and chic boutiques cluster together in the vibrant district that houses the impressive university.

The town is rich with architectural styles: 15th-century timber-framed houses bracket place Plumereau; Gothic and Renaissance architecture lines rue Briçonnet; and the mansion of the dukes of Touraine stands in rue du Change. Two towers of the original basilica can still be seen, as can the Gothic-Renaissance concoction of buttresses and spires that make up Cathédrale St.-Gatien, dedicated to Saint Gatien, its first bishop, on rue Colbert.

C5

Tourist information 78–82 rue Bernard-Palissy, 37042 02 47 70 37 37; www.tours-tourisme.fr

The verdant vegetable garden laid out below the grand Château de Villandry

Troglodyte Villages

If you believe the last cave dwellers in western France were primitive clansmen, then think again. The caves of the Loire have washing machines and cable TV. The soft white tufa used for building châteaux hides hundreds of caves. Quarries created semi-underground villages, houses, churches and schools carved into the rock face. Most were active communities until inexpensive ground-level housing lured underground families to the surface in the 1940s and the 1950s.

Visit Doué-la-Fontaine, near Saumur, and Rochecorbon, near Tours. Exhibitions show images of 20th-century troglodyte village life. Since the 1990s, many of these caves have been developed as vacation homes and restaurants. Don't expect primitive fireplaces. The caves have all the usual facilities, including electricity. Tufa, cool in summer and warm in winter, is considered ecologically sound. Spend a night or two lodging in a comfy cave, complete with kitchenette, and use it as a base for exploring château country.

🚩 C5

Tourist information ✉ 30 place Fontaines, Doué-la-Fontaine, 49700 ☎ 02 41 59 20 49; www.ot-douelafontaine.fr

Tourist information ✉ place Croissant, Rochecorbon, 37210 ☎ 02 47 52 80 22; www.mairie-rochecorbon.fr 🕐 Apr.–Sep. only

Troglodyte accommodations ☎ 02 41 40 20 60

Villandry, Château de

The other châteaux may have greater staircases, tapestries and grandeur, but nowhere else in the Loire will you find gardens like those of Villandry. Dr. Joachim Carvallo, whose descendants still live here, was the 19th-century historian who decided to recreate great 16th-century English gardens *à la française*. Magnificent terraces surround the château, as neat box and yew hedges create geometric patterns. Admire the design of the gardens of Love and Music, and breathe in the aromatic sensations of a herb garden, where a brush against wild thyme and rosemary releases fresh fragrances.

Climb to the upper tier, where a shimmering lake, enveloped within a cloister of lime trees, collects rainwater to feed the gardens and fountains below. Canals and water features irrigate the estate. The lowest level is a well-stocked kitchen garden. Replanted twice a year, but no less decorative than the other gardens, the crops are clustered in attractive shapes. Pergolas abound for those who wish to linger in such beautiful surroundings.

🚩 C5

✉ Villandry, 37150 ☎ 02 47 50 02 09; www.chateauvillandry.com 🕐 Daily 9–7:30, Jul.–Aug.; 9–7, late Mar.–Jun. and Sep.–Oct.; 9–6, early to mid-Nov. and mid- to late Feb.; 9:30–5, late Dec.–early Jan. Gardens: daily from 9 a.m. year-round (closing time varies seasonally) 🍴 $$

Drive
Château Country

Distance: 260 miles
Time: 3 to 4 days

The fashion for building Renaissance châteaux in the Loire region came with a surge of national pride after the expulsion of the English from France in 1453. The nobility hired Italian architects and gardeners, and design schools were set up from Tours to Fontainebleau as each great family created its dream palace.

From Tours take the D751 east.
The well-preserved remains of the great Château d'Amboise are noteworthy for the queen's chapel on the ramparts and Aubusson tapestries in the king's apartments. Nearby Clos Lucé has a museum devoted to Leonardo da Vinci, who died here.
Follow the D31 south toward Loches.
The road climbs behind Amboise and two miles along is the Pagode de Chanteloup, a remnant of an 18th-century imitation of Versailles built by the Duke of Choiseul. Views are great.

Continue on the D31; turn left to the D40. Visit the Château de Chenonceau (see page 93) from the village, spelled Chenonceaux.
Take the D40 toward Chisseaux, turning right for the D80 to Francueil. Bear left to the D81. Drive south to turn left onto the D760 at Nouans-les-Fontaines. Then take a left on the D960 to Valençay (the D960 is the D760 until the Berry border).
Actually in Berry rather than the Loire region, the stunning Renaissance and baroque Château de Valençay is worth the long detour. Patrolled by peacocks, the grounds are as regal as the interior.
Go north on the D4 then the D128 and turn right on the D724.
The heart of the Sologne region is the town of Romorantin-Lanthenay on the Sauldre river – a good starting point for an hour or two exploring the surrounding countryside.
The D49 takes you to the Sologne area, with its thatched red-brick houses, heaths and woodland. At St.-Viâtre, turn right on the D93 to Nouan-le-Fuzelier. Take the D44 to turn right onto the D923. At Clémont, turn right on the D176 toward the Étang du Puits. Go right on the D948 to Argent-sur-Sauldre, then left on the D940.
The château at Gien is a river stronghold, unusual in eschewing the

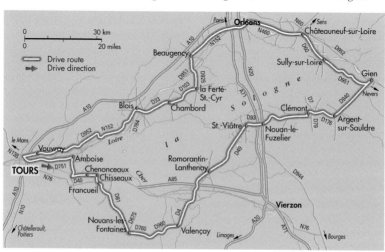

The beautiful, fairy-tale Château de Chambord dates to the 16th century and was a royal favorite

local white stone in favor of sturdy red brick. The 15th-century château was restored after World War II bombing and since 1952 has housed the Musée International de la Chasse (International Museum of Hunting). The modern pink-brick church nearby is dedicated to Joan of Arc. The tower of the original church remains.

Return back across the river and turn right on the D951.

Beautifully maintained, the fabulous moated Château de Sully-sur-Loire retains its original timber roofs. To create the 30-foot arches, chestnut trees were tied together as saplings so that the wood would grow in the right shape. Here, at this lovely château, Voltaire staged his early plays, and Joan of Arc met King Charles VII.

Follow the D948 north and the D952 west via Châteauneuf-sur-Loire, then take the N60 to Orléans.

Although May is the prime season for commemorations of the Maid of Orléans, Joan of Arc, plenty of year-round monuments honor the woman who broke the English siege of Orléans in 1429. Follow her story through the cathedral's stained-glass windows. **Be careful as you leave the city not to filter onto the highway; watch for signs for the N152 toward Blois. At Beaugency, cross the river on the D925 to la Ferté-St.-Cyr, then go right onto the D103, filtering onto the D33 through the walled estate of Chambord.**

The epitome of the Loire valley châteaux, Chambord is the jewel in this royal region's crown. Constructed in the heart of a hunting forest with no views nor even a convenient water supply, the "simple" lodge ordered by François I incorporated 440 rooms, 63 staircases and a roof studded with 365 ornate chimneys, spires, gables and dormer windows. It became home to huge regal hunting parties, plots, intrigues and scandals. Eventually it received a moat and glorious furnishings, including a riddle of a double spiral staircase, attributed to Leonardo da Vinci, which allows people to ascend and descend without crossing each other's paths. It is said the king loved Chambord so much he spent money on its finery rather than pay ransom for his two sons.

Follow the D33 under the bridge of St.-Gervais-la-Forêt, then turn right on the D956.

Blois, the city of Louis XII, bustles as much today with visitors as it did in the days of the court. The splendid Renaissance château has as many styles of decoration as there were kings and queens in the Loire. Followers of Médicis intrigues will delight in discovering secret cupboards and doors behind the panels in Catherine's private rooms. Like Chambord (see page 102), this is a château to be enjoyed through summer sound-and-light shows, which recount the gore and the glamor of the past. Blois is a useful base for exploring the region on guided tours.

Follow the N152 toward Tours, then turn right on the D65 and left to the D58, which becomes the D1. Follow signs for Vouvray, coming into town on the D46.

A wine-tasting stop, Vouvray lets you discover white, sparkling aperitifs and sweet dessert wines, and visit troglodyte houses (see page 100).

The N152 leads back to Tours.

In the round: A superb external spiral staircase extends to the full height of the Château de Blois

Dordogne

Opposite: Beynac-et-Cazenac, one of the most beautiful villages in France

Dordogne

Shaded from the rest of France by its vast forests, the Dordogne region is a timeless sanctuary where simple country values hold sway and city life is held firmly at bay. The Dordogne river itself flows from the mountains of the Massif Central to join the Gironde estuary at Bordeaux, through countryside of unmatched fertility, variety and incredible beauty.

The traditional regions of Périgord and Quercy are today known as the Dordogne and Lot departments. Quercy is the country of winemakers and shepherds. Rivers divide Périgord into four colorful areas: Black Périgord, with its walnut forests and treasured truffles; White Périgord, grazing ground of veal herds; Green Périgord, with lush farmland; and Purple Périgord, home to the vineyards of Bergerac. To the north of Périgord is Limousin, a rural region of arable farms, oak forests and lakes.

Secret History

For years, people spoke of the history of Périgord as contemporary to its neighbors. Gallic dry-stone huts, called *bories*, and Roman remains were believed to date from the start of the region's history and were taken up again with repopulation in the 11th century. Until the end of the Middle Ages, the land batted between the French and English during the Hundred Years War and the Wars of Religion between the Catholics and Protestants. Thus, the tree-topped skyline gained round French-style towers, square towers in the English style, fortified towns and many châteaux.

In the 19th century came the discovery of Périgord's secret life in the Stone Age. Simple tools and caves announced a civilization that flourished tens of thousands of years ago. The early years of the 20th century brought about the revelation of cave paintings, proving that prehistory, surprisingly, had an artistic tradition to match any period over the past millennium.

A major political pawn, Périgord became French when it was added to the dowry Eleanor of Aquitaine brought to her 1137 marriage to Louis VII. But when the marriage was dissolved in 1152, Eleanor presented the land to her new husband Henri, Count of Anjou, Lord of Maine, Touraine and Normandy, and eventual Plantagenet King Henry II of England. The land wouldn't be French for another 300 years.

The fertile valley of the River Isle, close to Périgueux

Rivers of the Region

The best way to explore the Dordogne is by water. The Dordogne river is a mighty waterway that flows westward through changing but always beautiful scenery, passing villages, castles, vineyards and dense woodland. In places a raging torrent, elsewhere peaceful and slow-moving, the Dordogne river is popular for canoeing, kayaking and rafting. There are also plenty of companies offering boat trips for the less energetic. In addition, the river provides a significant amount of hydroelectric power to the region.

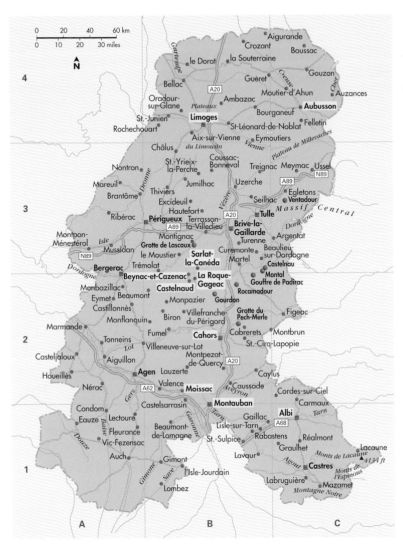

0 20   40   60 km
0   10   20   30 miles

N

4

Aigurande
Crozat
Boussac
le Dorat la Souterraine
Bellac Guéret Gouzon
A20 Auzances
Oradour- Ambazac Moutier-d'Ahun
sur-Glane *Plateaux* Bourganeuf **Aubusson**
St.-Junien **Limoges** Felletin
Rochechouart St-Léonard-de-Noblat
Aix-sur-Vienne Eymoutiers
Châlus *du Limousin* *Vienne* *Plateau de Millevaches*

3

Coussac-
Nontron St.-Yrieix- Bonneval Treignac Meymac Ussel
la-Perche N89
Mareuil Jumilhac Uzerche A89
Brantôme Thiviers Seilhac Ventadour
Excideuil *Massif Central*
Ribérac Hautefort **Tulle**
Périgueux Terrasson- A20 *Dordogne*
A89 la-Villedieu **Brive-la-**
Montpon- Montignac **Gaillarde** Argentat
Ménestérol *Isle* Grotte de Lascaux Turenne Beaulieu-
Mussidan le Moustier Curemonte sur-Dordogne
N89 **Sarlat-** Martel Castelnau
Bergerac Trémolat **la-Canéda**
Dordogne **La Roque-**
Beynac-et-Cazenac **Gageac** **Montal**
Gouffre de Padirac
Monbazillac **Castelnaud** Rocamadour
Eymet Beaumont
Castillonnès Monpazier Gourdon

2

Marmande Monflanquin Biron Villefranche- Grotte du
du-Périgord Pech-Merle
Fumel **Cahors** Cabrerets Montbrun
Tonneins Villeneuve-sur-Lot St.-Cirq-Lapopie
Casteljaloux *Lot* Montpezat-
Aiguillon de-Quercy A20
Houeillès **Agen** Lauzerte Caylus
Nérac Valence **Moissac** Caussade Cordes-sur-Ciel
A62 *Aveyron*
Condom Castelsarrasin **Montauban** Carmaux
Eauze Lectoure Gaillac **Albi**
Fleurance Beaumont- Lisle-sur-Tarn A68
Vic-Fezensac de-Lomagne St.-Sulpice Rabastens Réalmont
Douze Graulhet Lacaune
Auch Gimont Lavaur *Monts de Lacaune* 4134 ft
Gers **Castres** *Monts de*
Baïse l'Isle-Jourdain *l'Espinous*

1

Gimone *Save* *Tarn* *Agout* Labruguière Mazamet
Lombez *Montagne Noire*

A B C

Since 30 miles of the lower reaches of the Lot river opened up to pleasure craft, it's now possible to sail from the plum orchards of Villeneuve-sur-Lot to the Garonne. Tourists may be towed by tugboats and take 39-foot lock drops, then chug between the Atlantic and the Mediterranean on the Canal des Deux Mers or float along the Baïse into Armagnac country, which lends itself perfectly to the prospect of fortifying brandy tastings.

Birth of the Forest

Périgord Noir (Black Périgord) gets its name from the vast forests that cover the land. However, at the time of the Roman occupation in the fourth century AD, much of this land was cultivated by farmers. For the next 800 years, successive barbarian invasions forced the local population away from southwest France, and thick forests grew where once stood small Roman walnut groves.

Sarlat-la-Canéda

The former capital of Périgord is so improbably beautiful it hardly seems real. In fact, Sarlat by night is nearly too gorgeous to believe. The main square and its side streets are so remarkably illuminated that the entire town resembles a cardboard cutout set from an expensive operetta.

The civic illumination, including picturesque gas lamps, is one of the more visible aspects of a conservation project started more than 30 years ago to guarantee that the town was no anticlimax after the long scenic drive through the dramatic Dordogne region. Well indicated along food- and

wine-tasting routes from Bordeaux and Bergerac, the compact, historic center of Sarlat-la-Canéda is restrained by a ring road, where it's best to find a parking space and then explore on foot.

The medieval center of town is full of narrow stone-paved streets that slope steeply up and down between houses and mansions of golden and gray stone. Every corner provides inspiration for another snapshot. In the early 19th century, rue de la République divided the town into two unequal halves. The larger section is a haven of wonderful little houses, terraces, gardens and tiny squares. The old quarter (Quartier des Clercs), no mere museum piece, remains very much a thriving community with

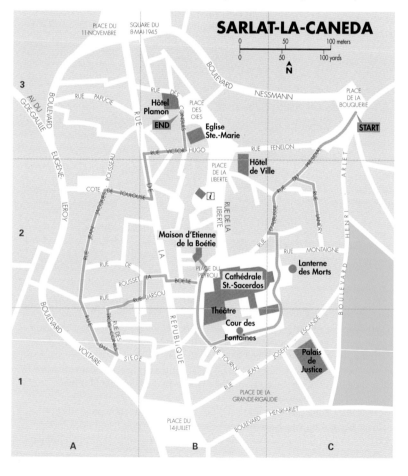

people as full of local character as their surroundings. Sarlat folk have strong country faces, with the weathered complexion of the south. See an elderly widow in black sitting in her doorway or an open window with a cat purring on her lap and a caged canary on the windowsill. Watch old men in caps exchanging greetings as they puff their way up steep stepped streets.

In the heat of the summer, a siesta break isn't uncommon during the afternoon. Some local farmers have even been known to spend the early evening in the city deep in conversation with their friends and neighbors, before heading off to work their fields after midnight, when temperatures drop to a more tolerable level.

Rather than retreating to your hotel, slip into a museum when it's too hot for climbing hilly streets or find a shady table, order a coffee or glass of wine, and simply watch the somnolent town wake from its early afternoon siesta.

Whether it's early or late in the day, take time to explore and look for the details. There is a fascinating variety of stone-carved doorways, from Classical to high Gothic, that cry out to be

Rooftops in the old center of town

photographed. Wednesday and Saturday morning markets on place de la Liberté sell local produce (see page 114), and summertime brings international music and theater festivals.

Essential Information

Tourist Information

The main office is in a late-Renaissance house ✉ 3 rue Tourny, 24203 ☎ 05 53 31 45 45; www.sarlat-tourisme.com. English is spoken, and maps/walking tours (Apr.–Oct.) provided.

Urban Transportation

There are three bus routes serving the city (Infobus ☎ 05 53 59 01 48). Rail services travel from Paris and Bordeaux to Sarlat ☎ 36 35 (toll call); www.voyages-sncf.com. Taxis ☎ 05 53 59 02 43.

Airport Information

The airport at Bergerac (☎ 05 53 22 25 25; www.bergerac.aeroport.fr) has domestic and UK flights. The closest international airport is Bordeaux, two and a half hours away by rail.

Climate – average highs and lows for the month

Jan.	Feb.	Mar.	Apr.	May	Jun.	Jul.	Aug.	Sep.	Oct.	Nov.	Dec.
9°C	11°C	14°C	16°C	19°C	23°C	26°C	26°C	23°C	18°C	13°C	10°C
48°F	52°F	57°F	61°F	66°F	79°F	79°F	79°F	73°F	64°F	55°F	50°F
2°C	4°C	5°C	6°C	10°C	13°C	15°C	15°C	12°C	9°C	5°C	4°C
36°F	39°F	41°F	43°F	50°F	55°F	59°F	59°F	54°F	48°F	41°F	39°F

Dordogne

Sarlat Sights

Cathédrale St.-Sacerdos

The Cathedral of St. Sacerdos is interesting as much for its surroundings of courts and chapels – which are clustered near the one-time abbey that ran the town – as for the building itself. The bulky monument, with its slate-capped tower, dominates the town, appropriate since Sarlat had been the seat of a bishop from the 14th century until the Revolution.

The present church dates from the late-16th to 17th century. An ancient sculpture over the main door and a Romanesque tower remain from the original building. The effects of glittering stained glass soften the cavernous and stern interior. Note the handsome organ and large wooden pulpit. On the south side is the Bishop's Palace. Behind the cathedral is a strange 12th-century bullet-shaped building with a conical roof. Called the Lanterne des Morts (Dead Men's Lantern), it's believed to have been used for funeral purposes, although its actual history is unknown.

➕ B2 ✉ place du Peyrou, 24200

Maison d'Etienne de la Boétie

Opposite the cathedral, this splendid stone house was built in 1525 by a local magistrate, father of the poet Etienne de la Boétie, who grew up to inspire Jean-Jacques Rousseau's celebrated *Social Contract*. Step across the road to get the full effect of the facade, with its exuberant sculpture, stone pilasters and medallions. Compare and contrast it with the Gothic windows and trailing flowers of the quaintly medieval Hôtel Plamon, on rue des Consuls. Enter the courtyard, once a covered market, to admire an elegant staircase.

Unfortunately the house is the office of the Sarlat Chamber of Commerce and Industry, and the interior is closed to most visitors.

➕ B2 ✉ place du Peyrou, 24200

There are plenty of opportunities to purchase the produce of Périgord in Sarlat

Walk
Exploring Secret Sarlat

Refer to route marked on city map on page 108

From place de la Bouquerie, walk down rue du Présidial and then turn left onto rue Landry.
Continue up a narrow stone-flagged passage to peer through a gate into the gardens of the 17th-century Palace of Justice, now a grand restaurant. Return to rue Présidial, and note the handsome Classical doorway at No. 6.

Turn left onto rue d'Albusse, with its corner Gothic doorway, then take a left behind the church to admire some wrought-iron balconies and follow a narrow winding stepped passage that leads to the Lanterne des Morts (see page 110). Keep following the path down into the churchyard behind the cathedral and then cross into cour des Fountaines to view a Classical stone arch. Turn right on rue Tourny. Continue onwards to place du Peyrou.
Here, pause by the Maison d'Etienne de la Boétie (see page 110). To the right is rue de la Liberté with ancient wooden houses. For a small circular tour, follow along this road and turn left at the tourist office, which takes you through a lovely quarter of old houses returning to place du Peyrou.

Head along rue de la Boétie, cross rue de la République, and enter the western section. Turn left and then right to climb rue Liarsou, then wind up rue des Trois-Conils.
This street is notable for its modern shops cunningly tucked into old buildings. Old city walls still border the main boulevard and surround the town. A nearby 16th-century tower is one of only two remaining from a set of 18 that once studded the fortifications.
Turn right onto rue du Siège.

The three bronze geese are a well-known landmark

Enjoy the view down to the town and a charming towered house. Steps take you along the narrow and unusually straight rue Jean-Jacques-Rousseau, which is noteworthy for its handsome gold stone houses.
Turn right where Côte de Toulouse crosses and go down to rue de la République, and swing a swift left and right down rue Victor-Hugo.
Take a left before the large Église Ste.-Marie, with the cloth-makers' house, Hôtel Plamon, and the old well and sculpture of three bronze geese opposite. Turn left at the church and climb the street for a fine view down to the marketplace.

Regional Sights

Dordogne

Albi

Count Henri Marie Raymond de Toulouse-Lautrec (1864–1901) was born into minor nobility in the fiery red-brick town of Albi. The medieval Pont Vieux spanning the Tarn river, as well as the flour mills, ocher dusty lanes and cypress trees of the hardy wine-producing area, may have kindled the young artist's passion for painting. However, it was the debauched fleshpots of Paris' Montmartre that lured him away from the family château in Naucelle and took him to the city where he was to find fame and wealth. Crippled and stunted at the age of 14, Toulouse-Lautrec had been sheltered by his family. Life among the outcasts of Paris stimulated both the artist and his art. His paintings of prostitutes and showgirls at the Moulin Rouge and other public balls made his name even more famous than the dancers Jane Avril and La Goulue, whom he immortalized in the posters that defined late-19th-century nightlife.

Imposing Cathédrale Ste.-Cécile, the world's largest brick building, represents the restraint of his hometown. Apart from the flamboyant 16th-century porch, the edifice is austere. There are not many stained-glass windows, merely fortress slits keeping daylight from the sumptuous interior, whose treasures include a masterly fresco of the Last Judgment, slightly damaged in the 17th century but still impressive.

Below the cathedral is Old Albi, with houses of timber and brick. Make your way to rue Toulouse-Lautrec to see the artist's birthplace, the Hôtel du Bosc. The Palais de la Berbie, a 13th-century

The Palais de la Berbie is a museum devoted to the life and works of Toulouse-Lautrec

palace fortified because of civil unrest, is now a museum devoted to Toulouse-Lautrec. The collection of his work before Paris features family portraits and local landscapes and offers clues to the compassion he later showed for harsher subjects.

A 30-mile drive northeast of the town, the Château du Bosc, as well as its estate at Naucelle, was the artist's childhood home and also his lifelong summer retreat. Here, his descendants welcome visitors to the family's richly furnished medieval château.

✚ C2

Tourist information ✉ place Ste.-Cécile, 81000 ☎ 05 63 36 36 00; www.albi-tourisme.fr

Musée Toulouse-Lautrec ✉ Palais de la Berbie, place Ste.-Cécile ☎ 05 63 49 58 97; www.museetoulouselautrec.com 🕐 Daily 9–6, Jul.–Sep.; 9–noon and 2–6, Jun. (from 10 a.m., Apr.–May); Wed.–Mon. 10–noon and 2–6, Oct. (closes 5:30 p.m., Feb.–Mar., Nov.–Dec.; 5 p.m. Jan.). Gardens: daily 8–7, Apr.–May (closes 6 p.m. Oct.–Mar.) ℹ Audio-guided tours available in English ($$) 💷 $$

Château du Bosc ✉ Camjac, 12800 Naucelle
☎ 05 65 69 20 83; www.naucellois.com ⏰ Daily 9–7,
in summer; 9–6, rest of year ✋ $$

Aubusson

A town whose name is synonymous
with the world's finest tapestries,
Aubusson had its fame assured when
Flemish weavers set up shop on the
banks of the Creuse river in the 14th
century. With each century, new
crafts-people came to town, and each
reign brought fresh royal orders to
weave more ornate hangings for the
châteaux and palaces being built along
the Loire and around Paris. From the
reigns of Louis XIV to Louis XVI, noble
clients commissioned needlework copies
of famous paintings. The popularity of
pastoral and mythical themes is
explained at the town's museum of the
history of weaving, the 16th-century
Maison du Tapissier. Modern tapestries
can be seen at the Musée Départemental
de la Tapisserie, which exhibits
contemporary examples as well as

Cubist-inspired work by the modern
master Lurçat himself.

➕ C4

Tourist information/Maison du Tapissier ✉ rue
Vieille, 23200 ☎ 05 55 66 32 12; www.ot-aubusson.fr
⏰ Mon.–Sat. 9:30–1 and 2–6:30, Sun. 10–noon and
2:30–5:30, Jul.–Aug.; Mon.–Sat. 9:30–12:30 and 2–6,
Sun. 10–noon and 2:30–5:30, Jun., Sep. and Easter;
Mon.–Sat. 9:30–2:30 and 2–6, rest of year ✋ $$

Musée Départemental de la Tapisserie ✉ avenue des
Lissiers ☎ 05 55 83 08 30 ⏰ Wed.–Mon. 10–6, Tue.
2–6, Jul.–Aug.; Wed.–Mon. 9:30–noon and 2–6, rest of
year. Closed three days before and after exhibitions
ℹ Demonstrations by appointment only ($$$) ✋ $$

Beynac-et-Cazenac

If you like a romantic and extravagant
view of history and its heroes, then drive
out to see the improbably spectacular
Château Féodal de Beynac looming atop
rugged limestone rocks and soaking up
the sunshine that blesses the village
rooftops on the riverside below. The
fortress, known locally as Satan's
Archway, comes complete with
legendary heroes. Richard the Lionheart

The village of Beynac-et-Cazenac is dominated by the château, perched high above

Dordogne

Taste of Périgord

The Dordogne provides nearly half of France's luxury foods. The welcome is open and warm to guests who wish to taste, buy or learn to cook legendary poultry and mushroom dishes. However, the locals jealously guard their sources, and too many questions as to where to find your own wild mushrooms and truffles will be met with a polite smile and determined silence.

The gathering and traditional preparation of conserves are an essential part of family life here, and each household has its secret supply of raw materials. Sunny mornings after rain in early autumn are spent trudging into the forest to collect cèpes and other wild mushrooms. The inexperienced take their finds to the nearest pharmacy to confirm identification. While some mushrooms are enjoyed immediately, most are cooked, bottled and stored for the rest of the year.

In December, geese and ducks are plucked and prepared for the pot. Anglo-Saxon sensibilities often recoil at the force-feeding that creates foie gras, but here, what elsewhere might be considered cruelty is regarded as merely a process of food production. The liver is weighed separately and put aside for the alchemy of foie gras. Wings and legs are preserved in fat based on recipes as old as the woods. Some birds are served *demoiselle*, deliciously grilled whole over a wood fire.

Mid-winter is the time for farmers to snuffle for truffles. Some use pigs and others hunt with hounds to find the rare fungi. Back at the farm, these nuggets are bottled in their own juice. Pigs are slaughtered in the winter and the meat preserved. Walnuts and chestnuts are harvested in season, and these too find their way into bottles, cans and jars. The intensely flavored preserves are deployed year round in small doses to enliven simple foods and create gastronomic delights at little expense. Even an omelet becomes an occasion with a dash of truffle juice. Just a mist of *liqueur de noix* (walnut liqueur) can transform a summer ice cream into a culinary treat.

In summer months, farmers grow asparagus, winemakers tend their vines, and farmers' wives open their kitchens to visitors for half-day and weekend cookery courses that teach vacationers how to make the most of pre-cooked confits and succulent *magret de canard* (duck breast). You can obtain details from the local tourist offices.

Glacé fruits are among the cornucopia of fresh produce for sale in Périgord markets

Medieval Pont Valentré gracefully spans the Lot river at the wine town of Cahors

captured the original building in the 12th century, and Simon de Montfort destroyed it during his crusades. It was rebuilt and changed hands several times during the Hundred Years War. When peace was restored, Beynac became a stronghold of the barons of Périgord and was embroiled in local rivalries with the Château de Castelnaud (see pages 115–116).

It's worth the climb for the views and to see a fresco of the Last Supper in the principal stateroom. Bronze Age and Roman history can be discovered in a small museum in the town below.

✠ A3

Château Féodal de Beynac ☎ 05 53 29 50 40
⏰ Daily from 10 (11 in winter). Closing times vary seasonally 🎟 $$

Cahors

Cahors is best known overseas for the hardy red wine that bears its name. It was the holy spring, worshiped by the ancient Gauls and Romans, that led to a town developing in this natural moat formed by the Lot river. Coveted

and taken by the English during the Hundred Years War, the town sustained little damage to its buildings and walls. Many early turrets and battlements are still dotted around town. Today, visitors come to admire the 14th-century Pont Valentré, with its seven arches gracefully sweeping across the river and three square towers standing sturdily atop. For years, no one could place the final stone on top of the central tower, known as the Devil's Tower, because, it is said, the devil quarreled with the architect and was appeased only when his image was carved on the tower. Cross the bridge into town to visit the Renaissance cloisters of the cathedral. The old quarter is famed for its ornate doorways.

✠ B3

Tourist information ✉ place François-Mitterrand, 46003 ☎ 05 65 53 20 65; www.tourisme-cahors.com

Château de Castelnaud

The château was rescued from virtual ruin when it was declared a national monument in 1966. Now it's the Musée de la Guerre au Moyen Âge (Museum of Medieval Warfare), with many fascinating exhibits. Its history is indelibly linked with that of its neighbor across the water, Beynac (see pages 113, 115). Both shared similar fluctuating fortunes during the Hundred Years War as the lords of the two houses bitterly vied for control of the region, spying on each other and splitting the loyalty of the community without ever actually declaring war. In 1317, Pope Jean XXII ordered a marriage between the families to end the conflict. As the château fell into disrepair, the family moved to nearby les Milandes (see page 120), abandoning Castelnaud to the ravages of the weather and builders seeking local stone. It was finally restored in 1998, and visitors come as much for the wonderful views as for the museum. On summer evenings (July through August), actors recreate scenes from the castle's glory days. Summer courses for children include calligraphy, heraldry and siege strategy.

⊹ B3

Château de Castelnaud ✉ Castelnaud-la-Chapelle, 24250 ☎ 05 53 31 30 00; www.castelnaud.com ⊙ Daily 9–8, Jul.–Aug.; 10–7, Apr.–Jun. and Sep.; 10–6, Feb.–Mar., Oct.–Nov. 11; 2–5, Nov. 12–Jan. except Christmas holidays 10–5 (2–5 Dec. 25 and Jan. 1) 🍴 Tavern (Jul.–Aug. only) 🎟 $$

Limoges

Elegant blue-and-gold tableware bearing the Limoges name is recognized throughout the world, but before the porcelain industry was even conceived, this town on the banks of the Vienne river had discovered another sought-after talent: *champlevé*. From the 12th to 18th centuries, Limoges was the world center of the art, which involves multilayering enamel onto copper to create perfect luster and sheen. The Musée des Beaux-Arts has an extensive collection of classic pieces, while modern works are on display at the Cité des Metiers et des Arts on rue Règle. The town's tradition of ceramic- and porcelain-making is celebrated at the Musée National de la Porcelaine Adrien Dubouché.

Take a look at the eight-arch 13th-century bridge and visit the nearby Gothic Cathédrale St.-Étienne, which was inaugurated in the same era and completed 600 years later. The old streets, especially around rue des Bouchers, make for a pleasant stroll. Not surprisingly, plenty of shops sell genuine Limoges porcelain.

⊹ B4

Tourist information ✉ 12 boulevard de Fleurus, 87000 ☎ 05 55 34 46 87; www.tourismelimoges.com

Detail of a Limoges porcelain sauceboat, decorated with anemones

Musée National de la Porcelaine Adrien Dubouché
✉ place Winston-Churchill, 87000 ☎ 05 55 33 08 50;
www.musee-adriendubouche.fr 🕒 Wed.–Mon.
10–12:25 and 2–5:40 👆 $

Moissac

World Heritage Site canals, bustling
farmers' markets and fruit orchards;
modern Moissac has all of this. But it's
Abbatiale St.-Pierre (St. Peter's Abbey
Church) that entices people into this
modest settlement between the Tarn and
Garonne rivers. Despite serious bruising
during the French Revolution, the
remains of the Benedictine abbey church
and cloisters are among the most
treasured in France, with ornate carved
capitals from the 11th through 13th
centuries. A museum next door displays
remaining stonework from the abbey.
The monks acquired many great
artworks since its founding in the
seventh century. Most impressive is the
southern doorway (12th-century)
depicting St. John's vision of the
apocalypse. Some street names appear in
the old language of Occitan.
➕ B2

Tourist information ✉ 6 place Durand-de-Bredon,
82200 ☎ 05 63 04 01 85; http://tourisme.moissac.fr
Abbatiale St.-Pierre ✉ place Durand-de-Bredon,
82200 ☎ 05 63 04 01 85 🕒 Cloisters open daily 9–7,

Jul.–Aug.; 9–6 Sep.; Mon.–Fri. 9–12 and 2–6, Sat.–Sun.
10–12 and 2–6, Apr.–Jun. and Oct.; Mon.–Fri. 10–noon
and 2–5, Sat.–Sun. and holidays 2–5 rest of year
ℹ Guided tours some Sundays. For information, call
the tourist office 👆 $$

Montauban

Ignore the bland suburbs surrounding
the original old *bastide* – a medieval new
town. The rose-tinted brickwork is most
striking at dawn and dusk. Garlands of
arcades border place Nationale with
angled porticoes linking 17th-century
houses. The quarter's alleys and bars
provide an evocative setting for the
fringe events of a jazz festival in July.
The festival attracts musicians from
Louisiana to the Paris suburbs, with
main events taking place in the park
below the old town walls (www.
jazzmontauban.com). The civic history
of this Protestant stronghold that held
out for 100 days against Louis XIII's
forces in 1621 has been overshadowed
by its art collection. The Bishop's Palace,
by the banks of the Tarn, houses a lavish
collection of religious and melodramatic
canvases by the popular 19th-century
painter Jean-Auguste-Dominique Ingres.
➕ B2

Tourist information ✉ 4 rue du Collège, 82002
☎ 05 63 63 60 60; www.montauban-tourisme.com

Elegant and ornate, the cloisters at Abbatiale St.-Pierre in Moissac

The medieval Manoir de Tarde is set into limestone cliffs in the pretty town of La Roque-Gageac

La Roque-Gageac

Nestled among old trees at the foot of a limestone cliff, with the river flowing gently by, the picturesque town of La Roque-Gageac is the epitome of the Dordogne. Tourists are escorted on trips down the river on flat-bottomed boats, known as *gabares*. Logs were floated downstream in the days when the town's fortunes depended on the lumber trade.

The town has many interesting buildings and looks its finest from the water. The seemingly 15th-century Château de la Malartrie was built in the 20th century, but the Manoir de Tarde is an authentic medieval building.

The towering cliffs crumbled too far in 1956, leading to tragedy when falling rock killed several people. Nowadays, all is safely shored up, and the town receives a steady flow of visitors to explore its steep, narrow streets. ✚ B3

Tourist information ✉ Contact office at Sarlat-la-Canéda, 3 rue Tourny, 24203 ☎ 05 53 31 45 45; www.sarlat-tourisme.com

Drive
Historic and Prehistoric Tour

Distance: 238 miles
Time: 4 days

From prehistoric caves to Roman streets, medieval miracles to the home of a 20th-century American heroine, this drive starts and finishes at Périgueux, the old capital of Périgord.

Taking the N2089 toward Brive, go right on the N221, pass beneath autoroute A89, then turn right onto the D710. Continue south then take the D45, turning right along the D47.
Pause on the steps leading to the first cave of the tour, Grotte du Grand Roc, and gaze at breathtaking views over the Vézère valley.
Continue along the D47.
The heart of prehistoric Dordogne is les Eyzies-de-Tayac, with the Musée National de Préhistoire (National Museum of Prehistory) housed in a 13th-century castle guarded by a giant statue of Neanderthal man. The Vézère

river created the caves that make this one of the world's key prehistoric regions. The tourist office will direct you toward the main sights: cave paintings at Font de Gaume or the caving museum at Tayac.
On the D706 toward Montignac, you will pass the 20 reconstructions of Neanderthal and Cro-Magnon sites. Turn right on the D704, then right again.
Known as the "Sistine Chapel of Périgord," Lascaux cave was discovered by four boys and a dog in 1940. The dog fell into a hole, and the boys scrambled after it to find themselves unwittingly facing the greatest prehistoric art collection known to man. The boys went back and told their teacher, who told expert Abbé Breuil, who then told the world. The ravages of tourism, light and moss led to the cave being sealed in 1963, but an exact replica was opened in 1983 at Lascaux II. Painstakingly precise reproductions of the 25,000-year-old drawings use the original pigments. Once again, visitors may marvel at the famous picture of a man being chased by a wounded bison and other scenes from another world.
From Montignac, take the D704 to Sarlat-la-Canéda (see pages 108–111). Follow the D46 to Vitrac, turning left on the D703.

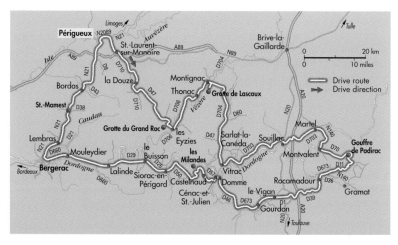

Dordogne

Enjoy Souillac's museum of automated toys, which houses 1,000 of them, then visit the 12th-century Romanesque church.

Take the D803 to Martel, turning right on the N140 and left on the D70. Take a right for the D11 to Miers then left on the D91. Turn left and continue along the D60, taking the right fork by a stone cross. Turn right again at the intersection.

At Gouffre de Padirac, take a boat trip along an underground river from the cave where Edward Martel discovered 200,000-year-old bones and human remains from nearly 50,000 years ago. Walk the 455 steps down or use the elevator to descend into an underworld of eerie and fascinating beauty.

Take the D90 to Padirac, then turn onto the D673 to Rocamadour.

Yet another superlative photo opportunity (from the Belvedere of l'Hospitalet on the D32 below), the medieval village of Rocamadour clings to its cliff face. The town flourished in the 12th century when the body of a man – thought to be Zaccheus, the tax collector who turned philanthropist after meeting Jesus – was discovered. Miracles and pilgrims came, and when the Protestants seized the village and tried to burn the body, it remained untouched by the flames. Rocher des Aigles nearby has displays of flying birds of prey.

Follow the D32 to Couzou, turning right on the D39 through St.-Projet. Turn right on the D801 to Gourdon. Leave Gourdon on the D673, turning right on the D6/D46 to Domme.

Browse the quaint covered market for picnic supplies and visit the history museum here.

From Cénac, take the D50 toward Siorac-en-Périgord. In Pont de Cause, go straight on for Castelnaud, then continue straight toward Fayrac and les Milandes. Turn left on the D53 toward Siorac-en-

Périgord. After a bend sign, make a sharp right uphill to the château.

The star of the 1926 all-black cabaret Revue Nègre, Joséphine Baker left racism in America to find adulation in the Folies Bergères. The one-time topless dancer and French Resistance worker bought this 15th-century château at les Milandes to care for her Rainbow Tribe, the children of many races she adopted after the war. The family became a tourist attraction, and she built a golf course, hotel and restaurant to cater to the visitors. When bailiffs came to evict her, she sat on the doorstep, holding the children and refused to leave. Princess Grace saw news film of the event and offered them a home in Monaco.

Continue along the road, bearing left to turn right on the D53. Take the D50 then the D703 to Siorac-en-Périgord, then follow signs from the D25 for Lalinde and then Bergerac.

A center of wine production and once home to the French tobacco industry, Bergerac has museums of wine and tobacco. Enjoy the statue of Cyrano, who, despite his name, in fact had nothing to do with the town.

Finally, join the N21 to take you back to Périgueux.

Musée National de Préhistoire ✉ 1 rue du Musée, les Eyzies-de-Tayac, 24620 ☎ 05 53 06 45 45; www.musee-prehistoire-eyzies.fr 🕓 Daily 9:30–6:30, Jul.–Aug.; Wed.–Mon. 9:30–6, Jun. and Sep.; Wed.–Mon. 9:30–12:30 and 2–5:30, rest of year 💷 $$

Grottes de Lascaux II ✉ Montignac, 24290 ☎ 05 53 05 65 65; www.semitour.com 🕓 Daily 9–8, early Jul.–Aug.; 9–6, Apr.–Jun. and Sep.–Oct.; Tue.–Sun. 10–noon and 2–5:30, rest of year 💷 $$

Musée de l'Automate ✉ place de l'Abbaye, Souillac, 46200 ☎ 05 65 37 07 07; www.musee-automate.fr 🕓 Daily 10–6, Jul.–Aug.; Tue.–Sun. 10–12 and 3–6, Apr.–Jun. and Sep.; Wed.–Sun. 2:30–5, rest of year 💷 $$

Opposite: An archway in the attractive town of Castelnaud-la-Chapelle

Pyrénées

Opposite: The village of Arvens nestles among trees in a fold of the foothills of the Pyrénées

Pyrénées

To most strangers, the Pyrénées are the "other" mountain range of France. Its ski resorts are less well-known than the glitzier destinations across the country. But the southwest corner of France boasts more than just peaks. The Pyrénées themselves rise from the plains of southwestern France to form a natural border with Spain. They span 250 miles between two seas, and though the highest peaks are on the Spanish side of the border, the French Pyrénées lure hikers in all seasons.

The most spectacular scenery is preserved within an area that is defined as a national park. Here, ibex, chamois and a few bears roam the hills, as golden eagles and three species of vulture – Egyptian, griffon and the rarer lammergeier – patrol the skies.

Where there are rocks, there are caves, and these encompass prehistoric paintings and picturesque stalactite-bordered subterranean waterways.

Particularly notable are the cavernous shrines at Bétharram and Lourdes, where miraculous events have fueled the faith of millions of pilgrims who are drawn here from all over the world.

The snow-capped mountain of Pic de Font Vive, east of the Col de Puymorens

Cordes-sur-Ciel
Carmaux
Lisle-sur-Tarn   Gaillac   **Albi**   *Tarn*
Villemur-sur-Tarn
St.-Sulpice   Rabastens   Réalmont
Graulhet   *Monts de Lacaune*   Lacaune
A62   A68
Lavaur   *Agout*
TOULOUSE
St.-Lys   Portet-sur-   Labruguière   Mazamet   **Castres**
Muret   Garonne   *Montagne Noire*
Vic-en-Bigorre   Villefranche-de-Lauragais
Garonne   Carbonne   Auterive   Castelnaudary
Tarbes   Cazères   *Ariège*   **Carcassonne**   Lézignan-Corbières
Lannemezan   St.-Gaudens   Grotte du   A66   A61   Fontfroide   **Narbonne**
Grottes des   Montréjeau   Mas-d'Azil   Pamiers   Mirepoix   *Aude*   Réserve Africaine
Médous   St.-Bertrand-   St.-Lizier   Limoux   Sigean   A9
9400 ft   de-Comminges   St.-Girons   **Foix**   Lavelanet   Puivert   Arques   Salses   Port-Leucate
Pic du   Arreau   *Massif de l'Arize*   Peyrepertuse   Port-Barcarès
Midi de   Tarascon-sur-Ariège   Montségur   Quillan   Quéribus   **Perpignan**
Bigorre   St.-Lary-   Aulus-   Grotte de Niaux   Axat   Puilaurens   Rivesaltes
Gèdre   Soulan   Bagnères-   les-Bains   Ax-les-Thermes   *Têt*
Cirque de   de-Luchon   10,220 ft   6282 ft   Eus   Serrabone   Thuir   Elne
Gavarnie   *Pic d'Estats*   *Col de*   St.-Martin-   St.-Michel-de-Cuxa   Collioure
   ANDORRA   *Puymorens*   du-Canigou   Céret   le-Perthus
   Bourg-   9134 ft   Cerbère
   Madame   Llo   *Pic du*
   Canigou
   C   D   E

Spanish Connection

The southwest of France is a funnel that distills all the Spanish influences that make the country such an intriguing and intoxicating cocktail. Just beyond are Catalan towns and villages, the principality of Andorra and the Basques. Summer bullfights, country dancing and cross-border pilgrim routes owe as much to Barcelona as to Toulouse.

French kings and leaders have long married Spanish princesses. This area recalls royal weddings and honeymoons from Louis XIV and Marie-Thérèse to the legendary pairing of Eugénie of Montijo with Emperor Napoléon III. Wars of religion and invasion have brought new blood from conquerors and refugees alike. The Romans opened spas, the Jews brought chocolate and the English gave the region foxhunting.

Two very different seas add to the mix: the Atlantic, where surfers take on the turbulent Bay of Biscay, and the calmer Mediterranean, rich with history.

Cutting-edge Tradition

Hikers often carry a traditional *makila* as they ascend the steepest paths. The Basque walking stick, used by shepherds and pilgrims since the Middle Ages, has been manufactured for centuries in the

Hikers enjoy the high pastures of the Pyrénées, along the border between France and Spain

French village of Larressore. The name means "death giver," since the handle contains an ornate blade said to have inspired the blacksmiths of Bayonne to invent the bayonet. The stick is carved from a living tree six months before the branch is removed, and details include a metal band on the handle with the owner's name and family motto. The country's highest honor is to be publicly presented a *makila*. Recipients have included several popes, Ronald Reagan and Winston Churchill.

Sports

The region is said to have been the first in France to popularize golf, and today there are plenty of courses and spectacular scenery. The Roman form of tennis (*pila*) is the main sport of the Basque country. Pelota is a type of jai alai played in the open air against one or more high walls, called a *fronton*. Variants of the sport use specific mitts or gloves, but the most strenuous is indoor, bare-handed *cesta punta*, one of the world's fastest sports.

Crossing Borders

If you fancy a diversion across the border, follow the coastal route along the Bay of Biscay down to Bilbao in northern Spain. A major attraction here is the remarkable Guggenheim Museum of avant-garde 20th-century and contemporary art (☎ [Spain 0034] 94 435 90 80; www.guggenheim-bilbao.es). North American architect Frank Gehry's writhing combination of limestone, titanium and glass is a landmark collaboration between Americans and the Basques.

Pioneers

The lush hills and scrubland of the plains form an unlikely backdrop for an international center of business and technology. Yet, Toulouse (see pages 127–131) has pioneered the Continent's conquest of the skies, from the first airmail services to the Concorde airplane and the European space program. The exhibition halls of Toulouse's City of Space make a fascinating day out.

A player gets ready to hit a fast-moving ball during a game of pelota in this single-wall court

Toulouse

Toulouse is the fourth-largest city in France and the capital of the skies. Since World War I, it has conquered flight, with legendary aviators such as Antoine de St.-Exupéry and Jean Mermoz. It is also home to the largest space center in Europe – Matra, now merged with German and Spanish companies to form the European Aeronautic Defence and Space Company. But ask any Frenchman about Toulouse's contribution to his country's wealth, and he will answer: *"cassoulet et rugby."* Cassoulet, the bean-and-meat stew of the south, is served in every restaurant in town. And rugby is practically a religion, with the local team one of the best in France. During championships, locals throng the streets dressed in the team's colors.

Lively Nightlife

Youthful exuberance keeps Toulouse from becoming just another industrial and commercial center. The second-largest university in France brings fresh faces to the bars and cafés. The mood is decidedly Latin, with more than a hint of the Mediterranean and Spain. This hexagonal city along the Garonne river is ringed by boulevards and has seven theaters, popular nightclubs and stylish bar patrons lingering until well after midnight. Evenings begin just before sundown, when the sky adds its special hues to the rosy tint of the buildings to cast warm shadows outside the Hôtel de Ville at the Capitole.

The Pink City

The Ville Rose (Pink City) gets its nickname from the red bricks used to build its magnificent houses and public buildings when local quarries were exhausted in the Middle Ages. The pink building boom also was funded by another color. Trade in the bluish-black dye plant, woad, revived city fortunes in the 16th century. Previously the city had been foremost an academic center, with literary societies promoting the ancient language of southern France, the langue d'oc.

The red bricks used in the construction of many of Toulouse's buildings gave rise to its nickname "Pink City"

Pyrénées

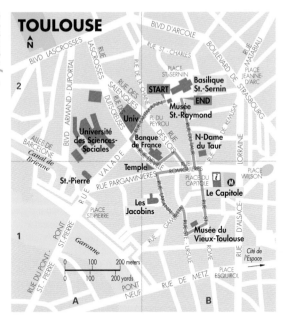

TOULOUSE

Shopping

Although commerce today centers around fashionable shops by the main squares, the markets are more fun. The main food market, where you can experience a melange of sights, sounds and aromas, is held every day but Monday outside the Capitole. A good book and prints market takes place at St.-Sernin. For books, crafts and jewelry, try the market on place St.-Étienne all day Saturday.

Essential Information

Tourist Information

Donjon du Capitole ☎ 0892 18 01 80 (toll call); www.toulouse-tourisme.com. The office has English-speaking assistants, and tours and river cruises can be booked here.

Urban Transportation

The two-line subway system has several stops around the city center. Capitole station is the most useful. Tickets should be validated before travel. A new tramway is under construction, with phase one (T1) already in service, operating from Aéroconstellation to Arènes (4:50 a.m. to 12:30 a.m.). There is a good bus service that runs from 5:30 a.m. to midnight ☎ 05 61 41 70 70; www.tisseo.fr. SNCF Gare Matabiau, to the northeast, has major national and local train connections ☎ 36 35; www.sncf.com. Taxis can be hailed on the street or ☎ 05 62 21 20 00; www.allotaxi31.com.

Airport Information

Toulouse Blagnac airport is close to the city and has flights from many European cities ☎ 08 25 38 00 00; www.toulouse.aeroport.fr. Shuttle buses into town operate every 20 minutes from the first to the last flight ☎ 05 61 41 70 70; www.tisseo.fr.

Climate – average highs and lows for the month

Jan.	Feb.	Mar.	Apr.	May	Jun.	Jul.	Aug.	Sep.	Oct.	Nov.	Dec.
9°C	11°C	14°C	16°C	19°C	23°C	26°C	26°C	23°C	18°C	13°C	10°C
48°F	52°F	57°F	61°F	66°F	73°F	79°F	79°F	73°F	64°F	55°F	50°F
2°C	4°C	5°C	6°C	10°C	13°C	15°C	15°C	12°C	9°C	5°C	4°C
36°F	39°F	41°F	43°F	50°F	55°F	59°F	59°F	54°F	48°F	41°F	39°F

Toulouse Sights

Key to symbols

✚ map coordinates refer to the Toulouse map on page 128 🅘 admission charge:
$$$ more than €10, $$ €5–€10, $ less than €5
See page 5 for complete key to symbols

Basilique St.-Sernin

Among the most famous pilgrimage churches in France during the Middle Ages, this wedding-cake-like edifice attracted hordes of devout travelers en route to Santiago de Compostela in western Spain. You can still see their clearly marked route around the Romanesque basilica. Its twin-colored spire and long, brick nave are noteworthy. There is an uncluttered and airy sense of space and many chapels inside. The church stands amid well-tended gardens. It was consecrated in 1096, having been built to house the relics of St. Saturnin, who was martyred in AD 250. The Basilique St.-Sernin is an impressive sight and is the largest and one of the prettiest of its type in the West.

✚ B2 ✉ place St.-Sernin, 31000 ☎ 05 61 21 80 45; www.basilique-st-sernin-toulouse.fr 🕐 Mon.–Sat. 8:30–7, Sun. 8:30–7:30, Jun.–Sep.; Mon.–Sat. 8:30–6, Sun. 8:30–7:30, rest of year. Crypt closes earlier
🅟 Capitole 🖐 Crypt $

The wedding-cake tiered spire of the 11th-century pilgrims' church, Basilique St.-Sernin

Pyrénées

Le Capitole

This grand building in the middle of town is a full city block long. Containing both the city hall and the main theater, it's a particularly cheery place to be on a Saturday, as a constant procession of brides, grooms and bouquets spills out of the main doors on wedding days. Looking as good as it has since the present building opened in 1759, the brick and stone have been restored and cleaned, and the eight marble columns positively gleam in the sunlight. Enter through the main entrance to cour Henri-IV. On non-wedding days, climb the main staircase to some splendid staterooms adorned with 19th-century paintings. The Galerie des Illustres (Marriage Room) contains a fabulously restored painted ceiling. The theater is grandly gilded and draped. By the garden behind the Capitole, the fortified donjon houses the tourist office. The Capitole takes up one side of the wide square that bears its name. The other three sides are mostly hotels and shopping arcades.

➕ B1 ✉ Galerie des Illustres, place du Capitole, 31000 ☎ 05 61 22 34 12; www.theatre-du-capitole.fr 🕐 Mon.–Sat. 8:30–7, Sun. 10–7, Easter to mid-Nov.; Mon.–Sat. 8:30–7, first Sun. of the month 10–7, rest of year 🚇 Capitole 🎫 Free

Cité de l'Espace

Since the area around Blagnac Airport is the hub of Europe's aerospace industry, it should come as no surprise that Toulouse boasts a City of Space.

Just on the outskirts of town (exit 17 of the Périphérique orbital road), the Cité de l'Espace is easily recognizable by the launch pad for the *Ariane 5* – flagship of the European space program. A massive expansion has doubled the exhibition area, including a spectacular new planetarium and wide-format 3D IMAX theater. There is also now a "junior astronauts" area for young visitors and interactive displays, including simulated rocket launches, weather forecasting and close-up views

Ariane 5 at Cité de l'Espace

of NASA and Russian space vehicles. A full day out includes tours of the Mir space station and a first-generation Russian Soyuz craft, and close encounters with satellites and stars.

➕ Off map B1 ✉ Parc de la Plaine, avenue Jean-Gonord, 31560 ☎ 08 20 37 72 23 (infoline); www.cite-espace.com 🕐 Daily 9:30–7, late Jul. to late Aug.; varied hours rest of year 🚇 37 💰 $$$

Les Jacobins

The spectacular vaulting of this Gothic church might never have been created but for a fiery accident in a church in nearby Narbonne. Dominican friars who rebuilt their preaching base in Toulouse, from 1275 to 1292, remembered the destruction at Narbonne and fireproof brick vaults rose from seven tall columns running along the center of the church, culminating in a "palm-tree" vault that springs from the final eastern pillar. A high altar of gray marble contains the relics of St. Thomas Aquinas. The cloister, a haven of peace in a busy town center, comes into its own every September with a month-long season of weekend piano recitals. The Piano aux Jacobins concert season attracts the world's finest musicians.

➕ B1 ✉ Parvis des Jacobins, 31000 ☎ 05 61 22 21 92; www.jacobins.mairie-toulouse.fr 🕐 Daily 9–7 🚇 Capitole 🎫 Church free; cloister $

Walk
Cloisters and Courtyards

Refer to route marked on
city map on page 128

This walk around Toulouse will
take about two to three hours.

Starting at place St.-Sernin, visit the
pilgrims' church (see page 129) and the
Musée St.-Raymond, a 16th-century
college with high, light rooms, for its
Roman and medieval treasures.
Take narrow rue Emile-Cartailhac.
Admire brick courts that open out
into the busy student quarter of tall
slender houses with shutters, lively
cafés and bookshops.
**Cross place du Peyrou to rue Albert
Lautmann and the Law Faculty on your
right. Turn left on rue Antoine-Déville.**
The facades on this street have been
cleaned and have typical wrought-iron
balconies. At the end on the left is the
Banque de France, with its elegant court
and frontage.
**Turn left here on rue du Collège-de-Foix,
noting the massive broken arch and a tall**
ruined window of an ancient college, then
right onto rue des Lois, and take another
sharp right to rue Romiguières.
Strolling through this typical, old-town
street with red brick and courtyards,
note the Vieux Temple on your right,
then turn left on rue Joseph-Lakanal to
the Jacobins' church (see page 130).
**At the end of rue Joseph-Lakanal, turn left
on rue Léon-Gambetta, then right on rue
Ste.-Ursule. Turn left onto rue du May.**
The fine brick Hôtel du May at No. 7
houses the Musée du Vieux-Toulouse.
Seize the opportunity to see the inside
of a typical aristocratic house. This
is right in the heart of the ancient
residential quarter.
**Go left on rue de St.-Rome to return to the
shopping center and place du Capitole.**
Walk around the arcades of the square
and take in a visit to the Capitole (see
page 130). The main central subway
station and tourist office are nearby.
Take the atmospheric rue du Taur and
allow old streets and courtyards to lure
you off course. On the right is the gaunt
brick facade of Notre-Dame du Taur.
Step inside to see mosaics and faded
19th-century wall paintings. Browse
the many small antiques shops and
galleries. The best buy is the celebrated
Toulouse earthenware. The road ends
at place St.-Sernin.

Les Jacobins church has brick vaulting that spreads from seven tall columns

Pyrénées

Basque Country

The most independently minded of the many lands that time has absorbed into France, the Basque Country straddles France and Spain. While the larger part of this nation is on Spanish land, the French Pays Basque consists of three provinces: Basse Navarre, Labourd and Soule. Fishing and farming occupied daily life here until the advent of tourism.

The modern world knows the Basque Country through terrorism. The militant Basque separatist group ETA announces periodic cease-fires from its constant campaign for independence, but violent political activity tends to center on the Spanish section of the land. Within France, aside from occasional marches, Basque culture is predominantly folkloric.

A traditional male Basque costume

Country dancing, sports, such as pelota (see page 126), and shops selling berets and rope-soled espadrille shoes – these are the picturesque elements of Basque life in southwest France.

The convoluted Euskara language dates back at least to the original tribes of eighth-century mountain men who fought Charlemagne's armies. Local legend claims it predates the Tower of Babel. Don't worry if you can't pick up the basics: The same tradition declares the devil himself managed to learn only three words. Although Euskara is spoken by many people in the Basque country, particularly in remoter places inland, everyone also speaks French.

Cuisine combines peppers, pimentos, tomatoes, garlic and onions. Mixed with eggs, these make *piperade*, similar to an omelet. Pepper and garlic sauces are traditional *à la basquaise* accompaniments to grilled tuna or chicken with kidneys. Ham from Bayonne is famous (see page 134). The local dessert is *gâteau Basque*, a lemon and cherry cake. In fishing ports such as St.-Jean-de-Luz, taste the savory monkfish-rich mariners' stew, *ttoro*.

St.-Jean-de-Luz is the prettiest resort in the Labourd coastal region. Once a key port for the Atlantic whaling industry, today St.-Jean provides a picturesque stopover for travelers driving along the coast toward Spain. Stroll the old town, with its echoes of piracy and royal romance. See the harborside house where Louis XIV spent the month before his marriage to the Spanish infanta Marie-Thérèse, and the ornate église St.-Jean-Baptiste, where they exchanged their vows.

Green hills, sandy beaches and neat red-and-white timbered villages – such as Sare, Ascain and Aïnhoa – line the coast. Inland look for *pottocks*, half-wild horses that roam the hills and are traded at the end of January during a colorful fair at the town of Espelette.

➕ A2

St.-Jean-de-Luz tourist information ✉ 20 boulevard Victor-Hugo ☎ 05 59 26 03 16; www.saint-jean-de-luz.com

Regional Sights

Andorra

The other principality, across the country from Monaco, boasts two princes, stunning scenery, the best skiing in the Pyrénées and some of the top shopping bargains to be found in western Europe.

Myths blur Andorra's history. A popular tale is that the original Gallic inhabitants fought Hannibal. The generally accepted view is that Charlemagne granted independence in the ninth century and that its princes have nominally governed the country since the 12th century. Princely honors are still shared between the French president and the Spanish bishop of Urgel. However, the result of a 1993 referendum handed real power to an autonomous assembly.

Measuring just 16 by 20 miles, Andorra is little more than a loop in the border between France and Spain, midway between Toulouse and Barcelona. Its official languages are French, Spanish and Catalan; the latter two are the most widely spoken. You are likely to hear English only at top hotels or in the crush of liquor, hi-fi and electronic stores that crowd the main streets of the capital, Andorra la Vella.

Since the principality isn't a member of the European Union and imposes no taxes, prices are on average 30 percent below those of the rest of the Continent. Trade all but dominates life in the capital, though the original old quarter, the Barri Antic, retains much of the charm of the original Pyrenean village. Among the whimsical stone houses lining cobbled streets is the 16th-century Casa de la Vall (House of the Valley), which has been the Parliament building since 1702. Recognize it by the arms of the principality over the door. The house contains Andorra's only courtroom on the first floor; the Parliament chamber, Sala del Consell, is upstairs.

Ski season runs from December to Easter, but many peaks are capped with snow well into the warm summer, when hiking becomes the main sporting activity. The goal for many visitors is the highest point, the magnificent 9,650-foot Pic de Coma Pedrosa on the Spanish border. Caldea at les Escaldes is a large, modern spa resort of baths fed by natural thermal springs.

Catalan cuisine, which reflects strong French and Spanish influences, dominates. Try *cunillo* (rabbit cooked in tomato sauce) or *escudella* (a stew of chicken, sausage and meatballs). Since Andorra has no international rail or air links, the only access is by road. From France, pass through the highest pass in the Pyrénées, the 7,900-foot Port d'Envalira.

✛ D1

Tourist information: Office du Tourisme de la Principauté d'Andorre ✉ 26 avenue de l'Opéra, 75001 Paris, France ☎ 01 42 61 50 55; www.andorre.fr
Tourist information ✉ Doctor Vilanova, 13 Edifici Davi, escalera B, 3º, AD500 Andorra la Vella

Soldeu is a popular skiing area in Andorra

Pyrénées

Facades of buildings in the old town of Bayonne

Bayonne

Capital of the French Basque Country (see page 132), Bayonne is the gastronomic highlight of the region. The town that gave the world the bayonet won fame through its pig farmers and chocolate makers – locally cured ham and chocolate, brought to France by Jews fleeing Spain, is on sale.

Rue Neuve has quaint tearooms and *confiseries*, where the local confectionery is best enjoyed as a mid-morning or mid-afternoon snack. Place de la Liberté is lively in the early evening.

Two sights for any itinerary are the impressive Cathédrale Ste.-Marie – with its 14th-century cloister, 16th-century stained glass and twin towers from the 19th century – and the Musée Bonnat, with works by Francisco José de Goya, Sandro Botticelli and Peter Paul Rubens. The museum is currently closed while undergoing renovations.

Learn more about the language and culture of the Basque people, not to mention berets, folklore and bayonets, at the Musée Basque (Basque Museum), which outlines the history of the town. Or learn about the manufacturing of chocolate at the Atelier de Chocolat.

⊕ A2

Tourist information ⊠ place des Basques, 64108 ☎ 08 20 42 64 64 (toll charge); www.bayonne-tourisme.com

Musée Basque ⊠ Maison Dragourette, 37 quai des Corsaires, 64100 ☎ 05 59 59 08 98; www.musee-basque.com 🕐 Daily 10–6:30 (Thu. 6:30–8:30 p.m.), Jul.–Aug.; Tue.–Sun. 10–6:30, Apr.–Jun. and Sep.; Tue.–Sun. 10:30–6, rest of year 🎫 $$ (free first Sun. of the month Sep.–Jun.)

Atelier du Chocolat ⊠ 7 allée de Gibeléou, 64100 ☎ 05 59 55 70 23; www.atelierduchocolat.fr 🕐 Mon.–Sat. 9:30–6:30, Jul.–Aug.; Mon.–Sat. 9:30–12:30 and 2–6, rest of year 🍴 Café 🎫 $$

Bétharram, Grottes de

Considered something of a sideshow to the more serious pilgrimage to Lourdes (see pages 137–138), 7 miles to the east, this slick underground excursion gets absolutely packed with tourists during the high season and the sheer noise can detract from the spirit of the occasion. However, a well-run transportation system keeps visitors flowing steadily through the attraction. More than 3 miles of stalactite- and stalagmite-packed chambers feature in a highly

The last rays of sun bathe the ramparts of the medieval Cité de Carcassonne at dusk

entertaining journey. The caves are reached by cable car, then passengers transfer to a boat and train to follow the course of the underground river and its phosphorous-coated stone figures.

The name *bét arram* means "beautiful branch," and the story is told of a young girl who slipped and fell in the nearby Gave de Pau. As she started to drown, a vision of the Virgin Mary threw her a branch and the girl was saved.

✚ B1

✉ Bétharram, 65270 St.-Pé-de-Bigorre

☎ 05 62 41 80 04; www.grottes-de-betharram.com

🕑 Daily 9–noon and 1:30–5:30, late Mar.–late Oct.; Mon.–Fri. 2:30–4, mid-Feb. to late Mar. 🍴 Café

💶 $$$

Carcassonne

Like an ornamental cake, Carcassonne is so much nicer on the outside than within. Views of the completely walled old town dominate the countryside,

seemingly promising a great deal. Unfortunately, the city is more than aware of the fact, and a barrage of Kodak signs, T-shirt racks and souvenir stands clogs a warren of winding lanes inside the walls.

Just to the southeast of the modern town, the old Cité stands 485 feet high and is marked by 2 miles of double walls fortified with 52 towers. Round and square towers from the 12th and 13th centuries appear in pristine condition. This is because in the 19th century – on the orders of *Carmen* author Prosper Merimée (then government inspector of ancient monuments) – architect Eugène Emmanuel Viollet-le-Duc renovated the entire edifice as a lasting reminder of the golden age of fortification.

Like most memories, this recreation is somewhat hazy on details, adding pretty pepper-pot roofs to some towers to please contemporary tastes. This

scrubbed image of medieval defenses inspired Hollywood to film actor Kevin Costner here in the blockbuster movie *Robin Hood, Prince of Thieves* (1991), with Carcassonne standing in for medieval Nottingham, England.

In the space between the twin walls, known as les Lices Hautes and Basses (the upper and lower lists), knights of old would practice jousting. Lively re-enactments of tournaments, sound-and-light shows, concerts and theatrical presentations are highlights of summer evenings, and the end of October finds locals from within the region celebrating the wine harvest at various locations inside the old stone walls.

The town is entered through two gateways: the Porte d'Aude by the river and twin-towered Porte Narbonnaise. Take a horse-drawn carriage (from April through September), or explore on foot. After visiting the tomb of Simon de Montfort (one of the fathers of parliamentary democracy), climb to the top of the ramparts, turn away from the tourist hordes and gaze out on vineyards producing *vin du pays d'Aude*.

Likewise, visitors will do better to stay in hotels outside the Cité to appreciate views of what Carcassonne might have been, rather than to wake up to the commercial reality.

Across the Aude river, the Ville Basse, modestly wealthy from the wine trade, offers a pleasant Fine Arts Museum, the Gothic Église St.-Vincent with its unfinished tower, and the 14th-century Cathédrale St.-Michel.

➕ D1
Tourist information ✉ 28 rue de Verdun, 11890 ☎ 04 68 10 24 30; www.carcassonne-tourisme.com
Château Comtal de la Cité de Carcassonne ✉ 11000 Carcassonne ☎ 04 68 11 70 70; www.carcassonne.monuments-nationaux.fr ⏰ Daily 10–6:30, Apr.–Sep. (last admission 45 minutes before closing); 10–5, rest of year ℹ Guided tours in English are available ($$) 💷 $$

Opposite: The shrine at Lourdes, one of the most-visited religious sites in the world

Castres

Castres owes its fortune to a heritage of textile manufacturing, and industry rings today's sprawling city. Its early wealth enabled the city fathers to commission the good and the great of the 17th century to design the public buildings. Thus the Hôtel de Ville has the stamp of the legendary architect Jules Hardouin-Mansart, who worked on the palace of Versailles (see page 52) and Paris' place Vendôme.

Mansart also is responsible for Castres' main attraction, the 1675 former Bishop's Palace (Evêché). This elegant building, on the edge of the old quarter, stands on grounds landscaped by royal favorite Le Nôtre. The palace is now the Musée Goya, with a small yet superb collection of paintings and drawings by Francisco José de Goya, as well as an impressive collection of other Spanish canvases. The striking cathedral also dates from the 17th century.

Castres is a useful base for touring the Midi-Pyrénées region and the Haut Languedoc Regional Park of which Sidobre forms a part. The Sidobre is known for its unusual granite boulders, the *roches-tremblantes* (shifting rocks), which actually sway gently when touched. A product of natural erosion, this movement is said to help psychics or sensitive souls predict the future.

➕ D2
Tourist information ✉ 2 place de la République, 81100 ☎ 05 63 62 63 62; www.tourisme-castres.fr
Musée Goya ✉ L'Evêché de Castres, 81100 ☎ 05 63 71 59 27 ⏰ Daily 10–6, Jul.–Aug.; Tue.–Sat. 9–12 and 2–6, Sun. 10–12 and 2–6, Apr.–Jun. and early–late Sep.; Tue.–Sat. 9–12 and 2–5, Sun. 10–12 and 2–5, rest of year 💷 $

Lourdes

The marvel of Lourdes – with its 4 million annual visitors, 300 hotels, three dozen campgrounds and efficient support system – is that despite the huge pilgrimage traffic, one may still find the spirit of Bernadette. The town of Lourdes, which graces both banks of the

Gave de Pau, is the summer residence of the bishop of Tarbes. Even now that the shrine has taken over the town, the overall elegant image remains one of a gracefully arched bridge and gleaming church spire set against green trees, snowcapped peaks and crystal clear blue skies.

On February 11, 1858, 14-year-old shepherdess Bernadette Soubirous (1844–79) had the first of 18 visions of the Virgin Mary at a nearby cave, the Grotte de Massabielle. Against her parents' wishes, Bernadette, frail and consumptive, returned time and again. Eventually Mary led Bernadette to a natural spring within the cave, which later was found to have healing qualities. Although Bernadette wasn't beatified until 1925 nor was she canonized until 1933, the pilgrimages began during her lifetime.

Nowadays, a nightly candlelit procession passes along the 550-yard Esplanade des Processions to the Esplanade du Rosaire for the blessing of the sick. Here is the basilica, reached by two curving ramps. Down below the church is the crypt and the cave itself, with its marble figure of Mary according to Bernadette's description. Open-air masses are held nearby. Below the esplanade is the remarkable Basilique souterraine St.-Pie X (underground Church of St. Pious X), which can accommodate 20,000 pilgrims at a time.

Look beyond the sea of retail candles, holy water and plastic icons to discover the true town. Lourdes clusters around its place Peyramale. See Bernadette's birthplace, the Moulin de Boly, at 2 rue Bernadette-Soubirous. Take the elevator 260 feet above the town to the fortress, parts of which date back to the 13th century. The château's Pyrenean Museum has folk costumes, and its terrace offers fine views of the mountains.

Lourdes pioneered disabled accessibility, with the pilgrimage route designed to welcome those with restricted mobility. Appropriate dress is expected around the grotto area.

✚ B1

Tourist information ✉ place Peyramale, 65100 ☎ 05 62 42 77 40; www.lourdes-infotourisme.com

Musée Pyrénéen ✉ Château Fort de Lourdes, 65100 ☎ 05 62 42 37 37; www.chateaufort-lourdes.fr 🕐 Daily 9–noon and 1:30–6:30, Apr.–Sep.; Sat.–Thu. 9–noon and 2–6, Fri. 9–noon and 2–5, rest of year 💶 $$

Luchon

Something of a Roman holiday resort, Luchon (or to give it its full name, les Bagnères-de-Luchon) was the fashionable mountain spa resort favored by Roman invaders. Even today, the place exudes elegance and sophisticated leisure. The thermal baths are still reached through a well-maintained park with statues of visitors past.

The local museum recalls the town's golden eras, with stories of such illustrious figures as mountaineer Count Henry Russell, who dynamited caves in the nearby mountains. Russell used one such artificial cavern near the top of the Vignemale for exclusive dinner parties. Naturally enough, Luchon boasts a casino to generate enough excitement and stress to guarantee a regular flow of customers to take to the calming, curative waters. A breathtaking drive from the valley climbs past waterfalls and mountain views, and leads to the winter resort of Superbagnères.

✚ C1

Tourist information ✉ 18 allées d'Étigny, 31110 ☎ 05 61 79 21 21; www.luchon.com

Niaux, Grotte de

Another well-preserved collection of cave paintings was discovered in 1906 in the Grotte de Niaux. Although copies of these 13,000-year-old images of bison are displayed nearby at Tarascon-sur-Ariège's Parc de l'Art Historique, the original works may be seen by torchlight. No free roaming is permitted, however; small, organized groups are escorted through the huge gaping mouth of the cave.

The Salon Noir has black painted animal scenes, among the best preserved in Europe. Experts are divided as to the significance of dots and splashes accompanying the illustrations. Many believe this to be a primitive form of alphabet although none of the symbols has yet been deciphered. Perhaps because access is so restricted and there are few of the usual trappings, this setting brings visitors closer than ever to individuals who lived and painted here so long ago. The floor of the cave has amazingly preserved the footprints of the original artists – dating to 11,000 BC.
✛ D1

Grotte de Niaux ✉ Tarascon-sur-Ariège ☎ 05 61 05 10 10; www.sesta.fr/grotte-de-niaux ◷ By reservation only: daily, Feb.–Dec.; Sat.–Sun., Jan. ✋ Tours by reservation only (most tours in French, however tours in English scheduled regularly) ✋ $$

St.-Jean-Pied-de-Port
St.-Jean-Pied-de-Port has welcomed travelers since the days before tourists.

A rallying point for pilgrims on the popular trail to Santiago de Compostela, the port isn't a harbor but a mountain pass, and the name recalls the pious travelers who once walked the route. Today, it's one of the prettiest Basque towns in France, with old stone walls and clay tiles set against the lush greenery of a textured horizon of hazy hills and the peak of Roncevaux. The original cobbled path of the pilgrims' way, from the Porte St.-Jean to the Porte d'Espagne, is a favorite with hikers. Over the years, the way has been fortified, most notably by Louis XIV's builder of citadels, Sébastien Le Prestre de Vauban. The ramparts hold the reinforced Notre-Dame du Pont, overlooking the Nive river itself. St.-Jean manages the balancing act of retaining both its individual charm and a healthy tourist industry, and its souvenir shops sell walking sticks and climbing gear as well.
✛ A1

Tourist information ✉ 14 place Charles-de-Gaulle, 64220 ☎ 05 59 37 03 57; www.saintjeanpiedeport-paybasque-tourisme.com

Flower-bedecked buildings line the banks of the river Nive at St.-Jean-Pied-de-Port

Pyrénées

Drive
The High
Pyrénées

Distance: 220 miles
Time: 3 to 4 days

Since parts of this route are impassable in winter, save this drive for the summer months, when the spectacular scenery, hairpin bends and picturesque mountain passes make for some of the more dramatic moments of the Tour de France (see page 17). This tour starts in Tarbes.

Home to a French song festival in late spring and a celebration of the humble bean in September, Tarbes spends its summer months basking in culture. The bandstand and open-air theater of the charming Jardin Massey provide a varied program of concerts. Within the park, peacocks strut and call outside the Musée Massey, with its cavalry exhibition and art galleries.

From Tarbes take the D935 to Bagnères-de-Bigorre.

The fashionable spa town of Bagnères-de-Bigorre was popular in the Roman era and again in the 19th century. You can take a white-water canoe ride along a stretch of the Adour river, which later goes underground and flows through the Grottes de Médous. Cave visits include escorted boat rides along the subterranean waterway.

Take the D938 toward Toulouse, turning right on the D26 and again on the D929 through Hèches. As soon as you see the sign for Rebouc over a railroad crossing, take a sharp left on the D26. Once at St.-Bertrand-de-Comminges, take a right uphill along the D26.

A medieval village of timbered houses, St.-Bertrand-de-Comminges owes its charm and name to the 12th-century bishop Bertrand de l'Isle. He inspired the restoration of the village after years of neglect and oversaw the building of the impressive cathedral where he is buried.

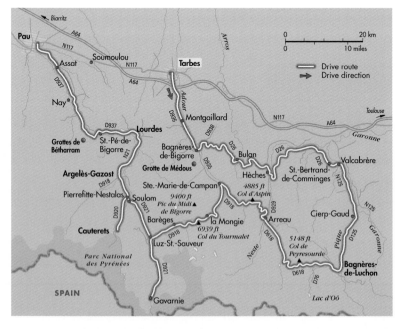

Continue along the D26 through Valcabrère. Turn right on the N125, following signs to les Bagnères-de-Luchon (see page 138.) From Luchon, the D618 goes west over the Col de Peyresourde. At Arreau, go right on the D929, then bear left opposite the gas station, climbing uphill on the winding D918 over the Col d'Aspin. At Ste.-Marie-de-Campan, turn left following the D918 toward the Col du Tourmalet.

Do check local weather reports for the Haute-Pyrénées region (toll call 08 92 68 10 20) to ensure the road is open. At 6,939 feet, the Tourmalet is the highest pass in the French Pyrénées – and views are spectacular. The highest museum of astronomy in Europe is the 100-year-old Pic du Midi Observatory at 9,439 feet. Take a cable car from La Mongie ski resort (on the way up to the Tourmalet) to the planetarium-style observatory, which affords views from Biarritz to the Monts du Cantal. Models, telescopes and special glasses help visitors discover the secrets of the skies, and exhibitions explain France's space program.

Continue straight after the summit through Barèges to Luz-St.-Sauveur.

A delightful spa town with a 14th-century fortified church, Luz-St.-Sauveur was established by the Knights of the Hospital of St. John at Jerusalem (or Knights Hospitallers), a military and religious order that offered travelers both spiritual and physical protection.

Take the D921 south to Gavarnie.

Gavarnie is to the Pyrénées what Chamonix is to the Alps. Its great natural treasure is the Cirque, an hour of challenging hiking or 20 minutes on horseback from Gavarnie. A glacial virtual amphitheater of rock with a sheer drop of 4,600 feet, the cliff face is awash with running water. The Grande Cascade plummets 1,450 feet to constitute one of Europe's longest falls. A statue of eccentric mountaineer Henry Russell can be seen in Gavarnie. His eyes are wistfully raised toward his beloved Vignemale mountain, which he climbed for the 33rd time at the age of 70. The mountain was presented to him as a gift.

Head back along the D921 past Luz-St.-Sauveur toward Lourdes, doubling back sharp left on leaving Soulom on the D920 to Cauterets.

Another spa town, Cauterets, houses an information center for the Pyrénées National Park. Use the town as a base for exploring as far as Pont d'Espagne and the Vignemale.

Back on the D920, turn left for Lourdes (see pages 137–138) on the D921-N21. Follow signs on the D937 for Grottes de Bétharram, passing through St.-Pé-de-Bigorre. Turn left and left again to reach the Grottes de Bétharram (see pages 134–135). The D937 leads to Pau.

Once capital of the Béarn region, Pau (pronounced "poe") was the hometown of one of France's favorite monarchs, Henri IV. Born a Protestant in 1553, he found his route to the capital barred when he came to take the throne, as the establishment insisted on a Roman Catholic king. He converted, with the immortal line, "Paris is well worth a Mass." His cradle, a turtle shell, is in the museum, a medieval château.

Grottes de Médous ✉ 60 route des Cols, 65200 Asté ☎ 05 62 91 78 46; www.grottes-medous.com ⏲ Daily 9–12 and 2–6, Jul.–Aug.; 9:30 a.m.–11:30 p.m. and 2–5, Apr.–Jun. and Sep. to mid-Oct.; by appointment only, rest of year 🍴 Café ♿ $$
Observatoire du Pic du Midi de Bigorre ☎ 08 25 00 28 77; www.picdumidi.com ⏲ Daily. Cable car ascents: 9–4:30, Jun.–Sep.; 10–3:30, rest of year 🍴 Café ♿ $$$ (includes cable car)
Cauterets tourist information ✉ place Foch, 65110 ☎ 05 62 92 50 50; www.cauterets.com
Pau tourist information ✉ place Royale, 64000 ☎ 05 59 27 27 08; www.pau-pyrenees.com
Musée National du Château de Pau ✉ rue du Château, 64000 Pau ☎ 05 59 82 38 00; www.musee-chateau-pau.fr ⏲ Daily 9:30–12:30 and 1:30–6:45, mid-Jun. to mid-Sep.; 9:30–11:45 and 2–5, rest of year ℹ Visit by guided tour only. Tours every 15 minutes ♿ $$; gardens free

Provence and the Côte d'Azur

Opposite: Menerbes village was the setting of Peter Mayle's book *A Year in Provence*

Provence and the Côte d'Azur

The French know the far south of France as the Midi. When you pass through the town of Valence on the long drive or fast rail journey south, something happens. The unmistakable air of the south overtakes the inconstancy of northern Europe. Even more than 100 miles from the Mediterranean, the area is warmer, drier, slower and of another age and culture.

Landscape

The region of Provence covers most of the ground, but Languedoc-Roussillon, with its Roman settlements and rugged scrubland, gives its own style to the countryside and coast west of Marseille.

The postcard image of Provence may be gentle, sun-kissed landscapes of olive groves and lavender fields, but the region has harsh mountainous terrain, dramatic gorges and some merciless winds – including the mistral, which whistles along the Rhône Valley to the coast, scattering roof tiles in its wake from late summer onward.

Vineyards – from the fine Châteauneuf du Pape and Côtes du Rhône, to the stronger country vines that thrive along rare strips of flat land in rocky valleys around Narbonne – mark the countryside. On slopes, chestnut trees are kept for candied chestnuts and hundred-year-old olive groves for the oil. Rice is harvested in the Camargue wetlands, and farms grow melons, peaches and strawberries.

The People

Locals tend to be laconic. Conversation is not courted, and curt answers to questions should not be taken as a sign of rudeness. There is a notorious wariness of outsiders moving permanently into their towns and villages – anyone living 10 miles away is considered a foreigner – but visitors are assured a genuine welcome.

All caricatures of the Latin temperament have been applied to the folk of Provence: fiery jealousy and lazy procrastination. This makes for entertaining films and good reading, from the stories of Marcel Pagnol (see page 147) to Peter Mayle's *A Year In Provence* (1991). The truth is the people here guard their family and village histories and ways of life. That very resistance to change makes the region so attractive.

Provence has always been a summer retreat for Parisians. The major festivals in July and August bring the cultural establishment to the region when the capital closes down. Since the first high-speed train links brought the region within hours of Paris, main cities

are far more open to year-round visitors. The area's rich heritage of arenas, temples and theaters from the Roman occupation of Gaul are the main attraction However, a turbulent history of dukedoms, principalities and long-forgotten monarchies has left a rich and varied architectural legacy, with buildings that range from Italianate to Gothic to Moorish.

Languages

The distinctive Provençal accent itself is hard for many French people to understand (*vin* sounds like "ving," for example), and individual towns and districts have their own dialects and argots. The Catalan community near the Spanish border is essentially bilingual. Nice's original Italian argot is not widely spoken. The old langue d'oc that gives the southwestern region its name is still taught in local schools. In Marseille, the old Provençal language

is undergoing something of a revival, being used in tourism brochures and websites, and taken up by young musicians and a café subculture. Many street signs are now bilingual.

Sport

When afternoon shadows are long, older men take to the dusty squares to play boules or *pétanque* (slang for "feet together"), a traditional bowling game in which each player has two, three or four steel balls (depending on the number of players) to roll toward a small wooden aim ball, called a *cochonnet* (little piggy). The closest ball wins. Notices in cafés and bars announce serious tournaments.

If watching from a bar, remember the local aperitif is *pastis*, a liqueur flavored with licorice and aniseed, taken with a carafe of water. If picnicking, inexpensive country wines can be bought from the local cooperative.

A yacht anchored off the coast where the Massif de l'Estérel plunges into the sea, near Cannes

Lagoons

To understand what the Riviera was like before fashion reinvented it, go west from the Camargue (see page 156) to the Spanish border and lose yourself in the beautiful rugged coast of Languedoc. Vast lagoons (*étangs*) separate the shore from the hinterland where vineyards grow rich *corbières* and *banyuls* wines. Cathar fortresses top precipitous peaks and the Canal du Midi wends through the lowlands. Molière's home town of Pézenas, the stunning coastal lookout town of Agde and many quaint fishing villages guard the past, while modern resorts such as Leucate and Palavas sprout vacation lodgings and villas. The African game reserve at Sigean, the Cistercian abbey of Fontefroide and the cities of Narbonne and Beziers serve sensation seekers, but the unspoiled land and the lagoons seduce the soul.

Pagnol

The cinema's love affair with the light, landscape and people of Provence is probably best seen in more than a dozen recreations of the tales of author and filmmaker Marcel Pagnol (1895–1974). His *Jean de Florette* (1986) and *Manon des sources* (1986), a two-part story starring Yves Montand and Gérard Depardieu, is the most famous. The town of le Castellet features in several movies. Aubagne is home to Le Petit Monde de Marcel Pagnol museum – featuring *santons* (see below) of his characters and stories. The tourist office in cours Barthélémy offers a walking tour that incorporates Manon's fountain and Pagnol's grave.

Christmas

Christmas in Provence is a wonderful occasion. The Christmas Eve meal (*gros souper*) has 13 traditional desserts. Nativity scenes are re-enacted on December 24 and local people come in costume for the midnight Mass. Every town, village and family has a crèche, a model stable with characters of Jesus, Mary and Joseph. These figurines are sold at the *santon* markets. *Santons* (models of saints) have been made here for more than 300 years. Crafters' workshops in Aubagne are open year-round, and Christmas markets in most towns and cities take place from late November until early January.

Capital of Culture 2013

Marseille-Provence – incorporating the towns of Aix-en-Provence (see pages 149–152), Arles (see page 153), Aubagne, Gardenne, Istres, la Ciotat, Martigues, Salon de Provence and the city of Marseille (see pages 160–161) – has been chosen by the E.U. as European Capital of Culture for 2013. This year-long celebration means a packed program of festivals, arts exhibitions and live performances. Reserve hotels extra early. Details at www.mp2013.fr.

Stars of the Med

The bulk of the coastline is famous as the French Riviera. Intellectuals claim that true magic left when the film stars arrived, and the Cannes Film Festival is blamed as the beginning of the end. Hollywood movie moguls and starlets came first in 1947, treading the bulb-popping steps of hyperbole, spoon-feeding glamor to the press and crushing the soul of the Côte d'Azur, they say.

Baloney, of course. Brash Cannes (see pages 156–157) never had a sensitive soul. Never let anyone tell you Cannes was a lady. She has a certain style, but remember the twin cupolas on the celebrated Carlton Hotel were modeled on the breasts of a well-known courtesan. Here, a supermarket check-out boy can earn more in one week fluttering his lashes as gigolo to the stars than he does the rest of the year blinking bar codes.

No one comes from the Riviera. Rather, it's a place to which people go. Graham Greene and Noël Coward came, stayed and gossiped in print here. Henri Matisse discovered the azure blues that he painted into legend. And the rich and famous played, hid behind high walls and swam in the sea off the Cap Ferrat (see pages 157–158).

Then Cannes created Woman. Led by Brigitte Bardot (star of the 1956 film *And God Created Woman*), who eventually

---

Discount Pass

The French Riviera Pass, valid for three or seven days, gives visitors access to museums, monuments and gardens on the Riviera, as well as free rides on the Nice Le Grand Tour panoramic bus. It is on sale in participating museums and monuments, tourist offices and FNAC stores.

Office de Tourisme et des Congrès

✉ BP 4070 Promenade des Anglais, Nice, 06302

☎ 08 92 70 74 07; www.frenchrivierapass.com

fled to the very public obscurity of St.-Tropez with only her cars, dogs, donkeys and a troupe of paparazzi for company, females were paraded on the front page of the *Croisette* newspaper.

Nowadays, the Riviera is a haven for the nipped, tucked and liposucked – in summer months, when the roads are bumper to bumper with traffic, this paradise becomes a hell for those not blessed with a private villa. Yet, during the off-season, the Azur Coast is where deities take their sabbatical. Land at the whisper-thin airstrip on the beach; take the train past the ocher cliffs of St.-Raphaël (see page 173), which reflect a never-ending sunset; and breathe the heady perfume that is the secret soul of the late summer sun: citrus blossom, pine, violet and lavender. Sniff the air, the fruit and the mimosa in the breath of

> ### Survival Tip
> Hedonists should be aware that unlike Cap d'Agde, where naturists are welcome in specialty supermarkets and banks, flesh isn't served on all streets of the Riviera. It is illegal to walk through the town of St.-Raphaël unless the upper and lower body is properly covered, and in Ste.-Maxime, bikini-clad sunbathers who stray from the beach may be fined.

a New Year and see the dancing sea clean and bright. Take to the hills, and wine and dine in one of the cliff top perched villages. A world away from film festivals, overguarded royals, fast-buck merchants and hangers-on, in springtime or fall you will discover the true soul of the South.

Stone carvings on the columns of the cloister in Abbaye de Montmajour, Provence

Aix-en-Provence

The city of fountains was, until 1790, capital of Provence, and parliamentary and judicial history feeds what is still a cultural, artistic and social hub.

Its early fame came from thermal springs. In the 12th century, it was chosen as a civilized oasis in a rugged landscape to be the seat of the counts of Provence. The last of the line to live in the city was Good King René (1409–80), duke of Anjou, Lorraine and Bar and king of Naples. He completed the cathedral and was a patron of the arts. When Provence became part of France in 1486, its cultural life continued.

Known as the city of the waters, Aix-en-Provence bore the Latin name Aquae Sextiae. The streets of Aix are

> ### Eggs and Aches
> Although the French word Aix is pronounced midway between the English words "eggs" and "aches," locals pronounce the city as "Ais." The local candy of choice is *calissons*, a confection that is made with almonds and fruits.

studded with nearly 100 fountains, refreshing in the hot summer sunshine.

In the 17th century, under the guidance of Cardinal Jules Mazarin, the city was expanded. Medieval ramparts were torn down and cours Mirabeau was created in their place (see page 151), which neatly divides Aix between the old town to the north, with its cathedral and market squares where residents

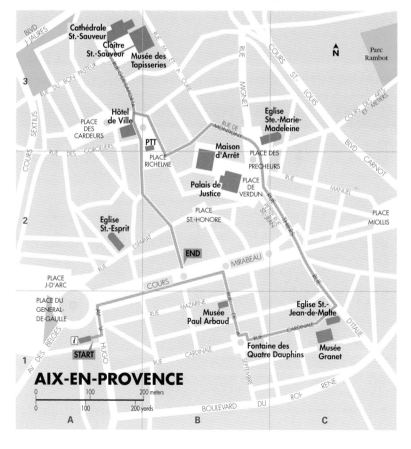

come to sit under parasols, and the elegant residential quartier Mazarin below, with elegant town houses and mansions of the good and the great.

City of Artists

A fine university town since 1413, Aix has never been allowed to stagnate. The annual Lyric Art Festival showcases the finest young operatic talent in the world. Émile Zola (1840–1902) spent his youth here, and the Sainte-Victoire mountain that looms above the city inspired the great Impressionist painter Paul Cézanne (1839–1906), who reproduced the mountain in more than 60 of his paintings.

Aix has held on to many of the artist's greatest works, and the city is liberally sprinkled with reminders of the time he spent here. Using commemorative bronze plaques in the sidewalk as a guide, you can stroll through the streets to follow the Cézanne trail. The culmination of the tour is 9 avenue Paul-Cézanne, the

A marker on the Cézanne trail

artist's garden and studio, L'Atelier des Lauves, built in 1901 and where he spent the final years of his life. Everything is kept exactly as he left it: his old black hat, paints, still-life props and unfinished canvases.

Essential Information

Tourist Information

✉ les allées Provençales, 300 avenue Giuseppe-Verdi, 13100 ☎ 04 42 16 11 61; www.aixenprovencetourism.com 🕐 Guided tours (in English) Wed. and Sat. 10 a.m., Apr.–Oct.; Sat. 10 a.m., rest of year

Urban Transportation

Bus services link central Aix-en-Provence with outlying towns. The bus station *(gare routière)* is at avenue de l'Europe ☎ 08 21 20 22 03 (toll call). In the city center, all sights can easily be reached on foot. Taxis can be hailed at stands, in the streets or by calling ☎ 04 42 27 71 11; www.taxisradioaixois.com.

Airport Information

The nearest airport is Aéroport Marseille-Provence ☎ 04 42 14 14 14; www.marseille. aeroport.fr. Shuttle buses leave the airport every 30 minutes for Aix; journey time is 30 minutes. Regional, national and international rail services are available from Aix-en-Provence Gare SNCF ☎ 36 35; www.sncf.fr.

Climate – average highs and lows for the month

Jan.	Feb.	Mar.	Apr.	May	Jun.	Jul.	Aug.	Sep.	Oct.	Nov.	Dec.
2°C	3°C	9°C	14°C	19°C	22°C	25°C	24°C	20°C	14°C	7°C	4°C
36°F	37°F	48°F	57°F	66°F	72°F	77°F	75°F	68°F	57°F	45°F	39°F
-3°C	-2°C	2°C	5°C	9°C	13°C	15°C	15°C	12°C	6°C	2°C	-1°C
27°F	28°F	36°F	41°F	48°F	55°F	59°F	59°F	54°F	43°F	36°F	30°F

Aix-en-Provence Sights

Key to symbols
➕ map coordinates refer to the Aix-en-Provence
map on page 149 💲 admission charge:
$$$ more than €10, $$ €5–€10, $ less than €5
See page 5 for complete key to symbols

Cathédrale St.-Sauveur

An architectural history lesson in its
own right, the cathedral has a fifth-
century baptistery, an 18th-century
octagonal cupola supported by eight
columns from a Roman temple of
Apollo, a Romanesque doorway from
the 12th century, a 15th-century
belfry and an extravagant Gothic facade
dating from the 16th century. In the
nave is the 1475 *Buisson Ardent*, a
triptych by Nicolas Froment that
combines the Old Testament burning
bush of Moses with an image of the
Madonna and Child. The tranquil
cloisters are built on the site of the
original Roman forum. The Archbishop's
Palace is now home to a museum of
tapestry and its courtyard is transformed
into a theater each summer for the
Festival d'Aix (see page 154), which
draws people from all over France.
➕ A3 ✉ 34 place des Martyrs-de-la-Résistance,
13100 ☎ 04 42 23 45 65; www.cathedrale-aix.net
Musée des Tapisseries ✉ 28 place des Martyrs-de-la-
Résistance, 13100 ☎ 04 42 23 09 91 🕐 Wed.–Mon.
10–6, mid-Apr. to mid-Oct.; 1:30–5, rest of year 💲 $

Cours Mirabeau

A promenade in every sense of the word
since 1651, cours Mirabeau is more than
a street – it's an occasion. From late
afternoon until well into the small
hours, the very European phenomenon
of *passeggiata* takes place, in which
people dress in their best clothes and
walk up and down the sidewalk to see
and be seen. After midnight, the peacock
parade is augmented by young motorists
in open-top cars cruising slowly in front
of café tables in Aix's peculiar blend of
fashion show and mating ritual. During
the day, old men relax on benches, and
far from impoverished would-be artists
hold animated discussions in the Café
des Deux Garçons. At festival time,
people dine here very early or very late.
The posing takes place on the north
sidewalk, and narrow alleyways lead up
to the old town.
➕ B2

Musée Granet

One room containing eight paintings by
Paul Cézanne – including his *Nude at the
Mirror* and the famous *Bathers*, all
belatedly donated by the state to his
hometown in the 1980s – is the main
lure of Aix-en-Provence's main museum
and gallery. A pleasant collection of
18th- and 19th-century art from France,
Flanders and Italy, including works by
Peter Paul Rubens and Rembrandt,
Giacometti, Picasso, Léger, de Staël and
Klee that mostly were collected by local
painter François Granet (1775–1849), is
overshadowed by archeological finds
displayed in the basement. Of note are
statues and masks from the settlement
known as Oppidum d'Entremont, which
existed here before the Roman
occupation of the area, as well as Roman
remains from Aquae Sextiae.
➕ C1 ✉ place St.-Jean-de-Malte, 13100 ☎ 04 42 52
88 32; www.museegranet-aixenprovence.fr
🕐 Tue.–Sun. 11–7, Jun.–Sep.; noon–6, rest of year
💲 $ (temporary exhibitions $$)

Decorative ironwork on a balcony in cours Mirabeau

Experience the colors and aromas of the farmers' market in place Richelme

Walk

Fountains and Markets

Refer to route marked on city map on page 149

Begin this 2.5-mile walk at the tourist office on place du Général-de-Gaulle, at the foot of the fountain built in 1860.

Walk along the right side of cours Mirabeau (see page 151) and turn right onto rue du 4-Septembre, with its collection of fine earthenware, statuary and rare books in the Musée Paul-Arbaud.

In front is the beautiful 1667 Fontaine des Quatre Dauphins by Jean-Claude Rambot. A left on rue Cardinale leads to the Musée Granet (see page 151). Next door is the 13th-century Église St.-Jean-de-Malte.

Turning left on rue d'Italie, return toward cours Mirabeau.

A fountain dedicated to the city's patron, Good King René, stands in the middle of cours Mirabeau. Across the boulevard, a sign at No. 55 announces the site of the Chapellerie du cours-Mirabeau,

Cézanne's father's hat shop, where young Paul spent much of his childhood. A narrow passageway that runs beside the present-day shop here leads to place de Verdun, where the morning flea market in front of the 18th-century Palais de Justice spills across to the edge of place Richelme. A flower market blooms at place des Precheurs every morning. Succumb to the aromatic lures of lavender, thyme, rosemary and mint. Salt cod, olive oil and Provençal herbs are the essential flavors of Aix. Climb steps to see the Peter Paul Rubens piece and other artwork displayed in the Église Ste.-Marie-Madeleine.

Take rue de Montigny opposite, then turn left through narrow streets and go into place Richelme, where you can explore the daily farmers' market.

Behind the old corn market, now a post office, is the Italian-style 17th-century Hôtel de Ville, with its splendid 16th-century clock tower that announces the seasons as well as the time.

Follow rue Gaston de Saporta to the Cloître St.-Sauveur, where occasionally chamber concerts are staged, and the cathedral (see page 151). Retrace your steps to place Richelme and filter through the little alleyways back to cours Mirabeau.

Regional Sights

Key to symbols

✚ map coordinates refer to the map on pages
144–145 🏛 admission charge: $$$ more
than €10, $$ €5–€10, $ less than €5
See page 5 for complete key to symbols

Arles

On the banks of the Rhône sits the
Roman capital of Provence. Plenty of
reminders of the days of imperial
occupation remain, most notably the
remnants of the old theater and the vast
Arènes, the largest amphitheater in the
country at almost 450 feet in length and
with a capacity of 20,000 gladiator-
cheering visitors. Although the top tiers
of marbled galleries are long gone, the
stadium today hosts bullfights. Another
ancient place of entertainment was the
Cirque Romain, where chariot races
once were held.

Now a base for archeological research,
the site holds the Musée Départemental
de l'Arles Antique, which tells the story
of the town from the Romans to the
Christian era.

On the edge of the Roman settlement
is Les Alyscamps, which like its Parisian
namesake, Champs-Élysées, is a
tree-lined avenue. Unlike the more
famous bustling thoroughfare in Paris,
the quiet street is bordered with
moss-covered stone coffins. This city of
the departed once boasted 19 temples
and thousands of great tombs. So
prestigious was the cemetery that bodies
would be floated down the river with
gold in their mouths to pay the
grave-diggers of Arles.

The artist Vincent van Gogh is forever
linked with the town, as it was here that
he cut off his own ear. The hospital and
gardens where he recovered are now the
Espace van Gogh. The courtyard, laid
out as it was in the artist's day, is free
to visit.

✚ C2

Tourist information ✉ boulevard des Lices, 13200
☎ 04 90 18 41 20; www.arles.org

Arènes ✉ rond point-des-Arènes, 13200 ☎ 04 90 49
36 74 🕐 Daily 9–7, May–Sep.; 9–6, Mar.–Apr. and
Oct.; 10–5, rest of year 🏛 $$

Musée Départemental de l'Arles Antique ✉ Presq'île
du Cirque-Romain, 13200 ☎ 04 13 31 51 30
🕐 Wed.–Mon. 10–6 🏛 $$

Les Alyscamps ✉ avenue des Alyscamps, 13200
☎ 04 90 49 36 74 🕐 Daily 9–7, May–Sep.; 9–noon
and 2–6, Mar.–Apr. and Oct.; 10–noon and 2–5, rest of
year 🏛 $

Espace van Gogh ✉ place du Docteur-Felix-Rey,
13200 ☎ 04 90 49 37 53 🕐 Open access 🏛 Free

Les Alyscamps offers welcome shade from the hot Provençal summer sun

Avignon Festival

Don't blame the sunshine, the heat or the last pastis on the café terrace. That really was a star of *Jean de Florette* (Golden Globe-nominated French movie) addressing a TV camera in the hotel lobby. Believe the improbable: Avignon is en *fête*. In July, the world of arts and entertainment has a Provençal postal code. The reason for this is the Avignon Festival, now more than 60 years old, with 50 official productions and fringe events.

The old papal city bursts at its fortified seams with a glorious crush of talent and revelers. Every espresso at a sidewalk table is accompanied by eager performers promoting one-man versions of Voltaire. So fascinating is the eavesdropping in restaurants that people nibble olives and forget to peruse the menu. Shady trees lining dusty, breezy streets are dressed in handbills, posters and enticements to sample something new and daring.

All the arts have their moment in the spotlight. Nonetheless, the heart of the festival is quality drama. The top names in French theater and cinema appear in new productions of the classics, and the most successful transfer to Paris for the fall. Legendary productions of William Shakespeare may grab the headlines, but search the listings to find works by Eugene O'Neil, Tennessee Williams and Henry James, given a European twist.

Everything will be previewed and reviewed, and all Paris papers and TV shows move to Avignon for the festival. Hotel bars and restaurants are called into service as makeshift studios, with arc lamps and movie stars as commonplace as mini-bars and chambermaids.

Intoxicating stuff, but for a respite visit the two neighboring opera festivals. At Orange, pageant-scale productions of *Carmen, Aida* or *Tosca* are staged in the Roman theater in a season known as the Chorégies. The Festival d'Aix, begun in 1948, is famous for discovering the great divas of the future, the strains of works by George Frederic Handel and Wolfgang Amadeus Mozart ringing out from a specially constructed playhouse within the courtyard of the Archbishop's Palace.

Street performers play with fire in front of the Palais des Papes

Avignon

Visitors knowing the song *"Sur le pont d'Avignon"* may feel shortchanged on first viewing the famous 13th-century Pont St.-Bénézet, with its tiny Chapelle St.-Nicolas. A fraction of the bridge remains, and just four of the original 22 arches stand lamely in the waters, with the rest destroyed by floods in the 17th century. Despite the lyrics "on the bridge of Avignon," locals traditionally danced under the bridge on the riverbanks.

Step inside the walled city to discover a wealth of architectural treasures. Known as the City of the Popes since Pope Clement moved his court here from the Vatican in 1309, Avignon developed as the church's center of power. Even when the papacy returned to Rome in 1377, a breakaway group continued to follow rival papal authority for four decades in what became known as the Great Schism. Walk around the ramparts to experience the intimacy and power of the old city, and look out on the sprawling suburbs across the river.

The essential visit is a tour of the Palais des Papes, actually a complex of two palaces: the old palace of 1334 – austere and monastic, a place of prayer – and the newer grander chambers of 1348, reflecting the power of a wealthy church and patron of the arts. Although much of the ornate decoration has been lost, the Stag Room frescoes are worth seeing. To see medieval artwork and Italian paintings from the 13th through 16th centuries, visit the Petit Palais, former residence of bishops of Avignon and a museum since 1958.

More recent works are displayed at the Musée Anglandon. The collection has works from Impressionists to Pablo Picasso and includes one of the few Vincent van Gogh paintings that remain in Provence.

Throughout the year, especially during festival time (see opposite), you can enjoy watching the world go by from a table on place de l'Horloge.

➕ C2

Tourist information ✉ 41 cours Jean-Jaurès, 84000 ☎ 04 32 74 32 74; www.ot-avignon.fr or www.avignon-tourisme.com

Palais des Papes ✉ 6 rue Pente-Rapide, 84000 ☎ 04 90 27 50 50; www.palais-des-papes.com 🕐 Daily 9–9, Aug.; 9–8, Jul. and early to mid-Sep.; 9–7, late Sep. to 1 Nov. and mid-Mar. to end Jun.; 9–6:30, early to mid-Mar.; 9:30–5:45, rest of year. Last admission one hour before closing 💶 $$$; combined ticket available with the Pont St.-Bénézet

Musée du Petit Palais ✉ place du Palais-des-Papes, 84000 ☎ 04 90 86 44 58; www.petit-palais.org 🕐 Wed.–Sun. 1–5:30 💶 $$

Musée Anglandon ✉ 5 rue Laboureur ☎ 04 90 82 29 03; www.angladon.com 🕐 Tue.–Sun. 1–6, Jul.–Aug.; Wed.–Sun. 1–6, rest of year 💶 $$

Pont St.-Bénézet ✉ rue Ferruce ☎ 04 90 27 51 16 🕐 Daily 9–9, Aug.; 9–8, Jul. and early to mid-Sep.; 9–7, late Sep.–1 Nov. and mid-Mar. to end Jun.; 9–6:30, early to mid-Mar; 9:30–5:45, rest of year 💶 $

Biot

Biot is to Provence what Murano is to Venice. But even without the glass workshops, the pretty arcaded main square, the window boxes ablaze with geraniums and steep cobbled streets in the orange-roofed village, perched high above Antibes-Juan-les-Pins, would merit a detour. Biot has long been home to potters and silversmiths who for centuries have created charming jars and bowls. Since the 1950s, it has been a center of glass-blowing, and the glass workshop is a popular attraction. Biot glassware is sold in countless small galleries. The craft was pioneered by Cubist Fernand Léger, whose own museum of glass and ceramics, the Musée National Fernand-Léger, is at the edge of the village.

Outside the museum is Léger's bright mosaic designed for the Hanover Olympic Stadium. At the southern side of place des Arcades, a doorway leads to the village church containing 16th-century altarpieces.

➕ E2

Tourist information ✉ 46 rue St.-Sébastien, 06410 ☎ 04 93 65 78 00; www.biot.fr

Musée National Fernand-Léger ✉ chemin de-Val-de-Pome, 06410 ☎ 04 92 91 50 20; www. musee-fernandleger.fr ⊙ Wed.–Mon. 10–6, Jun.–Oct.; 10–5, rest of year 🍴 Café (Apr.–Oct. only) 💲 $$

Cagnes-sur-Mer

Pretty painted fishing boats, known as *pointus*, bob in the harbor and terra-cotta roofs top whitewashed buildings. This looks like a typical busy coastal town, like so many others. But climb the hill to Haut-de-Cagnes to find the real charm of the medieval fortified village, with a 14th-century castle built by the Grimaldis as a lookout for pirate ships.

Nicely gentrified with earthenware pots on sunny windowsills and bougainvillea-dappled shadows, the walk is a leisurely diversion after lunch at a fish restaurant in the port. Attractions in the château include the Olive Tree Museum and an art gallery boasting pieces by Marc Chagall, Henri Matisse and Pierre-Auguste Renoir, who came here when he was struck by rheumatoid arthritis. Renoir's villa, in ancient olive groves outside town, preserves his studio and art collection.
➕ E2

Tourist information ✉ 99 promenade de la Plage, 06800 ☎ 04 93 07 67 08; www.cagnes-tourisme.com
Grimaldi Château-Musée ✉ 7 place Grimaldi, Haut-de-Cagnes, 06800 ☎ 04 92 02 47 30 ⊙ Wed.–Mon. 10–noon and 2–6, mid-Jun. to mid-Sep.; 10–noon and 2–5, rest of year. Closed one week in early Nov. 💲 $
Musée Renoir ✉ 19 chemin des Collettes, 06800 ☎ 04 93 20 61 07 ⊙ Wed.–Mon. 10–noon and 2–6, May–Oct.; 10–noon and 2–5, rest of year. Closed for renovation until summer 2013 💲 $

Camargue

White horses run free here through the waters, pink flamingoes flaunt their plumage in the lagoons, and beautiful sunsets color the horizon. The Camargue is a spectacular nature reserve that spreads across the Rhône delta. The waterways, salt marshes and coastline are home to more than 400 species of birds and half-wild sheep,

black bulls and horses, all managed by local cowboys known as *gardians*. The *gardians* work the ranches (*manades*), where visitors can enjoy riding vacations.

Local legend has it that the fishing village of les Stes.-Maries-de-la-Mer is where Maria Jacobé and Maria Salomé, half sisters of the Virgin Mary, arrived with their black serving maid Sarah, patron saint of gypsies. Their graves are marked by the Église Notre-Dame-de-la-Mer. Every year for two days around May 25, gypsies from all over Europe make their pilgrimage here. In colorful traditional costumes, gypsies and *gardians* carry statues of Ste.-Sarah and the Marias into the sea for a blessing, then into the night, the revelers celebrate with rodeos, flamenco dancing, bullfights and fireworks.
➕ C2

Tourist information ✉ 5 avenue Van-Gogh, Stes.-Maries-de-la-Mer, 13460 ☎ 04 90 97 82 55; www.saintesmaries.com
Parc Ornithologique de Pont de Gau ✉ route d'Arles, Stes.-Maries-de-la-Mer, 13460 ☎ 04 90 97 82 62; www.parcornithologique.com ⊙ Daily 9–sunset, Apr.–Sep.; 10–sunset, rest of year 💲 $$

Cannes

Cannes exists only for pleasure. What other town would have two branches of the same jeweler on opposite sides of the street to save clients the trouble of crossing a road? The city is famous for its May International Film Festival (see page 147), where big-screen icons, such as Brigitte Bardot and Angelina Jolie, have dutifully stopped traffic to pander to paparazzi. The parade of starlets along the main thoroughfare, boulevard de la Croisette, launches the vacation season. The only free beach is the area in front of the concrete Palais des Festivals et des Congrès; the rest of the sand is divided into private strips reserved for guests staying at the seafront hotels – with the famous Carlton InterContinental probably the best known symbol of the town.

Luxury villas nestle among the verdant vegetation of Cap Ferrat

To escape high prices, shop either in the backstreets around rue Maynadier or take a boat trip to the Îles de Lérins. The larger island, Ste.-Marguerite, has a fortress said to have held the Man in the Iron Mask. The smaller, St.-Honorat, is a tranquil haven where Cistercian monks make liqueurs and honey, and where visitors forget that Cannes is just 30 minutes away.

✚ E2

Tourist information ✉ Palais des Festivals et des Congrès, La Croisette, 06400 ☎ 04 92 99 84 22; www.cannes.travel

Ferries to Îles de Lérins ✉ Compagnie Planaria, Promenade Pantiero, 06400 ☎ 04 92 98 71 38; www.cannes-ilesdelerins.com 🕐 Timetables vary seasonally (15 minutes to Ste.-Marguerite, 25 minutes to St.-Honorat)

Cap Ferrat
Formerly home to the Duke and Duchess of Windsor, David Niven, Charlie Chaplin and others who could afford absolute privacy, the villas of Cap Ferrat are all hidden from view by lush greenery. The casual visitor can do little more than gaze at treetops and imagine the splendors that exist behind imposing gateways. Fortunately, one of the finest estates is open to the public.

The remarkable Villa Ephrussi, an exquisite pink belle-époque palace, was commissioned by Beatrice, Baroness Ephrussi de Rothschild, of the great banking family. With the sea on three sides and nestling among recreations of the great gardens of the world, the Italian-style villa houses the Rothschild collection of art and porcelain. Visitors must be escorted through the house but can wander the grounds on their own. If you aren't fortunate enough to be invited to a house party, then wine and dine in the former fishing village of St.-Jean-Cap-Ferrat.

✚ E2

Tourist information ✉ 59 avenue Denis-Séméria, St.-Jean-Cap-Ferrat, 06230 ☎ 04 93 76 08 90; www.saintjeancapferrat.fr

Villa et Jardins Ephrussi de Rothschild ✉ 1 avenue Ephrussi de Rothschild, St.-Jean-Cap-Ferrat, 06230

☎ 04 93 01 33 09; www.villa-ephrussi.com 🕐 Daily 10–7, Jul.–Aug.; 10–6, Feb.–Jun. and Sep. to early Nov.; Mon.–Fri. 2–6, Sat.–Sun. 10–6, rest of year
💰 $$$

Corsica

Known as the birthplace of Napoléon, this rugged individual island is no stranger to conquest. Invaded by just about everyone who ventured into the Mediterranean in Classical times – Phoenicians, Greeks, Etruscans, Carthaginians and Romans – Corsica has been taken and influenced since then by barbarian, Byzantine, Saracen, Italian, Spanish, German and even English conquerors. French since 1768 and a region of the country in its own right since 1970, Corsica boasts many listed parks on land and at sea and has a distinct identity. On the south and west coasts is a succession of wild rocky coves, fine sandy beaches and white chalky cliffs. Less rugged are the eastern shores, strewn with pools and long beaches. Inland are fast-flowing streams and waterfalls. The fragrant heather and myrtle that grow here led Napoléon to declare he could sense Corsica before her shores came into view.

The strongest image is of vivid bright colors: reds and blacks of penitants' Good Friday parades, when the Easter sunshine of Holy Week lights a million colorful fires on Cargèse's whitewashed walls; and ocher Genoese fortifications and watchtowers that contrast with the shimmering slate rooftops of Cap Corse. And then there are the flecks of granite, vast red rocks, white cliff faces and lush, rich greens, which are framed as ever by a silver and blue horizon. It is no wonder the Greeks called the island Kalliste – the most beautiful one.

The tourist office suggests good drives, depending on the season. Winter snow creates cross-country ski resorts from December to April and hikers could spend 15 grueling days on the best-known mountain hiking path, the GR20. Known locally as Fra I Monti, the path links Calenzana and Porto-Vecchio. Year-round sporting attractions include hang gliding, horseback riding and white-water rafting. Others may prefer comfortable inns and hotels in the resorts and towns of Bastia, Ajaccio, Bonifacio and Calvi. Each has its own museum with remnants of its religious and military past. The island has four airports and six ports. Car ferries from Marseille, Nice and Toulon cruise overnight. Express ferries from Nice cut the trip to less than three hours. Summer excursions to the neighboring Italian island of Sardinia are popular.
➕ Off map E1
Tourist information ✉ 17 boulevard du Roi-Jérôme, Ajaccio, 20000 ☎ 04 95 51 00 00; www.visit-corsica.fr
Ferries 🚢 Société Nationale Maritime Corse Méditerranée (SNCM) ✉ 61 boulevard des Dames, Marseille, 13226 ☎ 0825 88 80 88 (toll call) or 32 60 within France; www.sncm.fr

Côte d'Azur

The ribbon of coastline along the skirts of Provence, from Marseille to the Italian border, is known as the Côte d'Azur, a combination of sea and sky that wooed the rich and nurtured some of the Mediterranean's most charming resorts.

In many cases, the landscape itself stops picturesque coves from becoming too built up and losing their charms. Resorts may sprawl and drip proof of their fantastic wealth, but it's the many bays and rocky cliffs that, despite the unattractive rash of concrete apartment buildings that mar city limits, stop the ports, towns and villages from merging into one homogenized vacation park.

Nice (see pages 166–167), the main city of what is also called the French Riviera, has the bustle of any capital but with the added pleasure of the sweeping coastline of the Baie des Anges. Other beaches are more compact, providing marinas for millionaires' yachts and wharfside markets for fishermen.

The great headlands are still the preserve of the rich and famous. Cap Ferrat's fairy-tale Rothschild estate (see page 157) is fantastic opulence. Cap d'Antibes juts out into the Mediterranean, with its private beaches and exclusive villas. The eastern side of the peninsula has a good-sized public beach. The cap separates Juan-les-Pins – the party side, where a fabulous July jazz festival takes place in the pine grove – from Antibes, which is more reflective. Visit its ramparts, flower markets heady with the scent of mimosa or lavender, and the Picasso Museum, located in the artist's 13th-century Château Grimaldi. High above the coastline are perched villages (see page 172). Strung along the rock face like garlands of white-knuckle rides are the three tiers of the *corniches*, daredevil mountain roads with harrowing hairpin bends and unrivaled

views between Nice and Menton. And touching the sky are the Alps. Few people realize that in early spring, less than an hour's drive separates the exhilaration of the ski slopes and an all-over tan on the Med.

No greater contrast exists than that between the neighboring towns on the coast itself. A local maxim says, "I sin in Cannes, I work in Nice, I play in Monte Carlo, and I will die in Menton."

E1–E2

Tourist information 11 place de Gaulle, Antibes, 06601 04 97 23 11 11; www.antibesjuanlespins.com

Musée Picasso Château Grimaldi, place Mariejol, Antibes, 06600 04 92 90 54 20 Tue.–Sun. 10–6, mid-Jun. to mid-Sep. (Wed. and Fri. also 6–8 p.m., Jul.–Aug.); 10–noon and 2–6, rest of year $$

Bonifacio, the most southerly town in Corsica, perches on limestone cliffs, high above the Mediterranean

Grasse

Grasse has been the center of the perfume industry for 400 years. Born of local Italian glove-makers' tradition of perfuming their creations with blossoms, the manufacture of scent soon overtook the leather-tanning industry as the source of the town's wealth. Light breezes now waft aromas of jasmine, roses and lavender from the acres of cultivated fields around town. At the perfume museum, the story of scent is told, and two main perfume factories – Parfumerie Fragonard and Parfumerie Galimard – welcome tourists. The latter invites visitors to create their own personal fragrance, but at a price. Elsewhere, see the town's two Peter Paul Rubens paintings, *The Crucifixion* and *Crown of Thorns*, in the cathedral, and discover local culture at the Musée d'Art et d'Histoire de Provence.

➕ E2

Tourist information ✉ 22 cours Honoré-Cresp, 06130 ☎ 04 93 36 66 66; ✉ place de la Foux ☎ 04 93 36 21 68; www.grasse.fr

Musée International de la Parfumerie
✉ 2 boulevard du Jeu de Ballon, 06130 ☎ 04 97 05 58 00; www.museesdegrasse.com 🕐 Daily 10–7, May–Sep.; daily 11–6, Apr.; Wed.–Mon. 1–6, rest of year. Closed mid- to late Nov. 🎫 $

Villa-Musée Jean-Honoré Fragonard ✉ 23 boulevard Fragonard, 06310 ☎ 04 97 05 58 00; www. museesdegrasse.com 🕐 Daily 10–7, May–Sep.; daily 11–6, Apr.; Wed.–Mon. 1–6, rest of year. Closed mid- to late Nov. 🎫 $

Parfumerie Galimard ✉ 73 route de Cannes, 06130 ☎ 04 93 09 20 00; www.galimard.com 🕐 Daily by appointment only 🎫 Free; $$$ to make your own perfume (appointment required)

Musée d'Art et d'Histoire de Provence ✉ 2 rue Mirabeau, 06310 ☎ 04 97 05 58 00; www. museesdegrasse.com 🕐 Daily 10–7, May–Sep.; daily 11–6, Apr.; Wed.–Mon. 1–6, rest of year. Closed mid- to late Nov. 🎫 $

Marseille

Don't expect Riviera glamor. Marseille is a true mariners' port with a notorious underworld and the constant traffic of ships heading off to the wide world beyond. In 1996, the city embarked on the ambitious "Euroméditerranée" revitalization program, modernizing a whole stretch of city from place de la Joliette to St. Charles station. With the project nearing completion, fine examples of modern architecture have sprung up around place de la Joliette and the docks. The city will be at the heart of European Capital of Culture 2013 celebrations (see page 147). Many of the city's museums have been spruced up in preparation for the event.

The visitor shops are on La Canebière, the main boulevard leading down to the port. The name does mean "cannabis," but it has nothing to do with drug running – the city is well-established in the hemp rope-making industry. You will sense 26 centuries of the city's history as a port, from ancient civilizations to today's popular diversion for cruise liners, while eaves-dropping on conversations among old sea salts in Vieux Port bars or while browsing museum displays. A bronze plaque on quai des Belges marks the point where the Greeks first landed. The Musée d'Archéologie Méditerranéenne has a collection of artifacts from the ancient world, some found locally. The museum at the Vieille Charité center displays collections of art from Africa, Oceania, and Central and South America.

Like Paris, Marseille is divided into districts. Use the subway, tram and bus system to get around as taxis can be something of an adventure. There are several beaches away from the ferry, freight and fishing ports. Take a trip to the island Château d'If, where the Count of Monte Cristo was imprisoned.

The magnificent and commanding Église Notre-Dame-de-la-Garde (1853–64) stands 525 feet above the port. A 32-foot gold Madonna balances above the dome of the Byzantine-style basilica. Inside the sailors' church, model ships and paintings created by mariners serve as votive offerings. Above the modern docks is the similarly exotic

19th-century Cathédrale de la Nouvelle-Major. The smaller, more-interesting 11th-century Romanesque cathedral it replaced is tucked behind it.

Marseille boasts an excellent cultural life, with a respected opera season, concerts and a famous biennial dance festival in June and July.

✚ D2

Tourist information ✉ 4 La Canebière (1e), 13001 ☎ 08 26 50 05 00 (toll call); www.marseille-tourisme. com ℹ The tourist office runs a wide range of escorted tours

Musée d'Archéologie Méditerranéenne ✉ Centre de la Vieille Charité, 2 rue de la Charité, 13100 ☎ 04 91 14 58 59 🕐 Tue.–Sun. 11–6, Jun.–Sep.; Tue.–Sun. 10–5, rest of year 🎫 $

Menton

A mile from Italy and half a century from the rest of the Riviera, Menton is a delightful curiosity. Its 19th-century heyday welcomed consumptive writers advised to take the sea air rather than risk city winters. A very English style of seaside resort (see the memorial to Queen Victoria), Menton reveals architecture that is pure Italian: ocher mountainside houses and baroque churches. By the 1920s, overtaken by rival resorts Nice and St.-Tropez, Menton settled into faded gentility.

Happily, Menton's famous son was artist and filmmaker Jean Cocteau, whose little artistic scandals brought back the thrill last felt in the era of Britain's Prince of Wales, later Edward VII. Cocteau decorated the wedding room of the Hôtel de Ville with scenes of bacchanalian orgies, animal-print carpets and the face of his male lover as Marianne, emblem of France. Musée Jean Cocteau–Collection Séverin Wunderman is housed in an innovative building, designed by Rudy Ricciotti. It features 300 of Cocteau's works. A small museum at the bastion in the town harbor was decorated by the artist. The Jardin des Biovès lemon grove is Europe's biggest citrus garden, home to the annual Lemon Festival (see page 165).

✚ E2

Tourist information ✉ Palais de l'Europe, 8 avenue Boyer, 06500 ☎ 04 92 41 76 78; www.tourisme-menton.fr

Musée du Bastion ✉ Bastion du Vieux Port, 06500 ☎ 04 93 57 72 30 🕐 Wed.–Mon. 10–6 🎫 $

Salle des Mariages ✉ Hôtel de Ville, place Ardoïno, 06500 ☎ 04 92 10 50 00 🕐 Wed.–Mon. 10–6 🎫 $

Musée Jean Cocteau–Collection Séverin Wunderman ✉ 2 quai Monléon, 06500 ☎ 04 89 81 52 20 🕐 Wed.–Mon. 10–6 🎫 $$ (combined ticket with Musée du Bastion)

The picturesque, Italianate old town of Menton rises on terraces above the harbor

Monaco, Monte-Carlo

The world's longest-reigning royal family still holds sway in one of Europe's smallest principalities, midway between Menton and Nice. Prince Albert II is the present head of the Grimaldi family following the death of his father Prince Rainier III in 2005. The family has governed here since 1297.

Once stretching from Antibes to Italy, the principality shrank to its present size in the 19th century when citizens revolted against high taxes. In response, Prince Charles III created the new town of Monte-Carlo, opening the casino to create additional revenue. It was such a success that all taxes soon were abolished. Casino profits funded the 1875 Romanesque-style cathedral in Monaco-Ville. The casino – and the tax-free status for residents – ensures Monte-Carlo's reputation as the playground of the fabulously wealthy. The casino building was designed by Charles Garnier, architect of the Paris Opéra, and a miniature opera house within the building, the Salle Garnier, allows the elite to enjoy world-class performances. The decor throughout is as extravagant as the high rollers it attracts – marble floors, onyx columns and crystal chandeliers. Passports are needed for admission. The "man who broke the bank" of popular song was Charles Deville Wells, who turned $400 into $40,000 back in 1891. Less fortunate gamblers have been known to end their misery by plunging from the cliffs behind the casino.

In Monaco-Ville other attractions include the audiovisual *Monte-Carlo Story* and the Oceanographic Museum. You can take a tour of the royal palace – closed to the public when the Prince is in residence (indicated by the royal flag flown from the tower). Changing of the guard takes place daily at 11:55 a.m.

Opposite: Monte-Carlo, seen from the Jardin Exotique

Princess Grace, the former Hollywood actress Grace Kelly who died in a car accident on the Moyenne Corniche in 1982, is immortalized by a bronze statue in the rose garden bearing her name in the district of Fontevieille. Her tomb can be seen in the cathedral.

Present-day "stargazing" takes place in the marina, where only the select few may moor their yachts. From their boats, they may watch the famous May Formula One Grand Prix motor race, which commissioned Europe's first paved roads.

E2

Tourist information 2a boulevard des Moulins, 98000 (Monaco 377) 92 16 61 16; www.visitmonaco.com

The facade of Garnier's famous casino

Montpellier

A buzzing university town, Montpellier is the kind of place in which a well-chosen café table on place de la Comédie – with its fountain of the Three Graces and 19th-century theater – can give you a better sense of the town than a trek around the museums. The town grew around the medieval spice trade, and its early medical faculty. The gardens of esplanade Charles-de-Gaulle honor the past at the Musée Fabre, refurbished and one of the largest museums in France, with a collection of works by Italian and Dutch masters. Promenade du Peyrou is a park with an aqueduct, water tower, triumphal arch and sea views. A tramway makes getting around this town a breeze.

🚩 B2

Tourist information ✉ 30 allée de Lattre-de-Tassigny, 34000 ☎ 04 67 60 60 60; www.ot-montpellier.fr

Musée Fabre ✉ 39 boulevard Bonne-Nouvelle, 34000 ☎ 04 67 14 83 00; http://museefabre. montpellier-agglo.com 🕐 Tue.–Sun. 10–6 💵 $$

Narbonne

Narbonne is a delightful sea port that stands 10 miles away from the sea. Centuries of silting means Narbonne Plage is now a spectacular drive away through an undulating country of vineyards and the inland cliffs of La Clappe. The town itself, often overlooked by tourists, stands on the Canal de la Robine, which serves the Aude river and disappears under the shops of the old quarter; boats may be rented for an hour's exploration. The ramparts of the 13th-century Archbishop's Palace – within which nestles today's town hall, tourist office and a museum of art and history – dominate the splendid place de l'Hôtel-de-Ville. The Madeleine Courtyard in the oldest part of the palace shouldn't be missed. Abutting the town hall is the unfinished 13th-century Cathédrale St.-Just. The 135-foot Gothic-style choir is one of the highest in France. Narbonne is liberally sprinkled with references to 2,000 years of uprisings and intrigues, from the memorial by the main square to the martyrs of a peasant revolt to the Renaissance-style Maison des Trois-Nourrices, where the Marquis of Cinq Mars was arrested for conspiring against Cardinal Richelieu.

🚩 B2

Tourist information ✉ 31 rue Jean-Jaurès, 11100 ☎ 04 68 65 15 60; www.narbonne-tourisme.com

The cloisters at the fascinating, but unfinished, Cathédrale St.-Just in Narbonne

Carnival Time in Nice and Menton

Just when the rest of France is muffling and snuffling in blizzards and hardship, winter ends early on the Riviera – proclaimed by the centuries-old Mardi Gras tradition of Carnaval. Nice goes to town during February with its Carnaval (www.nicecarnaval.com). Magnificent floats are papier-maché fantasies parading along promenade des Anglais. Huge caricature heads skip beside trucks as marching bands "out-Disney" Disney along streets lined with grandstand seating. Streamers, whistles and singing fill the air.

Daytime battles of the flowers are breathtaking shows, and nightly parades are a cue for open-air partying until the wee hours. On the last night, the massive figures take their final ride through place Masséna to the beach, to be set afire and adrift at sea in the Bay of the Angels. The Mardi Gras tradition dates back to the 13th century, but the modern burlesque procession, with its figures of the king and queen of Carnival, began in 1873.

During February, the glamor continues but with less hullabaloo and more grace at the border town of Menton. The Lemon Festival is an unusual carnival (www.feteducitron.com). There's no papier-maché here: Dozens of floats, scores of statues and countless street decorations are all constructed from half a million oranges and lemons. Locals spend dark winter months attaching fruit to chicken wire and unleashing citrus aromas throughout town. Local legend has it that Eve herself gave the fruit to the town, and Menton pays homage to her generosity with parades aplenty in the teasing, breezing 70-degree sunshine of late winter. The undoubted highlight of each of these events is the carnival ball, a joyous occasion when locals dressed in their Sunday best dance the night away.

The carnivals are essentially parties for the locals, although visitors are always welcome to join in. In summer, Nice and Antibes Juan-les-Pins invite the biggest names from the U.S. to come to France and perform at world-class jazz festivals to cater to a more international crowd.

Statues and displays made from lemons and oranges during the Lemon Festival in Menton

Nice

Nice combines all the thrills and pleasures of the Côte d'Azur in its picturesque old port, grand town center for shopping and gambling, broad seafront and the coast's principal airport. French only since 1860, Nice has its rich Italian heritage – from its years as part of the duchy of Savoy.

The town is blessed with the sweep of the wide Baie des Anges, named for angels who are said to have carried the town's 15-year-old saint into the harbor after her martyrdom. The English discovered the bay in the late 18th century, and built the promenade des Anglais in 1822. Today, the walk is lined with palm trees and hotels, from modern monstrosities to the extravagance of the 1912 Hôtel Négresco.

At the eastern end of the promenade, the road spills onto place Masséna and its gardens, which make up the city's main square. Here is the more modern and swanky shopping district and the focus of music festivals and Carnaval (see page 165). The old town (see page 168) is just across the square and behind quai des États-Unis, named for the town's American fans. Follow the coast road to its sudden sweep into the Quartier du Port, where 18th-century buildings and the Classical Église Notre-Dame line the quay.

Between the port and the old quarter is the Colline du Château (Castle Hill), which despite its name can boast no castle. The French destroyed it in the 18th century. Climb the hill for pleasant gardens and views over the port and the rooftops of old Nice. Some remains of Classical times, housed in a small museum on the hill, are reminders that although the resort was a 19th-century creation, the ancient Greeks founded the town in the fourth century BC.

The Romans settled in the Cimiez district, an area that later found favor with Britain's Queen Victoria and became the most fashionable residential quarter. Here is the Musée Matisse, a stylish villa that houses works from all of Henri Matisse's periods in the location that inspired his brilliant blues.

There are many art collections in Nice, and the tourist office sells the French Riviera Pass, which gives access to museums and tourist sights. The Musée National Marc-Chagall displays the nation's major collection of the great 20th-century artist's work. Located at the foot of the Cimiez hill, the museum is renowned for a series of 17 canvases inspired by Old Testament tales. The third of Nice's local heroes was Raoul Dufy, who until recently had a seafront

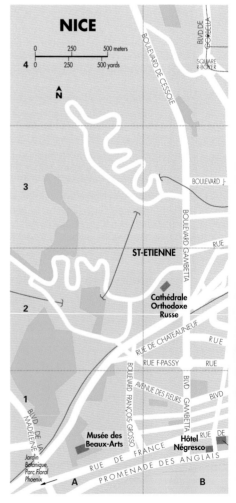

museum devoted to his work. Fears of damage by the sea air led to the collection being moved to the Musée des Beaux-Arts. Here is a superb fine arts collection spanning the Italian old masters to contemporary works.

The home of modern and contemporary art is the Musée d'Art Moderne et d'Art Contemporain (MAMAC), a marble and glass temple to American and French avant-garde art.

🛡 E2

Tourist information ✉ 5 promenade des Anglais, 06302 ☎ 0892 70 74 07 (toll call); www.nicetourism.com

Musée Matisse 🛡 D4 ✉ 164 avenue des Arènes-de-Cimiez, 06000 ☎ 04 93 81 08 08; www. musee-matisse-nice.org 🕐 Wed.–Mon. 10–6, 🛡 Free

Musée National Marc-Chagall 🛡 C3 ✉ avenue du Docteur-Ménard, 06000 ☎ 04 93 53 87 20; www.musee-chagall.fr 🕐 Wed.–Mon. 10–6, May–Oct.; 10–5, rest of year 🛡 $$

Musée des Beaux-Arts 🛡 A1 ✉ 33 avenue des Baumettes, 06000 ☎ 04 92 15 28 28; www. musee-beaux-arts-nice.org 🕐 Tue.–Sun. 10–6 🛡 Free

Musée d'Art Moderne et d'Art Contemporain (MAMAC) 🛡 D2 ✉ promenade des Arts, 06300 ☎ 04 97 13 42 01; www.mamac-nice.org 🕐 Tue.–Sun. 10–6 🛡 Free

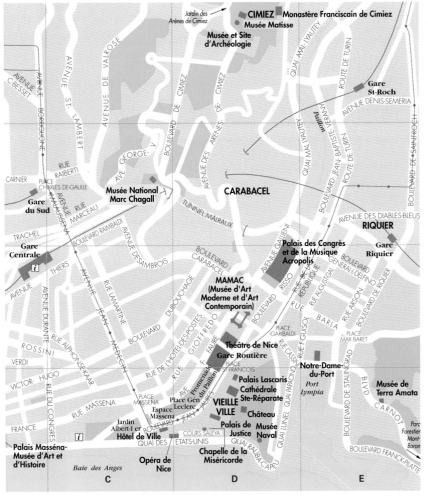

Nice: The Old Town

The old town of Nice was dismissed as a slum for most of the postwar years until the inevitable gentrification of the 1970s. Nowadays, it is a picturesque, atmospheric place that is ideal to explore on foot. Its Italian-like side streets are bedecked with garlands of laundry, cascades of flowers on windowsills, quaint red-painted row houses and small chapels. Place Garibaldi is named after the Italian military hero who was born in Nice in 1807. His statue in the square is now on a busy traffic circle.

To gain the real flavor of this area, stop by a street café and breathe in the aromas of the market in cours Saleya: flowers, of course, but also fresh fruits, honey and Provençal herbs. If you're here on a Monday, however, you'll miss all of this, as Mondays welcome the flea market.

The yellow house in cours Saleya was once home to Henri Matisse. Look, too, for the trompe l'oeil mural on the Palais Annibal Grimaldi. On the south side of the square are the squat houses known as *ponchettes*, many of which are now seafood restaurants. On the north side of the square, visit the 18th-century rococo Chapelle de la Miséricorde.

On place Rossetti is the distinctive, green-domed Cathédrale Ste.-Réparate, a 17th-century baroque tribute to the patron saint who was martyred in Asia Minor at around the age of 15.

A more secular treat is the glorious Italian ice cream served from 9 a.m. until midnight every day, March to November, at Fenocchio. For a different kind of aroma, follow your nose along rue Mascoïnat and rue du Collet to place St.-François, site of the morning fish market.

Check out some of the excellent art galleries and antiques shops on rue Droite. Then visit the beautiful Palais Lascaris at No. 15. Restored by the town, the former palace of the counts of Castellar boasts a 1738 pharmacy on the first floor and state rooms, adorned by fine tapestries, that are reached up a magnificent staircase decorated with paintings and statues. The nearby baroque Église du Jesus dates from the early 17th century.

Palais Lascaris ✉ 15 rue Droite, 06300 ☎ 04 93 62 72 40 🕐 Wed.–Mon. 10–6 💶 Free

One of the plants for sale at the flower market in cours Saleya

The Roman Théâtre Antique in Orange provides a magnificent setting for drama

Nîmes

Although its greatest gifts to the world are the blue jeans made from the textile that bears its name (*serge de Nîmes = denim*), real-life Nîmes is ancient Rome in Provence. For 500 years, gladiators fought to the death in the Arènes, an exceptionally fine example of a Roman amphitheater. The preservation is remarkable considering that generations of local families built houses inside the arena. The site was restored in the 19th century. Well worth a visit is the Maison Carrée, a first-century temple with neat Corinthian columns. Opposite, a 20th-century reinterpretation of the Classical design is architect Norman Foster's Carré d'Art, home of the contemporary art museum. The Jardins de la Fontaine were France's first public park. The pedestrian-friendly historic center has charming cafés and little shops. Cathédrale Notre-Dame et St.-Castor is nearby.

Seasonal bullfights (*ferias*) take place during the February Carnaval, Easter, Pentecost and the September harvest.

➕ C2

Tourist information ✉ 6 rue Auguste, 30020
☎ 04 66 58 38 00; www.ot-nimes.fr
Musée d'Art Contemporain ✉ Carré d'Art,
16 place de la Maison-Carré, 30000 ☎ 04 66 76 35 70
🕐 Tue.–Sun. 10–6 🍴 Restaurant 🍷 $$

Orange

On summer nights, 10,000 people climb the steep stone steps of a playhouse that first opened nearly 2,000 years ago. The figure of Emperor Augustus dominates a red sandstone wall 337 feet long and 118 feet high – the only Roman theater backdrop that survives. Three ranks of seating divided early audiences by social status and divide today's visitors by budget. The Théâtre Antique of Orange is one of the town's two great reminders of the Roman heritage of Provence. The other is a fine 73-foot Arc de Triomphe, the first Roman monument in France, erected around 20 BC at the gateway to Provence across the old Via Agrippa. It illustrates imperial might, with carvings showing natives in chains, and the supremacy of the Roman fleet. Carefully cross the busy main road (Route 7) if you would like a closer look, as the triple arch now stands in the center of the intersection.

➕ C3

Tourist information ✉ 5 cours Aristide-Briand, 84100
☎ 04 90 34 70 88; www.otorange.fr
Théâtre Antique ✉ rue de Madeleine-Roch, 84100
☎ 04 90 51 17 60; www.theatre-antique.com
🕐 Daily 9–7, Jun.–Aug.; 9–6, Apr.–May and Sep.;
9:30–5:30 Mar. and Oct.; 9:30–4:30, rest of year
🍷 $$ (includes Musée d'Art et d'Histoire d'Orange,
opposite the theater)

Drive Jewish Heritage Trail

Distance: 240 miles
Time: 3 days

Jewish communities have existed in Provence for nearly 2,000 years, and they faced a turbulent history of exile and welcome. Some ghettos (*carrières*) were created during the influence of the papal state as sanctuary from persecution; others were virtual prison townships.

Start the tour in Avignon (see page 155).
In 1221, the bishop of Avignon granted Jews the right to live within the city walls. The main synagogue by place de Jérusalem, rebuilt in 1848 after a fire, is a national monument. Its white colonnades and walnut furnishings are striking features. Nearby, rues Abraham and Jacob testify to the old Jewish quarter, as does rue Vieille-Juiverie.
Take the D225 northeast out of town. Turn right on the D942 for 6 miles to Carpentras.
Notorious for 1980s fascist attacks on the city's 15th-century Jewish Cemetery that brought widespread condemnation of the National Front, Carpentras has one of the oldest Jewish communities in France. A synagogue has stood on place de la Mairie since 1367. The present building, restored in 1741, is considered the most beautiful in France.
Take the D938 south to nearby Pernes-les-Fontaines.
Take a quick detour at Pernes-les-Fontaines to see the old stone mikvah baths of this spring town.
Take the D28 toward Avignon, turning left on the D31 south until it rejoins the D938 into Cavaillon.
In 1453, Jews were forced into the ghetto in Cavaillon. The state seized the 1772 synagogue above rues Hébraïque and Chabran in 1793, and now it is a museum. The building had an external

staircase and a grille between the women's level and the main prayer room that could be raised so women could see the Torah (scrolls of the law). Two fine staircases reach an ornate pulpit for the rabbi. Important texts are preserved at the Inguimbertine Library.
Take the A7 for 41 miles to Marseille.
Marseille (see pages 160–161) is home to around 40 synagogues. Jews settled here beginning in the 12th century until expulsion in 1501. At the start of the 20th century, refugees fled here from the pogroms of eastern Europe, and as a free zone beginning in 1939, it became a sanctuary for Jews escaping Nazi persecution until the German regime arrived in 1942. Marseille later became a major port for concentration-camp survivors leaving for Israel. On the plage du Prado, see the sculpture *Marseille:*

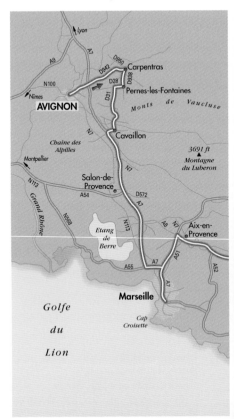

Gateway to the East, a symbol of Israeli gratitude to the city. A memorial to deportees may be seen on quai St.-Jean. The oldest synagogue is an 1864 Romano-Byzantine temple.

Take the A7 north for 7 miles, following signs for Aix-en-Provence. Merge onto the A51 for 10 miles, then continue on the A8 in the direction of St. Maximin–Cannes–Nice for 60 miles. At exit 36, turn left on the N555 into Draguignan.

Draguignan was "haven of the Hebrews," its ghetto a thriving community. On rue Jutarié, 75 feet of the medieval synagogue wall can be seen, and many religious images adorn stonework.

Back along the N555 to the A8, continue in the direction of Fréjus–Nice for 42 miles. Take exit 50 for Nice center, following the N202 for 250 yards and then the N7 for a mile into Nice (see pages 166–167).

The community settled around Nice's rues Droite and Mascoînat from 1408 until the Nazi roundups in 1942 – there is a commemorative plaque on rue Benoît-Bunico. The cemetery on Colline du Château is filled with generations of Jewish families. The principal synagogue on rue Deloye has fine windows by Théo Tobiasse and the Musée National Marc-Chagall (see page 166, 167) shouldn't be missed.

Synagogue ✉ place de Jérusalem, Avignon 84000 ☎ 04 90 85 21 24; **Synagogue** ✉ place de Maurice-Charretier, Carpentras 84200 ☎ 04 90 63 39 97; **Synagogue** ✉ rue Hébraïque, 52 place Castil-Blaze, Cavaillon 84300 ☎ 04 90 76 00 34; **Synagogue** ✉ 117 rue Breteuil, Marseille 13006 ☎ 04 91 37 49 64; **Synagogue** ✉ 15 rue Observance, Draguignan 83300; **Synagogue** ✉ 7 rue Gustave-Deloye, Nice 06000 ☎ 04 93 92 11 38

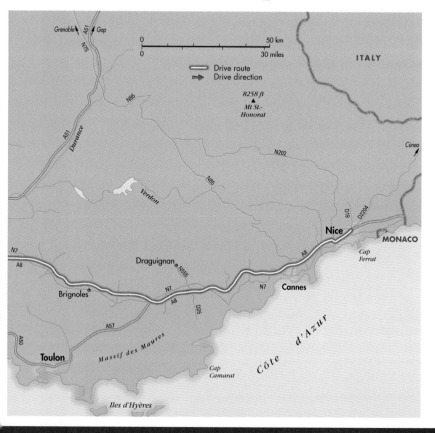

Perched Villages

Known as villages *perchés* and *nids d'aigles* (eagles' nests), the small towns and hamlets literally perched on the rocks high above the Côte d'Azur are the last remaining outposts of ordinary life before the arrival of the Riviera. Originally created out of the reach of opportunist invaders, the villages remain difficult to access but are well worth the effort. Roads are so steep and winding that some houses have several addresses, with each story of the houses being on a different street. Experienced motorists should pick one or two to visit on the map: Roquebrune, Vence (see page 175) and Èze. Èze, an outpost of the counts of Savoy, was fortified in the 12th century and belonged to Monaco until its citizens voted in the 19th century to join France. The exotic garden of cacti and palms is worth a visit. Although St.-Paul-de-Vence is famous for its 16th-century walls and tower, not to mention its Provençal Museum, most people come to visit the hotel La Colombe d'Or. In the 1920s, it was a humble inn and the customers were struggling artists who paid the owner in paintings rather than cash. The shrewd hotelier amassed what is probably France's greatest collection of modern art: Henri Matisse, Amedeo Modigliani, Georges Braque, Pablo Picasso and Paul Signac. Dozens of the 20th century's greatest artists handed over works in exchange for a room. Inevitably, St.-Paul-de-Vence is now overrun with art galleries and high-priced shops.

Tourist information ✉ 2 rue Grande, St.-Paul-de-Vence, 06570 ☎ 04 93 32 86 95; www.saint-pauldevence.com

The highest village in Provence – Èze is perched 1,410 feet above the coast

Perpignan

The second city of Catalonia – the capital is Barcelona, within Spain – is something of a curiosity. The town is home to the oldest palace in France – a French residence that served as the seat of the king of the island of Mallorca. Lasting only 68 years, it was created in 1276 by James I of Aragon as a treat for his youngest son.

The palace, now standing within a pink brick citadel, still has its chapel, great hall and royal apartments. The Gothic Cathédrale St.-Jean boasts a 15th-century bell housed in an 18th-century cage. Next door, the Campo Santo, France's only cloistered cemetery, has four marbled galleries. Église St.-Jacques, built in two parts in the 14th and 18th centuries, stands in some charming gardens. Salvador Dalí proclaimed Perpignan's train station "the center of the universe." He painted his own vision of the building and inspired the decor of the roof and paving outside the modern station.

➕ B1

Tourist information ✉ Palais des Congrès, place Armand-Lanoux, 66000 ☎ 04 68 66 30 30; www.perpignantourisme.com

Pont du Gard

This magnificent triumph of Roman engineering is an imposing three-tiered aqueduct spanning the Gard river. Bringing fresh water to Nîmes (see page 169) from the spring at Uzès, about 6 miles away, the bridge was part of a 30-mile complex of man-made waterways constructed at the end of the first century BC. Rightly acclaimed as one of the unofficial wonders of the ancient world, it has recently been renovated to stunning effect. The triple row of arches complements the landscape and soars 160 feet into the sky. Its top level spans a remarkable 902 feet. The massive blocks of stone, weighing up to 6 tons each, were assembled without the use of mortar. There's an extensive museum and activity center close to the site,

One of the wonders of the ancient world: the Pont du Gard

where displays explore this engineering marvel and describe Roman life at the time of its construction.

➕ C2

Tourist information ✉ route du Ponte-du-Gard, 30210 ☎ 04 66 37 50 99; www.pontdugard.fr 🌐 Site: open access. Museum and visitor center: daily 9–7, May– Sep.; 9–6, Mar., Apr. and Oct.–early Nov.; 9–5:30, rest of year 💶 $$$ (for up to five people)

St.-Raphaël

St.-Raphaël is unable to flaunt the evidence of its heyday, when Alexandre Dumas, Hector Berlioz and Guy de Maupassant discovered its charms, since many of its 19th-century buildings were destroyed in World War II bombing. The salons and hotels where literary giants once vacationed are long gone.

A fashionable seaside resort since the beginning of the 19th century, when Napoléon landed on its beaches after his Egyptian campaign, St.-Raphaël still attracts sun worshipers by day and casino lizards by night. Keep in mind, however, that beachwear isn't allowed in the town streets (see page 148). Even more modest attire is required to visit the Byzantine Cathédrale Notre-Dame-de-la-Victoire and the Romanesque Église St.-Pierre, with its hint of the original medieval village that grew up here in the days before seaside resorts.

➕ E1

Tourist information ✉ quai Albert 1, 83700 ☎ 04 94 19 52 52; www.saint-raphael.com

The mausoleum and arch at Les Antiques is a Roman site at St.-Rémy-de-Provence

St.-Rémy-de-Provence
The prophet Nostradamus was born in St.-Rémy-de-Provence and the composer Charles Gounod moved here, but the town's fame comes from the fact that Vincent van Gogh came to the St.-Paul de Mausole hospital in May 1889 to recover from depression when he cut off his own ear. Attracted by the light and landscapes around St.-Rémy, the artist warmed to the calm world of the nuns and nurses and created more than 150 paintings and numerous sketches during his year here – *The Irises* and *Starry Night* among them. He left St.-Rémy for Auvers-sur-Oise (see page 50), where he died about two months later.

Visit Église St.-Paul-de-Mausole to see the cloister and a permanent exhibition (Centre Culturel Valetudo) of pictures painted by patients and fine van Gogh reproductions, all of which are for sale; proceeds go toward the hospital upkeep. Each year, the Musée Estrine in the Hôtel Estrine has an exhibition on a different theme, using full-size reproductions of his paintings and slide shows. Upstairs, there are exhibitions of contemporary artists. A marked trail (follow the reproduction paintings) takes in places the artist painted during his stay in St.-Rémy. Escorted 90-minute tours leave the tourist office Tuesday,

Thursday, Friday and Saturday at 10 a.m., mid-April to mid-September. Maps and self-guided audio tours are available.

➕ C2

Tourist information ✉ place Jean-Jaurès, 13210 ☎ 04 90 92 05 22; www.saintremy-de-provence.com

Centre Culturel Valetudo ✉ rue des Baux-de-Provence, 13210 ☎ 04 90 92 77 00; www. cloitresaintpaul-valetudo.com 🕐 Daily 9:30–7, Apr.–Oct.; 10:15–4:45, rest of year 🎫 $

Musée Estrine ✉ rue Estrine, 13210 ☎ 04 90 92 34 72 🕐 Tue. and Thu.–Sun. 10–12:30 and 2–7, Wed. 10–7, May–Sep.; Tue.–Sun. 10–12:30 and 2–6, mid-Mar. to Apr. and Oct.–late Nov. 🎫 $

St.-Tropez
Forever linked with screen siren turned animal-rights activist Brigitte Bardot and promoted by the more salacious tabloid press for pioneering topless bathing, this former fishing village has a reputation as the playground of Hollywood in exile.

Named after a decapitated Roman martyr, the city's quaint streets and pretty market have long been appreciated by the good and the great. Here, 19th-century writers and composers escaped from city life. Raoul Dufy, Henri Matisse and Pierre Bonnard set up their easels; Jean Cocteau and Colette held house parties between the wars; movie stars moved in, beginning in the 1950s. First-timers to St.-Tropez often come to glimpse the glitterati among locals at the fruit and fish markets. Regulars frequent the Musée de l'Annonciade to view paintings by fauvists and pointillists.

There are two addresses for the well-heeled and well-dressed to loiter with a glass of something cool. Place des Lices is where locals play boules and visitors hang out in arty cafés. Down by the Vieux Port, the merely well-off watch the filthy rich dine on board the extravagant yachts moored just a few yards away. Detach yourself for photo opportunities, looking up at the town from the harbor walls, or down from the ramparts of the citadel.

✚ D1

Tourist information ✉ 40 rue Gambetta, 83990 ☎ 08 92 68 48 28 (toll call); www.ot-saint-tropez.com

Musée de l'Annonciade ✉ quai de l'Epi-Le-Port, 83990 ☎ 04 94 17 84 10 ◷ Daily 10–noon and 2–6, Jul.–Oct.; Wed.–Mon. 10–noon and 2–6, rest of year. Closed Nov. 🖉 $$

Musée de la Citadelle ✉ Montée de la Citadelle, 83990 ☎ 04 94 97 59 43 ◷ Daily 10–12:30 and 1:30–5:30 🖉 $

Salon-de-Provence

The great riddler and seer Nostradamus moved to Salon in 1547 and spent the last two decades of his life in a house that is now a museum dedicated to his life. An eminent doctor and astrologer, Michel de Nostredame was born in the town of St.-Rémy-de-Provence (see page 174) into a family of new converts from Judaism to Catholicism. His immortality was guaranteed by cryptic predictions reappraised by successive generations to reveal visions of tyrants and natural disasters. The Maison de Nostradamus offers an audio-guided tour of his life and times. Nostradamus is buried in the town's Église St.-Laurent.

Also worth seeing are the clock tower and Musée Grévin, featuring unusual waxworks depicting episodes from Provence's history. Handmade soap is a specialty of the town.

✚ C2

Tourist information ✉ 56 cours Gimon, 13300 ☎ 04 90 56 27 60; www.visitsalondeprovence.com

Vence

Two miles north of St.-Paul-de-Vence (see page 172) is Vence – in its day, a great artists commune. Here D. H. Lawrence lived and died and Marc Chagall spent his final years. His mosaic is one of the sights of France's tiniest cathedral, Cathédrale St.-Véran, dating from the 10th century. Roman tombs are embedded in the walls.

Henri Matisse declared that his finest work was the *Chapelle du Rosaire*, a labor of love created in gratitude to the Dominican sisters who nursed him when he was dangerously ill in 1941. He spent five years creating drawings of the stations of the cross, washed with light from stained-glass windows.

✚ E2

Tourist information ✉ 8 place du Grand-Jardin, 06140 ☎ 04 93 58 06 38; www.ville-vence.fr

Chapelle du Rosaire ✉ 466 avenue Henri-Matisse, 06140 ☎ 04 93 58 03 26 (tourist office) ◷ Tue. and Thu. 10–11:30 and 2–5:30, Mon., Wed. and Sat. (also Fri. during school holidays) 2–5:30. Closed mid-Nov. to mid-Dec. 🖉 $

The pretty harbor at St.-Tropez, bathed in sunshine

Massif Central

Opposite: The spectacular Millau Viaduct

Massif Central

For lovers of the great outdoors, the Massif Central always comes as a surprise. Despite claiming a sixth of the country's land mass, the area boasts few major cities and therefore often fails to make it onto most travel itineraries. However, this mountainous region is the missing link between the Alps and the Pyrénées, and it trickles out through the Loire, Dordogne and Lot rivers. The image the region has presented to the world is of vast expanses of volcanic landscapes, usually printed on plastic bottles containing mineral water that are sold throughout France and the wider world. This anonymity works in vacationers' favor. Untouched by some of the regrettable urban development of the 1960s, destinations are, for much of the year, free from crowds of tourists. Plenty of churches and museums provide cultural enlightenment, and splendid late 19th-century spa resorts and casinos dole out satisfying entertainment.

Gorges du Tarn from Pointe Sublime

Activities

Sailing, windsurfing, canoeing, fishing and hiking are the main activities for summer visitors. Winter sees the gentle slopes called into service with ski resorts well known to the French but less vigorously marketed internationally than the Alpine stations. In the fall, a hot-air balloon event takes place among the volcanoes.

Food

Local cuisine includes a great deal of freshwater fish: pike, perch, carp and trout. A noble tradition of sausage making, cured ham and all kinds of pork products dates from days when preserving meats was the only way to keep them through the long winter months. Light summer dishes are matched in winter by warming stews, such as *potée auvergnate*, a hearty pot of cabbage and potatoes with bacon and sausages. Cabbage is matched in popularity only by the celebrated green lentils from le Puy (see page 188).

Outstanding desserts include delicious puréed chestnuts from Ardèche and glazed shortcrust apple pie from Auvergne. Wines that once graced the tables of kings are gradually coming back into fashion. Order a St.-Pourçain from the Bourbonnais region, home of the royal house of Bourbon.

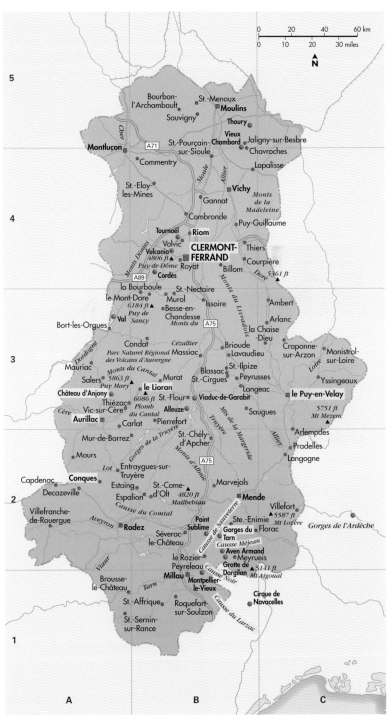

0   20   40   60 km
0   10   20   30 miles
N

5

Bourbon-
l'Archambault   St.-Menoux
Souvigny   **Moulins**
                 Thoury
                 Vieux
                 Chambord   Jaligny-sur-Besbre
Montluçon   St.-Pourçain-   Chavroches
                sur-Sioule
Commentry   Lapalisse

St.-Eloy-
les-Mines   **Vichy**   Monts
              Gannat   de la
                                         Madeleine
              Combronde
                              Puy-Guillaume

4

Tournoël   **Riom**
Volvic   Thiers
Vulcania   **CLERMONT-**
4806 ft   **FERRAND**   Courpière
Puy de Dôme Royat   Billom   *5361 ft*
Cordès   Dore

la Bourboule   St.-Nectaire
le Mont-Dore   Murol   Ambert
6184 ft   Besse-en-   Issoire
Val *Puy de* Chandesse   Arlanc
Sancy   *Monts du*   la Chaise
Bort-les-Orgues   -Dieu   Craponne-
                                          sur-Arzon Monistrol-
                Condat   *Cézallier*   sur-Loire
                Parc Naturel Régional Massiac Brioude
Mauriac   *des Volcans d'Auvergne*   Lavaudieu
                                    St.-Ilpize
3 Salers *5863 ft* Murat Blassac
       Puy Mary **le Lioran** St.-Cirgues Peyrusses Yssingeaux
Château d'Anjony *6086 ft* St.-Flour **Viaduc-de-Garabit** Langeac
       Thiézac   *Plomb*   **le Puy-en-Velay**
       Vic-sur-Cère *du Cantal* **Alleuze**   Sauges   *5751 ft*
Aurillac   Carlat   Pierrefort   *Mt Mézenc*
                                                             Arlempdes
       Mur-de-Barrez   St.-Chély-
                        d'Apcher   Pradelles
  Maurs   Langogne
         Lot Entraygues-sur-
               Truyère   St.-Côme-   Marvejols
Capdenac **Conques** Estaing d'Olt *4820 ft*
       Decazeville   Espalion *Mailhebiau*   **Mende** Villefort
2   *Causse du Comtal*   *5587 ft*
Villefranche-   Ste.-Enimie *Mt Lozère* Gorges de l'Ardèche
de-Rouergue   *Aveyron* **Rodez** **Point** Gorges du Florac
                         Séverac-   **Sublime** Tarn
                         le-Château   *Causse Méjean*
       Viaur   le Rozier- Aven Armand
Brousse-   Peyreleau Meyrueis
le-Château *Tarn* **Millau** **Montpellier- Grotte de *5141 ft*
                               le-Vieux** Dargilan *Mt Aigoual*
       St.-Affrique   Roquefort-   Cirque de
                      sur-Soulzon *Causse du Larzac* Navacelles
       St.-Sernin-
       sur-Rance

1

A   **B**   **C**

Clermont-Ferrand

A town built on and of volcanic rock –
even the Gothic Cathédrale Notre-
Dame-de-l'Assomption is made of black
lava – Clermont-Ferrand welcomes
visitors but isn't overrun by them.

Ideally, visitors should divide their
time between the two historic quarters:
Vieux (Old) Clermont and Montferrand.
Old Clermont is busy and attractive but
for the occasional lapse into a modern
color scheme. It's famous for its
fountains great and small (see page
184). Nearby Montferrand, founded by
the counts of Auvergne, has lovely
rust-colored rooftops and neatly planned
streets. It was originally a town in its
own right before royal decree united it
with Clermont in the 17th century.

Strolling by Colors

Walking is a pleasure and an education.
Old quarters are color-coded, with
themed signs and panels offering
historic walks. Three trails begin from
the main tourist office by Clermont's
cathedral, the fourth by the art museum
in Montferrand. Medallions featuring
local heroes are embedded in the
sidewalks to keep you on the right path.

Local Heroes

The figure set in the streets of
Montferrand is the Countess G. Her
husband bequeathed this amiable widow
the city in 1196, and she in turn gave
the citizens a charter and freedom to
trade. Countess G., who suffered from
leprosy, then devoted the rest of her life
to charity work and running a leper

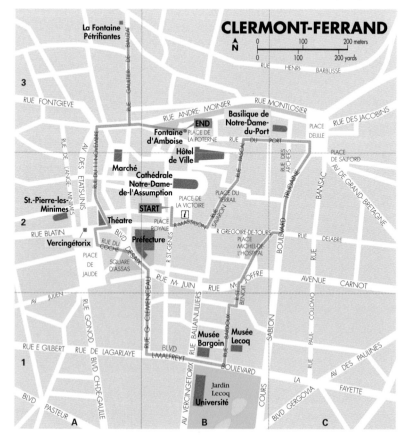

The town's towering, Gothic cathedral was constructed from the local black volcanic lava

colony with her son, Count Guillaume VIII of Auvergne. Other faces set in paving stones are those of Pope Urban II, Vercingétorix (see page 183), and the 17th-century mathematician and philosopher Blaise Pascal, who invented the world's first adding machine.

The city has long bred pioneers, such as the Michelin brothers, who created tires here. The tradition of a city of thinkers continues at Café des Augustes, 5 rue Sous-les-Augustins, where books,

newspapers and magazines are swapped among tables as everyone muses on the meaning of life and Pascal's view that "the heart has its reasons."

An art market is held the first Sunday of each month in place Salins, a Sunday flea market takes place here and at the bus depot, and market merchants gather Monday to Saturday at place St.-Pierre. Other passions are well served by the casino in Royat, the theater-opera house and the circus school at Riom.

Essential Information

Tourist Information
✉ place de la Victoire, 63000
☎ 04 73 98 65 00;
www.ot-clermont-ferrand.fr
Information and advice is available in English.

Urban Transportation
Although central Clermont-Ferrand is manageable on foot, the tramway and bus services are frequent and reliable. Tickets are available individually from the driver or in books (carnets) of 10 from tobacconists

(tabacs). Taxis may be hailed in the streets or ☎ 04 73 31 53 15. SNCF rail operates to Paris ☎ 36 35, toll call; www.sncf.fr.

Airport Information
Clermont-Ferrand Auvergne Airport, just outside town at Aulnat, has scheduled domestic and European flights ☎ 04 73 62 71 00; www.clermont-aeroport.com.
A shuttle bus links the airport with the center of Clermont-Ferrand ☎ 04 73 28 70 00; www.t2c.fr.

Climate – average highs and lows for the month

Jan.	Feb.	Mar.	Apr.	May	Jun.	Jul.	Aug.	Sep.	Oct.	Nov.	Dec.
5°C	7°C	13°C	16°C	20°C	24°C	27°C	26°C	23°C	16°C	10°C	6°C
41°F	45°F	55°F	61°F	68°F	75°F	81°F	79°F	73°F	61°F	50°F	43°F
-1°C	0°C	3°C	6°C	9°C	13°C	15°C	14°C	12°C	7°C	4°C	0°C
30°F	32°F	37°F	43°F	48°F	55°F	59°F	57°F	54°F	45°F	39°F	32°F

Of True Love and Blue Cheese

Once upon a time on a hillside in the heart of France, a young shepherd boy was sitting at the entrance to his cave, lunching and munching on a tasty sandwich. In the distance he saw a beautiful shepherdess and ran to meet her, leaving his bread and cheese in the cave.

History doesn't tell whether the lovers found a happy ending, but the sandwich lived happily ever after. For the passionate swain returned to the caves some months later to find that the cool moist atmosphere had turned the moldy bread into blue veins, and so Roquefort cheese was born. By the time the Romans arrived in France, those caves were already full of cheeses for a discerning market. Today, the queen of blue cheese is still made in Roquefort-sur-Soulzon in the same way, although many of the commercially manufactured faithful imitations are now produced in factories as far south as Corsica.

The distinctive foil label stamped with a red sheep distinguishes the traditional blend of milk from Lacaune ewes and natural mold from two-month-old bread. The original cool damp caves under the village are open to lactose-tolerant visitors who marvel at the endless shelves of ripening cheeses. Central France is duly proud of its cheese board; the beautiful Auvergne in particular has five distinguished cheeses: the widely appreciated Cantal; the lesser-known Salers; creamy St.-Nectaire, the long-matured favorite of King Louis XIV; and the veined specialties Fourme d'Ambert and Bleu d'Auvergne, a saltier alternative to Roquefort made from cow's milk.

The cheeses feature in such regional specialty dishes as *tarte de St.-Nectaire*, and duck breast prepared with honey and Fourme d'Ambert. Every month from May to October finds at least one town or village hosting a cheese fair.

Hardy motorists may scorn the healthy spa-town trail in favor of the cardiovascular white-knuckle thrill of a five-day drive along the cheese routes of the Puy-de-Dôme and Cantal areas. Road signs marked "Route des Fromages A.O.C. d'Auvergne" promise farmhouses, dairies, cellars and caves, châteaux, parks and restaurants. Maps are available from most regional tourist offices.

Traditionally produced blue cheeses are a specialty of the Massif Central

Clermont-Ferrand Sights

Basilique de Notre-Dame-du-Port

With splendid Romanesque architecture, Notre-Dame-du-Port justifiably is a World Heritage Site. A well from an earlier church on the site may be seen in the crypt. This spacious building dates from 1150, and its 1843 octagonal tower perches proudly above the curves and right angles of this many-tiered classic of its type. A figure of Christ the King surrounded by cherubim sits above images of John the Baptist and Isaiah at the south entrance to the basilica.

Within, there is true delight to be had in tracing the popular Bible stories carved into the capitals of the pillars. The most entertaining is the story of Adam and Eve, detailed in depictions of Eve eating the forbidden fruit of the vine (no apples in this Eden) and of a moment of anger in which Adam grabs hold of Eve by the hair and kicks her in an earthy manner.

➕ C3 ✉ rue Notre-Dame-du-Port, 63000 ☎ 04 73 98 65 00 🕐 Daily 8–7 ✋ Free

Vercingétorix

In 52 BC, a brave, 20-year-old Gallic chieftain held off Julius Caesar's army as the Romans prepared to march through the Auvergne. Since then, the name Vercingétorix has been hailed with pride in the region despite him later being hauled off to Rome and imprisoned for six years before being executed by strangulation in 46 BC. In October 1903, he literally rode again when the town finally erected a statue of Vercingétorix on horseback, sculpted by Frédéric Auguste Bartholdi (1834–1904), who created the *Statue of Liberty*.

Vercingétorix stands today, looking toward Puy-de-Dôme. Bartholdi's original bronze study is displayed beside art and artifacts from the medieval to the contemporary at Montferrand's Musée d'Art Roger-Quilliot. Musée Bargoin takes us back to Vercingétorix with a collection of local Gallo-Roman finds.

➕ A2

Vercingétorix Statue ✉ place de Jaude, 63000

Musée d'Art Roger-Quilliot ✉ place Louis-Deteix, Montferrand, 63100 ☎ 04 73 16 11 30 🕐 Tue.–Fri. 10–6, Sat.–Sun. 10–noon and 1–6 🚌 TC2: 20, 21, 25; 25 from Gare SNCF; tram: Line A to Musée d'Art Roger-Quilliot ✋ $$ (free first Sun. of the month)

Musée Bargoin ✉ 45 rue Ballainvilliers, 63000 ☎ 04 73 42 69 70 🕐 Tue.–Sat. 10–noon and 1–5, Sun 2–7 ✋ $$

Bartholdi's equestrian statue of Vercingétorix

Walk
Among the Fountains

Refer to route marked on city map on page 180

Begin this 1.5-mile walk at place de la Victoire's fountain of Pope Urban II, pointing toward the Holy Land.

Take rue St.-Genès to place Royale, with its 19th-century Renaissance-style Fontaine Royale. Rue Massillon twists into rue Savaron and place du Terrail, with galleried windows overlooking the cherubim of a 17th-century fountain.

On rue Pascal, admire the elegant 18th-century house at No. 4 and the scalloped basin at the intersection with rue du Port.

Take rue Notre-Dame-du-Port to the church (see page 183).

You can see Fontaine du Port's twin spouts from here. The road leads to place Delille, home to the chubby cheeks, thighs and pitchers of the Fontaine Delille.

Walk right on boulevard Trudaine. Fontaine de la Flèche is on the corner with rue des Archers. Farther along, turn right on place Michel-de-l'Hospital.

The 1661 Fontaine des Cercles is set into a wall.

Cross rue Maréchal-Joffre, taking rue St.-Benoît and rue Bardoux to pass the Musée Lecoq (natural history).

Across boulevard Lafayette is the charming Jardin Lecoq. By the gardener's hut is Jean Camus' white stone *Byblis Weeping*.

Leave the park toward boulevard Malfreyt and see the Egyptian obelisk known as la Fontaine de la Pyramide.

This is dedicated to the Egyptian campaigns of local General Louis Desaix, and is opposite the archeological Musée Bargoin (see page 183), which has a collection of Gallo-Roman finds.

Continue to Fontaine de l'Hôtel-Dieu, erected in 1989, and take a right to rue Clemenceau.

On the square d'Assas, the Fontaine du Roi-des-Eaux features a baroque-style Poseidon.

Rue du Coche leads to place Jaude and its modern water features. Note the Wallace drinking fountains with their signature caryatids (draped female figures) by the theater, named after Englishman Richard Wallace, who financed their construction. Follow rue du 11-Novembre and cross rue André-Moinier to rue Gaultier-de-Biauzat to see the site of the town's eccentric thermal spring grotto, La Fontaine Pétrifiante, now closed to the public. Then return to rue André-Moinier and place de la Poterne.

This is the best photo opportunity of the day, the pretty Amboise Fountain set against the mountain-peaked skyline.

Musée Lecoq ⊞ B1 ✉ 15 rue Bardoux, 63000 ☎ 04 73 42 32 00 🕐 Tue.–Sat. 10–noon and 2–6, Sun. 2–6, May–Sep.; Tue.–Sat. 10–noon and 2–5, Sun. 2–5, rest of year 🚌 3, 4, 6, 7, 8, 9, 10, 12, 13; tram: A 💶 $$ (free first Sun. of the month)

Fontaine Pétrifiante ⊞ A3 ✉ rue Gaultier de Biauzat

Place Jaude features modern fountains

Regional Sights

> **Key to symbols**
> ⊕ map coordinates refer to the Massif Central
> map on page 179 🍴 admission charge:
> $$$ more than €10, $$ €5–€10, $ less than €5
> See page 5 for complete key to symbols

Aurillac

The man who gave the West the zero is honored with a statue in the main square of Aurillac. Pope Sylvester II is the most famous son of this town at the foot of the mountains. Monks educated the shepherd boy, who went on to study mathematics and medicine at the schools of Córdoba. Among his innovations was the concept of a clock worked by a system of weights and the introduction of Arabic numerals. In AD 999, he became the first French pope.

Aurillac has an art collection, museums of local culture and a museum of volcanoes to explore away from the heat of the sun or the rain. Outside, stroll through the old narrow streets and admire some fine houses in the historic quarter on the banks of the Jordanne river, with its Pont Rouge, named for the original red-painted wooden bridge that once stood here. Great Auvergnat produce is sold at the Wednesday and Saturday markets.

⊕ A3

Tourist information ✉ 7 rue des Carmes, 15000
☎ 04 71 48 46 58; www.iaurillac.com

Les Causses

The great river valley plateaux are known as les Causses, and the four great spaces between the Lot and the Languedoc's Mediterranean coast make for dramatic scenery, each plain ripped from its neighbors by great river gorges. The Causses de Sauveterre, Méjean, Causse Noir and Larzac offer wild, windswept countryside that serves as grazing ground for the sheep whose milk makes Roquefort cheese (see page 182). Rock formations protect towns

The village of Navacelles in the Cirque, les Causses

and villages from the winds, and sweeping courses of long-gone glaciers and rivers have hewn vast natural amphitheaters out from the limestone, the best known being the Cirque de Navacelles. The other main attraction is underground, where potholes and caves open up into vast cathedral-like spaces. These areas were relatively unknown outside the region until France's first great environmental protest in the 1970s, when the government's plan to develop a huge military base at Larzac eventually was defeated by the weight of public opinion.

Once many of these strange landscapes were considered largely inaccessible, with passage restricted to stone steps carved from the rock face and the old pilgrims' road across Larzac. Today, drivers can take the road along the Tarn Gorges (see pages 187–188) and the A75 highway from St.-Flour to Montpellier, through dramatic landscapes and across the world's tallest road bridge, spanning the Tarn Valley near Millau.

⊕ B1–B2

Château d'Anjony

Lavish Renaissance frescoes, sumptuous tapestries and the rich tones of paintings from generations past bid you welcome not merely to a château, but to a genuine family home. Just as bookcases or CD racks inform you about new acquaintances, here solid wooden furnishings and extravagant decorative styles lend a personal insight into the fortunes and fashions of the Anjonys. Family portraits through the centuries go back to the days of the château's founder, the valiant and belligerent Louis II of Anjony.

The 15th-century château has four round towers and overlooks Tournemire village, with its church built of volcanic stone. Tournemire and the Anjonys have had a turbulent relationship over the years. After a quarrel over the land on which Louis II had built his château, the Tournemire and Anjony families fought a tournament to settle the dispute. The Tournemires were the victors, with Louis and his sons slain. The families maintained hostilities until the 17th century, when Michel II of Anjony proposed to Tournemire heiress Gabrielle de Pesteils, and they all lived happily ever after.

✚ A3

✉ Tournemire, 15310 ☎ 04 71 47 61 67; www.anjony.com ⏰ Mon.–Sat. 11–11:30 and 2–6:30, Sun. 2–6:30, Jul.–Aug.; daily 2–6, Apr.–Jun. and Sep.; 2–5, mid-Feb. to end Mar. and Oct. to mid-Nov. Closed mid-Nov. to mid-Feb. ✋ $$

Conques

The twin towers of Église St.-Foye once welcomed pilgrims to this picturesque hillside village in the Aveyron region, south of the Lot river. Today, the charms are no less a lure to vacationers, wooed and won by dainty stone cottages, sloping rooftops and delightful country gardens. The name refers to the conch-shell shape of the site.

Pilgrims on their way to cross the Pyrénées made the fortunes of the village as they paid their respect at the shrine to the Christian martyr for whom

Fine furnishings and frescoes are on show in the magnificent Château d'Anjony

the 11th-century church is named. A golden statue reliquary embossed with precious stones dates from the ninth century, and a superb interpretation of the Last Judgment is carved over the main doorway.

✚ A2

Tourist information ✉ Le Bourg, 12230 ☎ 05 65 72 85 00; www.tourisme-conques.fr

Gorges de l'Ardèche

The very image of a rural French summer day is the sight of families by the waterside under the Pont d'Arc. This magnificent natural arch makes a 111-foot-high stone bridge spanning the Ardèche Gorge and is the undisputed star of the rugged Ardèche mountains between the Rhône and Cévennes valleys. Through the centuries, the river has carved a spectacular canyon, now classified as a natural park.

Excellent views are guaranteed along the gorge, and not only for drivers taking the D290 from Vallon-Pont-d'Arc to the Rhône, with its 12 designated viewing points en route. Lazy sunbathers tickle their toes in the water under the arch, and solo fishermen cast their lines from the rocks. Canoeists shoot the 25 rapids that cover 19 miles from Vallon to Pont-St.-Esprit. The adventure can take up to two days. Canoes can be rented at Vallon-Pont-d'Arc, where minibus shuttles link with Sauze, near St.-Martin-d'Ardèche, some 20 miles downstream.

Less energetic water travel is also available at a price. *Barques* carrying four to six passengers, and steered by two boatmen, may be reserved at the Vallon-Pont-d'Arc tourist office. The office can also advise on excursions to the various caves of the region (the Grottes d'Aven), where guides take visitors down to underground chambers of glistening stalactites and stalagmites. The hillsides, with their steep paths above 1,000-year-old chestnut groves, are popular with hikers and mountain bikers in search of the perfect panorama.

If the heat of the summer sun is too much, step into the cool shade of one of the 100 caves.

Many attractive towns and villages offer shady squares for a long, cool drink and a leisurely snack. At the delightful town of Aubenas, you can visit the elegant château, with its 12th-century donjon, and see the dome of the Benedictine Chapelle St.-Benoît.

Don't leave the area without buying a can of the famous chestnut paste, *crème de marrons*. Delicious for cooking, it's available from shops or farmers' markets. Because of the afternoon heat, several towns hold midweek markets at night, an enchanting otherworldly experience marked by a wonderful atmosphere in local bars and sidewalk cafés. Check dates and addresses with tourist offices.

✚ C2

Ardèche tourist information www.ardecheendirect.com

Privas tourist information ✉ 3 place General-de-Gaulle, 07000 ☎ 04 75 64 33 35; www.paysdeprivas.com

Aubenas tourist information ✉ 4 boulevard Gambetta, 07200 ☎ 04 75 89 02 03; www.aubenas-vals.com

Vallon-Pont-d'Arc tourist information ✉ place de l'Ancien-Gare, 07150 ☎ 04 75 88 04 01; www.vallon-pont-darc.com

Château d'Aubenas ☎ 04 75 87 81 11 🕐 Guided tours daily 11, 2, 3, 4 and 5, Jul.–Aug.; Tue.–Sat. 10:30 and 2:30, Jun. and Sep.; Tue. and Thu.–Sat. 2, rest of year 🎫 $

Gorges du Tarn

The most popular section of the Causses (see page 185) is this canyon dividing the *causses* of Méjean and Sauveterre. In summer, what is otherwise a peaceful and charming drive along the riverside D907b can resemble a crowded parking lot, as seemingly everyone around appears to have decided to take the same trip. Either grin and bear it in your quest for natural beauty, or try to do the trip before mid-July or after early September.

The main attraction is the riverbank that runs from le Rozier-Peyreleau to

Ste.-Énimie, wedged between 1,600-foot cliffs teeming with waterfalls. If you are fit and suitably shod, follow marked trails up the rocks to gaze down on the shimmering waters. A more leisurely way to enjoy the river is on a boat trip from la Malène through les Détroits (the straits).

✚ B2

Le Rozier-Peyreleau tourist information ✉ Siège au Rozier, route de Metreuls, 48150 ☎ 05 65 60 60 89; www.officedetourisme-gorgesdutarn.com

Maison du Parc National des Cévennes
✉ 6 bis, place du Palais, Florac, 48400 ☎ 04 66 49 53 01; www.cevennes-parcnational.fr

Boat trips ✉ La Malène, 48120 ☎ 04 66 48 51 10; www.gorgesdutarn.com ✋ $$$

Le Lioran

From December to April, le Lioran is the capital of winter sports in the Cantal area. Nestled in pine forests just below the 4,245-foot Col de Cère, it attracts visitors year round. In winter, much of the attention is focused on nearby Super-Lioran. The largest ski resort in the Massif Central, it's more a family destination than a chic jet-set spot. A cable car, chairlifts, drag lifts and 22 ski lifts serve 40 miles of slopes and plenty of cross-country ski trails in winter and carry hang gliders and hikers to the crest of the 6,086-foot Plomb du Cantal and other peaks during summer and fall.

Tailor-made itineraries for touring the area – from torchlight ski rambles to mountain-bike trails – are available year round. In the resort, as well as the usual pizzerias, rustic taverns serve traditional mountain dishes.

✚ B3

Tourist information ✉ 15300 le Lioran
☎ 04 71 49 50 08; www.lelioran.com

Le Puy-en-Velay

Crane your neck from the enchanting town, built in an old volcanic crater, to see the chapel perched high on a rocky outcrop, way above the streets of le Puy-en-Velay. The 11th-century

Chapelle St.-Michel-d'Aiguilhe sits like an eagle's nest on the horizon and upstages the town's cathedral, a Moorish-style edifice with a rare vault of oblong domes and exquisite cloisters. Look above the cathedral for another rocky peak, capped by a 52-foot statue of the Madonna and Child. Climb up to the statue's viewing platform to look down at the many levels of this quaint town. For more than 300 years, le Puy has been a center of lace-making and classes are available.

✚ C3

Tourist information ✉ 2 place du Clauzel, 43000
☎ 04 71 09 38 41; www.ot-lepuyenvelay.fr

A glimpse of some of the spectacular scenery to be enjoyed in the Gorges du Tarn

Riom

Until Clermont and Montferrand united to form Clermont-Ferrand (see pages 180–184), this city was the prime candidate for capital of the Auvergne. Its blend of volcanic rock and Renaissance architecture creates elegant streets and impressive residences. Visit the local museum of the Auvergne and the Église Notre-Dame-du-Marthuret, with its 14th-century statue of the infant Christ caressing a goldfinch. The Musée Francisque Mandet has a good collection of fine and applied arts. There are fine views from the city's clock tower and you can see the workings of the clock. Near the town is the ruined fortress of Tournoel, overlooking the source of the Volvic mineral water spring.

🔁 B4

Tourist information ✉ 27 place de la Fédération, 63200 ☎ 04 73 38 59 45; www.tourisme-riomlimagne.fr

Musée Régional d'Auvergne ✉ 10 bis rue Delille, 63200 ☎ 04 73 38 17 31 🕐 Tue.–Sun. 10–6, Jul.–Aug.; 10–noon and 2–5:30, Apr.–Jun. and Sep–Nov. Closed Nov. 1–11 and Dec.–Mar. 🚻 $

Musée Francisque Mandet ✉ 14 rue de l'Hôtel-de-Ville, 63200 ☎ 04 73 38 18 53 🕐 Tue.–Sun. 10–6, Jul.–Aug.; Tue.–Sun., 10–noon and 2–5:30, rest of year 🚻 $

Land of Volcanoes

Far from the lunar landscape that its name evokes, Parc Naturel Régional des Volcans d'Auvergne is a verdant natural park, home to chamois, marmots and wild sheep. Kites and peregrine falcons patrol the skies around the highest peak, Puy de Sancy, and rare butterflies are attracted to colorful wild flowers. This largest ensemble of volcanoes in Europe boasts dome-shaped hills and craters shaped like egg cups. Although the volcanoes have been dormant for centuries, they still course with heat far below the surface – as the hot springs of the spa towns prove.

The biggest and best on the visitor trail, the 4,806-foot Puy de Dôme, has some remnants of a Roman temple, several postcard and souvenir hawkers and – best of all – a spectacular view over the city of Clermont-Ferrand (see pages 180–184) and south toward the Monts Dore.

Puy de Sancy, at 6,184 feet, has more than an hour's hike from the top of the cable-car route to reach the highest views over the Cantal massif. On the eastern slopes of the Monts Dore massif is the delightful village of Besse-et-St.-Anastaise, with its 15th-century houses and a museum of skiing. Real-life action takes place on Super-Besse, a few miles away.

Fields edged with trees stretch away toward Puy de Peyre Arse

Rangers organize short walks and week-long treks through the park, but individuals seeking a briefer taste of scenery should drive on the D680 to the Pas de Peyrol. Here, follow a walk to the 5,863-foot Puy Mary. Most of the area is unspoiled, unchallenged by town planners and commandeered for use by the army. Hikers will notice the lava stone huts and shelters, known as *burons*, where livestock herdsmen live during summer when they bring their flocks up from the valleys.

The story of the Auvergne volcanoes is told at Vulcania, the European vulcanology science park near Clermont-Ferrand, which has 30 live events and films in two movie theaters exploring the role of volcanoes in the creation of our solar system.

Centre d'Information du Parc Naturel Régional des Volcans d'Auvergne

✉ Château Monlosier, 63970 Aydat ☎ 04 73 65 64 26; www.parc-volcans-auvergne.com

Vulcania, Parc Européen du Volcanisme ✉ route de Mazaye, 63230 St.-Ours-les-Roches ☎ 08 20 82 78 28 (toll call); www.vulcania.com 🕐 Thu.–Tue. 10–7:30, Wed. 10 a.m.–11 p.m., Aug.; Thu.–Tue. 10–7, Wed. 10 a.m.–11 p.m., Jul.; daily 10–6, late Mar.–Jun.; Wed.–Sun. 10–6, Sep. to mid-Nov. Closed mid-Nov. to late Mar. 🍴 Restaurant, café, bar 🚌 Shuttle bus from Clermont-Ferrand Jul.–Aug. Contact tourist office for details 💶 $$$ (varies with season)

Drive
Spas of the Belle Époque

Distance: 195 miles
Time: 3 to 4 days

This summer drive through the Auvergne's countryside (some roads are closed in winter) starts in Vichy and takes in many of the bubbling springs where generations have come to enjoy the waters.

Ornate pergolas and regal architecture reflect the golden age of each resort. Even if you've no desire to sample the curative spring waters, you still may appreciate the ritual of afternoon tea, enjoying music at the park bandstand and evening entertainment. Nightfall means dressing up for the casino, indulging at an elegant restaurant or enjoying a night at the opera or at the racetrack in Vichy. The queen of the spa towns, Vichy, pampers with all the pomp and splendor of the belle époque and Second Empire.

From Vichy, drive west on the N209. At Gannat, turn right on the N9, then left on the D42. Turn left again to the D35, pausing in the exquisite village of Charroux. Continue on the D35 to St.-Bonnet-de-Rochefort then turn left on the D37 to rejoin the N9, going south. Bypass Aigueperse on the D448, then rejoin the N9 to Riom (see page 189). Follow the D446 west until taking a right turn on the D985 to Châtel-Guyon.

At the spa resort of Châtel-Guyon, the style could best be described as art nouveau meets Hollywood. Guy de Maupassant was inspired to write *Mont-Oriol* after staying here.

Back to the D446, then take the D986 to Volvic (see page 189). Take the D15 south, turn right on the D762 and left on the D941

to skirt Clermont-Ferrand (see pages 180–184). Take the D68 into Royat.

Just outside Clermont is the Roman-favored spa resort of Royat. Its Source Eugénie spring is popular with French women concerned about cellulite, and visitors can take a day's treatment to break the busy touring schedule.

Back on the D68, turn left on the D941C, then left again on the D941A, stopping at the Col de la Moreno. On reaching the N89 intersection, take the second exit onto the D216, later taking the D27 south. Join the D983, then the D996 toward Mont-Dore, stopping at the magnificent Col de Guéry, landscaped by volcanoes and glaciers.

In the heart of volcano country (see pages 190–191), the mountain resort of Mont-Dore was a place of worship long before the era of the body beautiful. Celts believed gods lived in the crater; Romans built their largest temple, parts of which remain, to Mercury; 19th-century scientists built an observatory; and the 20th century brought golf. Every generation comes for the views and baths. The neo-Byzantine spa and funicular railway are listed monuments.

Continue along the D130 to la Bourboule.

With the "rock of the fairies," the wooded Park Fenêstre's little railroad and lake, pastel-tinted bridges over the Dordogne and discreet grandeur, la Bourboule would be a joy at any altitude. Take the cable car to the Charlannes plateau at 4,100 feet. In winter, sports lovers come here to ski. In summer, parents bring asthmatic children here to breathe.

Head back to le Mont-Dore via the D130, then take the D996, turning left after Col de la Croix Morand on the D617. Take a right on the D5, pausing at Murol-Château, then turn left onto the D996. A left on the D150 leads into St.-Nectaire.

St.-Nectaire is a spa resort that boasts an interesting 12th-century church in the village of St.-Nectaire-le-Haut. The waters here are said to help with weight loss and relieve stress.

Follow the D996 east to Issoire, then go south on the A75. Take the exit at intersection 28, for St.-Flour center. Leave St.-Flour on the D921 to Chaudes-Aigues.

Europe's warmest natural springs produce 180-degree waters – hot enough to heat the whole town of Chaudes-Aigues. The town is delightful and worth taking time to explore.

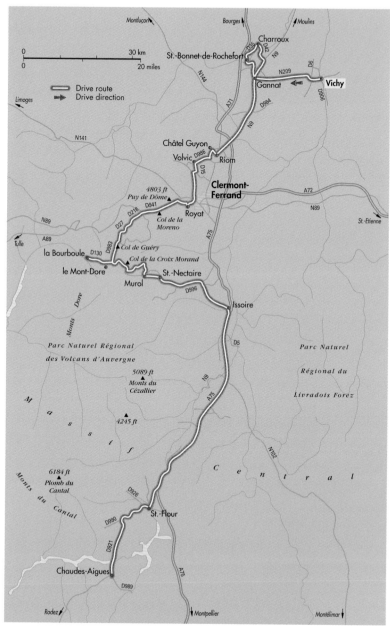

Alps and the Rhône Valley

Opposite: The village of Combloux, with stunning views of the Chaîne des Aravis mountains

Alps and the Rhône Valley

For the would-be adventurer, this is the region of soaring glaciers and mountain ranges. For the down-to-earth trencherman, it's the pinnacle of haute cuisine. Whatever the lure, a vacation here is presented in wide screen. The grandeur of nature, lakes, mountains, gorges and vast areas of woodland may have been reined in by cable cars, modern roads and the architecture of electricity. Although electricity lines and power stations mar the occasional view, they do allow other vistas to be appreciated in comfort. In addition, since the Mont-Blanc tunnel fire in 1999, restrictions have been placed on its use by heavy-duty trucks and this has greatly reduced the traffic fumes that previously tended to spoil the panorama. The pristine waters of Lake Geneva (Lac Léman) show Swiss concern for cleanliness. The truth is that the region of the Rhône benefits from the environmental overspill of its neighbors, as well as from its own majestic Alpine pleasures of lakeside spas and ski resorts. All around the nougat town of Montélimar is the stunning scenery of Provence. The Drôme and Ardèche landscapes are the continuation of the splendors of the Massif Central. Beaujolais and Mâcon have much in common with the slopes of Burgundy.

Grapes growing in a verdant Côtes du Rhône vineyard ripen as they soak up the sun

Cosmopolitan Pleasures

The contrast between town and country, mountain resort and nature park is the main attraction of the area. Lyon (see pages 200–205) is a city with a rich cultural and architectural heritage, yet it's just a short drive from many a rural idyll. Its key high-speed train link between Paris and the Mediterranean, and the famous Autoroute du Soleil guarantee Lyon's cosmopolitan mix of movers and shakers, as in its trading heyday on Roman tin and silk routes.

However, the regional capital has no monopoly on culture. In winter, the money moves to the mountains, and leisure resorts woo the arts. Great paintings by artists of centuries past line gallery walls in towns such as Grenoble, and modern artists have set up a colony in Pérouges.

Raise a Glass

A heritage of good food in cities and villages alike (see page 199) means that local wines may be found wherever you visit. Besides the wine of Beaujolais, the region has its red wines of Côtes du Rhône, the best known of which are Crozes-Hermitage and Condrieu. A small area of the Savoie produces splendid white wines. Try the clear and fruity Cruet or Crépy, with its light intriguing bouquet from the Altesse

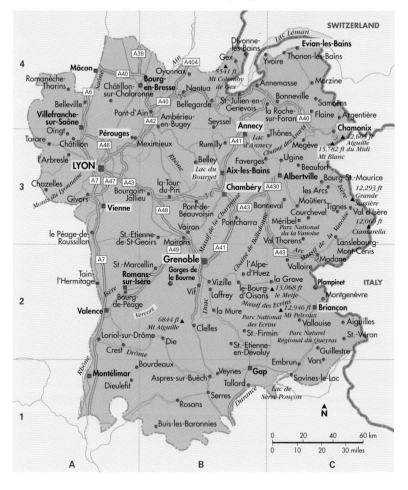

Snowcapped Mont-Blanc stands proud above a cool and shady alpine meadow

vines. Locally popular everyday rosés and reds are produced here, too.

Capital of Winter Sports

Three Winter Olympic seasons – at Chamonix (1924), Grenoble (1968) and Albertville (1992) – and dozens of annual championship skiing events keep the French Alps in top form. With 180 resorts serving 3,600 miles of courses, this is the world's largest fully equipped skiing area. Three massive interconnected circuits offer unrivaled scope, each for the price of a single pass: les Portes de Soleil, with 400 miles of linked runs along the Franco-Swiss border; les Trois Vallées, a similar circuit; and l'Espace Killy, named for Olympic gold medalist Jean-Claude Killy. The latter contains 190 miles of connected slopes for serious downhill skiers.

The vast ski country has color-coded runs suitable for every ability: green for beginners, blue for intermediates, red for experienced skiers and black for James Bond-standard sports enthusiasts. Lifts and cable cars are continually renewed and improved. Weekly passes are the

sensible option. Resorts range from the traditional mountain village, with its slate-roofed wooden chalets and cheery, old-fashioned knitwear boutiques, to the functional complexes built since the 1950s. Slopes and lifts reach the front doors of modern hotels. Megève, St.-Gervais and Val d'Isère (see page 215) are among traditional destinations safely wrapped in environmental protection orders. Contemporary resorts include Avoriaz (a motorist-free zone), la Plagne and les Arcs.

Snowboarding is as well catered to as conventional skiing, and dog-sled rides, snowshoe hikes and adrenaline sports feature on many itineraries. Larger destinations now market themselves to non-skiers as well, packing the winter season with festivals on themes from film to stand-up comedy.

The region is big enough to appeal to the lone adventurer as much as the sporting package tourist. Plenty of locations away from the ski hubs attract those who like to challenge the elements. Against the snows of winter and rock faces of summer, bright day-glo colors easily identify adventure-sports enthusiasts. The winter season is from early December to April, with good-value weekend rates available except during French school holidays. There is no guarantee of good weather, but most destinations are equipped with snow-making machinery. Recent years have found winters that are milder and later than the calendar assumes. Higher resorts are open earlier and continue into May. In summer, glacier skiing is an option at Val Thorens, Val d'Isère, Tignes, la Plagne, les Deux Alpes and Alpe d'Huez.

Tables of the Rhône

Food matters in the Rhône Valley. Where Paris sways between fashions, Lyon manages the complex balancing act of maintaining the finest traditions of gastronomy and steering each new wave. Maybe the common sense stems from the fact that the original innovators of Lyonaise cuisine were women (*les Mères*, the mothers).

There is life outside the important kitchens of the city. Lyon's bistros, known as *bouchons*, are lively, informal and welcoming establishments, serving up the famous *andouillette* (small sausage made of chitterlings) in mustard sauce; and *quenelles* (pike dumplings) in pink Nantua sauce.

After skiing, savor Savoyard favorites, including cheeses for all courses: Tomme de Savoie, Beaufort, Emmental or Reblochon; a *fondue* with bread or raclette of melted cheese with ham as a warming fireside treat; or *tartiflette* (baked cheese and potatoes) as an informal snack. At the end of a meal, order walnut pie from Grenoble, a chocolate dessert from a Lyon confectioner, or, in the fall, fresh wild berries from the woods.

Nyons produces one of the few *appellation d'origine contrôlée* olive oils in France. In the district of Drôme, the oil is outshone only by the value of the legendary truffles. You will sometimes hear of a "truffle market"

Gourmet City

Lyon (see pages 200–205) is famed as a source of great chefs and world-class cuisine, and one of the most prominent names today is that of Paul Bocuse, a seventh-generation master chef. As well as operating his own restaurant and five brasseries in the city, he is the founder of the Institut Paul Bocuse, École Superieur d'Hotellerie et Restauration, where graduates of the three- or five-year courses are pretty much guaranteed top jobs in the hospitality industry. Short courses of six or 12 weeks are available for food-lovers to develop their culinary skills (☎ 04 72 18 02 20; www.institutpaulbocuse.com).

being held in town, but you will search in vain for neat tables of the sought-after delicacy. Chefs come with wads of bills to buy the best available, but the cash-only transactions take place in cafés and bars. Truffle farmers keep their wares discreetly tucked away in their deep coat pockets.

Gastronomy is considered to be an art in Lyon

Lyon

Lyon has scores of unmissable sights, but the greatest of all is the city itself. Just like the Pyramids, St. Petersburg and Venice, the entire historic center of Lyon has been declared a UNESCO World Heritage Site.

Almost 1,250 acres have been awarded monument status, so rich are the streets, hills and waterfronts in fabulously preserved memories of 2,000 dramatic years. Unlike ordinary museums, this area is the vibrant, pulsating heart of

France's second-busiest city. Rather than preserving the past under glass, the city center continues to develop with a keen eye on conservation. Parking lots are moved underground, and views remain unspoiled – except perhaps by the uninspiring pencil-shaped Credit Lyonnais tower.

The tower, along with the business and conference district, needn't concern you. With distinctive hills and a medieval quarter almost entirely surrounded by water, Lyon boasts enough historic landmarks to make the visitor feel

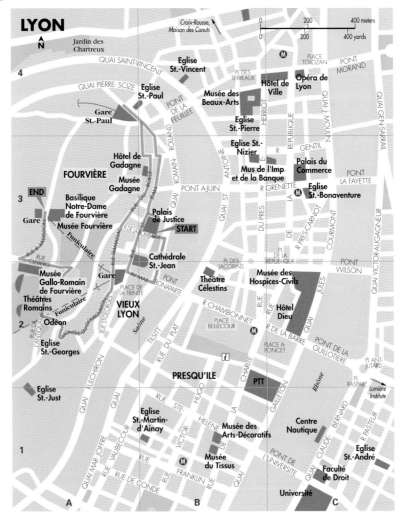

Basilique Notre-Dame de Fourvière looks down over the old town and the statue of Louis XIV

comfortable about exploring the city on foot or by the well-organized public transportation system.

Since the city has never had time to stagnate, each era has seen the development of a new section of Lyon. First to flourish were the hills of Fourvière and Croix-Rousse in 43 BC, when Romans and Gauls coexisted as the city proved a rallying point for Roman colonial armies marching north and west. As Rome declined and France grew, so did medieval Vieux (Old) Lyon, below and between the hills.

The very center of this section is the Presqu'île, or peninsula (literally "nearly an island"). The dangling strip of land is almost completely surrounded by two rivers, the Saône and the Rhône. Most main sites of interest are to be found here and on the Fourvière bank of the Saône.

The church controlled medieval Lyon. Renaissance prosperity led to merchants and the monarchy taking over the city. Highly ostentatious houses were built during this period. The silk trade led to the development of the Croix-Rousse district, and 19th-century civic confidence brought grand boulevards.

Arts and Pleasures

Throughout its history, Lyon has garnered a deserved reputation as a center of good living. Gastronomically, the city is without equal (see page 199). Food is presented with a flourish, and shop windows and market stands inspire unseemly drooling among passersby.

Top-grade opera, ballet, concerts, theater and exhibitions run either in their formal fall-to-spring seasons or in world-class festivals, such as the biennial Contemporary Art Festival, held in odd-numbered years. Besides the great sights and monuments, there are at least two dozen fine museums to visit.

Street culture is best seen in spectacular murals, painted on the outside of buildings. Trompe-l'oeil fantasy worlds and famous faces from the city's past and present are favored themes. Bars and fashionable cafés buzz well into the night in the streets of Vieux Lyon. This is also the only French city, other than resorts, to nurture a casino. Great shopping abounds around town, especially near place Bellecour and Part Dieu station.

As far from Hollywood as you could imagine, Lyon was the birthplace of cinema. Antoine Lumière encouraged his sons Louis and Auguste in their experiments, which in March 1895 resulted in the launch of the Lumière

Pick a Card

The essential companion for a visit to this city with so much to see and do is the Lyon City Card. Valid for one, two or three days and sold at the tourist office, the leisure pass gives you admission to the main museums, guided tours and river cruises, as well as unlimited use of public transportation.

Cinématographe. The family's first film, *Workers Leaving the Factory Gates*, was an instant hit. The story of the brothers and the cinematic revolution that their work inspired is the theme of the Lumière Institute, a combined movie theater and museum complex that stands on the site of the family's groundbreaking first picture show.

Essential Information

Tourist Information

✉ place Bellecour, 69005 ☎ 04 72 77 69 69; www.lyon-france.com 🚇 Bellecour

Urban Transportation

An excellent bus, tramway and subway system runs from 5 a.m. to midnight, and a funicular railway climbs Fourvière hill. Recognize stations by the sign M. Tickets, sold individually, in discounted books *(carnets)* of 10 or a one-day pass *(Ticket Liberté)* may be used on buses or the subway ☎ 04 26 10 12 12 (toll call); www.tcl.fr.
The Lyon City Card (see above) offers additional travel on riverboats. Taxis may be hailed in the streets, or ☎ 04 78 28 23 23. The tourist office provides a taxi service for visitors, *(taxis touristiques)*, in which

drivers double as guides to the sights. A high-speed train service from Perrache and Part-Dieu stations links Lyon with the rest of France – Paris in two hours and Marseille in two hours 45 minutes ☎ 36 35; www.sncf.fr.

Airport Information

Aéroport International de Lyon-St.-Exupéry (☎ 0826 80 08 26 (toll call); www.lyonaeroports.com) is 16 miles east of the city at Satolas. Rhonexpress offers a tram service between the airport and downtown (Part Dieu train station), between 5 a.m. and midnight, with a journey time of 30 minutes ☎ 08 26 00 17 18; www.rhonexpress.fr. A "Moto Taxi" service offers a fast transfer between the airport and the city center by motorbike. Book at the tourist office.

Climate – average highs and lows for the month

Jan.	Feb.	Mar.	Apr.	May	Jun.	Jul.	Aug.	Sep.	Oct.	Nov.	Dec.
5°C	8°C	12°C	14°C	20°C	23°C	27°C	26°C	22°C	17°C	10°C	7°C
41°F	46°F	54°F	57°F	68°F	73°F	81°F	79°F	72°F	63°F	50°F	45°F
0°C	1°C	3°C	5°C	10°C	14°C	17°C	16°C	12°C	8°C	4°C	2°C
32°F	34°F	37°F	41°F	50°F	57°F	63°F	61°F	54°F	46°F	39°F	36°F

Lyon Sights

Cathédrale St.-Jean

Built between the 12th and 15th centuries, the cathedral has the expected Gothic facade and a grand rose window, dating from 1393. St.-Jean still has its original 13th- and 14th-century stained glass. The main attraction for visitors is a 16th-century astronomic clock by Swiss craftsman Lippius. It chimes at noon, 2 p.m., 3 p.m. and 4 p.m.

➕ B3 ✉ place St.-Jean, 69005 ☎ 04 78 42 11 04; http://cathedrale-lyon.cef.fr 🕐 Mon.–Fri. 8:15–7:45, Sat. 8:15–7, Sun. 8 a.m.–9 p.m. 🚇 Vieux Lyon ✋ Free

Croix-Rousse

The Croix-Rousse district rises above the neck of the Presqu'île and it grew rich on the back of the silk trade.

The fabulous Maison des Canuts (Silk Weaver's House) workshop and museum showcases the old ways of working and offers silk-weaving demonstrations. The Musée du Tissus (Fabric Museum) on rue de la Charité, near place Bellecour (see page 204), has displays of fine "canut" workmanship.

➕ Off map B4

Maison des Canuts ✉ 10–12 rue d'Ivry, 69004 ☎ 04 78 28 62 04; www.maisondescanuts.com 🕐 Guided tours only, Tue.–Sat. 11 a.m. and 3:30 p.m. 🚇 Croix-Rousse ✋ $$ (combined tickets with Musée du Tissus available)

Fourvière

A funicular train saves your breath for the breathtaking views from the top of the hill that dominates every other view of the city. A good place to start or finish any tour of Lyon, the hill shows off the rooftops of Vieux Lyon, the slopes of the Croix-Rousse and the Presqu'île to form the ultimate panorama. The views continue along a walkway to the Hauteurs Park and Jardin du Rosaire, which link the districts of St.-Jean and Loyasse. At the crest of the hill is the chunky fortresslike Basilique Notre-Dame de Fourvière, opened in 1896. It's noteworthy for Byzantine mosaics, Gothic stained-glass windows, marble statues and its crypt.

Nearby, the 12th-century oratory and 18th-century chapel, with its

Cathédrale St.-Jean has a fine Gothic exterior and some original interior features

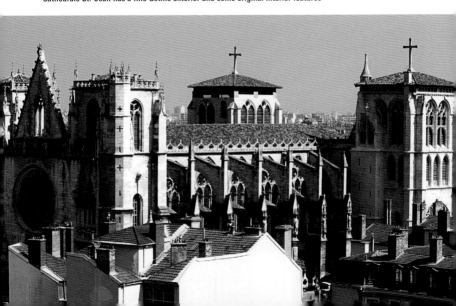

Alps and the Rhône Valley

statue of the Virgin, are worth a visit. The Fourvière Museum has a splendid collection of sacred art. Television is beamed courtesy of a transmission tower reminiscent of Eiffel's in Paris.

➕ A3
Musée de Fourvière ✉ 8 place Fourvière, 69005 ☎ 04 78 25 13 01; www.fourviere.org 🕐 Daily 10–12:30 and 2–5:30 🚇 Vieux Lyon, then funicular to Fourvière 💶 $–$$

Musée Gadagne

Two enchantingly different museums share an elegant, beautifully renovated, Renaissance home in the imposing mansion of the Hôtel de Gadagne: the Museum of Lyon History and the engaging International Puppet Museum.

The Museum of Lyon History tastefully presents the city from the Middle Ages to the 20th century.

The International Puppet Museum has all manner of puppets that

developed into the nation's favorite creation, the satirical and politically incorrect puppet show Guignol, which first was performed in the city.

➕ B3 ✉ 1 place du Petit-Collège, 69005 ☎ 04 78 42 03 61; www.gadagne.musees.lyon.fr 🕐 Wed.–Sun. 11–6:30 🚇 Vieux Lyon 🎭 Théâtre du Guignol de Lyon hosts performances for adults and children courtesy of the Zonzons company at 2 rue Louis-Carrand (☎ 04 78 28 92 57; www.guignol-lyon.com) 💶 $$

Musée Gallo-Romain de Fourvière

When Munatius Plancus founded the city of Lugdunum on the Fourvière hill in the ancient capital of Gaul, he simply wanted to provide shelter for the veterans of Julius Caesar's armies. He could not have imagined that so much of the original construction would still draw crowds 2,000 years later. Two Roman theaters from 15 BC still pull in huge audiences for summer classical and rock concerts.

The 10,000-capacity open-air Théâtre and the Odéon, which once had a bronze roof, as well as traces of public baths, can be explored free of charge. It's better, however, to pay to see the exhibitions at the adjacent Gallo-Roman Museum first to begin to understand life in Roman France. The museum is superbly designed, with underground passages to keep the 21st century out of sight. Intelligently displayed stone coffins, statues, bronze, mosaics, gold and silverware are all explained in English as well as French.

➕ A2 ✉ 17 rue Cléberg, 69005 ☎ 04 72 38 49 30; www.musees-gallo-romains.com 🕐 Tue.–Sun. 10–6. Theaters: daily 7 a.m.–9 p.m., mid-Apr. to mid-Sep.; daily 7–7, rest of year 🚇 Vieux Lyon, then funicular to Fourvière 💶 Museum $$ (free Thu.); theaters free

Place Bellecour

The sweeping expanse of place Bellecour is one of Europe's largest squares. It's an oasis of calm in the middle of the Presqu'île between the two rivers, graced by gardens by Robert de Cotte and a statue of Louis XIV.

➕ B2 🚇 Bellecour

The impressive Roman Théâtre at Lyon could seat up to 10,000 people

Walk
World Heritage Site

Refer to route marked on city map on page 200

This two-mile stretch of Renaissance houses, secret passages and Roman theaters gives a flavor of this World Heritage Site in the center of Lyon.

With your back to the Palais de Justice, turn right along quai Fulchiron and right again onto avenue Adolphe Max for the cathedral. Behind the cathedral, visit remains of St.-Etienne and Ste.-Croix churches. On rue de la Bombarde, pass Maison du Chamarier, the first Renaissance house in town. Cross rue St.-Jean, passing the Maison des Avocats and its magnificently arched gallery. **At 54 rue St.-Jean, enter the Grande Traboule through four buildings and courtyards before arriving at 27 rue du Bœuf. Double back to rue St.-Jean, and find the *traboule* (alleyway) opposite at No. 27, then walk through two small courtyards** with 16th-century galleries to 6 rue des Trois-Maries. Then, return to rue St.-Jean and admire the architecture, especially at Nos. 24 and 28. At place du Change, Maison Thomassin has a Gothic zodiac facade. **Follow rue Lainerie to the Gothic facade of No. 14. Continue to the Romanesque and Gothic Église St.-Paul. Cross the square from the church and take rue Juiverie. No. 4, the Maison Henri-IV, was built under the reign of François I.** At 8 rue Juiverie, the Maison Bullioud, with a gallery by Philibert Delorme, shows the skill of an architect who went to work for a king. **Continue to place du Petit Collège and the history museum (see page 204). Take rue du Bœuf to pause at No. 16 to see La Tour Rose (pink tower), with its famous hanging gardens and restaurant. Follow rue Tramassac to place de la Trinité. No. 2 rue St.-Georges leads you to some extraordinary oval galleries. Make your way up montée du Gourguillon, and then right up rue de l'Antiquaille. Turn left at rue Cléberg to the Gallo-Roman museum and Roman theaters (see page 204). Turn right on rue Roger-Radisson to get to place Fourvière, the basilica and to see panoramic views of the city from the esplanade.**

A long *traboule* (alleyway) in the St.-Jean district of the World Heritage Site

Beaujolais

Best known for its wines, Beaujolais country is a sunny distraction on the main highway to the south of France. Close enough to Lyon to benefit from the culture of gastronomy yet individual enough to retain its own flavors, this area of gentle hills and neat vineyards is pretty and welcoming. Parts of the region have been dubbed Beaujolais Tuscany for the effect of the sunlight on rich golden stone. In Haut Beaujolais, villages are built of sturdy granite. Everywhere little churches prod the skyline, and boards by the roadside invite drivers to stop and visit wine cellars.

The 54,000 acres between Mâcon and Lyon produce popular red wines. Unlike the vintages of neighboring Burgundy and the châteaux of Bordeaux, these don't change hands at hundreds of dollars per bottle. The vast majority of local wines are made to be shared informally.

There are three distinct types of Beaujolais: the highest-quality Beaujolais *crus*, the everyday Beaujolais *villages* and the famous Beaujolais *nouveau*. The Beaujolais *crus* consists of 10 fine wines – Brouilly, Chénas, Chiroubles, Côte-de-Brouilly, Fleurie, Juliénas, Morgon, Moulin-à-Vent, Régnié and St.-Amour. These are worth saving a few years. Brouilly, in particular, is one of few red wines best served chilled. On the edges of the better slopes grow the Beaujolais *villages*, good-quality, everyday wines.

The majority of vineyards produce Beaujolais *nouveau*, bright red, fun and fruity country wine that is best drunk young – so young, in fact, that the third Thursday in November finds the famous Beaujolais Nouveau race. When the new wine is released at the stroke of midnight, vehicles hit the roads in a race to be the first to bring the new wines to European cities, where commuters at railroad stations give their verdict to the press.

Every other town seems to have its modest wine museum. One of the best is Le Hameau du Vin (www.hameauduvin.com) in Romanèche-Thorins, which sits in the shadow of the windmill that gives its name to Moulin-à-Vent. Run by George Duboeuf, probably the finest name in Beaujolais viticulture, the tour features traditional winemaking and modern bottling, audiovisual presentations and a wine tasting in the cellar. Rhône Tourist Board provides itineraries and details of cellar visits.

Comité Départemental du Tourisme du Rhône ✉ 142 bis avenue de Sax, 69003 Lyon
☎ 04 72 56 70 40; www.rhonetourisme.com

One of the Beaujolais *villages* vineyards producing popular red wine

Alps and the Rhône Valley

Regional Sights

Key to symbols

➕ map coordinates refer to the map on page 197

✋ admission charge: \$\$\$ more than €10,
\$\$ €5–€10, \$ less than €5

See page 5 for complete key to symbols

Annecy

Postcard perfect, this charming town center – on the banks of the tourist-magnet lake of the same name – has a permanent air of having just been dusted. In summer, fresh flowers perch on every surface; windowsills, railings, bridges and even roadsides are ablaze with color. Bracing fresh air and numerous waterways add to the feeling of constant cleanliness. Once you've enjoyed the attraction highlights, take a stroll through the streets of the old town or along the lakefront and savor the atmosphere. In season, the international crowds that fill the streets and line up for boat trips take the edge off the glow, but there is plenty to enjoy in the quaint, canal-veined quarter where the Thiou river flows into the lake. Enjoy Renaissance frescoes in the Église St.-Maurice, the waterfront prison on the Palais de l'Île, and an interesting local museum in the château that once was home to the counts of Geneva and dukes of Savoy.

➕ B3

Tourist information ✉ 1 rue Jean-Jaurès, 74000 ☎ 04 50 45 00 33; www.lac-annecy.com

Bourget, Lac du

The spa town of Aix-les-Bains is the principal resort of this long, slender lake between high mountain ridges. With all the diversions of a 19th-century spa resort, and promenade gardens, Aix is conducive to taking mountain air. Modern water sports are available on the lake, and lunch cruises are ideal for admiring the scenery. Another interesting boat trip takes visitors to the final resting place of the dukes of Savoy, on the west bank of Lac du Bourget. Generations of the ruling family were interred at the mausoleum of Hautecombe Abbey at St.-Pierre-de-Curtille. The abbey was given a Gothic facelift in the 19th century and today it is popular with lovers of Gregorian chant, who come to enjoy the services here. A pleasant walking tour from le Bourget-du-Lac, which has a notable 11th-century priory, leads up the slopes of Mont du Chat and crosses the Col du Chat, culminating in excellent vistas.

➕ B3

Tourist information ✉ place Maurice-Mollard, Aix-les-Bains, 73100 ☎ 04 79 88 68 00; www.aixlesbains.com
Abbaye de Hautecombe ✉ 73310 St.-Pierre-de-Curtille ☎ 04 79 54 26 12; www.chemin-neuf.org
🕐 Wed.–Mon. 10–11:15 and 2–5, late Mar. to mid-Nov.; Wed.–Mon. 10–11:15 and 2:30–5, rest of year ✋ \$

A canalized section of the Thiou river flowing through an old quarter of delightful Annecy

A sundial decorates the vibrant facade of a building in the town of Briançon

Briançon

Occupied since the days of the Roman Empire, Briançon is the highest town in Europe. At 4,349 feet, the town is closer to the sun than any other on the continent and, accordingly, the walls are liberally decorated with sundials. In the 18th century, these were painted on public buildings and churches, but by the 19th century they became the fashion for private houses. Frescoes featuring hour lines and mottos in Latin, French or local dialect range from naive clock faces to lovely works of art in their own right.

The sundial on the Cordeliers church has Louis XV ribbons and wreaths. Later domestic examples by the artist Zarbulla have trompe-l'oeil birds and flowers, and young designers with a 21st-century take on tradition are rediscovering the old art.

Briançon stands at the crossroads of the Alps, with the Col de Montgenèvre kept open throughout the winter. The town is completely encased by citadel walls built by Louis XIV's legendary defensive architect Sébastien Le Prestre de Vauban, whose fortresses protected the entire nation's borders. This particular fortification has been embellished over the centuries, and additional forts have been added above the town. The town serves the ski resort of Serre Chevalier.

✚ C2

Tourist information ✉ 1 place du Temple, 05100 ☎ 04 92 21 08 50; www.ot-briancon.fr

Chambéry

No one has heard of the Shroud of Chambéry. The reason is that when the dukes of Savoy moved their seat of government away from this Alpine town in the mid-16th century, the famous relic went with the power and the glory to the new capital in Turin. Chambéry finally became a part of France in 1860 following the treaty of Turin and a referendum among its citizens brought Savoy back within France's borders.

Today's administrators busy themselves with the affairs of the Savoie district, but memories of the way things once were may be discovered at the ducal château that dominates the town. Constantly reinvented and extended from the 13th to 19th centuries, the château's buildings include a beautiful Gothic chapel. Try to hear the grand carillon – a majestic peal of 70 bells from the chapel tower.

The old town around the château is a splendid labyrinth of winding streets and secret passages, similar to the *traboules* (alleys) of Lyon. Grand houses reflect the Italian influences of the Savoy dynasty, with ornate baroque stucco facades and intricate wrought-iron decoration.

In the Curial quarter, just outside the medieval district, the state seized Franciscan, Ursuline and other convents after the French Revolution. Napoléon himself decided to convert them into military barracks, along the lines of Les Invalides in Paris. Since 1975, the town has adapted the buildings as administrative and cultural centers. Other museums include the Musée Savoisien; the home of the writer Jean-Jacques Rousseau, which presents costumed tours in summer; and the Musée des Beaux-Arts, home to France's finest collection of Italian art outside the Louvre, which reopened in March 2012 after a comprehensive two-year renovation program.

La Fontaine des Eléphants in Chambéry

Savoy boasts that it's the home of true French gastronomy. All the elements of the national cuisine have origins in the regal demands of the former kingdom that stretched across the modern national borders of the Alps.

✚ B3

Tourist information ✉ 5 bis place du Palais-de-Justice, 73000 ☎ 04 79 33 42 47; www.chambery-tourisme.com

Château des Ducs de Savoie ✉ place du Château, 73000 ☎ 04 79 33 42 47 🕐 By guided tour only. Contact tourist office for details 💷 $

Musée Savoisien ✉ Square Lannoy-de-Bissy, 73000 ☎ 04 79 33 44 48 🕐 Wed.–Mon. 10–noon, 2–6 💷 Free

Musee des Beaux-Arts ✉ place du Palais-de-Justice, 73000 ☎ 04 79 60 50 65 🕐 Wed.–Mon. 10–noon and 2–6 💷 $ (free first Sun. of the month)

Evian-les-Bains

Probably the source of France's best-known mineral water, Evian made its name as a spa resort and remains an elegant place to stay on the banks of Lake Geneva. Guests at luxurious hotels with views across the Swiss border still spend their money on rejuvenating health treatments to reduce the stress lines created at the roulette and blackjack tables of the flamboyant casino. Other visitors stay on their yachts in the marina. Those on modest budgets play miniature golf and enjoy the musical fountain.

Not all the thermal treatments are the exclusive province of the well-heeled. Simple rheumatic or postnatal cures are available at daily or single-session rates. Water sports, lake cruises and hikes are on offer for those wanting to explore. Regular festivals and exhibitions are among the on-site delights.

Evian is now developing as something of a conference destination, so out-of-season visitors might find themselves overwhelmed by convention delegates sporting laminated name tags.

✚ C4

Tourist information ✉ place de la Porte-d'Allinges, 74500 ☎ 04 50 75 04 26; www.eviantourism.com

Natural Splendor

The Rhône-Alpes, extending as far as the Ardèche gorges, boasts two national parks, six regional nature parks and 26 nature reserves. Chamois and ibexes live among the firs, rhododendron and edelweiss, otters and beavers busy themselves at the water's edge, and deer and wild boar hide in the dense forest. Bird sanctuaries welcome snow finches and eagles.

Parc National des Écrins

This high mountain park is the largest national park in France. Small shepherds' villages make useful bases for hiking. Tête de la Maye, at 8,465 feet, is a popular summer walk. Roads within the park link the eastern hamlets of Ailefroide, Pelvoux and Vallouise. A mountain path with stunning views links the Pré de Madame Carle to the Glacier Blanc. From the southern resort of la Chapelle-en-Valgaudémar, you can walk past waterfalls to the Lac du Lauzon. There is no road entry to the park, but walkers can approach via the Oisans, Valgaudémar and Vallouise.
B2–C2   www.ecrins-parcnational.fr

Parc Naturel Régional du Queyras

The charming, automobile-free village of St.-Véran, with its sundials, fountains and crosses, nestles in this protected wooded area. A pilgrims' route from St.-Véran to the Chapelle Notre-Dame-de-Clausis is among the paths through the peaks of the Italian border country. The Col d'Izoard route to Briançon (see page 208) is rocky and barren, the Casse Déserte.
C2   www.pnr-queyras.com

Parc National de la Vanoise

The ski resorts of Courchevel, les Menuires, Méribel and Val Thorens are found in the oldest national park in France. Protected since 1963, the park, with its Italian neighbor the Gran Paradiso, is one of the most beautiful nature reserves in Europe. To the west, climbers head for Pralognan. Along the southern edge are traditional villages. Hares, marmots and ermine live in la Grande Sassière.
C3   www.parcnational-vanoise.fr

A high meadow in the spectacular Queyras Natural Regional Park

Grenoble

Museums, parks, gardens and an air of civilization make Grenoble the perfect spot to recharge and reflect away from the ski society of the mountain resorts or hiker's solitude of the lake lands.

You can cross the Isère river by the gondola lift (*téléphérique*) from the quai Stéphane-Jay to the Fort de la Bastille, high above the university campus. Now home to a permanent exhibition of automobiles and motorcycles, the fort was originally a prison. City life begins behind the cable-car station. Here, from the neat Jardin de la Ville to the main square, place Grenette and place St.-André is the hub of city life. Famous author Stendhal is a native son and said of his home town: "At the end of every street, there is a mountain." This fact is appreciated by drivers who can be at the ski resorts within half an hour. The city's Musée Dauphinois records the development of this economically important sport.

Grenoble claims to have sown the seeds of the Revolution. When Louis XVI made moves to restrict local liberties, rioting citizens climbed onto the town roofs and attacked the army with tiles. The events of June 7, 1788, known as the Day of Tiles (*Journée des Tuiles*), directly led the king to convene the Estates General in May 1789. The French Revolution was under way.

The work of the French Resistance is celebrated in the modern Musée de la Résistance et de la Déportation de l'Isère, featuring accounts of life under the Nazi occupation during World War II.

The town is constantly modernized to meet new challenges and the capital of the Alps has developed a lively arts scene to complement its sporting attractions. In addition to theaters, a dance center and a respected chamber orchestra, the town has six museums. Visit the modern Musée de Grenoble, an example of 1990s architecture incorporating a medieval tower. It has a spectacular art collection from the Old Masters to the likes of Marc Chagall, Pablo Picasso and René Magritte. Take the tram to Le Magasin, the national contemporary art center housed in Gustave Eiffel's splendid 1900 industrial building. For two weeks in December, place Victor-Hugo hosts a Christmas market. One of the major seasonal fairs of the Alps, it attracts up to 150,000 visitors. Choirs singing carols, garlanded shopfronts and processions of children carrying lanterns set the scene, and many stands sell traditional handmade gifts, cakes, candies and decorations.

➕ B2

Tourist information ✉ 14 rue de la République, 38000 ☎ 04 76 42 41 41; www.grenoble-tourisme.com

Le Magasin ✉ 155 cours Berriat, 38000 ☎ 04 76 21 95 84; www.magasin-cnac.org 🕐 Tue.–Sun. 2–7 🚌 26; tram A 💷 $ 🛈 Reservations needed for guided tours in English

Musée de Grenoble ✉ 5 place de Lavalette, 38000 ☎ 04 76 63 44 44; www.museedegrenoble.fr 🕐 Wed.–Mon. 10–6:30 🚌 32; tram A 🍽 Restaurant and café 💷 $$ (free first Sun. in month) 🛈 Audioguide available ($)

Musée de la Résistance et de la Déportation de l'Isère ✉ 14 rue Hébert, 38000 ☎ 04 76 42 38 53; www.resistance-en-isere.fr 🕐 Mon., Wed.–Fri. 9–6, Tue. 1:30–6, Sat.–Sun. 10–6 💷 Free

The *téléphérique* **across the Isère river, Grenoble**

Alps and the Rhône Valley

Dining out in the cobbled square of a tranquil village in the Rhône Valley

Mont-Blanc and Chamonix

The highest peak in Europe at 15,782 feet, Mont-Blanc soars majestically above the granite needle peaks of the Aiguilles de Chamonix. Technically, it belongs to the neighboring town of St.-Gervais, but Chamonix, which incorporates the mountain in its name, has adopted the giant of the Alps. Chamonix is a hectic mixture of traditional Alpine chalets, serviceable hotel buildings and constant traffic clogging the road to the Mont-Blanc Tunnel to Italy.

Despite all this, and the tourist-ski-package industry that has all but swamped the town, Chamonix-Mont-Blanc remains a thrilling place to visit. This is due in part to the awe-inspiring peak that challenged the first Alpine mountaineers in the 18th century. When Geneva scientist Dr. Michel-Gabriel Paccard returned from the summit in 1786, he started a tradition of climbing that remained a local diversion until the railroads reached the Alps in the 1860s. Suddenly Chamonix became popular not only for mountaineers but also for their fashionable friends who would enjoy hotel hospitality while watching the climbers through specially provided telescopes. A triumphant wave from the summit of Mont-Blanc would be the cue for champagne corks to pop in the resort. Natural wonders still upstage commercialism – with breathtaking glaciers such as the Glacier des Bossons dropping nearly 12,000 feet. Don't forget your passport if you want to take the spectacular six-stage cable car ride over Mont-Blanc via the Aiguille du Midi to la Palud in Italy. You will need it for the bus ride back through the tunnel.

✠ C3

Tourist information ✉ 85 place du Triangle-de-l'Amitié, Chamonix-Mont-Blanc, 74400 ☎ 04 50 53 00 24; www.chamonix.com

Pérouges

Named for the Italian weavers from Perugia who founded the village, this imposing fortified settlement perches on a hilltop northeast of Lyon. Houses lining the picturesque narrow, cobbled streets have mullioned windows and overhanging roofs. A busy artists' community still thrives here, even if most of its output is designed for the tourist market. The central place du Tilleul is named after the old linden tree that still grows in the center. Visit the fortified church.

✠ A3

Tourist information ✉ Entrée de la Cité, 01800 ☎ 04 74 46 70 84; www.perouges.org

Opposite: Mont-Blanc, viewed from the Col des Saisies

Drive
Lakes and Peaks

Distance: 294 miles
Time: 4 days

Starting and finishing at the cultural oasis of Grenoble (see page 211), this drive takes in sophisticated resorts and nature's grandeur in equal measure. In general, thanks to various Olympic seasons, Alpine roads are first class. But, even in summer, it's important to check road and weather reports before embarking on a long drive. Local tourist offices can advise about snow and road forecasts and offer alternate routes for any leg of the itinerary.

Leave Grenoble on the north bank of the Isère, following the D512 to St.-Pierre-de-Chartreuse.

From their secluded monastery in the forest, the Carthusian monks gave the world the green liqueur known as Chartreuse. Made from a secret blend of 130 wild herbs and plants added to brandy and honey, the heady drink is now manufactured in Voiron (an easy drive west along the D520), where cellar tours and tastings of Chartreuse, both the green and milder yellow variety, are offered. At la Correrie, just northwest of St.-Pierre-de-Chartreuse, a museum tells the story of the 11th-century monastic order.

Continue on the D512, then take the D912 over the Col du Granier to Chambéry (see pages 208–209). The N201 follows the east bank of Lac du Bourget to Aix-les-Bains.

The popular resort (see page 207) has plenty of distractions for the active and passive visitor. A trip to the Roman remains provides insight into the lives of those who first exploited the potential of the town.

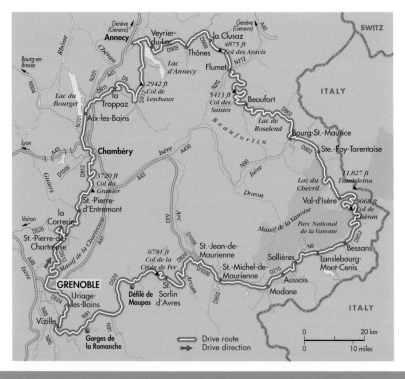

The popular spa resort of Aix-les-Bains sits by the Lac du Bourget

Leave town on the N201, then turn right onto the D911. After la Tropaz, turn left to cross the Chéran river on the D31, then right on the D5 to rejoin the D911. Turn left on the D912 then N508 to Annecy (see page 207), climbing the Montagne du Semnoz and crossing the Col de Leschaux. Follow the D909 via Thônes to la Clusaz.

Cheese and adventure sports keep the winter resort of la Clusaz, famed for its speed-skiing events, alive all through the summer. Skiing on grass is an option for the hardened athlete, and demonstrations of Reblochon cheese-making in large copper cauldrons, sampling matured cheeses and admiring traditional chalet-roofing skills are essential parts of summer festivals. Mid-September finds locals gathering chanterelles and other wild fungi.

The D909 continues over the Col des Aravis to Flumet, where the D218B leads over the Col des Saisies. At the D925, turn left toward Bourg-St.-Maurice, making the most of a thrilling drive featuring a veritable catalog of spectacular Alpine scenery.

Bourg-St.-Maurice, with its 15th-century wooden houses and Renaissance porches, is best known for les Arcs ski resort. The Academy Music Festival

takes place during the last two weeks of July. Gifted young musicians from France and abroad attend exclusive master classes, and 20,000 visitors enjoy a fabulous season of free concerts and recitals in churches and public squares in outlying villages. Golf, hiking and tennis are among the summer sports on offer, and the terrace cafés around Grand Rue bustle year round.

Take the D902 to Val d'Isère.

Ride the winter cable cars in summer for great views, or use this most popular of ski resorts in a narrow valley as a base for hiking or horseback riding through the spectacular countryside. Experts can take advantage of summer glacier skiing. In August, Val d'Isère is the venue of the L'Avaline traditional fete.

The same road continues to Col de l'Iseran.

One of the highest roads in Europe at 9,085 feet, the road up the Col de l'Iseran took 20 years to build and is often closed well past spring. It offers impressive views over the mountains of the Parc National de la Vanoise.

Still on the D902, pass through Bessans, Lanslevillard and Lanslebourg. Take a right on the N6, turning right at Sollières on the D83, then the D215 to Modane.

The mountainous slopes of the Vercors National Park offer challenging walks and cycle rides

Modane is mostly known as an intersection for hikers and travelers changing course in mid-Alps. This is a center of English language learning in the Alps. The old center is the quartier du Pâquier, clustered around the parish church with its simple belltower. Across town, Lutraz's Rizerie des Alpes is a Greek-style temple, built in 1929 to process raw rice imported from Italy on the new trans-Alps railroad.

Take the N6 and continue on this road to St.-Jean-de-Maurienne.

Three fingers of the hand that baptized Christ are represented on the coat of arms of St.-Jean-de-Maurienne, which acquired these relics of John the Baptist back in the sixth century. See the 11th-century portal of Église Notre-Dame and the 15th-century cathedral and cloister. Secular attractions include a museum of knives and the bustling Saturday market.

The D926 leads to Col de la Croix-de-Fer.

The austere iron cross gives its name to a leg of the Tour de France (see page 17). This section of the drive offers exciting driving, emerging from rock tunnels over the dramatic Arvan Gorge, leaning into sharp twists and turns of a mountain climb and fine views of the Combe d'Olle and Défilé de Maupas.

Take the D926-D526-N91 toward Grenoble. At Vizille, take the D101 to the D524 via Uriage-les-Bains and into Grenoble.

Musée de la Grande Chartreuse

✉ La Correrie, St.-Pierre-de-Chartreuse, 38380 ☎ 04 76 88 60 45; www.musee-grande-chartreuse.fr ⏰ Daily 10–6:30, May–Sep.; 1:30–6, Feb.; Mon.–Fri. 1:30–6, Sat.–Sun. 10–6:30 late Mar.–Apr. and Oct.–Nov. 💰 $$

Caves de la Chartreuse ✉ 10 boulevard Edgar-Kofler, Voiron, 38500 ☎ 04 76 05 81 77; www.chartreuse.fr ⏰ Daily 9–11:30 and 2–6:30, Apr.–Oct.; Mon.–Fri. 9–11:30 and 2–5:30, Nov.–Mar. 💰 Free

Aix-les-Bains tourist information

✉ place Maurice-Mollard, 73100 ☎ 04 79 88 68 00; www.aixlesbains.com

La Clusaz tourist information

✉ 161 place de l'Église, 74220 ☎ 04 50 32 65 00; www.laclusaz.com

Les Arcs-Bourg-St.-Maurice tourist information

✉ 105 place Gare, 73700 ☎ 04 79 07 12 57; www.lesarcs.com

Val d'Isère tourist information ✉ Maison de Val-d'Isère, place Jacques-Mouflier, 73115 ☎ 04 79 06 06 60; www.valdisere.com

Valfréjus-Modane tourist information

✉ Les Mélèzets, Valfréjus, 73500 ☎ 04 79 05 33 83; www.valfrejus.com

St.-Jean-de-Maurienne tourist information

✉ Ancien Évêché, place de la Cathédrale, 73300 ☎ 04 79 83 51 51; www.saintjeandemaurienne.com

Vercors

Pine-forested slopes and limestone river gorges mark this majestic mountain range. The largest regional nature park in France lies at the heart of the massif, with inland cliff faces and waterfalls. Local drivers fearlessly negotiate the narrow roads of the Grands Goulets, cut into the rock face. During World War II, Vercors became synonymous with the heroism of the French Resistance. The movement incurred the wrath of German forces, who bombed the region in 1944 and razed the villages of St.-Nizier, la Chapelle and Vassieux-en-Vercors. Rebuilt after the war, Vassieux is home to the Mémorial de la Résistance du Vercors.

At the very end of the gorges of the Bourne and Grands Goulets, the fast-flowing waters meet at Pont-en-Royans before spilling into the Isère river. Come here to walk the narrow streets and marvel at the perilously suspended houses.

✚ A2–B2

Pont-en-Royans tourist information ✉ Grande Rue, 38680 ☎ 04 76 36 09 10; www.ot-pont-en-royans.com

Mémorial de la Résistance du Vercors ✉ Col de la Chau, 26420 Vassieux-en-Vercors ☎ 04 75 48 26 00; www.memorial-vercors.fr 🕐 Daily 10–6, Jul.–Sep.; Mon.–Fri. noon–6, Sat.–Sun. 10–6, May–Jun.; Mon.–Fri. noon–5, Sat.–Sun. 10–5, Apr. and Oct.; Wed.–Sun. 10–noon and 2–5, mid-Nov. and late Dec.–Mar. Closed mid-Nov. to late Dec. 👤 $$

Vienne

South of Lyon, on the Rhône, Vienne is the second capital of Roman Gaul, after Lyon (see pages 200–205). The July jazz festival in the Théâtre Antique is the biggest and best of the town's treasures. Don't miss the fourth-century road and obelisk in the Jardin Public. In place du Palais is the Temple of Augustus and Livia, dating from 25 BC. A church in medieval times, it became a post-revolutionary Temple of Reason and a museum. Mosaics and sculpture are displayed in the Musée de l'Ancienne Église St.-Pierre. The Gothic Cathédrale St.-Maurice has 16th-century Flemish tapestries. In the nearby village of St.-Roman-en-Gal is the Musée Gallo-Romain, with Roman finds.

✚ A3

Tourist information ✉ cours Brillier, 38200 ☎ 04 74 53 80 30; www.vienne-tourisme.com

Théâtre Antique ✉ rue du Cirque, 38200 ☎ 04 74 85 39 23; www.musees-vienne.fr 🕐 Daily 9:30–1 and 2–6, Apr.–Aug.; Tue.–Sun. 9:30–1 and 2–6, Sep.–Oct.; Tue.–Fri. 9:30–12:30 and 2–5, Sat.–Sun. 1:30–5:30, rest of year 👤 $

Musée Archéologique Église St.-Pierre ✉ place St.-Pierre, 38200 ☎ 04 74 85 20 35; www.musees-vienne.fr 🕐 Tue.–Sun. 9:30–1 and 2–6, Apr.–Nov.; Tue.–Fri. 9:30–12:30 and 2–5, Sat.–Sun. 1:30–5:30, rest of year 👤 $

Musée Gallo-Romain ✉ D502, St.-Romain-en-Gal ☎ 04 74 53 74 02; www.musees-gallo-romains.com 🕐 Tue.–Sun. 10–6 👤 $

The village of Vassieux-en-Vercors sits at the foot of the Vercors massif

Burgundy and the East

Opposite: Early morning mist over the village of Sacy and its vineyards, Burgundy

Burgundy and the East

There is a gentle quality to this part of eastern France. Here, great vineyards spread over a softly undulating landscape, with none of the rugged scrubland of the south. The mountains of the Jura are strangers to the razzmatazz of the Alps. Even disputed border towns conjure quaint images from the pages of a children's book.

Disputed Lands

The regions of Alsace and Lorraine are an intriguing blend of French and German culture, for centuries pawed this way and that by warring neighbors. At the end of each 20th-century war, both were returned to France. The legacy is a wealth of contrasting influences on food, dialects and building style. Mixed parentage is a boon for the Alsace capital Strasbourg.

An international city like New York, Brussels and Geneva, Strasbourg is home to the European Parliament. Besides Teutonic timbered houses, Alsatian towns and villages, such as Riquewihr and Hunspach, are famed for the abundant floral displays decorating windows and storks nesting on chimney stacks.

The least-known region of France is Franche-Comté, a land of deep forests, running waters and the snowcapped peaks of the Jura mountains. Its sobriquets include: Little Scotland for its lakes; Little Ireland for its moors, bogs and streams; and Little Canada for its gorges and expanses of tall trees.

Endurance

The occupations of cheese making, freshwater fishing and wine producing are key to the region, as are its less trumpeted winter-sports resorts. But don't overlook another aspect that lends it character – the fierce independence of the people of the Jura. One of the

Thriving vines skirt the foot of a rocky outcrop near the Burgundian village of Époisses

region's most famous sons, Louis Pasteur (1822–95), spent a lifetime fighting disease on a micro level, and the fortified hill town of Belfort is known for holding out against invasion months longer than many bigger cities. Present-day endurance is typified by the February Transjurassienne – a 47.5-mile World Cup-class cross-country skiing rally along the Swiss border. The event attracts 3,000 competitors and 90,000 spectators who ring cowbells, light torches at nightfall and bake heart-shaped gingerbread to comfort the last brave finishers.

Burgundy should be enjoyed at a leisurely pace. Besides vines (see pages 232–233), the countryside is dotted with hilltop Romanesque churches and simple Cistercian abbeys. Even the cattle – cream-colored and elegant Charolais – are picturesque.

Canals

The ideal way to discover Burgundy is from the water. The Loire, Seine and Rhône rivers freshen a 750-mile network of canals. Small motor boats can be rented from a half-day to the full season, and many floating hotels ply the water and serve good local food. A recommended starting point is the town of Auxerre. The best sightseeing waterways are the canals de Bourgogne and du Nivernais. The French canal network extends as far as the Atlantic.

Strasbourg

Strasbourg redefines cosmopolitan. With the German border just across the Rhine, the city was a shuttlecock in the nationality tussles of Alsace, creating a unique Franco-German style from its architecture to its dinner plates. Strasbourg is also the site of the European Parliament. So as you admire trellised timbering on quaint old houses, your ears may ring to an international hum of voices and accents more usually heard in an airport lounge.

In countless atmospheric restaurants, waiters slip effortlessly from French to Spanish to Greek to English as they flourish trays of authentic Alsatian sauerkraut and beer.

Fortunately, the institutions of an international capital are far enough away from the historic center for the heart of Strasbourg to retain its centuries-old charm. Dominated by a magnificent cathedral (see page 224) and embraced by the meandering Ill river, the old quarter combines a striking German postcard image of charming cobbled streets and tall gabled buildings with unmistakably French warmth.

Getting Around

Strasbourg is a city for *flâneurs* (strollers). Take time to wander among the three main city squares: the places de la Cathédrale, Gutenberg and Kléber. Or for a more strenuous tour there are also facilities for renting bicycles for two-wheeled exploration. Trams are useful for crisscrossing the city, and taxis are plentiful.

The boat trip along the Ill and Rhine rivers is a scenic and relaxing option – and it's free to holders of the Strasbourg Pass, which offers a combination of free and discounted admissions to museums, sights, tours and concerts in the city over a three-day period. Obtain a pass from the tourist office or at your hotel.

Music

Music is essential in Strasbourg life, from the International Music Festival in June to the September contemporary

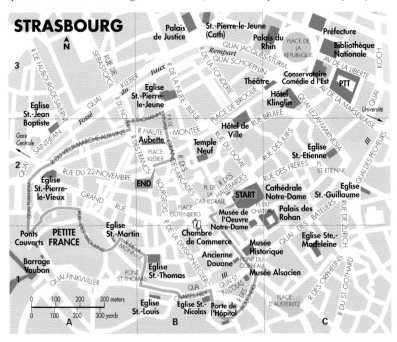

Musica festival. Opera and concerts are of a high standard. In summer, folk concerts are held outside the Palais des Rohan (see page 224), in the flood-lit Orangerie park and in some squares.

Christmas

St. Nicholas' Day is celebrated on December 6, with festivities also on the 5th. The Christmas season continues until Christmas Eve. The town prides itself on the size of its Christmas tree, adorned with massive mock fruits. The huge Christkindelsmärik (www.noel. strasbourg.eu) is a market of wooden chalets that sprawls from place de la Cathédrale to the other two squares. A month-long December tradition since 1570, the market is bathed in twinkling lights and offers an array of hand-carved toys and fragrant candles, and hot mulled wine and spiced cakes.

Shopping

Even beyond the Christmas season, most days of the year promise at least one

La Marseillaise
On April 24, 1792, Frédéric de Dietrich, the first elected mayor of Strasbourg, commissioned composer Rouget de Lisle to write a stirring marching song for the volunteer soldiers of the Army of the Rhine. The next morning, Rouget de Lisle had completed the song, which was adopted by the Federates of Marseille. And so the French national anthem, "la Marseillaise," was born.

market: flea markets at rue du Vieil-Hôpital; a book market at place Gutenberg; and various produce markets around town for local food specialties and souvenirs. Saturday is the farmers' market on place du Marché-aux-Poissons. Plenty of shops in the old quarter sell antiques, clothes and crafts, but prices are generally geared to the international market. Locals tend to stick to Les Halles shopping mall, across the river.

Essential Information

Tourist Information
✉ 17 place de la Cathédrale, 67802
☎ 03 88 52 28 28; www.otstrasbourg.fr

Urban Transportation
Trams and buses cross the city. Buy tickets from machines at bus and tram stops and validate before boarding. Route maps are available from the tourist office; for information ☎ 03 88 77 70 70; www.cts-strasbourg.fr. There are taxi stands

at the railroad station, and on place Kléber and place Gutenberg ☎ 03 88 36 13 13.

Airport Information
Strasbourg International Airport
☎ 03 88 64 67 67; www.strasbourg.aeroport. fr. Connections link to most European capitals. A taxi ride to the city center takes about 20 minutes. A shuttle train service operates every 15 minutes, travel time nine minutes (☎ 08 00 77 98 67; www.ter-sncf.com/alsace).

Climate – average highs and lows for the month

Jan.	Feb.	Mar.	Apr.	May	Jun.	Jul.	Aug.	Sep.	Oct.	Nov.	Dec.
4°C	5°C	10°C	15°C	19°C	22°C	24°C	24°C	20°C	14°C	8°C	4°C
39°F	41°F	50°F	59°F	66°F	72°F	75°F	75°F	68°F	57°F	46°F	39°F
-2°C	-2°C	1°C	5°C	9°C	12°C	14°C	13°C	10°C	6°C	2°C	0°C
28°F	28°F	34°F	41°F	48°F	54°F	57°F	55°F	50°F	43°F	36°F	32°F

Strasbourg Sights

Cathédrale Notre-Dame

Work started in 1176 and continued for
more than 250 years on the undisputed
masterpiece of the city. The Gothic
facade of the cathedral is beautifully
illuminated by floodlights at night. This
magnificent frontage is breathtaking,
from the ornate porch up past numerous
saintly statues to its single open-work
octagonal spire which, at 466 feet high,
is a landmark across the Alsace plain.
Inside, evocative shadows painted by
stained-glass windows pour on splendid
statuary. The showcase is the Pilier des
Anges, a pillar with ranks of angels
telling the story of the Last Judgment.

Behind the column is the famous
16th-century astronomical clock. Daily
at noon, except Sunday, a 30-minute
film precedes the main event, the
automated pageant of the Apostles and
Ages of Man, which takes place at 12:30.
The clock's main performance is
ticket-only. Purchase yours from the
postcard stand, from 9 a.m. to 11:30
a.m., or the cashier at the south
doorway, from 11:20 a.m. to 12:15 p.m.
During other times, there is no charge
for witnessing the figure of Death
announce that each of us is another
hour nearer the grave.

✚ B2 ✉ place de la Cathédrale, 67060 ☎ 03 88 21
43 34; www.cathedrale-strasbourg.fr ⏰ Daily 7–11:20
and 12:35–7, except during Mass 🚊 Tram: A, B, D, F
🖐 Free; tower $; clock $ (free Sun.)

Musée de l'Oeuvre Notre-Dame

Many of the greatest original
architectural treasures of the cathedral
are displayed here, free from the ravages
of pollution. The stone masons of
Chartres worked on the statuary, and
the elegant features of saints and biblical
characters can be fully appreciated in
close proximity. Modern copies have
taken their place within the cathedral.
Examples to seek out include *The Wise
and Foolish Virgins*, with the famous
image of the seduced maiden about to
undo her dress, and the architect's
original drawings of the spire. This 14th-
century building – originally used by
workers who built and cleaned the
cathedral – is worth a visit in its own
right. Discover graceful tiny spiral
staircases, pretty courtyards and a
medicinal herb garden.

✚ B2 ✉ 3 place du Château, 67060 ☎ 03 88 52 50
00; www.musees-strasbourg.org ⏰ Tue.–Fri. noon–6,
Sat.–Sun. 10–6 🚊 Tram: A, B, D, F 🖐 $$

Palais des Rohan

The one-time residence of the prince
bishops of Strasbourg, no strangers to
court intrigue, Palais des Rohan is a
typical example of mid-18th-century
Classical flamboyance. Balustrades and
galleries line the courtyard and
bull's-eye windows stud the roofs. It is
now home to a fine-arts museum on the
second floor, a decorative-arts museum
on the first floor and an archeological
museum in the basement.

✚ C2 ✉ 2 place du Château, 67060 ☎ 03 88 88 50
68; www.musees-strasbourg.org ⏰ Mon., Wed.–Fri.
noon–6, Sat.–Sun. 10–6 🚊 Tram: A, B, D, F 🖐 $$

Glorious stained glass in Cathédrale Notre-Dame

Walk

Medieval Churches and la Petite France

Refer to route on city map on page 222

Opposite the cathedral, the Boutique Culture (once France's oldest pharmacy) has fabulous 15th-century arches carved with branches and reptiles.

Take rue Mercière, then the second left onto rue du Vieux-Marché-aux-Poissons.
The Ancienne Douane, at the street end by the river, is largely a late 20th-century reconstruction of the original 14th-century bonded customs warehouse. It houses a good restaurant. **Cross over the river on Pont du Corbeau and follow rue des Bouchers to the hospital gateway.**
The hospital's 17th-century observatory is a remodeling of the 13th-century original. The 15th-century Chapelle St.-Erhard became the hospital's Anatomy Hall.
Rue St.-Nicolas leads to the riverbank; bear left past Église St.-Nicolas along quai Charles-Frey, then cross the river on Pont St.-Thomas onto rue Martin-Luther-King. Ahead to your right is Église St.-Thomas. Turn left on rue de la Monnaie, then take the first bridge on your left to rue des Moulins and the old tanners' district.
The twists and turns of the river proved ideal for powering the water mills, which were essential for leather workers. This former industrial district is now one of the prettiest corners of town.
The second promontory on the left is place des Moulins. Turn back, then left and left again onto square Louise Weiss and the yellow, blue, white and terra-cotta house fronts of la Petite France.

La Petite France is a very pretty district

Here, veterans of 16th-century battles with Italy were quarantined for venereal disease. Since locals blamed the French for the disease, "la Petite France" became the nickname for syphilis.

At the tip of quai de la Petite-France are the Ponts Couverts: once timber-covered bridges, now stone, with three defensive towers offering fabulous views of the river and the Barrage Vauban, a 17th-century defensive dam. The viewing platform is the perfect spot for photographs of la Petite France's low-sweeping Sleeping Beauty roofs, shady dappled banks reflected in still waters and panoramic vistas leading to the cathedral.
Follow quai de Tuckheim to place St.-Pierre-le-Vieux.
At Église St.-Pierre-le-Vieux, admire the 15th-century panels of Christ's Passion. **Turn right on rue du Vieux-Marché-aux-Vins, left on rue du Noyer and right on rue Thomann to place St.-Pierre-le-Jeune.**
Église St.-Pierre-le-Jeune has medieval frescoes and a 12th-century bell tower.
Petite rue de l'Église and rue des Grandes-Arcades lead into the Renaissance place Kléber.

Regional Sights

Key to symbols

➕ map coordinates refer to the Burgundy and the East map on page 221 🎟 admission charge:
$$$ more than €10, $$ €5–€10, $ less than €5
See page 5 for complete key to symbols

Beaune

Although Dijon may be the capital of the Burgundy region, Beaune is the capital of wine. This beautiful town in the midst of the area's grandest vineyards is simply exquisite. See for yourself the elegant patchwork of many-colored glazed tiles above the carved gables and palatial pillars of the Hôtel Dieu of the Hospices de Beaune. This building, with its courtyard and centuries-old pharmacy, was established as a hospital in 1443, a function it continued to fulfill until 1971. Visit the marvelous vaulted sick room, laid out like a church with 230-foot rows of wooden beds, each big enough for two patients and separated by heavy red drapes. Nuns still care for elderly residents in less public rooms.

The hospice hosts the annual charity wine auctions in October, setting the annual price for classic Burgundy wines and continuing until the last candle on the auctioneer's platform flickers out. An exhibition gallery contains treasures, such as Roger van de Weyden's polyptych *The Last Judgment*. There's more spiritual sustenance at the 12th- to 13th-century Collégiale Notre-Dame, which has remarkable tapestries displayed only in warm seasons. Opposite the Hôtel Dieu, the Marché aux Vins tempts the palate for wine tasting and shopping, and the town has plenty of first-class restaurants.

Walk around the town walls, which now hide wine cellars, and visit the Museum of Burgundy Wine. The tourist office can arrange excursions to the vineyards. July sees weekend baroque concerts at the principal sites. However, as air-conditioning isn't available, seasonal temperatures can make 90 minutes inside the Hôtel Dieu's sick room uncomfortable. Open-air performances in the courtyard are more advisable.

➕ A1

Tourist information ✉ Porte Marie-de-Bourgogne, 6 boulevard Perpreuil, 21203; also at 1 rue de l'Hôtel-Dieu 🕾 03 80 26 21 30; www.ot-beaune.fr

Musée de Hôtel Dieu ✉ 2 rue de l'Hôtel-Dieu, 21200 🕾 03 80 24 45 00; www.hospices-de-beaune.com 🕐 Daily 9–6:30, late Mar. to mid-Nov.; 9–11:30 and 2–5:30, rest of year 🎟 $$

Collegiale Notre-Dame (Tapisseries) ✉ place Général-Leclerc, 21200 🕾 03 80 24 77 95 🕐 Mon.–Sat. 9:30–12:30 and 2–7, Sun. 1–7, Jun.–Sep.; Mon.–Sat. 9:30–12:30 and 2–5, Sun. 1–5, Mar.–May and Oct.–early Nov. 🎟 $

Musée du Vin de Bourgogne ✉ Hôtel des Ducs de Bourgogne, rue d'Enfer, 21200 🕾 03 80 22 08 19; www.musees-bourgogne.org 🕐 Daily 9:30–6, Apr.–Nov.; Wed.–Mon. 9:30–5, rest of year 🎟 $$

A statuette in the Museum of Wine

Opposite: Hôtel Dieu's glazed roof tiles

Eastern Promise Delivers at the Table

Burgundy's wealth is displayed at its tables. Great chefs – such as Bernard Loiseau, a gourmet legend at Saulieu – are attracted here by excellent ingredients, and others arrive, retire and turn restaurateur, serving simple classics after careers in other fast lanes. MGM star Leslie Caron turned her back on Hollywood to run an inn, La Lucarne aux Chouettes, in Villeneuve-sur-Yonne. The star of *Gigi* and *An American in Paris* fell in love with the ruined building and converted it into a hotel, where guests can eat on the terrace overlooking the 13th-century bridge over the Yonne river.

The ultimate poultry comes from Bresse, where free-range birds are fed on creamy milk and wheat and prepared with reverence. Even in the simplest restaurant, menu favorites include *escargots* and the famous *boeuf Bourguignon*.

Alsace cuisine is hearty. Best known is *choucroute*, a dish of cabbage, pork and sausages. Try *baeckeoffe*, pork and mutton marinated for 24 hours in white wine. *Flammekueche*, or *tarte flambée*, is an essential part of tavern culture. Between a pizza and a pancake, the flat dough is covered with sweet or savory toppings and baked on a wooden board for 90 seconds. Traditionally, one tears a strip of the flam', rolls it like a cigar and munches it as an accompaniment to beer.

Lorraine is famous for its egg, cheese and bacon quiche. Patés and stews are prepared with fruits, such as local Mirabelle plums, which are also found in jams and desserts.

Franche-Comté's smoked meats and fish are staples. The true star of a meal is the cheese course. Mont d'Or is matured in a box of spruce wood, but the ultimate flavor is that of the Comté cheese, often compared to a fine wine. The herds and pastures that create the milk, as well as the 18-month ripening process, are strictly controlled.

Franche-Comté produces many excellent wines. *Vins jaunes* (yellow wines), in essence white wines that may be matured for up to 100 years, are something of a rarity. Beer-making Alsace is also famous for whites: Pinot Noir, Pinot Gris, Riesling and Gerwürztraminer. Toul and Moselle wines are served in Lorraine, where fruits flavor beers, ciders and liqueurs.

Burgundian snails are a delicacy enjoyed throughout the region

Colmar

With narrow streets, tall gabled merchant houses and 16th-century timbered fronts tapering up to sharply pointed roofs, Colmar is the ultimate Alsatian town. Each turn in the old quarter seems to lead to another storybook address. Most picturesque, with turrets, wooden galleries and cascades of seasonal flowers, is the Maison Pfister at the corner of the rues Mercière and des Marchands. Another photo opportunity is the early 17th-century Renaissance Maison des Têtes at 19 rue des Têtes, liberally decorated with images of faces and heads.

The town is one of those places that gives you a reason to gasp every few yards, but the effect is slightly marred by crowds in vacation season. Don't let it keep you from visiting the engaging Krutenau district in Little Venice, where small bridges span the Lauch and church towers and willow trees frame every snapshot. The Musée d'Unterlinden, in a former Dominican convent, has many fine German paintings and works by 20th-century artists. Its treasure is Matthias Grünewald's 1515 *Issenheim Altar*, with its vivid depiction of the Redemption of Christ.

C2
Tourist information ✉ 4 rue d'Unterlinden, 68000 ☎ 03 89 20 68 92; www.ot-colmar.fr
Musée d'Unterlinden ✉ 1 rue d'Unterlinden, 68000 ☎ 03 89 20 15 50; www.musee-unterlinden.com 🕐 Daily 9–6, May–Oct.; Wed.–Mon. 9–noon and 2–5, rest of year 💶 $$

Côte d'Or

An area of less than 10,000 acres of land produces some of the world's most sought-after wines. This area, south of Dijon, is known as the Côte d'Or (golden slopes). The northern section, the Côtes de Nuit, produces celebrated reds, while the southern half, the Côtes de Beaune, makes red and white wines. Each village is a legend among fine wines. Meursault, Montrachet, Chambertin – these familiar names are modest settlements since land is too valuable for vines to be built on. Roadside signs offer tastings (*dégustation*) in cellars (*caves*), and the winemakers may escort visitors to view the vines. Farmers often own rows of vines in different fields. Each row gets a unique degree of sunshine, and this results in the variation in taste and accounts for the small quantities produced and the huge difference in prices.

A1

Timber-framed buildings backing onto the river in the Little Venice area of Colmar

Dijon

The dukes of Burgundy ran an empire that extended as far north as Flanders, and their seat at Dijon is a rich and prosperous city. The former ducal palace at the 17th-century place de la Libération houses the Musée des Beaux-Arts (Fine Arts Museum), with fascinating Gothic kitchens and superb sculpture galleries. See paintings by Veronese, Rubens and Frans Hals among a collection encompassing several centuries and stroll through the oldest quarter, with 16th-century houses. The front of the church has a mechanical clock made in 1383. Dijon streets were among the first in France to have sidewalks. A former convent now houses an interesting folk museum, recounting everyday life in the region.

Gastronomy and wine have long been associated with the city. When besieged by the Swiss, the city ended the 16th-century conflict with a gift of wine. Attacking soldiers simply fell asleep after overindulging. Visit the Amora Museum of Mustard and buy a jar of the famous condiment. Or try *crème de cassis* (blackcurrant liqueur), which when mixed with white wine, ideally *bourgogne alligoté*, makes the aperitif Kir, named for a mayor of the city.

➕ A1

Tourist information ✉ 11 rue des Forges, 21000 ☎ 08 92 70 05 58 (toll call); www.visitdijon.com

Musée des Beaux-Arts ✉ Palais des États-de-Bourgogne, 21000 (entrance: cour de Bar) ☎ 03 80 74 52 09; www.mba.dijon.fr 🕐 Wed.–Mon. 9:30–6, May–Oct.; 10–5, rest of year. Ducal kitchens, Egyptian Gallery, Gallery d'Art Contemporain closed 11:30–1:45 🎫 Free

Musée de la Vie Bourguignonne ✉ Couvent des Bernardines, 17 rue Ste.-Anne, 21000 ☎ 03 80 48 80 90; www.musees-bourgogne.org 🕐 Wed.–Mon. 9–12:30 and 1:30–6, May–Sep.; 9–noon and 2–6, rest of year 🎫 Free

Fontenay

Burgundy was the cradle of the Cistercian movement, founded by St. Bernard of Clairvaux at Citeaux Abbey, near Dijon. St. Bernard rebelled against the ostentation of other abbeys and established a new order of simplicity for pure meditation. No site reflects his ideals better than the Abbey of Fontenay. Restored at the beginning of the 20th century, its cloisters and halls remain masterpieces of calm, even during the peak summer season. The architecture contrasts dramatically with medieval chapels elsewhere in France.

➕ A2

Abbaye de Fontenay ✉ 21500 Montbard ☎ 03 80 92 15 00; www.abbayedefontenay.com 🕐 Daily 10–6, mid-Apr. to early Nov.; 10–noon and 2–5, rest of year 🎫 $

Haut-Koenigsbourg

The largest château in Alsace is every inch the European castle: vast rose-red sandstone walls with tendrils of green creeper spreading across them, round and square towers, suits of armor, even spindly trees growing in tiny courtyards among the turrets. The Château du Haut-Koenigsbourg in the Vosges mountains has been rebuilt several times since its first incarnation as a stronghold of Emperor Frederick of Hohenstaufen in 1147. The castle was destroyed in 1462 and 1633, and the ruins eventually were presented in 1899 to the German Kaiser Wilhelm II, who commissioned a recreation of the medieval version. Work on the reconstruction lasted from 1900 to 1908. On a clear day, the views from the top are magnificent, across the Rhine valley. To the east, you can see the edge of Germany's Black Forest.

➕ C2

Château du Haut-Koenigsbourg ✉ 67600 Orschwiller ☎ 03 69 33 25 00; www.haut-koenigsbourg.fr 🕐 Daily 9:15–6, Jun.–Aug.; 9:15–5:15, Apr.–May and Sep.; 9:30–5, Mar. and Oct.; 9:30–noon and 1–4:30, rest of year 🎫 $$ (free first Sun. of month Nov.–Mar.)

Metz

Metz is a town with a long history but a young heart. The townsfolk became French only in 1918, after a long period of German rule. Chart the political fortunes of Metz through its buildings. Late 19th-century edifices, including the railroad station, have a Germanic appearance, while attractive Cathédrale St.-Étienne belongs to the great French Gothic period. The church now displays 1.5 acres of kaleidoscopic colored glass from the 13th, 15th and 16th centuries, as well as modern panes by Marc Chagall. Sébastien Le Prestre de Vauban fortified Metz (locals pronounce it "Mess") with a ring of châteaux; the last vestige is the imposing Porte des Allemands, a miniature castle gateway facing the German border.

Opened in 2010 and housed in a post-modernist cathedral-like space, which was designed by Shigeru Ban and Jean de Gastines, the prestigious Centre Pompidou-Metz brings high art to the regions. Avant-garde temporary exhibitions of 20th- and 21st-century art feature specifically selected pieces from the vast collection of the Centre Pompidou's Museum of Modern Art in Paris (see page 35). Artists such as Matisse, Dufy and Picasso are showcased in long-term displays but masterpieces are changed every two years.

✠ B3

Tourist information ✉ 2 place d'Armes, 57020 ☎ 03 87 55 53 76; www.tourisme.metz.fr

Centre Pompidou-Metz ✉ 1 parvis des Droits-de-l'Homme, 57020 ☎ 03 87 15 39 39; www.centrepompidou-metz.fr 🕓 Mon. and Wed.–Fri. 11–6, Sat. 10–8, Sun. 10–6 ✋ $$

The rose-colored fairy-tale Château du Haut-Koenigsbourg sits high up on a hill

St. Vincent Requests the Pleasure

It happens every year in a different village of the Côte d'Or (see page 229), surrounding the old walled city of Beaune. On a weekend in late January or early February, wine lovers from around the world descend in numbers on the chosen village to drink Chablis from the best vineyards.

While most of the year is spent producing wine, mid-winter is party time. The feast of St. Vincent, the patron saint of winegrowers, is celebrated with a stately procession, a solemn Mass and a formal dinner. It's known as the St.-Vincent Tournante (turn) de Bourgogne, because the venue changes every year, as Montrachet, Musigny, Fixin and Rully and others take their turn to host the event.

In preparation for the festival, wines are chosen for tasting and the children create thousands of paper flowers to bring summer to the winter streets. On Saturday morning, the red-robed brotherhood of the Chevaliers du Tastevin and members of the 19th-century Société d'Entre Aide des Vignerons begin to march somberly down the main road. Dozens of statues of the saint are hoisted through the crowds, in celebration of and homage to St. Vincent, with many a silent prayer for good weather during the upcoming summer and a good harvest. The fraternity then partakes of a long gastronomic feast at which the chosen wines are decorked, tasted and analyzed, with due deference. After that there's a grand ball, and on the Sunday there's another parade after Mass, followed

Robes are donned for celebrations toasting St. Vincent, the patron saint of winegrowers

by speeches on an open-air stage. Villagers and visitors all turn out to witness the ceremonies and partake in the wine tastings offered by local growers. There are 20 villages on the roster to host the festival. For information, visit www.st-vincent-tournante.fr.

The St.-Vincent Tournante de Bourgogne is one of many wine festivals that take place throughout the year. Most occur in the fall, from the folk festival around the centuries-old wine presses of the dukes of Burgundy in Chénove to the celebrations of the new wines at Nuits St.-Georges. Les Trois Glorieuses is a series of November events at Clos de Vougeot, Mersault and Beaune. Featuring the legendary auction at the hospice (see page 227), the event is considered the highlight of the serious wine lover's calendar.

Why St. Vincent?

It's a mystery why St. Vincent – a Christian clergyman martyred in Spain early in the fourth century – should become patron saint of winegrowers. Theories abound, the simplest being that the first three letters of his name are in the Latin *vino*, meaning wine. Another claims that the name can be interpreted as *vin sang* (blood wine), embodying the close relationship between wine and *bien être* (well being) in France. Yet another states that because one of Vincent's responsibilities would have been care of the sacramental wine, it is most fitting that he is now holy protector of the vines. Many other myths abound, but the Confrérie des Chevaliers du Tastevin guild of wine producers ensures his spirit is treated with the utmost respect.

Nancy

The historic capital of Lorraine is a masterpiece of 17th- and 18th-century town planning. Take in the baroque, ornate gilding on gateways and railings around the city, best appreciated in the main square, place Stanislas, a UNESCO World Heritage Site. The square is named after Stanislas Leczinski, duke of Lorraine and former king of Poland, who brought numerous artists to his court and gave the city its rococo flourishes. The gracefully proportioned square was laid out from 1752 to 1760, with fountains, several palaces and the Hôtel de Ville.

Despite this, baroque isn't the style for which Nancy acquired its reputation. To the world, Nancy is the city of art nouveau.

Gallé, Prouvé and Daum glass may be enjoyed around town, and many art nouveau architectural gems line the streets, even in banks. Jacques Gruber's 1901 glass roof of the Credit Lyonnais building brings a delicate and harmonious touch of green and purple coloring through the clematis that winds around the bank's initials "C. L." The BNP Paribas (Banque Nationale de Paris) is a nouveau take on a Germanic style that is more Alsace than Lorraine. The tourist office publishes an art nouveau itinerary to help visitors discover all the gems.

Houses worth photographing include the looming Villa Majorelle and the extravagantly shuttered Villa Marguerite. Visit the Brasserie Excelsior for its original furnishings and stained glass.

The School of Nancy Museum, a gift to the town by the owner of a department store who amassed an enviable collection of furniture and glassware, also has fascinating grounds with a remarkable collection of underground fish pools and an aquarium.

Other treats include a fine arts museum and some enchanting waterside gardens.

✚ B3

An art nouveau lamp in the Musée de l'École, Nancy

Tourist information ✉ place Stanislas, 54011 ☎ 03 83 35 22 41; www.ot-nancy.fr
Musée de l'École de Nancy ✉ 36–38 rue du Sergent-Blandan, 54000 ☎ 03 83 40 14 86; www.ecole-de-nancy.com 🕐 Wed.–Sun. 10–6 💶 $$

Verdun

Verdun is a small town in northeastern France that casts a long shadow over the 20th century. From February 1916 until October 1917, the German high command attempted to bleed France dry at a cost of 800,000 lives. More than 90 years after the Great War, visitors still come here to shake their heads and ponder the terrible cost of humanity. A center for world peace, the Verdun Monument in the heart of the battlefield is a worthy institution, but the most powerful and eloquent arguments come from the unending sea of graves at Douaumont, watched over by its stark white memorial tower. The massive memorial contains an ossuary of bones that could not be identified after the war had ended. This is their suitably somber and reverential resting place. Here, too, the Tranchée des Baïonnettes recalls the men of the 137th Infantry Regiment, who were buried alive in a trench. The Stars and Stripes fly alongside the tricolor outside the Citadelle Souterraine, an exhibition about the living conditions of soldiers during the battle, and at the Meuse-Argonne American Cemetery at nearby Romagne-sous-Montfaucon, which is the largest U.S. graveyard in Europe.

✚ B3

Tourist information ✉ place de la Nation, 55106 ☎ 03 29 84 14 18; www.verdun-tourisme.com

Vosges

The Vosges mountains, the sister range to Germany's Black Forest, neatly divide the regions of Alsace and Lorraine. An area rich in woodlands, ruined castles and health spas, it's a favored retreat in summer months and an alternative to the Alps during the ski season. Year round, wine lovers follow the Route du Vin, which takes in many enchanting medieval villages tucked among vineyards that produce the region's Riesling, Gewürztraminer and Tokay wines. Just north of the town of Colmar (see page 229), the jewel of the wine trail is the cobbled medieval village of Riquewihr. With pots of geraniums decorating windows of timbered houses and a 13th-century gate tower at the main entrance, it's the perfect spot to take a break from any journey. The northern Vosges are now a protected natural park, but some of the more spectacular views may be found in the southern Vosges. Here, summits known as *ballons* reach heights of up to 4,672 feet. Grand Ballon has a well-marked trail to the top.

✚ C2–C3

Riquewihr tourist information ✉ 2 rue de la 1ère-Armée, 68340 ☎ 03 89 73 23 23; www. tourismevosges.fr or www.ribeauville-riquewihr.com

Window boxes drip with colorful flowers in the lovely, medieval village of Riquewihr

Drive
Discovering the Franche-Comté

Distance: 209 miles
Time: 4–5 days

This drive takes you along two of this region's rivers, the Doubs and the Ognon, and features splendid towns and scenery. Multicolored roof tiles and wood piles outside farmhouses contrast with high city walls and imaginative architecture. Start and finish the tour in the watchmakers' city of Besançon, wrapped in a loop of the Doubs. Art festivals, a gallery and museums cover themes from the French Resistance to time itself.

Take the N83 northeast out of town along the Doubs, bearing right on the D463 after l'Isle-sur-le-Doubs. Follow signs into Montbéliard.
This city of princes is famed for its annual book fair and its 12th-century château with Renaissance adornments. Visit the 16th-century market buildings, and the Musée de l'Aventure Peugeot, which displays Peugeot cars and motorcycles, including competition models and concept cars, in surroundings appropriate to their particular era. There are vehicles dating back more than a century, as well as a few interesting items from Peugeot's pre-car days, including kitchen appliances, tools and crinolines.

From the D438 north, take the N83 via Argiesans, then the D47A into Belfort.
The huge 36-foot-high sandstone lion that guards the château from its perch on a rock 230 feet high is the symbol of plucky little Belfort. The territory has a history of heroism, and Frédéric Auguste Bartholdi, builder of the Statue of Liberty, sculpted its lion to guard the main route from the Vosges to the Jura.

Follow the N19 to Ronchamp.
On a hill to the west of Ronchamp is the remarkable 1950–54 Notre-Dame-du-Haut. The most famous creation of architect Le Corbusier, the church has a distinctive sweeping roof reminiscent of a melting Noah's ark. Within the church, find works of art by Marc

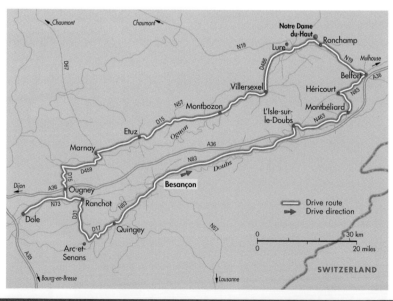

La Chapelle de Notre-Dame-du-Haut, designed by Le Corbusier, near Ronchamp

Chagall and Henri Matisse. The site has welcomed pilgrims for centuries.

The next long drive follows the Ognon river. Take the N19 toward Lure, turn left on the D64, then follow the D486 to Villersexel. Turn right onto the D9 and left onto the D49, which becomes the D15 at Montbozon. Continue on the D15 via Rioz and Etuz to Marnay. Go left on the D67 and right on the D29 leading to the D459, turning left after Ougney on the D10. Turn right on the N73/D973 to Dole.

Gateway to the Jura and capital of Franche-Comté until the 17th century, Dole gained new fame as the birthplace of Louis Pasteur (see page 221). His childhood home is now a museum. Picturesque narrow streets and carved doorways characterize the old quarter around the 16th-century church, with its 246-foot tower. Many buildings beckon you to explore. The town is a starting point for trips on the Doubs.

Back up the N73 to Ranchot, turn right for Rans and take the D31 to join the D17E to Arc-et-Senans.

It's incredible that Claude-Nicolas Ledoux's beautiful Classical architecture served as an industrial plant, but this World Heritage Site was the Royal Saltworks (Saline Royale). Built between 1775 and 1779, for 120 years it burned wood from the nearby forest to extract salt from the water of Salins les Bains.

Take the D17 northeast onto the N83, which leads back to Besançon.

Besançon tourist information ✉ Hôtel de Ville, place du 8-Septembre, 25000 (daily) and Parc Micaud, 2 place de la 1ère-Armée-Française, 25000 (Mon.–Fri.) ☎ 03 81 80 92 55; www.besancon-tourisme.com

Montbéliard tourist information
✉ 1 rue Henri-Mouhot, 25200 ☎ 03 81 94 45 60; www.ot-pays-de-montbeliard.fr

Musée de l'Aventure Peugeot ✉ Carrefour de l'Europe, 25600 Sochaux ☎ 03 81 99 42 03; www.musee-peugeot.com 🕐 Daily 10–6 ✋ $$

Belfort tourist information ✉ 2 bis rue Clemenceau, 90000 ☎ 03 84 55 90 90; www.belfort-tourisme.com

Ronchamp tourist information ✉ 14 place du 14-Juillet, 70250 ☎ 03 84 63 50 82; www.tourisme-rahin-cherimont.com

La Chapelle Notre-Dame-du-Haut
✉ 70250 Ronchamp ☎ 03 84 20 65 13; www.chapellederonchamp.fr 🕐 Daily 9:30–7, Apr.–Sep.; 10–5, Mar. and Oct.; 10–4, rest of year ✋ $$

Dole tourist information ✉ 6 place Jules-Grévy, 39100 ☎ 03 84 72 11 22; www.tourisme-paysdedole.fr

Maison Natale de Louis Pasteur ✉ 43 rue Pasteur-Dole, 39100 ☎ 03 84 72 20 61; www.musee-pasteur.com 🕐 Mon.–Sat. 10–6, Sun. 2–6, Jul.–Aug.; Mon.–Sat. 10–noon and 2–6, Sun. 2–6, Apr.–Jun. and Sep.–Oct.; Sat.–Sun. 2–6, rest of year ✋ $$

Saline Royale ✉ 25610 Arc-et-Senans ☎ 03 81 54 45 00; www.salineroyale.com 🕐 Daily 9–7, Jul.–Aug.; 9–6, Jun. and Sep.; Mon.–Fri. 9–12 and 2–6, Sat.–Sun. 9–6, May; 9–noon and 2–6, Apr. and Oct.; 10–12 and 2–5, rest of year 🍴 Cafeteria (Jun.–Sep.) ✋ $$

Champagne and the North

Opposite: Champagne vines on a hillside near Reims

Champagne and the North

Visitors often dismiss France north of Paris as little more than the route to Britain and Belgium. But shrug away these regions and you're missing out on some of the most charming corners of the country. Here will discover unspoiled walled towns, dramatic Gothic cathedrals and champagne bubbles.

From the Battlefields

This green land hides the scars of battles. The Somme and Flanders fields are dotted with poppies and broken by war cemeteries and memorials. Historic wars and treaties between France and England litter local history books – Agincourt, Crécy and the Field of the Cloth of Gold are indicated from the roadside. At Compiègne in Picardy, you can visit a replica of the railroad carriage where Germany signed the armistice of World War I and later, during World War II, forced France to surrender on the same site.

The fields that saw so much bloodshed are mainly farmland today, and fresh vegetables contribute to much of the rural economy. There are some industrialized developments outside principal towns though, and these center on pharmaceuticals in Reims (see page 252) and mail-order clothing in Lille Métropole (see page 247).

The area suffered considerably with the running down of the traditional mining industry. The former pit at Lewarde, near the bell-ringing town of Douai, is now an excellent museum showing the daily life of miners during the past 100 years. Spoil heaps have been redeveloped as dry ski slopes.

Food

Food is generally less ostentatious than in Paris, Lyon or Burgundy to the south, but it's full of delicious local flavors. You can still find some of France's best restaurants in rural locations, but simple local fare in family-run restaurants in the Nord-Pas de Calais is a cheering experience. Savory filled pastries (*tartes*) made with maroilles cheese or leeks (*poireaux*) are a particular favorite. The filling main course is *carbonade flamande*, a hearty stew. Along the coast, fresh fish is a specialty. Etaples, near Le Touquet, has a restaurant run by fishermen themselves (www.auxpecheursdetaples.fr), and the

In regimented rows, the Hautvillers vineyards cover the gently sloping hillside near Épernay

region has many local variants on *soupe de poisson* (fish soup). Ardennes pâté is legendary (see page 249).

Champagne and Beer

Champagne (see page 253), of course, produces its sparkling wines, and bars in the region will serve bubbly not only by the bottle but also by the glass (ask for a *coupe* or a *flute*). In Reims you can visit some of the great champagne houses – Mumm, Ruinart, Veuve Clicquot Ponsardin, Taittinger and Vranken-Pommery – and learn how champagne is made and see the cellars, many in tunnels carved out by the Romans. Elsewhere is beer country. The hops of Artois and Flanders create fabulous ales,

including monastic brews. The area around Cassel has great beers, and in Lille, Les Trois Brasseurs restaurant (www.les3brasseurs.com) brews its own. There are four main types of beer: *blonde, brune, rousse* and the local specialty, *blanche de Lille*, served with a slice of lemon.

Estaminets

Breweries and gin distilleries (see page 247) often organize guided tours and tasting sessions, but the place to stop for a drink in the north, especially near Cassel, is an *estaminet*. These are small local bars in towns and villages, often the front room of a private house, sometimes open for just a few hours.

Lille

For many years, Lille was the best-kept secret in France. Despite having charming cobbled streets of elegant 17th- and 18th-century houses, broad Flemish squares and the richest art gallery outside Paris, the city was tucked away in a coal-mining region and therefore scorned by Parisians and virtually ignored by foreign tourists. Then came the TGV high-speed trains, which connected all regions of France and brought Europe's key capitals within an easy commute of Lille. The city was reborn.

Shopping is a main attraction. The Euralille mall, by the station, and the pedestrian streets around the rue de Béthune have big stores, and the chic boutiques in Vieux Lille (the old quarter) have some of the top names in fashion.

The first weekend in September sees the *Braderie de Lille*, a citywide garage sale, with 125 miles of sidewalks taken over as every family in town trades around the clock. Subways run all night, and restaurants serve mussels and fries.

Eating out is a social occasion. Intimate and charming restaurants line rue de Gand in the old town, and lively bars and bistros cluster around the former market, Halles, on rue Solférino for the younger crowd. Forty percent of the population is under 25, many attending the city's respected universities. Louis Pasteur (see page 221) was the first dean of the science faculty at the University of Lille.

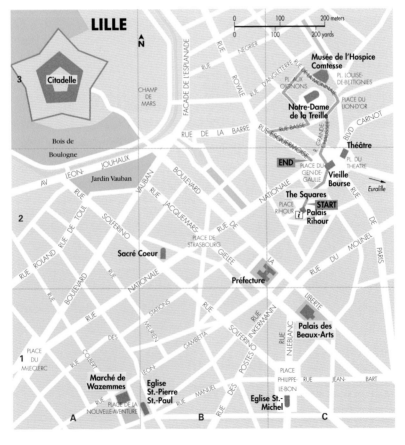

The cloistered courtyard in the Vieille Bourse serves as a book market

Essential Information

Tourist Information

✉ Palais Rihour, place Rihour, 59000 ☎ 03 59 57 94 00 (outside France) or 08 91 56 20 04 (within France); www.lilletourism.com
🚇 Rihour

Urban Transportation

Two subway lines and more than 60 bus routes serve central Lille and the metropolitan area as far as the Belgian border. Two tramways link the city with Tourcoing and Roubaix. Integrated ticketing means that any single trip may be taken using one or all of the bus, tram or subway lines. Tickets are sold individually or in books *(carnets)* of 10, and a 1-day Pass Journée and an evening pass are available (www.transpole.fr). The City Pass gives free access to museums, monuments and attractions and use of public transportation for 1, 2 or 3 days; available from the tourist office. Services run from 6 a.m. to midnight. No public transportation operates on May 1. Information, tickets and assistance are available from Lille-Flandres Station ☎ 0820 42 40 40. Taxis can be hailed from stands outside main stations. Or reserve AVS Taxis: ☎ 03 20 55 05 50. Lille-Europe Station has fast train links to northern Europe (Paris one hour and 12 minutes, Brussels 35 minutes, London via Channel Tunnel 80 minutes). Local services depart from Lille-Flandres Station (500 yards away); for information ☎ 36 35; www.sncf.fr. Rent a bicycle and electric scooters at Cyclogreen ✉ 58 rue Gustave Delroy ☎ 03 20 96 15 88; www.cyclogreen.fr.

Airport Information

Lille Airport, 5 miles south of the city at Lesquin, has international and domestic services ☎ 08 91 67 32 10; www.lille. aeroport.fr. A regular shuttle bus runs to Lille-Europe Station.

Climate – average highs and lows for the month

Jan.	Feb.	Mar.	Apr.	May	Jun.	Jul.	Aug.	Sep.	Oct.	Nov.	Dec.
5°C	6°C	9°C	12°C	17°C	20°C	22°C	23°C	19°C	15°C	9°C	7°C
41°F	43°F	48°F	54°F	63°F	68°F	72°F	73°F	66°F	59°F	48°F	45°F
1°C	1°C	3°C	5°C	8°C	11°C	13°C	13°C	11°C	7°C	4°C	2°C
34°F	34°F	37°F	41°F	46°F	52°F	55°F	55°F	52°F	45°F	39°F	36°F

Lille Sights

Key to symbols
✚ map coordinates refer to the Lille map on
page 242 🎫 admission charge:
$$$ more than €10, $$ €5–€10, $ less than €5
See page 5 for complete key to symbols

Citadelle
The magnificent fortress surrounded by
trees has been the hub of the French
army for 300 years. Louis XIV's "Queen
of Citadels" was a town in its own right
– its five-sided star-shape design
inspired the U.S. Pentagon. The main
entrance, Porte Royale, has a Latin-
inscribed regal facade and 13-foot-thick
walls. Designed for 1,200 men, the
garrison remains home to 1,000 soldiers,
including members of the French
Foreign Legion.
✚ A3 ✉ avenue du 43ème-Régiment-d'Infantrie,
59800 ☎ 03 59 57 94 00 (tourist office) or 08 91 56 20
04 (within France) ⏰ Tours (in French only) Sun at
3 p.m.; reserve through tourist office 🚇 14 ❗ To gain
entrance you need to show your passport 🎫 $$

Euralille
If you arrive in the city by high-speed
train, this modernist district created in
the 1980s will provide your first
impression. The glass towers house a
convention center and a huge shopping
mall with buildings designed by a
collection of Europe's finest architects.
In contrast to the man-made edifices,
Parc Matisse has an area left to nature
where local plants and animals thrive.
✚ Off map C2 🚇 Lille-Europe

Marché de Wazemmes
No mere market, this is an occasion – a
multicultural Sunday morning in the
streets around Église St.-Pierre St.-Paul
and place de la Nouvelle-Aventure.
Antiques and kittens are sold on the
sidewalks, and produce stalls are piled
high with plump, fresh chicory and ripe
tomatoes. For pâté and cheeses, try the
brick market hall. Sounds of an
accordion from a sidewalk café mingle
with the spiel of traders selling fresh mint
from old bicycles. All is handshakes,
backslapping and bonhomie. The smell
of Sunday lunch is overwhelming. Huge
pans of paëlla are stirred outside ethnic
restaurants, and giant rôtisseries turn
dozens of roast chickens.
✚ A1 ✉ place de la Nouvelle-Aventure, 59000
⏰ Sun. mornings and holidays 🍴 Bars, cafés and
food stands 🚇 Gambetta

Palais des Beaux-Arts
France's second national art collection
after the Louvre was originally built
from 1885 to 1892 and reopened in
1997 after six years of renovation. Don't
miss the museum's celebrated works by
Francisco José de Goya: a pair of wicked
portrayals of youth and old age, *Les*

Jeunes and *Les Vieilles*. Red walls and high ceilings provide the backdrop to a veritable banquet of French, Flemish and European masterpieces from the 17th century to the Impressionists. A Renaissance gallery and Sébastien Le Prestre de Vauban's original citadel models take up the basement.

➕ C1 ✉ place de la République, 59000 ☎ 03 20 06 78 00; www.pba-lille.fr 🕐 Wed.–Sun. 10–6, Mon. 2–6. Closed first weekend in Sep. 🍴 Café and restaurant with terrace 🚇 République Beaux-Arts 💵 $$ (free first Sun. of the month)

The Squares

The heart of Lille is the expansive place du Général-de-Gaulle. Transformed into a park or fairground when the city is in party mood, it's the venue for the Christmas Ferris wheel, which affords unrivaled views across the city. It's lively at any time of year, with its sidewalk cafés and the bustle of shoppers. The central fountain, with its statue of Déesse (Goddess), was a spiritual symbol of civic courage during a siege in 1792. The main theater is the former guardhouse. The tiered roof topped with golden figures next door is the 1936 home of the local paper *La Voix du Nord*, dominating the square along with Europe's largest bookstore, the Furet du Nord. Behind the elegant Vieille Bourse (see page 246) is place du Théâtre, the neoclassical Opera House and the magnificent belfry of the imposing chamber of commerce.

➕ C2 🚇 Rihour

The Ferris wheel, place du Général-de-Gaulle

Walk
Old Town

Refer to route marked on
city map on page 242

This 1.5-mile stroll is around the
17th- and 18th-century quarter.

**Leave the tourist office at Palais Rihour,
a former chapel of the dukes of Burgundy,
and cross place du Général-de-Gaulle. Walk
through the Vieille Bourse.**
Vieille Bourse is Lille's most beautiful
site. It is a cluster of private houses,

where merchant stalls in the cloistered
courtyard serve as a flower and book
market and refuge for chess players.
**Rue de la Bourse leads onward to rue
de la Grande-Chaussée.**
An iron arm above the corner shop
points you in the right direction. Charles
de Batz-Castlemore D'Artagnan, who
served as captain of the Muskateers of
the Guard under Louis XIV, lived at
Nos. 20 and 26.
**Turn right along rue des Chats-Bossus;
on your left you may admire the fabulous
Breton art deco mosaic frontage of
A l'Huitrière restaurant. Continue to place
du Lion-d'Or, then further on to rue de
la Monnaie.**
Visit Musée de l'Hospice Comtesse,
a 13th-century hospital that houses
a museum on Flemish life and art from
the 15th through 17th centuries.
**Continue along the road and turn left on
rue au Péterinck, past 18th-century
weavers' houses to place aux Oignons.**
The name has nothing to do with the
onions sold in the nearby market; rather
it's a corruption of *donjon* (dungeon).
Little alleyways lead to place Gilleson,
where long ago stood the château of the
counts of Flanders. The foundation stone
of Cathédrale Notre-Dame de la Treille
was laid in 1854. However, although the
chapel and apse were built by the end of
the 19th century and the city welcomed
its first bishop in 1913, construction
was abandoned in 1947, leaving Lille
with three-quarters of a cathedral until
1999. Notre-Dame now has an oddly
industrial modern frontage and
piazza, with magnificent doors by
Holocaust survivor, sculptor
Georges Jeanclos.
**Take rue du Cirque, and turn right on
rue Basse to see the antiques shops.
Then go left to the bustling rue
Esquermoise, with its legendary tearoom
Meert at No. 27, a few steps from place
du Général-de-Gaulle.**

A decorated clock tower overlooks buildings
bordering place du Général-de-Gaulle

Lille Métropole

The larger metropolitan area around Lille has a population of almost a million (compared to 150,000 residents in the city itself) and laps over the Belgian border. An integrated public transportation system of trams, buses and subways enables a local ticket to take you from one town to the next.

Pretty gardens line the roads to the two major satellite towns, Tourcoing and Roubaix, each 30 minutes away. Tourcoing is a major cultural center with music festivals and the MUba Eugène Leroy, consisting of works by Tourcoing-born Leroy (1910–2000), along with French, Flemish and Dutch artists. Roubaix is a mecca for clothes shopping – McArthur Glen sells top brands at discount prices. The prestigious 19th-century Museum of Arts and Industry is housed in a converted art deco swimming pool. Villeneuve d'Ascq, just 15 minutes from central Lille, is home to the Modern Art Museum, which has displays of all major art movements of the 20th century. The building is in a park with sculptures by Picasso.

A river trip along the Deûle from Lille includes a visit to the 200-year-old distillery at Wambrechies. Equipment from the early 1800s makes *genièvre* (a juniper gin) and an associated 40-proof Vieux Malt whisky.

Tourcoing tourist information ✉ 9 rue de Tournai, 59200 ☎ 03 20 26 89 03; www.tourcoing-tourisme.com

Roubaix tourist information ✉ 12 place de la Liberté, 59100 ☎ 03 20 65 31 90; www.roubaixtourisme.com

MUba Eugène Leroy ✉ 2 rue Paul-Doumer, 59200 Tourcoing ☎ 03 20 28 91 60; www.muba-tourcoing.fr 🕐 Wed.–Mon. 1–6 🚇 Tourcoing Centre 🖐 $$

McArthur Glen ✉ 44 Mail de Lannoy, 59100 Roubaix ☎ 03 28 33 36 00; www.mcarthurglenroubaix.fr 🕐 Mon.–Sat. 10–7 🚇 Roubaix Eurotéléport

Musée d'Art et d'Industrie André Diligent ✉ 23 rue de l'Espérance, 59100 Roubaix ☎ 03 20 69 23 60; www.roubaix-lapiscine.com 🕐 Tue.–Thu. 11–6, Fri. 11–8, Sat.–Sun. 1–6 🚇 Jean Lebas 🖐 $$

Musée de l'Art Moderne ✉ 1 allée du Musée, Villeneuve d'Ascq, 59650 ☎ 03 20 19 68 68; www.musee-lam.fr 🕐 Tue.–Sun. 10–6 🚇 Pont de Bois, then bus 41 to Parc-Urban-Musée 🖐 $$

Distillerie Claeyssens de Wambrechies ✉ 1 rue de la Distillerie, 59118 Wambrechies ☎ 03 20 14 91 91; www.wambrechies.com 🕐 Tours by reservation only 🚇 9 Wambrechies Château 🖐 $$

La Piscine (swimming pool) in the Museum of Arts and Industry, Roubaix

Champagne and the North

Regional Sights

Amiens

The miracle of Amiens is its vast Gothic
cathedral. During the bombings of the
20th-century wars, when much of
the surrounding medieval town was
destroyed, France's largest cathedral
remained untouched. Similarly, during
the Revolution, when images of saints
outside most churches and cathedrals
were decapitated, the faces on rows of
apostles and prophets around the three
main porches remained intact. Built in
less than 50 years, this 13th-century
marvel of engineering has a 139-foot-
high nave. Later treasures include 3,650
carved figures in the 16th-century choir
and an impressive baroque pulpit.
Explore the surviving medieval quarter
behind the cathedral and Jules Verne's
house. The town was a Celtic settlement
on the Somme river until taken by the
Romans under Julius Caesar as a
strategic point on routes to the north.
The Somme feeds Amiens' unusual
private market gardens, Les
Hortillonnages, which are floating plots
of land served by narrow canals (*rieux*).
Boat trips around the gardens provide a
delightful diversion.

Canalside restaurants on the Somme river in the town of Amiens provide a charming setting for lunch

A2

Tourist information ✉ 40 place Notre-Dame, 80000
☎ 03 22 71 60 50; www.amiens-tourisme.com

Ardennes

The town of Charleville-Mézières (see pages 250–251) is a perfect base for exploring the wooded countryside of the Ardennes. Deep forests straddle the border with present-day Belgium, and it's impossible today to imagine the huge tracts of woodland flattened during the last war in Germany's final assault on the Allies. By the 1970s, the forests were as rich as ever.

Following the route of the River Meuse takes you through spectacular scenery. The Massif Ardennais is a perfect backdrop high above, and the river plunges along its equally dramatic gorge below you. You can explore on horseback, by boat or on foot; details are available from Charleville tourist office (see below).

Each month, forest rangers lead escorted treks into the countryside to discover wildlife, wild fruits and mushrooms in the woods. Strong mushrooms and wild boar dominate the flavors in bistro and restaurant fare, which includes famous patés and smoked meats. Boar is best served with a potato and onion dish known as *la bayenne*. The health-conscious visitor will treasure one of the local Ardennes cheeses: Rocroi, which is strong in flavor but low in fat.

C2

Departmental tourist information: Comité Départemental du Tourisme des Ardennes
✉ 24 place Ducale, 08107 Charleville-Mézières
☎ 03 24 56 06 08; www.ardennes.com

Arras

Amid the countless World War I cemeteries, Arras, with its arcaded squares and high-gabled houses, was once the capital of Artois and gave its name to fine tapestries. The 17th- and 18th-century architecture in the wide squares, place des Héros and Grand Place, is a miraculous reconstruction since the original buildings were destroyed in the war. Fortunately, a network of passages connected the town's cellars, and the original plans for every building were discovered therein.

The 16th-century town hall, which was also rebuilt and boasts a fabulous belfry, stands over the entrance to these tunnels, known as Les Boves. During the war, the tunnels extended to the trenches and an underground railroad and telephone system communicated with the front. Visit the tunnels, then climb the belfry for good views over the town. The war memorial lists the names of 36,000 soldiers whose bodies were never found. The awe-inspiring Canadian Monument at Vimy Ridge is 7 miles away (see page 255).

🚩 B2

Tourist information ✉ Hôtel de Ville, place des Héros, 62000 ☎ 03 21 51 26 95; www.ot-arras.fr

Les Boves ✉ place des Héros, 62000 ☎ 03 21 51 26 95 🕐 Guided visits only starting at 10 a.m. Details at the tourist office. Closed for three weeks in Jan. 🎫 $$

Boulogne-sur-Mer

France's largest fishing port, Boulogne has a bustling commercial center with a lively market and one of the world's greatest cheese shops, Philippe Olivier, over on rue Thiers.

Climb Grande Rue to the upper town. Untouched by wartime bombings, the old town is completely walled, with just four entrances. Fortifications enclose the 19th-century domed basilica, attractive cobbled streets and the moated medieval château, now a museum. Summer sees a music festival on the ramparts. Down by the port is Nausicaá, a fascinating sea-life center with shark aquarium, and

The town hall in place des Héros, Arras

a wide beach. As a ferry port for Britain, English is spoken widely here.

🚩 A3

Tourist information

✉ Parvis de Nausicaá, 62203 ☎ 03 21 10 88 10; www.tourisme-boulognesurmer.com

Nausicaá ✉ boulevard Ste.-Beuve, 62203 ☎ 03 21 30 99 99, infoline: 03 21 30 98 98; www.nausicaa.fr 🕐 Daily 9:30–7:30, Jul.–Aug.; 9:30–6:30, rest of year. Closed early to late Jan. 🍴 Restaurant and bistro 🎫 $$$

Charleville-Mézières

The ninth-century town of Mézières was a fortified buffer zone between France and its enemies in the low countries. Bruised by the centuries, it declined when Charles de Gonzague, the Duke of Nevers and Mantua, built splendidly Ruritanian Charleville, and rivalry between the two towns ensued until they merged in 1966. Charleville's main square, place Ducale, with its honeyed buildings framed by forest treetops, looks like a fairy-tale illustration, never more so than during the biennial International Marionette Festival (www.festival-marionnette.com). Known as the City of Puppets,

Charleville hosts the Institut National de la Marionnette, the world's leading school for puppeteers, with its incredible clock called the Grand Marionnettiste (Puppet Master). A two-story delight, the clock transforms itself into a puppet show every hour from 10 a.m. to 9 p.m. The Arthur Rimbaud Museum evokes the life and work of the young poet, born in Charleville in 1854.

✛ C2

Tourist information ✉ 4 place Ducale, 08102 ☎ 03 24 55 69 90; www.charleville-mezieres.org **Musée Rimbaud** ✉ quai Arthur-Rimbaud, 08000 ☎ 03 24 32 44 65 🕐 Tue.–Sun. 10–noon and 2–6 💲 $ (free first Sun. of month)

Laon

The seven towers of the cathedral in Laon can be seen for miles around. On closer inspection, it is apparent that the glorious Notre-Dame (building started c.1155) inspired the Gothic design of its more famous namesake in Paris. The highlight of the walled town, the cathedral has brooding inset porchways that frown across the parvis under the twin towers of the west front. Inside, discover two rose windows, lovely old stained glass, a splendid 387-foot-long nave and a beautiful cloister. During the 9th and 10th centuries, Laon was the capital of France. There is plenty of medieval architecture to appreciate, including the leaning tower of the 13th-century Porte de Soissons. Upper town treasures are best explored on foot, so park and leave your car in the lower town and take the monorail to the top of the hill.

✛ B2

Tourist information ✉ Hôtel Dieu, place du Parvis-Gautier-de-Mortagne, 02000 ☎ 03 23 20 28 62; www.tourisme-paysdelaon.com

Detail of the upper west facade of the Cathédrale de Notre-Dame in Laon

Lens

This unprepossessing town, surrounded by reminders of two world wars, is the site of one of France's most exciting arts projects, the Louvre-Lens. A glass edifice designed by Japanese architects SANAA will exhibit an extended range of the Louvre Paris' monumental collection through regular temporary exhibitions.

➕ B3

Tourist information ✉ 28 rue de la Paix, 62300 ☎ 03 21 67 66 66; www.toursime-lenslievin.fr
🕐 Information not available at time of print

Reims

Reims is rich. The wealth of the city was built on the popping of champagne corks (see page 253), but its history is much richer than the fizz in its cellars. Clovis, France's first Christian king, was crowned here, and Joan of Arc led the dauphin to his coronation in Reims. The city has overseen 25 Sunday coronation processions to the cathedral, from Louis VIII in 1223 to Charles X in 1825.

That magnificent cathedral is the essential visit, the front combines the best of all of France's Gothic cathedrals: stone lacework on the twin towers and 56 statues of kings, each one 14.5 feet high, arranged above the rose window. The most famous figure on the facade is the Angel, the city symbol. The edifice was restored after artillery damage in World War I, and its 20th-century prize is the window by Marc Chagall, among some stunning 13th-century glass. Check out a fascinating 15th-century astronomical clock with moving figures depicting the Adoration of the Magi and the Flight into Egypt. A sound-and-light show, in July and August, relates the history of the cathedral.

Don't miss the Archbishops' Palace (Palais du Tau) nearby – a UNESCO World Heritage Site – where remains of many of the cathedral's original damaged statues can be seen close up.

The Roman era is recalled by the Porte de Mars, a splendid ocher-colored stone archway that now stands forlornly at the

French monarchs were crowned at Reims cathedral

heart of a traffic interchange on the edge of town. Horse-drawn carriage tours include a visit to the cathedral, lunch and a visit to the champagne vineyards.

Les Flâneries Musicales (www. flaneriesreims.com; late June to late July) is a season of free concerts established by Yehudi Menuhin. Some of the world's greatest musicians come to perform in Reims' churches and parks.

➕ B2

Tourist information ✉ 2 rue Guillaume-de-Machault, 51100 ☎ 0892 70 13 51 (toll call); www.reims-tourisme.com
Cathédrale Notre-Dame ✉ 3 rue Guillaume-de-Machault, 51100 ☎ 03 26 47 55 34; www. cathedrale-reims.com 🕐 Daily 7:30–7:30
Palais du Tau ✉ place du Cardinal-Luçon
☎ 03 26 47 81 79; www.monuments-nationaux.fr
🕐 Tue.–Sun. 9:30–6:30, May 6–Sep. 8; 9:30–12:30 and 2–5:30, rest of year 🕐 $$

Discovering Champagne

There is no such thing as French champagne; there is just champagne. If made anywhere else, it's simply sparkling wine. Only champagne from Champagne is champagne.

The unknown alchemy in the cellars and soil that creates this special wine (locals swear one may drink until dawn and never know a hangover) was discovered by Dom Pérignon, a monk who added yeast to speed up the winemaking process at the Hautvillers Abbey. Visit the abbey and the neighboring village as part of a trail through Champagne country. The tourist office in Reims provides routes that feature Châlons-en-Champagne and Château-Thierry, plus some small private cellars. Base yourself in Épernay or Reims, the location of the great champagne houses.

Many larger houses offer escorted tours of their cellars. Some are simple, educational walks through chalk tunnels where staff explain winemaking from pressing to blending red and white grapes with cane sugar. Stored neck down in wooden racks, bottles must be twisted an eighth of a turn every day in a process called *remuage*. Each *remueur* turns 40,000 bottles daily.

Tours of this special underworld vary from Mercier's laser-guided automatic miniature train ride past thousands of bottles and a gallery of 19th-century posters in Épernay to the sedate one-hour stroll through the tunnels beneath the Taittinger winery, where you'll have the services of an expert guide. Of course, whichever tour you choose – or maybe you'll take two or three – you'll have the chance to sample the bubbly end result.

Champagne Veuve Doussot, at Noë les Mallets in the Aube *département*, offers visitors a chance to join in the grape harvest for a day. The Journée Vendanges costs €40 per person, which includes lunch and champagne tasting after an hour's work in the vineyard. However, the season is hard to predict as it is dependent on the weather, and it is over quickly.

Reims tourist information (see page 252)

Épernay tourist information ✉ 7 avenue de Champagne, 51200 ☎ 03 26 55 33 00; www.ot-epernay.fr

Comité Régional du Tourisme de Champagne-Ardenne ✉ 50 avenue Général-Patton, 51000 Chalons-en-Champagne ☎ 03 26 21 85 80; www.tourisme-champagne-ardenne.com

Take a tour through the cellars of a champagne house to discover how the wine is made

Drive
The Opal Coast and Old Walled Towns

Distance: 160 miles
Time: 3 days

With a coast that has attracted pioneers, from aviation to the Channel Tunnel, and a countryside rich in history, the Pas de Calais has plenty of tales to tell along its pretty valleys and byways.

From Calais, with its famed Auguste Rodin statue outside the ornate town hall

belfry, take the D940 south toward Boulogne-sur-Mer.

Follow the Côte d'Opale (Opal Coast) of the English Channel, crossed by ferries and tunnel trains from Calais. Blériot-Plage is named for the aviator who first flew the Channel from here in 1909. The cliffs Cap Gris-Nez and Cap Blanc-Nez are marked from the road. Explore Boulogne (see page 250).

Continue on the D940 to Étaples, then take the N39 to Le Touquet.

The seaside and casino resort is known as Paris-Plage due to its popularity with wealthy weekenders from the city. Built by the British, who today take 20-minute flights from the U.K. to an airstrip by one of three golf courses, this early 20th-century playground remains fashionable. Enjoy thalassotherapy treatments, great food and shopping.

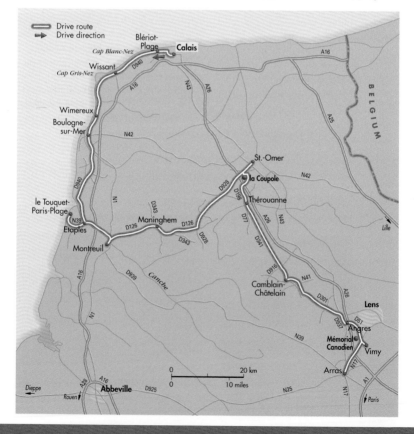

Sand yachts skim along the sand at speed on the beach at Le Touquet

Pine groves hide houses built in a fantastic array of vernacular styles. **Head inland on the N39, turn right to the N1 and right to the D138 and the D901 to Montreuil.**

High on a hill above the Canche river, the walled town of Montreuil-sur-Mer, with cobbled streets, is, despite the name, 10 miles from the sea. Victor Hugo's novel *Les Misérables* was set here, and townsfolk re-enact scenes from it on summer evenings. An 11th-century church and good restaurants are among quieter town alternatives. **Go north on the N1, then take the D907 to the D126. Turn right on D343 at Maninghem and continue for 3 miles. Rejoin the D126, then turn left on D928 into St.-Omer.**

Fast highways to Paris mean most travelers miss the delights of the walled town of St.-Omer, with a Gothic cathedral and unusual farms on waterlogged marshes, where farmers tend fields of lettuce from flat-bottom boats. **Leave St.-Omer on the D928 to Abbeville then take the D210 signed for Helfaut and La Coupole.**

A Nazi rocket bunker, La Coupole, serves as a moving museum, with two remarkable audiovisual presentations: one showing rocket science from wartime weaponry to the *Apollo* missions and the other revealing life in occupied France through thousands of home movies and family photographs.

Take the D198 to Thérouanne, picking up the D341. Just after Camblain-Châtelain, go left on the D301 and keep left to turn right on the D937. Turn left on the D51 through Angres to Vimy. After 4 miles, look for signs to the Mémorial Canadien.

On the battlefield of April 1917 – land that France later gave to Canada – Walter Allward's white stone cenotaph dominates the Douai plain. The inscription reads: "To the valor of their countrymen in the Great War and in memory of their 60,000 dead, this monument is raised by the people of Canada." At its foot, the figure of Mother Canada weeps for her sons. Visitors may walk front-line trenches and explore tunnels behind the lines. **Take the N17 for Arras (see page 250).**

Le Touquet tourist information ✉ Palais du Congrès, place de l'Hermitage, 62520 ☎ 03 21 06 72 00; www.letouquet.com

Montreuil-sur-Mer tourist information
✉ 21 rue Carnot, 62170 ☎ 03 21 06 04 27; www.tourisme-montreuillois.com

St.-Omer tourist information ✉ 4 rue du Lion-d'Or, 62500 ☎ 03 21 98 08 51; www.tourisme-saint-omer.com

La Coupole ✉ rue du Mont-à-Car (D210), 62570 Helfaut ☎ 03 21 12 27 27; www.lacoupole-france.com 🕐 Daily 10–7, Jul.–Aug.; 9–6, rest of year. Closed late Dec.–early Jan. 🍴 Café 💲 $$

Vimy Ridge National Historical Site of Canada
✉ 62580 Vimy ☎ 03 21 50 68 68; www.veterans. gc.ca 🕐 Site: daily dawn–dusk 💲 Free

Hotels and Restaurants

Opposite: The dome over the entrance to the Negresco hotel in Nice is a famous landmark

Hotels and Restaurants

The hotels and restaurants in this book were selected by local specialists and include establishments in several price ranges. Since price is often the best indication of the level of facilities and quality of service, a three-tiered price guide appears at the beginning of the listings. Because variable rates will affect the amount of foreign currency that can be exchanged for dollars (and thus affect the cost of a room or a meal), price ranges are given in the local currency.

Although price ranges and operating times were accurate at press time, this information is always subject to change without notice. If you're interested in a particular establishment, it is always advisable to call ahead for a reservation. The larger and more expensive hotels, and the better-known restaurants, are more likely to have someone who speaks English on staff; smaller establishments may not.

The ceiling of Le Train Bleu, Gare de Lyon, Paris

Facilities for travelers with disabilities vary greatly; it is advisable to contact an establishment directly to determine whether your needs can be met. Also, some older buildings may not be suitable for visitors with limited or impaired mobility.

Accommodations

Accommodations have been selected with two considerations in mind: a particularly attractive character or sense of local flavor, or a convenient or central location. Remember that centrally located hotels fill up quickly, especially during summer vacation periods; make reservations well in advance. In-room bathrooms (sometimes referred to as "en-suite facilities") may not be available in smaller budget hotels.

Room rates for French hotels sometimes include a light breakfast of rolls or croissants and coffee. Some hotels offer a rate that includes an evening meal (known as *demi-pension*).

Eating Out

Listed restaurants range from upscale places suitable for an elegant evening out to small cafés where you can stop and take a leisurely break from a busy day of sightseeing. Some are close to attractions; where this is the case, there is a cross-reference under the attraction listing. Other eating possibilities are the cafeterias and restaurants on the premises of museums and galleries.

French food has a justifiable reputation as among the best in the world. From the simplest offering of an oven-fresh baguette with a melt-in-the-mouth omelet to the most elaborate and imaginatively prepared *menu gastronomique* of a famous chef, you will be delighted by your meals in France. So relax and take your time as the French do; a meal here is not just a remedy for hunger, but an experience to enjoy at leisure and a feast for eye and palate, enhanced by the hospitality and good service of your host.

KEY TO SYMBOLS

	hotel
	restaurant
	address
	telephone number
	days/times closed
	nearest metro/tube/subway station(s)
AX	American Express
DC	Diners Club
MC	MasterCard
VI	VISA

Hotels
Price guide: double room with breakfast for two people
$ less than €130
$$ €130–€200
$$$ more than €200

Restaurants
Price guide: dinner per person, excluding drinks
$ less than €35
$$ €35–€65
$$$ more than €65

Haute Cuisine – Literally

In many places on earth, it could have been turned into an overpriced tourist trap, but this is Paris and it's food we are dealing with. Le Jules Verne (☎ 01 45 55 61 44; www.lejulesverne-paris. com), up on the third level of the Eiffel Tower, is a fabulous restaurant where the cuisine, under the direction of one of France's top chefs, Alain Ducasse, is more than a match for the stunning view. It is expensive, though no more so than any top Paris restaurant, and there's a good-value fixed-price lunch. In any event, for a special treat and an unforgettable Paris experience, it's money well spent. The chic 58 Tour Eiffel (☎ 08 25 56 66 62), on the first level of the tower, offers a less pricey alternative and a good brasserie-style menu.

PARIS AND THE ÎLE-DE-FRANCE

AUVERS-SUR-OISE
Sous le Porche $–$$
Stylishly simple and contemporary furnishings are combined with feature exposed brick walls, rugged old beams and rug-scattered worn wooden floors here. The restaurant sources local ingredients and traditional recipes are enriched with international influences. Outside of meal times, you can drop in for a relaxing coffee complemented with pastries or artisan ice creams.
 place de la Mairie ☎ 01 30 36 16 50 AX DC MC VI

CHARTRES
Grand Monarque $$
The former coaching inn is now a smoothly operated hotel, with individually decorated rooms.
 22 place des Épars
☎ 02 37 18 15 15 AX DC MC VI

La Passacaille $
Very good pizzas and pastas are served here. This restaurant in the town center is a good bet and has a non-smoking dining room.
 30 rue Saint-Même ☎ 02 37 21 52 10 Thu.–Tue. AX DC MC VI

FONTAINEBLEAU
Hôtel Napoléon $$
In a grand 19th-century building, the Napoléon has a refurbished interior and a lovely restaurant terrace.
 9 rue Grande, 77300
☎ 01 60 39 50 50 AX DC MC VI

PARIS
Agora $–$$
This budget-priced, mildly eccentric hotel is centrally located just yards from the Châtelet-Les-Halles RER train station. Cheerful staff are pleased to assist. Be aware that clients may be accommodated in the sister hotel in Saint Germain, which has better furnishings but is not so centrally located.
 7 rue de la Cossonnerie, 75001
☎ 01 42 33 46 02 Les Halles; RER Châtelet-Les-Halles AX MC VI

Au Chien Qui Fume $$
Founded in 1740, this restaurant serves a range of traditional French dishes including particularly good foie gras.
 33 rue du Pont-Neuf, 75001
☎ 01 42 36 07 42 RER Châtelet-Les-Halles AX DC MC VI

Au Pied de Cochon $$
Recently refurbished, this is the last great market restaurant in town. Join revelers for onion soup and pig's trotters at dawn – it is open 24 hours.
 6 rue Coquillère, 75001 ☎ 01 40 13 77 00 Open 24 hours
 Châtelet-Les-Halles AX DC MC VI

Brasserie Flo $$
In this boisterous backstreet restaurant hear the clatter of platters and yells of barmen as waiters negotiate the crowds.
 7 cour des Petites-Écuries, 75010
☎ 01 47 70 13 59 Château d'Eau AX DC MC VI

La Bretonnerie $$
Antique furnishings fill the old-style rooms of this family-run hotel. Parking may be arranged in advance.
 22 rue Ste.-Croix de la Bretonnerie, 75004 ☎ 01 48 87 77 63 Hôtel de Ville MC VI

Café Beaubourg $$
Watch the street entertainers outside the Pompidou Center while enjoying fresh, crisp salads and fashionable food options.
 100 rue St.-Merri, 75004 ☎ 01 48 87 63 96 Châtelet-Les-Halles AX DC MC VI

Chez Georges $$
Journalists and bankers dine elbow to elbow and lunch secrets are confided over turbot in a sauce *béarnaise* and good steaks.
 1 rue du Mail, 75002
☎ 01 42 60 07 11 Closed Sat.–Sun. Sentier AX VI

Chez Paul $–$$
Chez Paul is a traditional old bistro with original early-1900s decor. The classic menu is filled with French staples and portions are generous.
 13 rue de Charonne, 75011
☎ 01 47 00 34 57 Bastille AX MC VI

Chopin $
At the end of a glass-roofed gallery of toy shops, this homey spot has rooms looking out over the pretty courtyards.
 10 boulevard Montmartre, 46 passage Joufroy, 75009 ☎ 01 47 70 58 10 Grands Boulevards MC VI

Le Comptoir du Relais $$$
Yves Cambeborde's latest restaurant sits shoulder-to-shoulder

Paris and the Île-de-France

KEY TO SYMBOLS

🏨	hotel
🍽	restaurant
✉	address
☎	telephone number
🕐	days/times closed
Ⓜ	nearest metro/tube/subway station(s)
AX	American Express
DC	Diners Club
MC	MasterCard
VI	VISA

Hotels
Price guide: double room with breakfast for two people
$	less than €130
$$	€130–€200
$$$	more than €200

Restaurants
Price guide: dinner per person, excluding drinks
$	less than €35
$$	€35–€65
$$$	more than €65

Hôtel du Jeu de Paume

The Hôtel du Jeu de Paume, located on Île St.-Louis, is one of Paris' more imaginative conversions. From the archway leading to the 17th-century courtyard to the hotel's former royal *jeu de paume* – or indoor tennis court – the interior decor offers a change of pace for the visitor bored with efficient but dull whitewash and chrome. A glass elevator affords a superb view of the courtyard and its galleries, cleverly redone as comfortable breakfast and lounge areas, and centuries-old beams grandly support this airy central well. All rooms are individually decorated, and those under the eaves have little private spiral staircases to the sleeping area. The hotel also has a sauna (✉ 54 rue St.-Louis-en-l'Île, Île St.-Louis (Pont Marie) ☎ 01 43 26 14 18 Ⓜ Pont Marie AX DC MC VI).

---

with his new hotel. A brasserie by day and gastronomic restaurant with single menu in the evening, this is modern French cuisine at its best from one of the masters.
✉ Hôtel Relais Saint-Germain, 9 carrefour de l'Odeon, 75006 ☎ 01 44 27 07 97 Ⓜ Odéon

🏨 Crillon $$$
Arguably the most prestigious hotel in town, the Bernstein and Presidential apartments are ideal for those with elastic wallets.
✉ 10 place de la Concorde, 75008 ☎ 01 44 71 15 00 Ⓜ Concorde AX DC MC VI

🏨 The Five Hotel $–$$
This contemporary boutique hotel is decorated by award-winning French artist Isabel Emmerique and is located south of the downtown city core.
✉ 3 rue Flatters, 75005 ☎ 01 43 31 74 21 Ⓜ Les Gobelins, Censier Daubenton AX DC MC VI

🍽 La Fontaine de Mars $$
Red-check tablecloths and polished copper decorate this café. Lunches are good value.
✉ 129 rue St.-Dominique, 75007 ☎ 01 47 05 46 44 Ⓜ École Militaire AX DC MC VI

🍽 Le Fouquet's Barriere $$$
This upscale restaurant is a Champs-Élysées institution, where people-watching has been refined into an art form.
✉ 99 avenue des Champs-Élysées, 75008 ☎ 01 40 69 60 00 Ⓜ George V AX DC MC VI

🏨 Grand Hotel Francais $–$$
This contemporary hotel with cool decor is located close to the Bastille district, with its great eateries. There's a bar on site.
✉ 223 boulevard Voltaire, 75011 ☎ 01 43 71 27 57 Ⓜ Rue des Boulets AX DC MC VI

🍽 Le Grand Vefour $$$
At one of Paris' oldest restaurants, the decor is opulent, the wine cellar is great, and Guy Martin's cuisine is faultless. Reservations well in advance are essential.
✉ 17 rue de Beaujolais, 75001 ☎ 01 42 96 56 27 🕐 Closed Sat.–Sun., Aug., Dec. 24–31 Ⓜ Palais-Royal/Musée du Louvre AX DC MC VI

🏨 L'Hôtel $$$
Oscar Wilde died here, and cabaret-singer Mistinguette's boudoir is among the rooms in one of the most expensive hotels on the left bank.
✉ 13 rue des Beaux-Arts, 75006 ☎ 01 44 41 99 00 Ⓜ St.-Germain-des-Près AX DC MC VI

🏨 Hôtel Crayon $$
This funky, colorful small hotel, decorated by artist Julie Gauthron, is perfectly placed for all attractions.
✉ 25 rue de Bouloi, 75001 ☎ 01 42 36 54 19 Ⓜ Louvre, Palais-Royale/Musée du Louvre AX DC MC VI

🏨 Hôtel New Orient $–$$
Newly refurbished, with a personal touch, this little gem is located 10 minutes on foot from the Opéra.
✉ 16 rue de Constantinople, 75008 ☎ 01 45 22 21 64 Ⓜ Villiers AX MC VI

🏨 Meurice $$$
Fling open a tall bedroom window and look over the gardens of the Tuileries. The palatial hotel is furnished in lavish style.
✉ 228 rue de Rivoli, 75001 ☎ 01 44 58 10 10 Ⓜ Tuileries AX DC MC VI

🏨 Millennium Opéra Paris $$–$$$
The elegant hotel near the Opéra has a glass dome and country-house good taste in the rooms.
✉ 12 boulevard Haussmann, 75009 ☎ 01 49 49 16 00 Ⓜ Richelieu-Drouot AX DC MC VI

🍽 Les Papilles $–$$
This is an authentic little wine bar/bistro and delicatessen. The wine list is extensive, and has examples from around France in all price ranges.
✉ 30 rue Gay-Lussac, 75005 ☎ 01 43 25 20 79 Ⓜ RER Luxembourg MC VI

🏨 Pavillon de la Reine $$$
These converted royal apartments are a rarity among the garret-like accommodations of the Marais.
✉ 28 place de Vosges, 75003 ☎ 01 40 29 19 19 Ⓜ St.-Paul AX DC MC VI

🍽 Polidor $–$$
At this last of the traditional left bank eateries, students and visitors share long wooden tables and waitresses are honest about the dish of the day.

✉ 41 rue Monsieur-le-Prince, 75006
☎ 01 43 26 95 34 🚇 Odéon
No credit cards

🍴 Le Reservoir $$
Decorated in Italian Renaissance
style, this trendy eatery serves
traditional cuisine.
✉ 16 rue de la Forge-Royales ☎ 01
43 56 39 60 🕐 Closed lunch Tue.–
Sat., dinner Sun., and all day Mon.
🚇 Ledru Rollin AX DC MC VI

🏨 Le Rives de Notre-Dame $$$
This delightful 16th-century house on
the banks of the Seine has bright
decor and attentive service.
✉ 15 quai St.-Michel, 75005
☎ 01 43 54 81 16 🚇 St.-Michel
AX DC MC VI

🍴 Rotisserie du Beaujolais $$
Perhaps the best-kept secret in
Paris, the menu at this country-style
bistro includes fabulous regional
dishes that are prepared in the
traditional manner.
✉ 19 quai de Tournelle, 75005
☎ 01 43 54 17 47 🚇 Cardinal
Lemoine MC VI

🏨 St.-James Paris $$$
This is the only private château-hotel
in Paris, with a garden terrace
restaurant, faultless service and
comfortable rooms and suites.
✉ 43 avenue Bugeaud, 75016
☎ 01 44 05 81 81 🚇 Porte Dauphine
AX DC MC VI

🏨 St.-Merry $$–$$$
The Gothic interior is the former
presbytery of the 16th-century
church of St.-Merry. Original flying
buttresses plunge through room No.
9, which is located above the nave.
✉ 78 rue de la Verrerie, 75004
☎ 01 42 78 14 15 🚇 Hôtel de Ville
AX DC MC VI

🍴 Le Train Bleu $$$
This station restaurant is a mix of
luxuriant red drapes and extravagant
gilts and mirrors (see photo, page
258). Solemn mustached waiters don
ankle-length starched aprons.
✉ Gare du Lyon, place Louis-Armand,
75012 ☎ 01 43 43 09 06
🚇 Gare de Lyon AX DC MC VI

🏨 Vendôme $$$
Close to the Ritz and the best-kept
secret on the square, this small
hotel blends luxury with an informal
touch. English-speaking staff and

easy access to the highway.
✉ 1 place Vendôme, 75001
☎ 01 55 04 55 00 🚇 Concorde
AX DC MC VI

VERSAILLES
🍴 La Boeuf à la Mode $–$$
Simple but typical, this bistro has a
selection of dishes all at the same
price – the menu changes according
to market freshness. As the name
suggests, the menu concentrates
on meat dishes.
✉ place du Marché ☎ 01 39 50 31
99 🚇 RER C MC VI

🏨 Trianon Palace $$$
Opened in 1910, this luxurious,
Regency-style hotel offers sublime,
tranquil views over its extensive
landscaped grounds and the forest
of Versailles.
✉ 1 boulevard de la Reine, 78000
☎ 01 30 84 50 00 🚇 Versailles Rive
Droite AX DC MC VI

NORMANDY AND BRITTANY

BAYEUX
🏨 Churchill Hotel $–$$
Conveniently located for the
cathedral and tapestry, this hotel
has a pretty courtyard and offers
home-cooked meals.
✉ 14–16 rue St.-Jean, 14400
☎ 02 31 21 31 80 🕐 Closed
Dec.–Feb. AX MC VI

🍴 Le Lion d'Or $$
Step inside the airy, salmon-pink
dining room of this former post inn
for classic Normandy dishes cooked
with flair.
✉ 71 rue St.-Jean ☎ 02 31 92 06 90
🕐 Closed lunch Sat., Mon., Tue.
AX DC MC VI

CAEN
🍴 Le Carlotta $$
Historic art nouveau brasserie
serving traditional French cuisine.
It has views of boats moored at
Bassin St.-Pierre.
✉ 16 quai Vendeuvre ☎ 02 31 86
68 99 🕐 Closed Sun. and Mon.
AX MC VI

🏨 Ivan Vautier $$–$$$
In this cool, contemporary hotel with
minimalist decor, rooms are spacious
and bathrooms are luxurious. The
gastronomic Ivan Vautier restaurant
is on site.
✉ 3 avenue Henry-Chéron, 14000
☎ 02 31 73 32 71 AX MC VI

CARNAC
🏨 Hôtel du Tumulus $–$$
Built by archaeologist Zacharie Le
Rouzic as Carnac's first visitor center,
the building is now a hotel offering
comfortable accommodations.
✉ Chemin de Tumulus, 56340
☎ 02 97 52 00 21 🕐 Closed early
Nov.–early Feb. AX MC VI

🍴 Le Ratelier $$
This vine-covered house in a quiet
part of town has a loyal clientele who
treasure dishes such as pan-fried foie
gras with a rhubarb compote.
✉ 4 chemin du Douët, 56340
☎ 02 97 52 05 04 🕐 Closed
Tue.–Wed., Oct. to mid-Jan. and
mid-Feb. to end Mar. AX MC VI

CLÉCY
🏨 Au Site Normand $
Airy rooms make up the traditional
timbered house. The restaurant ($–$$)
offers a variety of vegetarian dishes.
✉ 1 rue des Châtelets, 14570
☎ 02 31 69 71 05 AX DC MC VI

DEAUVILLE
🏨 Normandy Barriere $$$
Traditional Norman timbering
accentuates the luxury seaside hotel.
An indoor pool, casino and golf are
among the attractions.
✉ 38 rue Jean-Mermoz, 14800
☎ 02 31 98 66 22 AX MC VI

🍴 Le Spinnaker $$–$$$
Wash down succulent Normandy
seafood with good wines or local
farmhouse cider.
✉ 52 rue Mirabeau ☎ 02 31 88
24 40 🕐 Closed lunch Mon.–Tue.,
Jul. to mid-Sep.; all day Mon.–Tue.,
rest of year; early Jan.–end Jan.;
early Jun. to mid-Jun.; one week late
Nov. AX DC MC VI

DINAN
🏨 Avaugour $–$$$
Two old stone buildings offer views
of the ramparts and the hotel garden.
There's also a good restaurant ($$).
✉ 1 place du Champ ☎ 02 96 39 07
49 🕐 Closed Nov. to late Feb.
AX DC MC VI

🍴 Chez la Mère Pourcel $$
This restaurant specializes in lamb
from Mont St.-Michel (summer only)
and is set in a 15th-century building.
✉ 3 place des Merciers ☎ 02 96
39 03 80 🕐 Closed Sun. dinner,
Tue. dinner and Wed. lunch and
dinner, Oct.–Apr. MC VI

Normandy and Brittany

KEY TO SYMBOLS

⊞	hotel
❚❚	restaurant
✉	address
☎	telephone number
◷	days/times closed
Ⓜ	nearest metro/tube/subway station(s)
AX	American Express
DC	Diners Club
MC	MasterCard
VI	VISA

Hotels
Price guide: double room with breakfast for two people

$	less than €130
$$	€130–€200
$$$	more than €200

Restaurants
Price guide: dinner per person, excluding drinks

$	less than €35
$$	€35–€65
$$$	more than €65

Discover the Logis

For a true taste of regional France, venture away from the international chain hotels and grand restaurants and watch for the yellow-and-green fireplace logo of Logis-de-France. Established by government initiative after World War II, these small, usually family-run establishments will prepare an unforgettable *menu de terroir* for around €25. These meals are inspired by and created from local ingredients, often by a son or daughter who has been sent to study at one of the great culinary schools and returned with skills to make the most of regional bounty. Dining rooms are furnished with a homey touch, and hotel facilities are graded from one to three fireplaces. The Logis-de-France website has English descriptions of member hotels and restaurants:
☎ 01 45 84 83 84; www. logishotels.com/en/html.

DINARD

⊞ Comfort Hôtel Balmoral $
A pleasant, old-style hotel, it is near the seashore and central attractions.
✉ 26 rue du Maréchal-Leclerc, 35800 ☎ 02 99 46 16 97 ◷ Closed early to mid-Dec. AX DC MC VI

❚❚ Didier Meril $$$
This restaurant, located in the town center with excellent views of the bay, specializes in fish and seafood.
✉ 1 place du Général de Gaulle, 35800 ☎ 02 99 46 95 74 ◷ Closed Sun. dinner, Mon. lunch and dinner, Wed. lunch, Oct.–Mar. AX MC VI

ÉTRETAT

⊞ Domaine Saint Clair – Le Donjon $–$$
This romantic, ivy-covered 19th-century château high above the town boasts a charming patio garden and elegant restaurant.
✉ Chemin de St.-Clair, 76790 ☎ 02 35 27 08 23 AX DC MC VI

GIVERNY

⊞ La Musardière $
Monet would have been familiar with this 1880 building, just 200 yards from his home.
✉ 123 rue Claude-Monet, 27620 ☎ 02 32 21 03 18 ◷ Closed late Dec.–end Jan. AX MC VI

HONFLEUR

❚❚ Auberge de la Lieutenance $$
With a pretty dining room and outside terrace, this *auberge* serves mainly seasonal cuisine.
✉ 12 place Ste.-Catherine ☎ 02 31 89 07 52 ◷ Closed early Jan.–early Feb. AX DC MC VI

⊞ La Chaumière $$$
This charming mansion is set in rolling countryside overlooking the Normandy coastline. The hotel enjoys direct beach access.
✉ route du Littoral, 14600 Honfleur ☎ 02 31 81 63 20 AX DC MC VI

⊞ L'Écrin $–$$$
The elegant manor house has regal rooms and a sumptuous salon.
✉ 19 rue Eugène-Boudin, 14600 ☎ 02 31 14 43 45 AX DC MC VI

LE MONT-ST.-MICHEL

⊞ Château Richeux $$$
Here, you can enjoy breathtaking views of the Mont Saint-Michel bay as well as direct access to the beach. The hotel has a gourmet restaurant.

✉ Le Bout, 35350 Saint Méloir-des-Ondes ☎ 02 99 89 64 76 AX DC MC VI

⊞ Le Relais du Roy $–$$
You'll find modern, comfortable rooms here and a location perfect for visits to the mount. There's a restaurant on site.
✉ route de Mont-Saint-Michel, 50170 ☎ 02 33 60 14 25 AX MC VI

NANTES

❚❚ L'Atlantide $$$
Enjoy gourmet cuisine mixing Asian flavors with traditional French fare while admiring the view.
✉ 19 quai Ernest-Renaud, 44100 ☎ 02 40 73 23 23 ◷ Closed Sat. lunch, Sun., Aug. and late Dec.–early Jan. MC VI

QUIMPER

❚❚ L'Ambroisie $–$$
Classic Breton dishes with fresh produce are prepared with flair by Monsieur Guyon. Try the excellent lunch menu, which is good value.
✉ 49 rue Elie-Fréron ☎ 02 98 95 00 02 ◷ Closed Mon. MC VI

⊞ Château de Guilguiffin $$
The enchanting 18th-century château is in the heart of a family-owned estate with four rooms, two suites and two cottages available for guests.
✉ 29710 Landudec; D765 from Quimper, 11 miles, then D784 ☎ 02 98 91 52 11 MC VI

RENNES

⊞ Lecoq-Gadby $$–$$$
In its own elegant gardens, the Lecoq-Gadby has well-furnished rooms with parquet floors and Oriental rugs.
✉ 156 rue Antrain, 35700 ☎ 02 99 38 05 55 AX DC MC VI

❚❚ La Taverne de la Marine $–$$
An institution for more than 25 years, this place serves a range of fish and shellfish, steaks, duck and *choucroute* (see page 228).
✉ 2 place de Bretagne ☎ 02 99 31 53 84 AX MC VI

ROUEN

❚❚ Gill $$$
Gill's chef Gilles Tournadre gained his first Michelin star in 1985. His menu reflects local specialties.
✉ 9 quai de la Bourse, 76000

☎ 02 35 71 16 14 🕓 Closed Sun. and Mon., 2 weeks in Jan. and 3 weeks in Aug. 🚇 Théâtre des Arts AX DC MC VI

🏨 Hôtel du Vieux Marché $$
This comfortable city-center three-star hotel has the advantage of a private garage for parking.
✉ 15 rue de la Pie, 76000 ☎ 02 35 71 00 88 🚇 Théâtre des Arts AX DC MC VI

🍴 Les Nymphéas $$–$$$
Good fish and game dishes are the mark of this small establishment with a beamed carriage entry and a pretty garden.
✉ 9 rue de la Pie, 76000 ☎ 02 35 89 26 69 🕓 Closed Sun., Mon. and end Aug. to mid-Sep. 🚇 Théâtre des Arts AX DC MC VI

ST.-MALO
🍴 Les Embruns $$–$$$
A long-established seafood restaurant which specializes in lobster and crab, it offers a vast range of fish dishes.
✉ 120 chaussée du Sillon ☎ 02 99 56 33 57 🕓 Closed Sun. dinner, Mon. lunch and dinner, Tue. lunch; early Jan. DC MC VI

🏨 France et Châteaubriand $–$$
Napoléon III-style salons and comfy rooms overlook the port in the house where the author Châteaubriand was born. English is spoken.
✉ place Châteaubriand BP 77, 35412 ☎ 02 99 56 66 52 AX DC MC VI

ST.-VAAST-LA-HOUGUE
🏨 Hôtel de France $
A remarkable climbing fuchsia envelops this family-run hotel. Its excellent kitchen ($$), serving the local catch, is popular with discerning locals and visitors alike.
✉ 20 rue du Maréchal-Foch ☎ 02 33 54 40 41 🕓 Closed Jan. AX DC MC VI

LOIRE VALLEY AND THE ATLANTIC COAST

AMBOISE
🏨 Choiseul $$–$$$
Just outside the royal estate, this luxury hotel has a pool and renowned restaurant ($$$) where Pascal Bouvier's cuisine may best be enjoyed at lunch ($$).
✉ 36 quai Guinot, 37400 ☎ 02 47 30 45 45 AX DC MC VI

ANGERS
🏨 Best Western Anjou $–$$
Art deco mosaics, ornate ceilings, stained-glass windows and elegant lounges adorn this imposing hotel. Rooms are spacious, and the Renaissance-style Salamandre gourmet restaurant ($$) specializes in regal hunting dishes.
✉ 1 boulevard Maréchal-Foch ☎ 02 41 21 12 11 AX MC VI

BIARRITZ
🍴 Campagne et Gourmandise $$–$$$
This Basque villa offers great views of the Pyrénées. The creative menu includes oxtail en croute, roast sea bass with wild mushrooms, a fish *pot-au-feu*, and a selection of traditional desserts.
✉ 52 avenue Alan-Seeger ☎ 05 59 41 10 11 🕓 Closed Sun. and Wed. dinner, Mon. and Wed. lunch AX MC VI

🏨 Palais $$$
The essential hotel of Biarritz was built for an empress. It has a hair salon and a heated seawater pool. The restaurant, Villa Eugénie ($$$), serves splendid Landais cuisine.
✉ 1 avenue de l'Impératrice, 64200 ☎ 05 59 41 64 00 AX DC MC VI

BLOIS
🏨 Holiday Inn Garden Court $–$$
All the international comforts are standard in the modern chain hotel.
✉ 26 avenue Maunoury, 41000 ☎ 02 54 55 44 88 AX DC MC VI

BORDEAUX
🏨 Best Western Grand Hôtel Français $–$$
Spacious air-conditioned rooms fill this imposing city-center hotel.
✉ 12 rue du Temple ☎ 05 56 48 10 35 🚇 Gambetta AX DC MC VI

🏨 Burdigala $$$
A comfortable hotel where you may enjoy a generous buffet breakfast. The hotel has a health center.
✉ 115 rue Georges-Bonnac, 33000 ☎ 05 56 90 16 16 🚇 Mériadeck AX DC MC VI

🍴 Pavillon des Boulevards $$$
Chef Denis Franc is widely regarded as a master of Bordelais cuisine. Innovative meals may be enjoyed in the dining rooms or the garden.
✉ 120 rue Croix-de-Seguey ☎ 05 56 81 51 02 🕓 Closed Mon.

and Sat. lunch and Sun., first week Jan. and mid-Aug. 🚇 Barrière du Médoc AX DC MC VI

🍴 La Tupina $$–$$$
Wholesome Gascon food and winter log fires add to the cozy mood.
✉ 6 rue Porte de la Monnaie ☎ 05 56 91 56 37 🚇 St.-Michel AX DC MC VI

CHAUMONT
🍴 La Chancelière $–$$
Gaze at the river and enjoy local Loire poultry and game while dining at this pleasant restaurant.
✉ 1 rue Bellevue ☎ 02 54 20 96 95 🕓 Closed Thu. AX MC VI

CHENONCEAUX
🏨 Le Bon Laboureur $–$$
Enjoy old-fashioned hospitality, shared by the superb restaurant ($–$$$).
✉ rue du Docteur-Bretonneau, 37150 ☎ 02 47 23 90 02 AX MC VI

CHINON
🏨 Hôtel Diderot $
A pretty period mansion (15th- to 18th-century) has been converted into a small hotel with particularly lovely gardens.
✉ 4 rue de Buffon, 37500 ☎ 02 47 93 18 87 MC VI

COGNAC
🏨 Hôstellerie les Pigeons Blancs $
You will find elegant and stylish rooms here and excellent cuisine is served in the popular restaurant ($$).
✉ 110 rue Jules-Brisson, 16100 ☎ 05 45 82 16 36 AX MC VI

FONTEVRAUD
🏨 Hôtel Abbaye Royale de Fontevraud $–$$
Surprisingly inexpensive, these comfortable accommodations are in a picturesque former priory. There's a restaurant in the cloister ($$).
✉ Le Prieuré Saint-Lazare, rue St.-Jean-de-l'Habit, 49590 Fontevraud l'Abbaye ☎ 02 41 51 73 16 🕓 Closed Feb. to mid-Mar. AX MC VI

🍴 La Licorne $$–$$$
This smart house is an ideal spot to discover Loire specialties, such as *sandre* (perch) and langoustine ravioli.
✉ allée Ste.-Cathérine ☎ 02 41 51 72 49 🕓 Closed Jan.; Mon., Wed. and Sun. dinner, Oct.–Apr. AX DC MC VI

KEY TO SYMBOLS

▦	hotel
▦	restaurant
✉	address
☎	telephone number
◔	days/times closed
Ⓜ	nearest metro/tube/subway station(s)
AX	American Express
DC	Diners Club
MC	MasterCard
VI	VISA

Hotels

Price guide: double room with breakfast for two people

$ less than €130
$$ €130–€200
$$$ more than €200

Restaurants

Price guide: dinner per person, excluding drinks

$ less than €35
$$ €35–€65
$$$ more than €65

Regional Delicacies

Provence's natural abundance of fresh fruits, vegetables and fish means that local food is both rich and healthy. Some foods are particular to the region, such as the delicious tapenade, a paste of black olives, capers and anchovies, and aioli, a rich garlic and olive oil mayonnaise. Both may be served with crudités, a selection of raw crunchy vegetables. Two classic soups come from Provence: *soupe au pistou*, a basil-rich minestrone, and the Marseille classic fish stew bouillabaisse. The latter is served with *rouille*, a spicy red paste that is spread on croutons, which are sprinkled with grated cheese and floated in the soup. The soup often is served as a main course. Most vegetable dishes are seasonal, except for ratatouille with zucchini and tomato, which is available year round. The most famous summer dish is *salade niçoise*, which varies but should include anchovies, tomato, potato, hard-boiled egg and beans.

ORLÉANS

▦ Le Lift $$–$$$

Chef Philippe Bardeau has an excellent reputation. His dining room is contemporary and has a menu that changes with the seasons.

✉ place de la Loire ☎ 02 38 53 63 48 ◔ Closed Sun. dinner AX DC MC VI

POITIERS

▦ Alain Boutin $$

This locally renowned chef produces gastronomic delights and regional dishes including guinea fowl and veal kidney.

✉ 65 rue Carnot ☎ 05 49 88 25 53 ◔ Closed Mon. lunch, Sat. lunch and Sun. MC VI

▦ Le Grand Hôtel $

Intricate art deco stylings and courtyard tranquility mark the hotel as desirable.

✉ 28 rue Carnot, 86000 ☎ 05 49 60 90 60 AX DC MC VI

LA ROCHELLE

▦ Best Western Hotel Champlain $–$$

This converted mansion in the heart of town has attractive, period-style rooms and a lovely garden. There is no restaurant.

✉ 30 rue Rambaud, 17000 ☎ 05 46 41 23 99 AX DC MC VI

▦ Richard et Christopher Cloutanceau $$$

This restaurant is a gastronomic delight. It has windows overlooking the beach and serves fine cuisine.

✉ Plage de la Concurrance, 17000 ☎ 05 46 41 48 19 ◔ Closed Sun. AX DC MC VI

SAUMUR

▦ Anne d'Anjou $–$$

By the banks of the River Loire, this charming 18th-century house has Louis XVI decor and a fabulous main staircase. The hotel also has a pleasant restaurant ($$) that can be found at the bottom of the garden.

✉ 32–33 quai Mayaud, 49400 ☎ 02 41 67 30 30 AX DC MC VI

▦ Auberge Saint-Pierre $–$$

Traditional cuisine of the region is served in a picturesque medieval building, with a grand old fireplace in the dining room.

✉ 6 place Saint-Pierre, rue de la Tonnelle ☎ 02 41 51 26 25 ◔ Closed Sun. AX MC VI

TOURS

▦ L'Odéon $$

This art deco dining room serves a menu of creative French dishes based on the freshest seasonal ingredients.

✉ 10 place Général-Leclerc, 37000 ☎ 02 47 20 12 65 ◔ Closed Sun. AX DC MC VI

VILLANDRY

▦ Le Cheval Rouge $

A modest village hotel and restaurant ($) is near Villandry's château.

✉ 9 rue Principale, 37510 ☎ 02 47 50 02 07 AX DC MC VI

DORDOGNE

ALBI

▦ La Réserve $$$

On the banks of the Tarn, this hotel has a pool, golf and tennis courts.

✉ Route de Cordes, 81000 ☎ 05 63 60 80 80 ◔ Closed late Oct. to early May MC VI

AUBUSSON

▦ Le Lion d'Or $

Patrick Soulière's modest hotel also has a dining room with inexpensive country food ($).

✉ 11 place d'Espagne, 23200 ☎ 05 55 66 65 71 ◔ Closed two weeks Jan., one week Jun. and one week Oct. AX DC MC VI

BEYNAC ET CAZENAC

▦ Pontet $

This family-run hotel has a good restaurant serving delicious local dishes ($).

✉ Village center, 24220 ☎ 05 53 29 50 06 ◔ Closed Jan. MC VI

CAHORS

▦ Le Balandre $$–$$$

Regulars savor pan-fried foie gras and truffles with poached eggs at tables dappled by sunlight through century-old windows.

✉ Hotel Terminus, 5 avenue Charles-de-Freycinet ☎ 05 65 53 32 00 ◔ Closed Sun., Mon. AX DC MC VI

▦ Château de Mercuès $$$

This former residence of the count-bishops of Cahors is now a château hotel-restaurant ($$$) serving fine duck, pâté and truffle-based cuisine.

✉ Mercuès, 46090; D911 from Cahors, 3 miles northwest ☎ 05 65 20 00 01 ◔ Closed mid-Nov. to Mar. AX DC MC VI

CASTELNAU-DE-LÉVIS
🍴 La Taverne $$–$$$
This former village bakery is now an intimate bistro overseen by chef Bruno Besson.
✉ Castelnau-de-Lévis, 81150
☎ 05 63 60 90 16 🕐 Closed Mon.
AX DC MC VI

LIMOGES
🏨 La Chapelle Saint-Martin $$–$$$
Set in the Limousin countryside outside Limoges, this stately mansion once belonged to a porcelain manufacturer.
✉ Saint-Martin-du-Fault, 87150
☎ 05 55 75 80 17 🕐 Closed Jan.–early Feb. and 1 week in Nov.
AX MC VI

🍴 Les Petits Ventres $$
This small restaurant set in a medieval house concentrates on country recipes of the Limousin, many of which include organ meats.
✉ 20 rue de la Boucherie, 87000 Limoges ☎ 05 55 34 22 90
🕐 Closed Sun. and Mon. MC VI

MOISSAC
🏨 Le Pont Napoléon $
Gaby Meouchi and Patrick Delaroux are the owners of this delightful hotel overlooking the Tarn. Patrick is also the chef, bringing international influences to a menu that features local traditional cuisine.
✉ 2 allées Montebello, 82200
☎ 05 63 04 01 55 AX DC MC VI

MONTAUBAN
🏨 L'Abbaye des Capuchins Hôtel-Spa-Resort $–$$
Well-furnished rooms, a spa and restaurant are housed in this refurbished abbey.
✉ 6–8 quai de Verdun, 82000
☎ 05 63 22 00 00 AX DC MC VI

🍴 Cuisine d'Alain $$
This restaurant's modestly priced dishes are prepared with local market products.
✉ Hôtel Orsay, 29 avenue Roger Salengro ☎ 05 63 66 06 66
🕐 Closed Sun. MC VI

PÉRIGUEUX
🏨 Hôtel l'Ecluse $
Set on the riverbank, this hotel has a restaurant serving regional dishes.
✉ Route de Limoges, 24420 Antonne et Trigonant ☎ 05 53 06 00 04
AX DC MC VI

ROCAMADOUR
🍴 Beausite $$–$$$
Regional specialties are beautifully prepared here. There's a lovely terrace for summer dining.
✉ Cité Medievale ☎ 05 65 33 63 08 🕐 Closed mid-Nov. to mid-Dec.
AX DC MC VI

LA ROQUE-GAGEAC
🏨 Belle Étoile $
This small hotel, set at the foot of La Roque-Gageac cliff, offers a garden and an air-conditioned restaurant ($). Eccentric rules allow dogs in the dining room but apparently not in the rooms.
✉ la Roque-Gageac 24250 ☎ 05 53 29 51 44 🕐 Closed Nov.–Mar. Restaurant closed Mon. and Wed. lunch, Apr.–Oct. AX DC MC VI

SARLAT-LA-CANÉDA
🏨 Plaza Madeleine Hotel and Spa $–$$
Flower-decked balconies welcome you to this stylish hotel located in the center of the town, with quiet and spacious rooms. There is also a restaurant ($).
✉ 1 place de la Petite-Rigaudie, 24200 ☎ 05 53 59 10 41
AX DC MC VI

BAYONNE
🍴 Auberge du Cheval Blanc $$–$$$
Jean-Claude Tellechea handles Basque dishes with modern flair at this charming *auberge*.
✉ 68 rue Bourgneuf ☎ 05 59 59 01 33 🕐 Closed Sun. dinner, Sat. lunch and Mon. (except Aug.), one week early Jul., one week late Jul., first two weeks Nov. and late Feb.–late Mar. AX MC VI

🏨 Best Western Le Grand Hôtel $–$$
Relish the warm welcome at this old-fashioned hotel with entirely renovated bedrooms near the river.
✉ 21 rue Thiers, 64100
☎ 05 59 59 62 00 AX DC MC VI

CARCASSONNE
🍴 Brasserie le Donjon $$
Enjoy a traditional southwestern cassoulet at this stylish restaurant.
✉ 4 rue Porte d'Aude, La Cité, 11000 ☎ 04 68 25 95 72
🕐 Closed Sun. dinner, Nov.–Mar.
AX DC MC VI

🏨 Hôtel de la Cité $$$
The luxury choice boasts Gothic furnishings. Its restaurant ($$$) is ideal for special celebrations.
✉ place Auguste-Pierre Pont, La Cité 11000 ☎ 04 68 71 98 71
🕐 Closed mid-Jan. to mid-Mar.
AX DC MC VI

CASTRES
🏨 Renaissance $
This 17th century-style building with red-brick bathrooms offers good value for money.
✉ 17 rue Victor-Hugo, 81100
☎ 05 63 59 30 42 AX MC VI

🍴 Le Victoria $–$$
This small bistro is set in the vaulted cellars of a 17th-century convent and serves a range of local dishes.
✉ 24 place du 8-Mai, 81100 ☎ 05 63 59 14 68 🕐 Closed Sat. lunch and Sun. dinner AX DC MC VI

LOURDES
🏨 Grand Hôtel de la Grotte $–$$
Fabulous mountain views and spacious rooms distinguish this place from other similar hotels in the same price range.
✉ 66 rue de la Grotte, 65100
☎ 05 62 94 58 87 🕐 Closed mid-Oct. to Mar. AX DC MC VI

LUCHON
🏨 Étigny $–$$
Opposite the spa is the comfortable hotel and restaurant ($–$$) specializing in regional dishes.
✉ 3 avenue Paul-Bonnemaison, Bagnères, Luchon 31110
☎ 05 61 79 01 42 🕐 Closed mid-Oct. to Apr. MC VI

ST.-JEAN-DE-LUZ
🏨 Parc Victoria $$–$$$
Attractively set in its own park, this hotel has rooms decorated in 1930s style. There is also an excellent restaurant ($$$).
✉ 5 rue Cépé, 64500 ☎ 05 59 26 78 78 🕐 Closed Nov. 15–Mar. 15
AX DC MC VI

ST.-JEAN-PIED-DE-PORT
🍴 Iratze Ostatua $–$$
Set on one of the small, steep alleyways, this Basque restaurant is building a reputation for consistently high-quality dishes.
✉ 11 rue de la Citadelle ☎ 05 59 49 17 09 🕐 Closed Tue. May–Sep., Mon. and Tue. Oct.–Apr. and Jan.–early Feb. MC VI

KEY TO SYMBOLS

🏨	hotel
🍴	restaurant
✉	address
☎	telephone number
🕐	days/times closed
🚇	nearest metro/tube/subway station(s)
AX	American Express
DC	Diners Club
MC	MasterCard
VI	VISA

Hotels

Price guide: double room with breakfast for two people

$	less than €130
$$	€130–€200
$$$	more than €200

Restaurants

Price guide: dinner per person, excluding drinks

$	less than €35
$$	€35–€65
$$$	more than €65

Two for One

Double your pleasure and your fun at more than 40 French regional cities and towns from Aix-en-Provence to Versailles. The promotional "Bon Week-end en Villes" offers two nights of hotel accommodations for the price of one for any stay beginning on a Friday or Saturday night. The offer is good from Nov. 1 through Mar. 31, although some cities/towns run it year-round. Reservations must be made through the town tourist office at least one day in advance. In return you will receive a welcoming gift plus details of discounted leisure and cultural activities. A directory listing all participating cities and hotels is available from the French Tourist Office or by contacting the Fédération Nationale des Offices de Tourisme et Syndicats d'Initiative ✉ 11 rue du Faubourg Poissoniere, 75009 Paris ☎ 01 44 11 10 30 or book through website www.villepassion.com.

🏨 Les Pyrénées $$–$$$

The Basque hotel offers accommodations with gracious standards and a restaurant ($$$) that serves the best in local cuisine.
✉ 19 place Charles-de-Gaulle, 64220 ☎ 05 59 37 01 01 🕐 Closed Jan. 5–28, Mon. dinner Nov.–Mar., Tue. Sep.–Jun. and Nov. 20–Dec. 22 AX DC MC VI

TOULOUSE

🍴 7 Place St.-Sernin $$–$$$

The fashionable dining room offers a lighter, stylish take on a variety of local dishes.
✉ 7 place St.-Sernin ☎ 05 62 30 05 30 🕐 Closed Sat. lunch and Sun. 🚇 Capitole AX MC VI

🏨 Grand Hôtel de l'Opéra $$$

The Florentine splendor of the brick facade continues in the tastefully decorated rooms.
✉ 1 place du Capitole, 31000 ☎ 05 61 21 82 66 🚇 Capitole AX DC MC VI

🏨 Hotel Beaux-Arts $$–$$$

Opposite the Pont Neuf and near the art museum, the hotel has windows that overlook the Garonne river.
✉ 1 place du Pont-Neuf, 31000 ☎ 05 34 45 42 42 🚇 Esquirol AX DC MC VI

🍴 Les Jardins de l'Opéra $$–$$$

This is the fine-dining address of Toulouse, where major deals are toasted and birthdays and anniversaries celebrated.
✉ 1 place du Capitole ☎ 05 61 23 07 76 🕐 Closed Sun.–Mon. lunch and dinner and early to mid-Jan. 🚇 Capitole AX DC MC VI

PROVENCE AND THE CÔTE D'AZUR

AIX-EN-PROVENCE

🍴 L'Amphitryon $$–$$$

Dine among magnolias and choose the market-fresh dish of the day.
✉ 2–4 rue Paul-Doumer ☎ 04 42 26 54 10 🕐 Closed Mon., Sun. and late Aug. MC VI

🏨 Augustins $–$$

This popular, small hotel sits on a side street off cours Mirabeau.
✉ 3 rue de la Masse, 13100 ☎ 04 42 27 28 59 AX DC MC VI

🍴 Clos de la Violette $$$

Truffle dishes are a specialty here in winter and *petits farcis* (stuffed

---

baked Provençal vegetables) in summer. Reserve well in advance.
✉ 10 avenue Violette ☎ 04 42 23 30 71 🕐 Closed Sun., Mon., Aug. and 2 weeks in Mar. AX MC VI

ANTIBES

🍴 Restaurant de Bacon $$$

This sophisticated establishment offers high-class seafood and spectacular views over the bay.
✉ boulevard de Bacon, 06160 Cap d'Antibes ☎ 04 93 61 50 02 🕐 Closed Mon., Tue. lunch, Mon. dinner and Nov.–Mar. DC MC VI

ARLES

🏨 Le Calendal $–$$

Pastel rooms overlook the garden. If you have a car make sure you reserve a garage space well in advance.
✉ 5 rue Porte de Laure, 13200 ☎ 04 90 96 11 89 AX DC MC VI

🍴 La Plaza $–$$

The simple dining room offers Provençal flavors and local wines.
✉ 28 rue du Dr.-Fanton ☎ 04 90 96 33 15 🕐 Daily lunch and dinner MC VI

AVIGNON

🏨 La Mirande $$$

This one-time cardinal's palace is now one of France's most elegant hotels, with a superb restaurant ($$–$$$$) supervised by a disciple of Alain Ducasse.
✉ 4 place de la Mirande, 84000 ☎ 04 90 14 20 20 AX DC MC VI

🍴 Restaurant Christian Etienne $$$

The master chef of this eponymous eatery abutting the Palais du Papes uses the finest Provençal ingredients to create delicious seasonal menus.
✉ 10 rue de Mons ☎ 04 90 86 16 50 🕐 Closed Sun.–Mon. and late Oct. to early Nov. AX DC MC VI

LES BAUX DE PROVENCE

🏨 Le Mas d'Aigret $$–$$$

This small, traditional stone hotel is built in the lee of a hillside in the heart of the Provençal countryside.
✉ D27, 13520 ☎ 04 90 54 20 00 🕐 Closed mid-Nov. to late Mar. AX DC MC VI

BIOT

🏨 Domaine du Jas $–$$

Comfortable rooms, efficient service, a pool and garage parking are all hotel features.

✉ 625 route de la Mer, 06410 ☎ 04 93 65 50 50 🕐 Closed mid-Dec. to mid-Jan. AX MC VI

🍴 Les Terraillers $$$
A 16th-century pottery is the unusual setting to showcase the sophisticated cuisine offered by the Fulci family.
✉ 11 route Chemin-Neuf ☎ 04 93 65 01 59 🕐 Closed Wed.–Thu. and Nov. AX MC VI

CALVI, CORSICA
🏨 La Villa $$–$$$
Set in the hills above Calvi, La Villa has spacious rooms and an excellent restaurant ($$–$$$).
✉ Chemin de Notre-Dame-de-la-Serra, 20260 Calvi ☎ 04 95 65 10 10 🕐 Closed early Jan. to mid-Feb. and Mon.–Tue. 2 weeks in Mar. AX DC MC VI

CANNES
🍴 Fouquet's $$–$$$
A Parisian brasserie is recreated on the sultry south coast at this luxury hotel.
✉ Hôtel Majestic Barrière, 10 boulevard de la Croisette ☎ 04 92 98 77 05 AX DC MC VI

🏨 Hôtel l'Olivier $–$$
This informal hotel in a wonderful setting overlooks the old town and is conveniently located near the Midi beach.
✉ 5 rue des Tambourinaires, 06400 ☎ 04 93 39 53 28 AX MC VI

🍴 Le Mesclun $$–$$$
Just a couple of streets from the bustling seashore razzmatazz, this charming restaurant offers a selection of delicious, well-prepared food and is the ideal setting for a romantic dinner.
✉ 16 rue St.-Antoine ☎ 04 93 99 45 19 🕐 Closed Wed. and mid-Nov. to mid-Dec. AX MC VI

GRASSE
🏨 🍴 Bastide St.-Antoine $$$
Jacques Chibois' renowned hotel-restaurant is a champion of the flavors of Provence.
✉ 48 avenue Henri-Dunant, 06310 ☎ 04 93 70 94 94 AX DC MC VI

🏨 La Rivolte $
This comfortable 19th-century mansion has well-tended gardens, a heated swimming pool and palm-fringed views of the town and

sea. Minimum two-night stay.
✉ Chemin des Lierres, 06130 ☎ 04 93 36 81 58 🕐 Closed mid-Dec. to early Jan. Two-night minimum booking throughout the year DC MC VI

MARSEILLE
🍴 Chez Fonfon $$$
This has been a temple to bouillabaisse – the king of French fish dishes – for more than 50 years. There is also a range of other fresh seafood.
✉ 140 vallon des Auffes ☎ 04 91 52 14 38 🕐 Closed Mon. lunch and Sun. lunch and dinner. Also Mon. dinner, Nov.–May AX DC MC VI

🏨 St.-Ferréol Hôtel $
On a pedestrian-friendly street near the old port, this hotel provides a good base to explore the city.
✉ 19 rue Pisançon, 13001 ☎ 04 91 33 12 21 AX MC VI

MENTON
🏨 Best Westen Prince de Galles $–$$
The pleasant hotel includes a modest restaurant ($).
✉ 4 avenue Général-de-Gaulle, 06500 ☎ 04 93 28 21 21 AX DC MC VI

🍴 Restaurant Mirazur $$$
Mauro Colagreco presides over his kitchen, utilizing the flavors of Provence. Excellent lunch and fixed-price menus are available.
✉ 30 avenue Aristide Briand ☎ 04 92 41 86 86 🕐 Closed Mon.–Tue., mid-Feb. to mid-Jul. and Sep.–early Nov.; Mon. and Sun dinner, mid-Jul. to end Aug.; early Nov. to mid-Feb. AX MC VI

MONACO – MONTE-CARLO
🏨 Hôtel de Paris $$$
Do Monaco in style at this luxurious 19th-century hotel where no stone is left ungilded.
✉ place du Casino, 98000 ☎ (00 377) 98 06 30 00 AX DC MC VI

MONTPELLIER
🍴 La Grillardin $–$$
In summer the town-center terrace provides a wonderful alfresco setting. You'll find contemporary French cuisine at a good price.
✉ 3 place de la Chapelle-Neuve, 34000 ☎ 04 67 66 24 33 🕐 Closed Tue. and Wed. lunch and dinner, Sat. lunch Oct.–Mar. MC VI

🏨 Le Guilhem $–$$
The stylishly restored rooms in one of these renovated old houses offer views of the cathedral gardens.
✉ 18 rue Jean-Jacques-Rousseau, 34000 ☎ 04 67 52 90 90 AX DC MC VI

🏨 🍴 Le Jardin des Sens $$$
Probably the finest meals served between Marseille and the Spanish border are encountered in the Pourcel twins' fashionable dining room. The four-star rooms are delightfully furnished.
✉ 11 avenue St.-Lazare, 34000 ☎ 04 99 58 38 38 🕐 Closed Mon. lunch, Wed. lunch and Sun. AX DC MC VI

NARBONNE
🍴 Agora $
The restaurant's generous platter of tapas or the value *plat du jour* are perfect for a simple lunch.
✉ 2 place de l'Hôtel-de-Ville ☎ 04 68 90 10 70 🕐 Daily lunch and dinner AC MC VI

🏨 Château l'Hospitalet $–$$
Relax in a room with a view in the heart of a wine-making estate. The pleasant restaurant ($$) offers excellent value.
✉ Domaine de l'Hospitalet, 11100; Route de Narbonne Plage, 6 miles east ☎ 04 68 45 28 50 🕐 Closed early to mid-Jan. AX DC MC VI

🍴 La Table de Fontfroide $$
Located in the Fontfroide abbey, the restaurant serves great-value priced lunches and quality dinners on the abbey's olive-tree-bordered terrace.
✉ Abbaye de Fontfroide ☎ 04 68 45 02 26 🕐 Closed Dec.–Feb. and dinner Sun.–Tue., Mar.–Jun. AX DC MC VI

NICE
🍴 L'Ane Rouge $$–$$$
Typical Provençal dishes from land and sea are served here. There's a lovely view over the old harbor from the terrace.
✉ 7 quai des 2-Emmanuel ☎ 04 93 89 49 63 🕐 Closed Wed. lunch and dinner and Thu. lunch AX MC VI

🏨 Negresco $$$
The Negresco's unusual green dome and pink roof are famous landmarks in Nice. The flamboyant doorman sets the tone for a hotel styled from

KEY TO SYMBOLS

⊞	hotel
🍴	restaurant
✉	address
☎	telephone number
🕐	days/times closed
Ⓜ	nearest metro/tube/subway station(s)
AX	American Express
DC	Diners Club
MC	MasterCard
VI	VISA

Hotels

Price guide: double room with breakfast for two people

$	less than €130
$$	€130–€200
$$$	more than €200

Restaurants

Price guide: dinner per person, excluding drinks

$	less than €35
$$	€35–€65
$$$	more than €65

Mastering the Menu

Since the French take their food so seriously, menus, even in modest bistros, are rarely dumbed down. Freely exploring the main à la carte selections can seriously bruise your wallet, but every restaurant must offer at least one fixed-price, set menu. With a restricted choice of two or three courses, this will provide not only the best value in the restaurant but usually the best reflection of the regional cuisine. Most places have two or three set menus, from the budget-minded "*menu express*" to a "*menu degustation*" offering haute cuisine at a set price. The latter might feature an appetizer, starter course, fish course, meat course, salad or vegetable dish, cheese, dessert and homemade candies. Lunchtime menus are often 20 to 50 percent cheaper than evening meals, and by going with bargain daily specials (*plat du jour*) you can enjoy a true taste of France for around €30 or less.

Hollywood's heyday. Memorable meals are served at Le Chantecler restaurant ($$–$$$).
✉ 37 promenade des Anglais, 06000 ☎ 04 93 16 64 00 🕐 Restaurant closed lunch Wed.–Sat., all day Mon. and Tue., and early Jan. to early Feb. AX DC MC VI

⊞ La Pérouse $$$
An unexpected quiet spot, just a stroll from the old town, the Pérouse offers unmatchable views.
✉ 11 quai Rauba-Capéu, 06300 ☎ 04 93 62 34 63 AX DC MC VI

⊞ Petit Palais $$–$$$
Prettily furnished rooms make up this charming house.
✉ 17 avenue E.-Bieckert, 06000 ☎ 04 93 62 19 11 AX DC MC VI

🍴 La Reserve de Nice $$$
The small, fashionable restaurant with a changing menu features seasonal, regional ingredients.
✉ 60 boulevard Franck-Pilatte at the Palais de la Reserve ☎ 04 97 08 14 80 🕐 Sun. dinner Nov.–Mar. AX DC MC VI

NÎMES

🍴 Aux Plaisirs des Halles $$–$$$
Fine cuisine with good-value fixed menus is available here. The courtyard is lovely for alfresco meals.
✉ 4 rue Littré ☎ 04 66 36 01 12 🕐 Closed Sun.–Mon., late Oct.–early Nov. and mid- to end Feb. AX MC VI

ORANGE

⊞ Arène $–$$
This central hotel has friendly staff and snug, tastefully furnished rooms.
✉ place de Langes, 84100 ☎ 04 90 11 40 40 AX MC VI

🍴 Le Parvis $–$$
Local herbs flavor the traditional meals presented in this stylish venue, close to the Roman theater.
✉ 55 cours Pourtoules ☎ 04 90 34 82 00 🕐 Closed Sun., Mon., Nov. and last two weeks of Jan. AX MC VI

PERPIGNAN

🍴 La Passerelle $$
Opened in 1975, this unassuming seafood restaurant has been growing in reputation, and is now a locally renowned eatery.
✉ 1 cours Palmarole ☎ 04 68 51 30 65 🕐 Closed Sun., and Mon. lunch AX DC MC VI

⊞ Villa Duflot $$
Big bedrooms and bathrooms are hallmarks of this establishment, as are the lovely breakfasts.
✉ rond-point Albert Donnezan (Serrat d'en Vaguer), 66000 ☎ 04 68 56 67 67 AX DC MC VI

ST.-JEAN-CAP-FERRAT

⊞ Grand-Hôtel du Cap-Ferrat $$$
The private estate sits on the tip of the peninsula, with its own park. The restaurant ($$$) is renowned.
✉ 71 boulevard Général-de-Gaulle, 06230 ☎ 04 93 76 50 50 🕐 Closed early Jan.–early Mar. AX DC MC VI

ST.-MAXIMIN

⊞ Hôtel le Couvent Royal $$–$$$
This historic convent, founded in 1295 has been converted into a comfortable and characterful hotel.
✉ place Jean-Salusse, 83470 ☎ 04 94 86 55 66 AX DC MC VI

ST.-RAPHAËL

🍴 La Brasserie Tradition et Gourmandisse $
A popular bistro serves Provençal dishes and good salads.
✉ 6 avenue de Valescure ☎ 04 94 95 25 00 🕐 Closed Sun. AX MC VI

⊞ La San Pedro $–$$
Deep in the heart of Valescure pine woodland, this elegant country house offers good value for money accommodations.
✉ avenue Colonel Brooke, 83700 ☎ 04 94 19 90 20 AX DC MC VI

ST.-REMY-DE-PROVENCE

🍴 Le Bistrot des Alpilles $–$$
A friendly bistro in the town center, this has a pleasant shady terrace.
✉ 15 boulevard Mirabeau ☎ 04 90 92 09 17 MC VI

⊞ Le Chateau des Alpilles $$$
A small family-owned hotel consisting of several beautifully renovated buildings set in a fragrant woodland.
✉ Route de Rougadou, 13210 ☎ 04 90 92 03 33 AX DC MC VI

ST.-TROPEZ

⊞ La Bastide de St.-Tropez $$$
An elegant hotel in a luxurious Provençal house near the port, with magnificent gardens and a famous restaurant.
✉ Route de Carles, 83990 ☎ 04 94 55 82 55 AX DC MC VI

¶ Chez les Garçons $$
This is a lively town-center bistro with bright pink decor. The menu concentrates on Provençal staples with a contemporary twist.
✉ 13 rue de Cépoun-San-Martin, 83990 ☎ 04 94 49 42 67 AX MC VI

¶ Tahiti $–$$
This famous beach restaurant and hotel ($$–$$$) once welcomed Brigitte Bardot and helped kick-start the reputation of the town.
✉ Tahiti Plage, 83350; 4 miles north of town ☎ 04 94 97 18 02 ◉ Closed mid-Oct. to May AX MC VI

SALON DE PROVENCE
⊞ Abbaye de Ste.-Croix $$–$$$
The fabulous 12th-century monastery offers glorious views and a top-class restaurant ($$$).
✉ Route du Val de Cuech, 13300 ☎ 04 90 56 24 55 ◉ Closed Jan. and Mon.–Thu., Nov.–Mar. Restaurant closed Mon.–Fri. lunch and Nov.–Mar. AX DC MC VI

VENCE
¶ Le Vieux Couvent $–$$
In a former chapel, this restaurant offers fresh lamb from Alpine slopes and delicious seafood.
✉ 37 avenue Toreille ☎ 04 93 58 78 58 ◉ Closed Wed. and Thu. lunch and dinner early Jan. to mid-Feb. MC VI

⊞ Villa Roseraie $–$$
This unique and welcoming hotel has a personality all of its own.
✉ avenue Henri-Giraud, 06140 ☎ 04 93 58 02 20 AX MC VI

AUBENAS
¶ Le Fournil $–$$
The comfort of the old stone dining room is reflected in Trésia Jeannata and Aurélieu del Rio's cuisine. Make sure you leave space for the *tarte au praline*.
✉ 34 rue de 4-Septembre ☎ 04 75 93 58 68 ◉ Closed Mon., Sun. dinner, first week in Jun. and all Jan. AX MC VI

⊞ La Pinède $
A warm welcome is waiting for you in this family-run hotel, which has a pool, parkland and restaurant ($–$$).
✉ route de Lazuel (D235), 07200 ☎ 04 75 35 25 88 ◉ Closed late Nov.–early Feb. MC VI

AURILLAC
⊞ Best Western Grand Hôtel de Bordeaux $
Rooms have been refreshed in this old-fashioned establishment. Service is always polite and impeccable.
✉ 2 avenue de la République, 15000 ☎ 04 71 48 01 84 ◉ Closed late Dec.–early Jan. AX DC MC VI

CHAUDES-AIGUES
⊞ Hôtel Arev $
Set in the center of this thermal spa, the Arev has a casino. Rooms are modern and simple but comfortable.
✉ 29 place du Gravier, 15110 ☎ 04 71 23 52 43 AX MC VI

CLERMONT-FERRAND
¶ Emmanuel Hodencq $$–$$$
Try pan-fried foie gras at Clermont-Ferrand's cutting-edge spot, both on the plate and in the decor.
✉ place St.-Pierre ☎ 04 73 31 23 23 ◉ Closed Sun. all day, Mon. lunch AX DC MC VI

⊞ Hôtel des Puys $–$$
Close to Notre-Dame-du-Port, the hotel has excellent views of the cathedral.
✉ 16 place Delille, 63000 ☎ 04 73 91 92 06 AX DC MC VI

¶ Restaurant Bath's $$
There's a contemporary metropolitan feel to this downtown restaurant which serves excellent classic cuisine using local ingredients.
✉ place du Marché Saint Pierre, 63000 ☎ 04 73 31 23 22 ◉ Closed Sun. and Mon. AX MC VI

CONQUES
⊞ Hôtel Ste.-Foy $–$$
This rustic hotel-restaurant ($$) sits opposite the historic abbey church.
✉ Conques 12320 ☎ 05 65 69 84 03 ◉ Closed Nov. 1–Easter AX DC MC VI

LEZOUZ
⊞ Château de Codignat $$$
In this wonderful medieval castle, set in 40 acres just west of Clermont-Ferrand, rooms are lavishly decorated with period furnishings.
✉ Bord l'Etang, 63190 ☎ 04 73 68 43 03 ◉ Closed Nov. to late Mar. AX DC MC VI

LE LIORAN
⊞ Le Rocher du Cerf $
Rooms at this *auberge*-style hotel with balneotherapy center were

refurbished in 2010. The hotel has the advantage of being adjacent to the ski station. Rates are for room, breakfast and evening meal.
✉ Super Lioran, 15300 ☎ 04 71 49 50 14 MC VI

LA MALÈNE
⊞ Manoir de Montesquiou $–$$
A dozen comfortable rooms make up the attractive 15th-century manor house. The restaurant ($$) offers views of the grounds.
✉ La Malène, 48210 ☎ 04 66 48 51 12 ◉ Closed late Oct.–early Apr. DC MC VI

LE PUY-EN-VELAY
¶ Tournayre $$
Try the inexpensive set menu here for delicious country dishes, or venture onto the main carte for delights such as lobster and red mullet cannelloni.
✉ 12 rue Chênebouterie ☎ 04 71 09 58 94 ◉ Closed Sun. dinner and Mon. AX MC VI

RIOM
¶ Le Flamboyant $$
Good food is tastefully presented by owner/chef Hervé Klein.
✉ 21 bis rue de l'Horloge ☎ 04 73 63 07 97 ◉ Closed Sun. dinner, Mon. and Wed. AX DC MC VI

SAINT ARCONS-D'ALLIER
⊞ Les Deux Abbesses $$–$$$
A medieval château and cottages of the surrounding hamlet make up this luxury hideaway. No TVs here.
✉ Le Château, 43300 ☎ 04 71 74 03 08 ◉ Closed early Nov.–early Mar. AX DC MC VI

SALERS
⊞ ¶ Hotel le Bailliage $–$$
A well-respected, small, family-run establishment, this place has simple yet contemporary rooms and a menu that uses the best in local ingredients.
✉ rue Notre-Dame, 15140 ☎ 04 71 40 71 95 AX MC VI

VICHY
¶ Table d'Antoine $$
The menu at this pleasant restaurant may suggest traditional cuisine, but the dishes have a modern presentation.
✉ 8 rue Burnol ☎ 04 70 98 99 71 ◉ Closed Sun. dinner, and all day Mon. Also Thu. dinner, Oct.–Apr., Feb., early Mar. and mid-Nov. MC VI

KEY TO SYMBOLS

▦	hotel
▯	restaurant
✉	address
☎	telephone number
◔	days/times closed
Ⓜ	nearest metro/tube/subway station(s)
AX	American Express
DC	Diners Club
MC	MasterCard
VI	VISA

Hotels

Price guide: double room with breakfast for two people

$ less than €130
$$ €130–€200
$$$ more than €200

Restaurants

Price guide: dinner per person, excluding drinks

$ less than €35
$$ €35–€65
$$$ more than €65

Simple Delight

Although they are often overshadowed by the gastronomic fireworks of the Burgundy region next door, Franche-Comté region's cuisine is also appetizing. Smoked meats and fish are staples, but the true star of a meal is the cheese course. Mont d'Or is matured in a spruce box, and the flavor of Comté cheese has often been compared to fine wine, so strictly controlled are the herds that create the milk and so long is the ripening process (up to 18 months). The region also produces excellent wines. *Vins jaune* (yellow wines) are quite a rarity: heady evaporated white wines matured a little over six years that may be kept for up to a century (see page 228).

▦ Vichy Spa Hôtel Les Célestins $$$

Rooms overlook the spa or the park, and the three restaurants include a simple bistro ($) or fine dining at Le N3 ($$$). Everything is smart, yet the hotel is still comfortably informal. ✉ 111 boulevard des États-Unis, 03200 ☎ 08 05 08 00 05 AX DC MC VI

VOLVIC

▦ La Rose des Vents $

A low-cost hotel that has lovely views as well as an attractive garden and swimming pool. ✉ Route de Pontgibaud, 63530 Luzet; D986 from Volvic, 2.5 miles west ☎ 04 73 33 50 77 ◔ Closed mid-Dec. to mid-Mar. AX MC VI

ALPS AND THE RHÔNE VALLEY

AIX-LES-BAINS

▦ Le Manoir $–$$

Le Manoir is a comfortable place to stay in the center of town. There is an indoor pool and a spa on site. ✉ 37 rue Georges 1, 73100 ☎ 04 79 61 44 00 AX DC MC VI

▯ Restaurant le 59 $$–$$$

Boris Campanella's creative French cuisine has given this restaurant a growing reputation. In the summer you can dine on the terrace. ✉ 59 rue du Casino, 73100 ☎ 04 79 88 29 75 ◔ Closed Sun. and Mon. AX DC MC VI

ANNECY

▦ Best Western Carlton $–$$

This 1930s-style hotel is close to the lake and the sights of the old town. ✉ 5 rue des Glières, 74000 ☎ 04 50 10 09 09 AX DC MC VI

▯ Le Freti $–$$

This restaurant specializes in Savoyard specialties, such as fondue, *raclette* and *tartiflette*. ✉ 12 rue Ste.-Claire (first floor), 74000 ☎ 04 50 51 29 52 ◔ Closed Mon.–Sat. lunch and holidays AX DC MC VI

BRIANÇON

▦ Vauban $

A genuine, warm family welcome awaits at this hotel. Reliable home cooking is served in the restaurant ($–$$). ✉ 13 avenue Gén-de-Gaulle, 05100 ☎ 04 92 21 12 11 ◔ Open all year AX MC VI

CHAMBÉRY

▦ Château de Candie $$–$$$

This 14th-century Savoyard castle is furnished with interesting frescoes. The hotel also has a pleasant restaurant ($$). ✉ rue du Bois-de-Candie, 73000 Chambéry-le-Vieux; N201 from Chambéry ☎ 04 79 96 63 00 AX MC VI

▯ L'Or du Temps $$

A gourmet hotel restaurant lies at the foot of the Alps, in a picturesque setting between Chambéry and Albertville. ✉ 814 route de Plainpalais, 73230 St.-Alban-Leysse ☎ 04 79 85 51 28 ◔ Closed Sat. lunch, Sun. dinner, Mon., mid-Aug. to early Sep. and first week of Jan. AX MC VI

CHAMONIX

▯ Atmosphère $–$$

Traditional dishes offer good value, but the stunning view of Mont-Blanc is priceless. ✉ 123 place Balmat ☎ 04 50 55 97 97 AX DC MC VI

▦ Jeu de Paume $$–$$$

The classic wooden chalet has a restaurant ($$), pool and sauna. ✉ 705 route du Chapeau, le Lavancher, 74400, N506 from Chamonix, 4 miles northeast ☎ 04 50 54 03 76 ◔ Closed May, Jun. and mid-Sep. to Nov. 30 AX DC MC VI

LA CLUSAZ

▦ Chalets de la Serraz $$–$$$

Popular with skiing enthusiasts, the traditional chalet's comfortable rooms pamper the sporty types who use the gym and pool when not on the slopes. Savoyard favorites are served in the restaurant ($$). Room prices are quoted with breakfast and dinner. ✉ Route du Col des Aravis, 74220; D909 from la Clusaz, 3 miles south ☎ 04 50 02 48 29 ◔ Closed Apr. to late May. and late Sep. to early Nov. AX DC MC VI

ÉVIAN-LES-BAINS

▦ La Verniaz $$–$$$

Guests who stay in chalets with lake views get a good taste of the high life. The restaurant menu ($$–$$$) features French favorites. ✉ avenue du Leman, 74500 ☎ 04 50 75 04 90 ◔ Closed mid-Nov. to mid-Feb. AX DC MC VI

GRENOBLE
🍴 Auberge Napoléon $$–$$$
A well-regarded, more formal restaurant, this place is run by a female chef. The menu is based on classic-style French cuisine.
✉ 7 rue Montorge ☎ 04 76 87 53 64 🕐 Mon.–Sat. dinner AX DC MC VI

🏨 Mercure Grenoble Grand Hôtel Président $$–$$$
This stylish hotel has an indoor pool. Regional cuisine is served.
✉ 11 rue Général-Mangin, 38100 ☎ 04 76 56 26 56 AX DC MC VI

LAC DU BOURGET
🏨 🍴 Ombremont $$–$$$
Set on the lake, this is a splendid small hotel that's a perfect luxury base for your regional explorations. Restaurant $$$.
✉ D1504, Le Bourget-du-Lac, 73370 ☎ 04 79 25 00 23 🕐 Hotel closed mid-Nov. to early Dec. and first three weeks in Jan. Restaurant closed Mon.–Tue., Dec.–Apr. AX DC MC VI

LYON
🍴 L'Auberge du Pont de Collonges $$$
This place is quite simply the best. It's run by Paul Bocuse, arguably the finest chef in the country.
✉ 40 rue de la Plage, Collonges-au-Mont-d'Or; D433, D51 from Lyon, 8 miles north ☎ 04 72 42 90 90 AX DC MC VI

🏨 Hotel Mercure Lyon Centre Château Perrache $–$$
Rooms are big and lounges reflect an art nouveau flair. A standard restaurant ($$) is on site.
✉ 12 cours de Verdun-Rambaud, 69002 ☎ 04 72 77 15 00 🚇 Perrache AX DC MC VI

🍴 Le Musée $
One of Lyon's most popular *bouchons* serves a range of local dishes and has a convivial atmosphere. Le Musée is popular for its small size and central location.
✉ 2 rue des Forces, 69002 ☎ 04 78 37 71 54 🕐 Closed Sun. and Mon. 🚇 Cordeliers MC VI

🏨 Royal $$$
This central historic hotel is renowned for its lavish rooms.
✉ 20 place Bellecour, 60002 ☎ 04 78 37 57 31 🚇 Bellecour AX DC MC VI

🏨 La Tour Rose $$$
The charming and beautifully converted 16th-century convent is also home to a renowned gourmet restaurant ($$$). French playwright Molière is known to have spent several years here.
✉ 22 rue du Bœuf, 69005 ☎ 04 78 92 69 10 🚇 Vieux Lyon AX DC MC VI

PÉROUGES
🏨 Hostellerie du Vieux Pérouges $$–$$$
One of the oldest hotels in France, this establishment has spectacular views. There is an excellent restaurant ($$$).
✉ place du Tilleul, 01800 ☎ 04 74 61 00 88 AX MC VI

ROMANÈCHE-THORINS – BEAUJOLAIS
🏨 Les Maritonnes $–$$
A useful overnight stop if you've overindulged in vineyard and cellar tours. The restaurant ($$–$$$) serves *escargot* and *quenelle-de-brochet* (pike patty).
✉ Route de Fleurie, 71570 ☎ 03 85 35 51 70 🕐 Closed late Dec. to early Jan. Restaurant closed Sun. and Mon., mid-Oct. to early Apr. AX DC MC VI

ST. VÉRAN
🍴 Grand Tétras $
Friendly service and home cooking can be expected in the restaurant of this small hotel ($) in Queyras' best-known village.
✉ Quartier la Sagne, 05350 ☎ 04 92 45 82 42 🕐 Closed Apr.–May and mid-Sep. to Nov. AX DC MC VI

VASSIEUX-EN-VERCORS
🏨 Auberge du Tetras Lyre $
This resort center hotel has rooms with balconies and offers a fitness center and restaurant.
✉ rue Abbé Gagnol, 26420 ☎ 04 75 48 28 04 🕐 Closed Nov.–early Dec. MC VI

VIENNE
🏨 Hôtel des 7 Fontaines $–$$
Spacious rooms fill this large house, set in parkland just out of town.
✉ Les 7 Fontaines, 38200 ☎ 04 74 85 25 70 🕐 Closed Sun., Dec.–Mar. AX DC MC VI

🏨 🍴 La Pyramide $$$
Although this hotel with beautiful gardens is lovely, the principal attraction is its excellent restaurant ($$$).
✉ 14 boulevard Fernand-Point, 38200 ☎ 04 74 53 01 96 🕐 Closed early Feb. to early Mar. Restaurant closed Tue., Wed., early Feb.–early Mar. and one week mid-Aug. AX DC MC VI

ARBOIS
🏨 Castel Damandre $–$$
Accommodations are in a restored water mill and outbuildings around a waterfall. There's an on-site restaurant ($$).
✉ Les Planches-en-Arbois, 39600 ☎ 03 84 66 08 17 Reservations recommended AX DC MC VI

🍴 Le Caveau d'Arbois $–$$
This is known for family cooking, popular fish dishes and terrines.
✉ 3 route de Besançon ☎ 03 84 66 10 70 🕐 Closed Sun. dinner, and Mon. lunch and dinner AX DC MC VI

BEAUNE
🏨 Hôtel de la Poste $$–$$$
The rooms of this lovely old house have wonderful views – either facing the ramparts of the old town or overlooking the local vineyards.
✉ 5 boulevard Clémenceau, 21200 ☎ 03 80 22 08 11 AX DC MC VI

🍴 Le Jardin des Remparts $$$
A constant local favorite, the restaurant boasts a great wine cellar and fabulous food – from mouthwatering beef and seafood to the delicate pear sorbet.
✉ 10 rue Hôtel-Dieu ☎ 03 80 24 79 41 🕐 Closed Sun., Mon. except national holidays and Jul.–Aug., Dec. to mid-Jan. AX MC VI

BELFORT
🏨 Grand Hôtel du Tonneau d'Or $
This place is popular during festivals; reserve in advance to avoid disappointment. A restaurant ($$) is on site.
✉ 1 rue Reiset, 90000 ☎ 03 84 58 57 56 AX DC MC VI

🍴 Le Molière $$–$$$
The flair of a woman's touch is evident in this popular restaurant's traditional dishes.
✉ 6 place de l'Étuve, 90000 ☎ 03 84 21 86 38 🕐 Closed Wed. AX DC MC VI

Burgundy and the East

KEY TO SYMBOLS

⌂	hotel
⊟	restaurant
⊠	address
☎	telephone number
⊘	days/times closed
Ⓜ	nearest metro/tube/subway station(s)
AX	American Express
DC	Diners Club
MC	MasterCard
VI	VISA

Hotels
Price guide: double room with breakfast for two people

$	less than €130
$$	€130–€200
$$$	more than €200

Restaurants
Price guide: dinner per person, excluding drinks

$	less than €35
$$	€35–€65
$$$	more than €65

Choosing a Wine

Whether choosing a wine or a stunning fall outfit, it pays to read the label in France. Unlike in the United States, the name of the grape variety tends not to be shown on the label; the main reference is more likely to be the region or the estate where the wine was produced. There are four main categories: *A.O.C. (appellation d'origine controlée)*, stating that the grapes were grown in a specified area to an agreed standard; *V.D.Q.S. (vin delimité de qualité superieure)*, or top-grade country wine; *vin de pays*, an honest open wine from a particular region; and *vin de table*, an everyday drinking wine that may be made from a blend of grapes from various sources. The major wine-producing areas are Bordeaux, Burgundy, Languedoc-Roussillon, the Loire and the Rhône Valley.

BESANÇON

⊟ Le Champagney $–$$
Local dishes are offered in this dining room in the old part of town.
⊠ 37 rue Battant ☎ 03 81 81 05 71
⊘ Closed Sun. MC VI

⌂ Château de la Dame Blanche $–$$
A beautiful château in its own grounds has bright bedrooms and a gourmet restaurant ($$–$$$). It is 10 minutes' drive from Besançon.
⊠ 1 route de la Goulotte, 25870 Geneuille ☎ 03 81 57 64 64;
AX MC VI

COLMAR

⊟ La Cocotte de Grandmere $–$$
A seasonal menu is served at this classic bistro which is run by a young, enthusiastic team.
⊠ 14 place de l'École, 68000 ☎ 03 89 23 32 49 ⊘ Closed Sat.–Sun. MC VI

⊟ Le Rendez-vous de Chasse $$–$$$
Regional and classic French standards are served in the finer of the Hôtel Bristol's two restaurants.
⊠ 7 place de la Gare
☎ 03 89 41 10 10 AX MC VI

DIJON

⊟ Le Bistrot des Halles $–$$
Flavorful food and wine are standbys at this reliable market restaurant.
⊠ 10 rue Bannelier ☎ 03 80 49 94 15 ⊘ Closed lunch and dinner Sun.–Mon. MC VI

⌂ Le Jacquemart $
Quaint streets run behind this 17th-century house; park away and walk.
⊠ 32 rue Verrerie, 21000
☎ 03 80 60 09 60 AX MC VI

METZ

⊟ Bistrot de G $–$$
Bistrot de G is a popular place to eat in the heart of town. Street tables are set out in the summer.
⊠ 9 rue de Faisin, 57000 ☎ 03 87 37 06 44 ⊘ Closed Sun. and Mon. AX MC VI

⌂ Cathédrale $
This hotel is a great base for sightseeing with the cathedral, marketplace and river right on your doorstep.
⊠ 25 place de Chambre, 57000
☎ 03 87 75 00 02 AX DC MC VI

MONTBARD – FONTENAY

⌂ Hôtel l'Ecu $
The restaurant ($–$$$) in the hotel has both budget and gastronomic menus featuring local dishes.
⊠ 7 rue Auguste-Carré, 21500; D905, D32 to Fontenay Abbey, 4 miles northeast ☎ 03 80 92 11 66
⊘ Hotel closed one week late Feb. Restaurant closed Fri.–Sun. dinner, mid-Nov. to Mar. AX DC MC VI

MONTBÉLIARD

⌂ ⊟ La Balance $–$$
Set in a 16th-century coach house, this restaurant (and hotel) provided headquarters accommodations for the French Army during the campaigns of 1944–45.
⊠ 40 rue de Belfort, 25200 ☎ 03 81 96 77 41 AX DC MC VI

NANCY

⊟ Brasserie Excelsior $$
This restaurant specializes in oysters and a visit will also please those interested in art nouveau decor.
⊠ 50 rue Henri-Poincaré
☎ 03 83 35 24 57 AX DC MC VI

⌂ Hotel d'Haussonville $$–$$$
This Renaissance palace in the heart of the old city provides elegant and comfortable accommodations.
⊠ 9 rue Monseigneur-Trouillet, 54000 ☎ 03 83 35 85 84 AX DC MC VI

RIQUEWIHR

⌂ Couronne $
Roomy accommodations fill the pretty 16th-century building. There is ample parking.
⊠ 5 rue de la Couronne, 68340
☎ 03 89 49 03 03 AX MC VI

⊟ Table du Gourmet $$$
Textbook Alsace cooking by award-winning chef Jean-Luc Brendel is served here. Let your waiter guide your discovery of the region's finer flavors.
⊠ 5 rue de la 1ère-Armée
☎ 03 89 49 09 09 ⊘ Closed all day Tue., lunch Wed. and Thu.
AX MC VI

STRASBOURG

⊟ Bierstub l'Ami Schutz $$
This traditional Alsace restaurant is located in the heart of the pretty waterside district.
⊠ 1 rue Ponts-Couverts ☎ 03 88 32 76 98 ⊘ Closed Christmas–Apr.
AX DC MC VI

¶ Buerehiesel $$$
Chef Antoine Westermann prepares inventive gastronomy for diners in this old farmhouse.
✉ 4 parc de l'Orangerie ☎ 03 88 45 56 65 🕐 Closed Sun.–Mon., three weeks in Aug. and first three weeks in Jan. AX DC MC VI

🏠 Cathédrale $–$$
Opposite the fine cathedral, this is an unrivaled central spot, especially during the popular and busy Christmas market season.
✉ 12–13 place de la Cathédrale, 67000 ☎ 03 88 22 12 12 AX DC MC VI

🏠 Dragon $–$$
Dragon is a 17th-century house situated on a quiet street; take an easy stroll to la Petite France and the markets.
✉ 12 rue du Dragon, 67000 ☎ 03 88 35 79 80 AX DC MC VI

VERDUN
🏠 Château des Montharirons $–$$$
This 19th-century château sits on extensive grounds. Dine well at the restaurant ($$–$$$).
✉ 26 rue de Verdun, 55320 les Montharirons, Dieve-sur-Meuse; D34 from Verdun, 10 miles south ☎ 03 29 87 78 55 🕐 Restaurant closed Mon. (open for dinner for guests of the château mid-Jun. to mid-Sep.), Tue. lunch and Sun. dinner AX DC MC VI

VOUGEOT
🏠 Château de Gilly $$–$$$
An historic estate of the Abbey of Cîteaux, this château is an ideal place to lay your head during your trips around the vineyards of the Côte d'Or.
✉ Gilly-les-Cîteaux, 21640 ☎ 03 80 62 89 98 AX DC MC VI

CHAMPAGNE AND THE NORTH

AMIENS
¶ Les Marissons $$
This excellent dining room is within a choir's chant of the cathedral.
✉ Pont de la Dodane ☎ 03 22 92 96 66 🕐 Closed Wed. and Sat. lunch AX DC MC VI

🏠 Mercure Amiens Cathédrale $–$$
Rooms are bright, spacious and well equipped at this modern downtown business hotel within walking distance of the main attractions.
✉ 21–23 rue Flarrers, 8000 ☎ 03 22 80 60 60 AX DC MC VI

ARRAS
¶ La Faisanderie $$
This popular restaurant serves arguably the best food in town, including a fabulous cheeseboard. Tables are arranged in the evocative 17th-century cellars of this establishment.
✉ 45 Grand-Place ☎ 03 21 48 20 76 🕐 Closed Sun. dinner, Mon. all day, Tue. lunch AX MC VI

🏠 Trois Luppars $
The oldest house on the main square in Arras has been lovingly restored by the owners.
✉ 49 Grand-Place, 62000 ☎ 03 21 60 02 03 AX MC DC VI

BOULOGNE-SUR-MER
🏠 Hotel de Londres $
This small family-owned hotel is a good budget option in a central location.
✉ 22 place France, 62200 ☎ 03 21 31 35 63 MC VI

¶ La Matelote $$–$$$
Tony Lestienne's superb fish-based menu never fails to please and always provides excellent value.
✉ 80 boulevard Ste.-Beuve ☎ 03 21 30 33 33 🕐 Closed Thu. AX MC VI

BUSNES
🏠 ¶ Le Château de Beaulieu $$–$$$
In this magnificent Empire-era château, you will find large, luxuriantly furnished rooms and a gastronomic restaurant ($$$). The château is set in acres of verdant parkland. It is a good base for touring the north.
✉ rue de Lillers, 62350 ☎ 03 21 68 88 88 🕐 Restaurant closed Sat. lunch, Sun. dinner, Mon. lunch and dinner and Tue. lunch AX DC MC VI

CALAIS
¶ Le Channel $–$$
Taste the best Dover sole this side of the Channel in this unpretentious seashore dining room.
✉ 3 boulevard de la Résistance ☎ 03 21 34 42 30 🕐 Closed Tue., Sun. dinner, late Jul. to mid-Aug. and late Dec. to mid-Jan. AX DC MC VI

🏠 Métropol $
This is probably the best budget hotel in town. It is situated close to the center of Calais. Bedrooms all have sea views.
✉ 45 quai de Rhin, 62100 ☎ 03 21 97 54 00 🕐 Closed Dec. 16–Jan. 6 AX DC MC VI

CHARLEVILLE-MÉZIÈRES
¶ Clef des Champs $$–$$$
The small restaurant serves inventive cuisine prepared by an enthusiastic, informal young team. The owners have five well-furnished rooms for bed-and-breakfast.
✉ 33 rue du Moulin, Waridon ☎ 03 24 56 17 50 🕐 Closed Sun. dinner and Mon. MC VI

CORBIE
🏠 Le Macassar $$–$$$
In a small village close to Amiens, this luxury bed-and-breakfast is an art deco treasure hidden behind a rather unassuming facade. Prices include evening cocktails.
✉ place de la Republique, 80800 ☎ 03 22 48 40 04 MC VI

ÉPERNAY
🏠 Hôtel Villa Eugène $$–$$$
It's only a short stroll to visit the finest champagne houses from this charming small hotel in a 19th-century mansion.
✉ 82–84 avenue de Champagne, 51200 ☎ 03 26 32 44 76 AX MC VI

¶ Le Théâtre $–$$
Highly rated menus are served at this popular local restaurant. In the evening, revelers take over from the more sober business lunchers.
✉ 8 place Mendès-France, 51200 ☎ 03 26 58 88 19 🕐 Closed Wed., Tue. dinner and Sun. dinner MC VI

LAON
🏠 Hostellerie St.-Vincent $
Comfortable rooms fill a modern building. Follow signs toward the industrial zone.
✉ avenue Charles-de-Gaulle, 02000 ☎ 03 23 23 42 43 AX MC VI

¶ Restaurant Zorn $$$
Taste a hint of the Mediterranean in the sauces and flavors of this bistro's dishes.
✉ La Petite Auberge, 45 boulevard Brossolette ☎ 03 23 23 02 38 🕐 Closed Sun. and Mon. dinner, two

KEY TO SYMBOLS

⊞	hotel
🍴	restaurant
✉	address
☎	telephone number
⊘	days/times closed
Ⓜ	nearest metro/tube/subway station(s)
AX	American Express
DC	Diners Club
MC	MasterCard
VI	VISA

Hotels

Price guide: double room with breakfast for two people

$	less than €130
$$	€130–€200
$$$	more than €200

Restaurants

Price guide: dinner per person, excluding drinks

$	less than €35
$$	€35–€65
$$$	more than €65

Breakfast at Paul's

Paul's doesn't have the biggest or most varied breakfast in Lille, but it does have the best. This bakery, part of a multinational chain, opposite the Vieille Bourse, is the place to go for fresh bread and croissants, homemade jelly and creamy, piping-hot chocolate first thing in the morning. Breakfast, served on solid wooden tables against the blue-and-white tiled walls and heavy tapestries of the bread and cake shop, is the perfect way to start the day. But meals also are served until the wee hours, and it would be a pity to dismiss this elegant bakery as a mere breakfast place or tearoom. Up a curving wooden staircase is the bright and airy second-floor dining room, which provides echoes of a more elegant era.
✉ Paul, 8 rue de Paris (Rihour) ☎ 03 20 78 20 78.

---

weeks in Aug., one week in Feb. and one week at Easter AX MC VI

LILLE

🍴 À l'Huîtrière $$$
Behind an art deco fish shop, this eatery offers renowned evening dining and also a lunch menu of excellent value.
✉ 3 rue des Chats-Bossus
☎ 03 20 55 43 41 ⊘ Closed dinner Sun. and holidays. Oyster bar closed late Jul. to late Aug. AX DC MC VI

⊞ Best Western Grand Hôtel Bellevue $$
The young Wolfgang Amadeus Mozart once stayed in this long-established hotel. Some rooms overlook the main square in the heart of the city.
✉ 5 rue Jean-Roisin, 59800
☎ 03 20 57 45 64 Ⓜ Rihour AX DC MC VI

⊞ Carlton $$$
This comfortable hotel has a fabulous cupola bedroom on the roof that affords the best panoramic view over the city center.
✉ 3 rue de Paris, 59026
☎ 03 20 13 33 13 Ⓜ Rihour AX MC VI

🍴 Le Compostelle $$–$$$
Charming little dining rooms and a Renaissance courtyard are delightful features at this one-time rest house for pilgrims heading for Santiago de Compostela in Spain.
✉ 4 rue St.-Étienne ☎ 03 28 38 08 30 Ⓜ Rihour AX MC VI

⊞ Couvent des Minimes Alliance Lille $$–$$$
This former convent has the benefit of air-conditioned rooms and is only 5 minutes from the center.
✉ 17 quai du Wault, Lille Couvent des Minimes, 59027 ☎ 03 20 30 46 08 Ⓜ Rihour AX DC MC VI

LUMBRES

⊞ Le Moulin de Mombreux $
This cozy, converted water mill, set in a verdant garden, has comfortable bedrooms and a good restaurant. WiFi is available throughout.
✉ chemin de Mombreux, 62380
☎ 03 21 39 13 13 AX MC VI

REIMS

⊞ Les Crayères $$$
This romantic mini-estate exudes the opulent champagne lifestyle.

The house is all marble and columns, with indulgent rooms.
✉ 64 boulevard Henri-Vasnier, 51100 ☎ 03 26 24 90 00 ⊘ Closed three weeks in Jan. AX DC MC VI

🍴 Le Vigneraie $$$
Classic French dishes with a modern touch are served here. For a seafood dish with a twist, try a specialty such as the cappuccino lobster.
✉ 14 rue de Thillois ☎ 03 26 88 67 27 ⊘ Closed Mon., Wed. lunch and Sun. dinner AX MC VI

ST.-OMER

🍴 Le Cygne $$
Ask for a table in the chic first-floor dining room, where locals lunch on traditional dishes.
✉ 8 rue Caventou, 62500
☎ 03 21 98 20 52 ⊘ Closed Sun. dinner, Mon., three weeks in Aug. and two weeks in winter
AX DC MC VI

SIGNY-L'ABBAYE

⊞ Auberge de l'Abbaye $
Monsieur Lefebre's welcome is always genuine, either in the agreeable restaurant ($) or showing guests around the eccentrically proportioned rooms.
✉ 2 place Briand, 08460
☎ 03 24 52 81 27 ⊘ Restaurant closed Wed. lunch. Serves set menu Tue. lunch and dinner and Wed. dinner MC VI

LE TOUQUET-PARIS-PLAGE

🍴 Les 2 Moineaux $$
This intimate and stylish restaurant offers contemporary French cuisine in a modern setting.
✉ 12 rue St.-Jean, 62520 ☎ 03 21 05 09 67 ⊘ Closed Mon., Tue. lunch AX MC VI

⊞ Westminster $$–$$$
Something of an institution with a spa and a fine restaurant ($$$), the Westminster is at the heart of le Touquet's social scene.
✉ 5 avenue du Verger, 62520
☎ 03 21 05 48 48 AX DC MC VI

TOURCOING

🍴 La Baratte $$
This family-run restaurant has contemporary decor and offers a refined dining experience.
✉ 395 rue Clinquet ☎ 03 20 94 45 63 ⊘ Closed Sat. and Mon. lunch, Sun. and Mon. dinner, and first two weeks in Aug. AX MC VI

Essential Information

U.S. CITIZENS

The information in this guide has been compiled for U.S. citizens traveling as tourists.

Travelers who are not U.S. citizens, or who are traveling on business, should check with their embassies and tourist offices for information on the countries they wish to visit.

Entry requirements are subject to change at short notice, and travelers are advised to check the current situation before they travel.

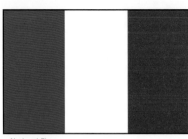

National Flag

Before You Go

Passports

Each person traveling must have a passport.
A visa isn't required for a tourist or business stay
up to 90 days.

Passport application forms can be obtained from
any federal or state court or post office authorized
to accept passport applications; apply early,
since processing can take several months. U.S.
passport agencies have offices in major cities;
check the Yellow Pages (U.S. Government, State
Department) for the nearest one. You also can
request an application form from the National
Passport Information Center: ☎ 1-877-487-2778.
Passport information and application forms are
available on the U.S. State Government internet
site at http://travel.state.gov.

Photocopy the identification page of your
passport; leave one copy with a relative or friend
in case of emergency, and carry one with you in
case the passport is lost or stolen while traveling.
If this occurs, inform the local police immediately
and contact the nearest U.S. embassy or consulate.
The U.S. State Department has a 24-hour traveler's
hotline: ☎ 1-888-407-4747; from overseas
202-501-4444.

Passports must be shown whenever you board
an international flight or cross an international
border. In practice, however, border controls have
been relaxed between many European Union (E.U.)
member countries.

Travel Insurance

Before departing, make sure you are covered by
insurance that will reimburse travel expenses if you
need to cancel or cut short your trip due to unfore-
seen circumstances. You also will need coverage
for property loss or theft, emergency medical and
dental treatment, and emergency evacuation if
necessary. Before taking out additional insurance,
check whether your current homeowners or medical coverage already includes travel abroad.

If you make a claim, your insurance company
will need proof of the incident or expenditure. Keep
copies of any police report and related documents,
or medical bills or statements.

Essential for Travelers

Required ● Recommended ● Not required ●

Passport	●
Visa	●
Travel, medical insurance	●
Round-trip or onward airline ticket	●
Local currency	●
Traveler's checks	●
Credit cards	●
First-aid kit and medicines	●
Health inoculations	●

Essential for Drivers

Required ● Recommended ● Not required ●

Driver's license	●
International Driving Permit	●
Car insurance	●
Car registration (for non-rental cars)	●

See also Driving section page 280.

When to Go

The northerly climate of France is affected by
various factors. The Gulf Stream has a warming,
sometimes wet, influence on its Atlantic coastline.
Mediterranean destinations have sunnier skies
and warm temperatures. Inland, the Pyrénées
and Alps bring cooler temperatures; the Alps are
popular with winter skiers. The southwest areas
of Aquitaine and the Dordogne have hot summers.
French school vacations are in July and August.
June and September offer fine weather and
fewer crowds.

Important Addresses

French Embassy U.S.A.
4101 Reservoir Road,
N.W. Washington DC, 20007
☎ (202) 944-6000
www.info-france-usa.org

French Government Tourist Office
Maison de la France/Atout France
79–81 rue de Clichy,
75009 Paris,
France
☎ 02 42 96 70 00
www.franceguide.com

American Embassy
2 avenue Gabriel
75382 Paris, France
☎ 01 43 12 22 22
http://france.usembassy.gov
American Citizens Services: An appointment
system, which can be arranged online, operates
in all but emergency cases.

Paris	New York	Chicago	Denver	Los Angeles	Time zones
12:00 noon	– 6 hrs	– 7 hrs	– 8 hrs	– 9 hrs	

277

Essential Information

Customs

 Duty-free limits on goods brought in from non-E.U. countries:

200 cigarettes or 100 cigarillos or 50 cigars or 250g tobacco; 4L wine; 1L alcohol over 22% volume; 2L alcohol under 22%; 16L beer; plus any other duty-free goods (including gifts) to the value of €430 if arriving by sea or air, €300 if arriving overland, €150 if under 15 years of age, whatever means of arrival. There is no limit on the importation of tax-paid goods purchased within the E.U., provided they are for your own personal use. There are no currency regulations. On returning to the U.S., you will be required to complete a customs declaration form. You are allowed $800 worth of goods or gifts (including items purchased in duty-free shops) providing you carry them with you; keep sales slips for inspection. The duty-free exemption can include 100 cigars and 200 cigarettes, as well as 1L of wine, beer or liquor if you are 21 or older.

✗ **No** unlicensed drugs, weapons, ammunition, obscene material, pets or other animals, counterfeit money or copied goods, meat or poultry.

Money

France's currency is the euro (€), a currency shared by 17 other E.U. countries. The euro is divided into 100 cents (¢). The denominations of euro bills are 5, 10, 20, 50, 100, 200 and 500 euros. There are coins of 1, 2, 5, 10, 20 and 50¢ and €1 and €2. You can exchange dollars or traveler's checks (chèques de voyage) at a bank (banque) or an exchange office (bureau de change) and some post offices.

Tips and Gratuities

Tips (pourboires) are welcomed, but not expected

Restaurants (service is almost always included)	change
Cafés/bars	change
Porters	€1–€2 per bag
Chambermaids	€2
Taxis	€1–€2
Cloakroom attendants	50¢–€1

Communications

Post Offices

Buy stamps (timbres) at a post office (un bureau de poste), newsstand (un marchand de journaux) or tobacconist (distinguished by its red Tabac sign). Hours of out-of-town post offices may vary. Mailboxes are yellow and are wall mounted or freestanding. For posting abroad, use the slot marked autres départements étranger.

Telephones

Phone booths with instructions in English are easy to find. All phones take phone cards (télécarte), which can be bought from post offices, newsstands and tobacconists. Some booths take credit cards.

Phoning within France

Most telephone numbers are 10 digits, and include the regional code, although some four-digit numbers have been introduced for businesses. Watch out for 08 numbers; some may be free (0800), some cheap, but others are premium rate. For national directory inquiries, dial 118 008 or visit www.pagesjaunes.fr.

Phoning France from abroad

The country code for France is 33. To phone France from the U.S. or Canada, omit the first zero from the French number, and add the prefix 011 33.

Example: 01 22 33 44 55 becomes 011 33 1 22 33 44 55.

Phoning from France

To phone the U.S. or Canada from France, prefix the area code and number with 00 1. Example: (111) 222-3333 becomes 00 1 111 222-3333.

To call international information dial 118 008

Emergency Numbers

	Police (police)	17
	Fire service (sapeurs-pompiers)	18
	Ambulance (ambulance)	15

Emergency calls are free from phone booths.

The pan-European emergency number **112** will also connect you to emergency services.

Essential Information

Hours of Operation

- Stores Tue.–Sat.
- Offices Mon.–Fri.
- Banks Mon.–Fri.
- Post offices Mon.–Fri.
- Museums/Monuments
- Pharmacies

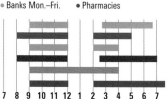

7 8 9 10 11 12 1 2 3 4 5 6 7

Most stores close on Sunday and all or half day on Monday, although opening hours are longer in resort areas and major towns and cities. Small stores close for lunch and, in the south of France in summer, lunch may extend to 4 p.m., but then the store will stay open later in the evening.
Many banks may stay closed on Monday, while some, particularly city banks, may open on Saturday morning.

Post offices close at noon on Saturday, some are shut all day on Monday; small offices close for lunch weekdays.

National museums are closed on Tuesday (except Versailles, the Trianon Palace and the Musée d'Orsay, which are closed Monday). Municipal museums are closed on Monday. Museum times vary considerably, and it's best to check before a visit.

National Holidays

Banks, businesses and most stores close on these days:

Jan 1	New Year's Day
Mar/Apr	Easter Monday
May 1	May Day
May 8	V.E. Day
May	Ascension Day
May/Jun	Pentecost Monday
Jul 14	Bastille Day
Aug 15	Assumption of the Virgin
Nov 1	All Saints' Day
Nov 11	Armistice Day
Dec 25	Christmas Day

Restrooms

Restrooms *(les toilettes* or WC, pronounced vay-say in French) are more common in larger towns, often located near a public amenity. You may still find the old-fashioned "squat" variety and hygiene is usually of a reasonable standard. There is a small fee to use facilities in railroad stations. If you need to use the restroom in a café or bar, buy a drink first. Note some places have unisex restrooms. Supermarkets usually have good, clean facilities.

Health Advice

Medical Services

Private medical insurance is recommended. Visitors from non-E.U. countries have to pay for all medical treatment; keep all receipts and medicine labels to claim on your travel insurance. If you wish to see an English-speaking doctor *(un médecin)*, ask at your consulate or hotel.

Dental Services

A dentist *(un/une dentiste)* charges for treatment. Emergency help is available from dentists listed in the Yellow Pages *(les pages jaunes)*. Check that your private medical insurance covers dental treatment.

Sun Advice

The yearly average for sunshine is high: 2,500 hours (3,000 hours along the coast). Summers, particularly July and August, can be dry and hot, especially in the south. When outside, wear a hat and drink plenty of fluids. On the beach, a high factor sunscreen is essential.

Drugs

Prescription medicines and medical advice can be obtained from a pharmacy *(une pharmacie)*, designated by a green cross sign. If you need medicines outside regular hours, information about the nearest 24-hour facility is posted on the door of all pharmacies.

Safe Water

It's safe to drink tap water, but never drink from a fountain marked *"eau non potable"* ("not drinking water"). Many French people prefer the taste of bottled mineral water *(eau minérale en bouteille)*, which is widely available. A less expensive alternative is *eau de source*, or spring water.

Personal Safety

To lessen the risk of theft or injury through crime, try not to be conspicuous by wearing expensive jewelry or carrying valuables. Criminals frequent tourist attractions, stores, markets and all transportation, while theft from rental vehicles with non-local license plates is common.

Your passport, money and credit cards should be kept hidden inside clothing, and only necessary money or cards carried.

If you should get into trouble, contact the police (see Emergency Numbers above), and if required the nearest U.S. embassy.

Essential Information

National Transportation

Air *(avion)*

Airports for the major cities in France are served by Air France, while many U.S. operators provide regular flights to Paris. For details on Air France flights, call ☎ (800) 237-2747 in the U.S. or contact your travel agent. For Air France information in France, call ☎ 36 54 (toll call); www.airfrance.com.

Paris has two airports – Roissy-Charles-de-Gaulle (Roissy-CDG) to the north, and Orly to the south. Both are connected to the center of Paris by the RER B (Orly is also connected by the RER C) railroad, and other public transportation is easily available. For daily flight information, call ☎ 39 50, (toll call), which serves all airports. General information about the airports is provided by Aéroports de Paris (ADP), who have customer service desks in the main terminals; www.aeroportsdeparis.fr.

Many of the main cities described in this guide can be reached from Paris by plane, including Bordeaux, Clermont-Ferrand, Lille, Lyons, Marseille, Nice, Rennes, Strasbourg and Toulouse. Other regional airports provide connections to smaller towns; contact Air France.

Train *(train)*

The state rail company is the Société Nationale des Chemins de Fer Français (SNCF). Trains are fast, reliable and comfortable, with numerous discounts available. A "round-the-clock" car-carrying service from Calais (Le Shuttle) and a Paris–London passenger train (Eurostar) both run through the tunnel under the English Channel. For SNCF details, ☎ 36 35 (toll call); www.sncf.fr. For Eurostar details, ☎ 08 92 35 35 39 (toll call); www.eurostar.com.

Bus *(autobus)*

Bus services in cities are excellent, but rural areas may be less well served. Long-distance bus stations are usually close to railroad stations, and major train and bus services usually coordinate (a long-distance bus is called a *car*). Bus services shown on train timetables are run by the SNCF, and rail tickets are often valid for them. The Eurolines international bus network operates in France; ☎ 08 92 89 90 91 (toll call); www.eurolines.fr.

Ferry *(ferry)*

There are frequent sailings to southern England from ports along the English Channel. P&O Ferries (☎ 08 25 12 01 56; www.poferries.com), and LD Lines (☎ 0825 30 43 04; www.ldlines.co.uk) operate from Calais in the north, and LD Lines also sail from Le Havre and Dieppe in Normandy. Brittany Ferries (☎ 08 25 82 88 28; www.brittanyferries.com) sail from Caen, Cherbourg, St.-Malo and Roscoff along the Normandy and Brittany coasts. DFDS Seaways (☎ +44 208 127 8303; www.dfdsseaways.co.uk) sail from Dover to Dunkerque, and Condor Ferries (☎ +44 845 609 1024, St. Malo office 0825 16 54 63, Cherbourg office 02 33 88 44 88; www.condor-ferries.co.uk) operate from Cherbourg in Normandy and St.-Malo in Brittany. Some Mediterranean ferries operate in summer only. SNCM sails to Corsica from Marseille, Toulon and Nice. For details, ☎ 32 60; www.sncm.fr.

Electricity

France has a 220-volt power supply. Electrical sockets take plugs with two round pins; American appliances will need a plug adapter and will require a transformer if they don't have a dual-voltage facility.

Photography

If you wish to take photographs inside a building, seek permission if possible. The same applies when you are photographing people.

Digital peripherals are widely available and every major town has at least one photographic store and developing stores with digital printing machines. Film and developing services can only be found in most cities, though this may not be a same-day service. Large stores, such as Leclerc and Carrefour, provide both digital printing machines and film developing for up to 30 percent less than specialized stores, but with a premium for quick service.

Media

France's national newspapers *(journaux)* include the conservative *Le Figaro*, the authoritative liberal *Le Monde*, the socialist *Libération*, the communist *L'Humanité*, the catholic *La Croix* and the sports paper *L'Équipe*. Regional newspapers are widely read.

In larger cities, U.S. newspapers (usually previous-day editions) and magazines are available; the most common are *USA Today*, the international edition of the *New York Herald Tribune* and *Time Magazine*. They can be bought at train stations, airports, newsstands and tobacconists.

The national radio and television network enters into competition with independent stations. *Le journal télévisé*, broadcast at 1 p.m. and 8 p.m. on France 2 and TF1, a news program, is watched by the majority of French people. France 24 is the country's first international news channel and is widely admired.

On the radio you can pick up "Voice of America," Radio Canada, or BBC broadcasts, and larger hotels often have satellite or cable connections that broadcast BBC channels, the British Sky network or CNN.

Driving Regulations

Drive on the Right

Drive on the right-hand side of the road; passing is on the left. At minor intersections in urban areas yield to traffic coming from the right, often shown by signs saying *Priorité à droite*. Major roads have priority over side roads or upcoming intersections, shown by the sign *Passage protégé* and/or a yellow diamond sign. Vehicles in a traffic circle *(rond-point)* have priority over traffic entering it, shown by the sign on the approach saying *Vous n'avez pas la priorité* or *Cédez le passage*.

Seat Belts

Must be worn in both front and back seats at all times.

Minimum Age

 The minimum age for driving a car is 18. However, most car rental agencies stipulate a minimum age of 21 years – some companies 25 years – and the driver to have held a driver's license for at least a year.

Blood Alcohol

The legal blood alcohol limit is 0.05 percent. Random breath tests are carried out frequently, especially late at night.

Tolls

There are tolls on many limited-access highways *(autoroutes à péage)*, which are identified on route signs with an A. Collect a ticket on entry and keep it in a safe place: you must show the ticket and pay when exiting. Cash and credit cards are accepted. Tolls are more expensive than in the U.S.

Additional Information

Although a valid American driver's license is acceptable, an International Driving Permit (IDP) is recommended; some rental firms require it, and it can speed up formalities if you are involved in an accident. An IDP contains your photograph and confirms you hold a valid driver's license in your own country; it has a standard translation in several languages (available from AAA travel agencies).

A Green Card (international motor insurance certificate) is necessary if you are driving a private car; see page 276 for more information.

A free road map of France can be obtained from garages displaying the sign *Bison Futé*. A driver flashing their headlights at you means they are claiming right of way and you should allow them to pass. Vehicles must carry an emergency pack containing a high-visibility vest, a warning triangle and a breath alcohol analyzer.

Speed Limits

Regulations

Traffic police can impose severe on-the-spot fines.

 Toll highways *(autoroutes à péage)*
130 k.p.h. (80 m.p.h.)
Outer lane minimum **80 k.p.h. (49 m.p.h.)**
Non-toll highways and divided highways
110 k.p.h. (68 m.p.h.) unless varied by signs.

 Main roads **90 k.p.h. (55 m.p.h.)**

Urban areas (indicated by place-name signs) **50 k.p.h. (31 m.p.h.) or 30 k.p.h. (18 m.p.h.)**

Speed limits are reduced by 20 k.p.h. on toll highways and 10 k.p.h. on main roads in wet weather, and by 80 k.p.h. on toll highways in foggy conditions (visibility less than 50 meters/55 yards).

Car Rental

The leading rental firms have offices at airports and train stations. Insurance is obligatory and a major credit card is usually required. Hertz offers discounted rates for AAA members. For reservations:

	U.S.	France (toll calls)
Alamo (Europcar)	(877) 222-9075	08 25 16 15 18
Avis	(800) 331-1212	08 20 05 05 05
Budget	(800) 527-0700	08 20 61 16 20
Hertz	(800) 654-3001	08 25 88 97 55

Fuel

Gas stations are generally easy to find, and highway service areas are open 24 hours. Gas *(essence)* is mostly unleaded *(sans plomb)* and sold in liters; diesel fuel also is easily available and many places have GPL (liquid petroleum gas). Credit cards are widely accepted; many pumps read cards directly, so the customer doesn't have to pay at the counter. Gas stations are less common in rural areas, and some close on Sunday. Supermarket gas stations have the best prices.

Parking

Parking is usually regulated in urban areas and is forbidden on many streets in central Paris. Only park in white spaces – unmarked spaces are free of charge, those marked *Payant* require payment – or green, which are for very short stays. Yellow or other markings are reserved for certain vehicles. A dotted yellow line on the edge of a sidewalk indicates you can drop off or pick up passengers. Coin-operated meters allow parking for up to two hours. Some pay-and-display areas are free over lunch from noon to 2 p.m.

AAA

 AAA AFFILIATED MOTORING CLUB
Fédération Française des Automobiles-Clubes et des Usagers de la Route (FFAC)
9 rue d'Artois, 75008, Paris, France
☎ 01 40 55 43 00;
fax 01 40 55 43 09

Not all automobile clubs offer full services to AAA members.

Breakdowns/Accidents

 If you are involved in an accident, call 17 or 112 for police assistance.
There are orange emergency telephones every 2km (1.6 miles) on highways.

Most car rental firms provide their own free rescue service; if your car is rented, follow the instructions given in the documentation.
Use of a car-repair service other than those authorized by your rental company may violate your agreement.

Road Signs

French traffic signs consist of six main types. Symbols in red triangles are warnings and those in a red circle state a ban. Red triangles also indicate the right of way at intersections. Blue circular signs give obligatory commands but symbols in blue rectangles only indicate or provide information. Red-and-blue circular signs declare parking restrictions: A red cross indicates no stopping, a slanted red bar no parking.

Ahead only

Keep right

No entry

No stopping

End of restriction

No passing

Oncoming vehicles have priority

No U turns

Route bends to left

Vehicles on traffic circle have priority

Give way

Route has priority at intersection

One-way traffic

No through road

Pronunciation

You'll be well received if you try to pronounce words correctly. However, don't worry too much about rolling your *r's* – the French realize how difficult it can be. Final consonants are seldom pronounced: the masculine adjective *ouvert* (open) is "oo-vair"; the feminine *ouverte*, "oo-vert." The final consonant in words like *vin* or *bon* makes the last vowel nasal.

h is silent	*hôtel* [o-tel]
th is t	*thé* [tay]
ch is sh	*chambre* [shombr]
ou is full	*vous* [vu]
u is tight	*menu* [meuh-nu]
c and *g* before *a, o, u*	*car* [car], *gare* [gar]
c and *g* before *i* or *e*	*merci, bagages* [si, gazh]
ç is soft before an *a*	*ça* [sa]
gn as in union	*agneau* [an-yo]

Airport

airport	*l'aéroport*
arrivals	*arrivées*
departures	*départs*
check-in	*l'enregistrement*
information	*information; renseignements*
ticket	*un billet*
flight	*un vol*
baggage	*les bagages*
baggage check	*contrôle des bagages*
passport	*le passeport*
passport control	*contrôle des passeports*
window seat	*place côté fenêtre*

Meeting People

hello, good morning	*bonjour*
good evening	*bonsoir*
Mr., Mrs., Miss	*monsieur, madame, mademoiselle*
excuse me	*excusez-moi*
Do you speak English?	*Parlez-vous anglais?*
yes, no	*oui, non*
I'm sorry	*Pardon*
please	*s'il vous plaît*
thank you	*merci*
I am American	*Je suis américain(e)*
We are American	*Nous sommes américain*
My name is...	*Je m'appelle...*
I don't understand	*Je ne comprends pas*
How are you?	*Comment allez-vous?*
That's fine, OK	*Ça va, d'accord*
goodbye	*au revoir*
see you later	*à bientôt*

Hotel

hotel, inn	*hôtel, auberge*
I have a reservation	*J'ai une réservation*
Do you have...	*Avez-vous...*
a room available?	*une chambre disponible?*
a single room?	*une chambre pour une personne?*
twin beds?	*une chambre à deux lits?*
a double room?	*une chambre pour deux personnes?*
What floor?	*À quel étage?*
Is there...	*Y a-t-il...*
an elevator?	*un ascenseur?*
room service	*service d'étage*
manager	*le directeur*
The check, please	*La note, s'il vous plaît*

Eating Out

A table for two, please	*Une table pour deux, s'il vous plaît*
Do you have a set menu?	*Avez-vous un menu à prix fixe?*
first course	*entrée*
main course	*plat principal*
cheese	*fromage*
dessert	*dessert*
wine list...	*carte des vins...*
red, white, rosé	*rouge, blanc, rosé*
a glass	*un verre*
bottle, half	*une bouteille, une demi-*
carafe, half	*un pichet, un demi-*
mineral water	*eau minérale*
What is that? (in menu)	*Qu'est-ce que c'est?*
bread	*du pain*
beef	*boeuf*
chicken	*poulet*
duck	*canard, caneton*
ham	*jambon*
lamb	*agneau*
pork	*porc*
pâté	*terrine/pâté*
mixed seafood	*fruits de mer*
mussels	*moules*
salmon	*saumon*
eggs	*oeufs*
coffee...	*café...*
small, black	*un expresso noir*
white	*au lait*
large white	*grand crème*
tea, with milk	*thé, au lait*
The restroom, please?	*Les toilettes, s'il vous plaît?*
The check, please	*L'addition, s'il vous plaît*
Thank you, that was very good	*Merci, c'était très bon*

Essential Information

Directions

Where is/are...	Où se trouve/ trouvent...
Turn left/right	Tournez à gauche/ à droite
Go straight ahead	Continuez tout droit
Take the first left/right	Prenez la première à gauche/droite

Post Office

post office	la poste
A stamp for... America, please	Un timbre pour... l'Amérique, s'il vous plaît
this letter	cette lettre
these letters	ces lettres
this postcard	cette carte postale
this parcel	ce paquet
mailbox	boîte aux lettres
for abroad	autres destinations

Telephone Calls

phone booth	une cabine téléphonique
phone card	une télécarte/carte de téléphone
operator	le/la standardiste
long-distance	interurbain (France), international
collect call	un appel en PCV

Shopping

bakery	une boulangerie
delicatessen	une charcuterie
newsstand	un tabac
bookshop	une librairie
grocery store	une épicerie
supermarket	un supermarché
Have you got...?	Avez-vous...?
How much?	Combien?
I'm just looking, thank you	Je regarde seulement, merci
change	la monnaie
a shopping bag, please	un sac, s'il vous plaît

Pharmacy

painkiller	un calmant
antiseptic	de l'antiseptique
bandage	un pansement
sanitary napkin	des serviettes hygiéniques
tampons	des tampons
razor blades	des lames de rasoir
suntan lotion	de la crème solaire
absorbent cotton	du coton hydrophile

Emergencies

police (17)	la police
ambulance (15)	une ambulance
fire service (18)	les sapeurs-pompiers
emergency (112)	police
services	secours
policeman	un gendarme
police station	une gendarmerie
first aid	les premiers soins
auto accident	un accident de voiture

Emergency calls are free from phone booths.

Transportation

railroad station	la gare
subway	le métro
train	le train
platform	le quai
ticket office	le guichet
bus station	la gare routière
bus	l'autobus, un bus
long-distance	un autocar, car
bus stop	un arrêt de bus
ticket	un billet
one-way to...	un billet simple pour...
round-trip to...	un aller-retour pour...
timetable	un horaire
Is this the bus/train to...	Est-ce bien le train/bus pour...

Money

Do you accept...	Acceptez-vous...
this credit card?	cette carte de crédit?
traveler's checks?	les chèques de voyage?
ATM	un guichet automatique

Numbers

1, 2, 3	un, deux, trois
4, 5, 6	quatre, cinq, six
7, 8, 9, 10	sept, huit, neuf, dix
11, 12, 13	onze, douze, treize
14, 15	quatorze, quinze
16, 17	seize, dix-sept
18, 19	dix-huit, dix-neuf
20, 21	vingt, vingt-et-un
30, 40	trente, quarante
50, 60	cinquante, soixante
70	soixante-dix
80	quatre-vingt
90	quatre-vingt-dix
100, 101	cent, cent-un

Acknowledgments
The Automobile Association wishes to thank the following photographers and organisations for their assistance in the preparation of this book.
Abbreviations for the picture credits are as follows – (t) top; (b) bottom; (l) left; (r) right; (c) centre; (AA) AA World Travel Library

3 Travel and Places / Alamy; 9 AA/J Tims; 10/11 AA/R Strange; 12/13 AA/Y Levy; 14 AA/J Tims; 15 AA/K Blackwell; 16/17 TDW / Corbis; 18 The Art Archive / Alamy; 21 AA/K Blackwell; 22 AA/Y Levy; 24 AA/K Blackwell; 26 AA/K Blackwell; 27 AA/K Blackwell; 31 AA/K Blackwell; 32 AA/K Blackwell; 34 AA/K Blackwell; 35 AA/K Blackwell; 36 AA/K Blackwell; 37 AA/K Blackwell; 39 AA/K Blackwell; 40 AA/K Blackwell; 42 AA/K Blackwell; 43 AA/J Tims; 44 AA/K Blackwell; 46 AA/K Blackwell; 47 AA/K Blackwell; 48 AA/K Blackwell; 49 AA/M Jourdan; 50 AA/D Noble; 51 AA/D Noble; 52 AA/D Noble; 54 AA/M Jourdan; 56 AA/C Sawyer; 58 AA/C Sawyer; 60 AA/I Dawson; 62 AA/R Moore; 65 AA/I Dawson; 66 AA/R Moore; 68 AA/I Dawson; 69 AA/S Day; 70/71 AA/C Sawyer; 72 AA/C Sawyer; 72/73 AA/I Dawson; 74 AA/A Kouprianoff; 75 AA/J Tims; 76/77 AA/S Day; 78 AA/I Dawson; 80 AA/R Moore; 84 AA/K Blackwell; 86 AA/P Kenward; 87 AA/N Setchfield; 89 AA/N Setchfield; 90 AA/N Setchfield; 91 AA/B Smith; 92 AA/R Moore; 93 Hemis / Alamy; 94/95 Hemis / Alamy; 96 AA/R Moore; 97 AA/P Kenward; 99 AA/R Moore; 100 AA/R Moore; 102 AA/J Edmanson; 103 AA/J Edmanson; 104 Hemis / Alamy; 106 AA/P Kenward; 109 AA/B Smith; 110 AA/B Smith; 111 Hemis / Alamy; 112 AA/N Setchfield; 113 AA/P Kenward; 114 AA/C Sawyer; 115 AA/N Setchfield; 116 The Art Archive / Alamy; 117 Hemis / Alamy; 118 AA/P Kenward; 121 AA/P Kenward; 122 AA/J Miller; 124 AA/K Reynolds; 125 AA/K Reynolds; 126 AA/P Bennett; 128 Art Kowalsky / Alamy; 129 AA/N Setchfield; 130 AA/N Setchfield; 131 AA/N Setchfield; 132 AA/P Bennett; 133 Ian Dagnall / Alamy; 134 AA/N Setchfield; 134/135 David Noton Photography / Alamy; 136 AA/B Smith; 139 R H Productions / Robert Harding; 142 AA/Y Levy; 146 AA/Y Levy; 148 AA/Y Levy; 150 AA/Y Levy; 151 AA/Y Levy; 152 AA/Y Levy; 153 AA/Y Levy; 154 Kate Diamond / Alamy; 157 Travel and Places / Alamy; 159 Peter Bowater / Alamy; 161 AA/A Baker; 162 AA/A Baker; 163 AA/A Baker; 164 George Munday / Alamy; 165 Chris Hellier / Alamy; 168 AA/J Tims; 169 AA/Y Levy; 172 AA/A Baker; 173 AA/B Smith; 174 AA/Y Levy; 175 AA/Y Levy; 176 Jon Arnold Images Ltd / Alamy; 178 Charles Bowman / Alamy; 181 Pierre Brye / Alamy; 182 AA/C Sawyer; 183 CW Images / Alamy; 184 CW Images / Alamy; 185 David Noton Photography / Alamy; 186 AA/T Oliver; 188/189 Jan Wlodarczyk / Alamy; 190/191 AA/R Moore; 194 AA/R Strange; 196 AA/R Strange; 198 AA/R Strange; 199 AA/C Sawyer; 201 Ian Dagnall / Alamy; 203 AA/J Wyand; 204 AA/J Wyand; 205 GM Photo Images / Alamy; 206 AA/R Strange; 207 AA/B Smith; 208 Guichaoua / Alamy; 209 AA/B Smith; 210 AA/R Strange; 211 AA/B Smith; 212 AA/R Moore; 213 AA; 215 AA/B Smith; 216 AA/T Teegan; 217 AA/R Strange; 218 AA/R Moore; 220 AA/M Short; 224 AA; 225 Paul H. Reinert / Alamy; 226 AA/M Short; 227 AA/M Short; 228 AA/C Sawyer; 229 AA/T Oliver; 231 AA/T Oliver; 232/233 JTB Photo Communications, Inc. / Alamy; 234 Adam Woolfitt / Robert Harding; 235 AA; 237 ImageState / Alamy; 238 Peter Bowater / Alamy; 240 AA/T Oliver; 243 AA/R Day; 244/245 Andia / Alamy; 246 AA/D Robertson; 247 Andia / Alamy; 248/249 AA/R Day; 250 AA/R Day; 251 Neil Thompson / Alamy; 252 John Kellerman / Alamy; 253 AA/K Blackwell; 255 David Jones / Alamy; 256 AA/J Tims; 258 AA/K Blackwell; 277t AA/K Blackwell; 277c AA/K Blackwell; 278 AA/K Blackwell

Every effort has been made to trace the copyright holders, and we apologise in advance for any unintentional omissions or errors. We would be pleased to apply any corrections in a following edition of this publication.